927 DAYS
of SUMMER

AROUND THE WORLD IN A VW VAN

Brad Van Orden
Sheena Van Orden

Go far, keep the rubber side down!

First published in 2015

Edited by Lynda Rice

Copyright © Brad Van Orden, 2015
All rights reserved

ISBN (Print): 978-0-9897665-3-1
ISBN (Kindle): 978-0-9897665-6-2
ISBN (ePub): 978-0-9897665-9-3

Contents

Drive Nacho Drive,

Brad and Sheena's first book, tells the story of their drive from Arizona to the tip of South America. It is a tale about stepping away from the American Dream to drive as far south as it is possible to drive in the world.

927 Days of Summer

picks up the story where Drive Nacho Drive left off. It is a documentary of patience, nerve, and adventure along the highways and backroads from Asia's east coast to America's west coast, seen through the windshield of an aging VW van.

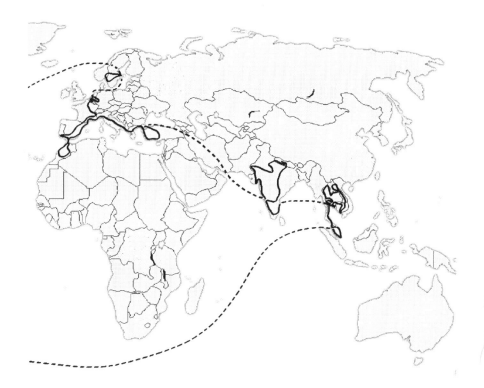

To the friends we made along the way

In the end it wasn't about the places, but the people

Part 1

The Far East

1

Xin Yan Tian Container Vessel
to Kuala Lumpur

Brad

There is one vehicle on Interstate 10 just west of New Orleans that is different from all the rest, its exterior cloaked by a patina of dust that looks permanent like leathery, sunburned skin. Its scarred body panels are a storybook of experiences, which it wears with a well-earned smugness; a shrapnel-torn tank returning triumphantly from the battlefield. A long gouge on one side terminates in a dramatic dent at the rear fender, evidence of having sideswiped a bus in the dense, sweltering hornet's nest of vehicular chaos in Varanasi, India. An ammunition can bolted to the front bumper bears the indentation of a concrete road marker from somewhere in the Cambodian countryside. The wind causes the passenger side mirror to rock loosely on its mount, the result of an overzealous Kathmandu bus driver with poor depth perception. The hurried drivers zipping past in the left hand lane of this American interstate pay no mind to the dented window frame on the old van's driver's side door, left there by the metal rod of an Argentinean thief.

I sit in the driver's seat, my left elbow propped on the windowsill, my hand resting loosely on the steering wheel much as I had over the course of the past two-and-a-half years since Nacho had last plied the roadways of North America. We are often asked why we chose to name our 1984 Volkswagen van Nacho, but there isn't a good story to tell. We had picked it up from a girl in Hollywood where it bore the name Whoopi. But every long distance traveling steed needs a strong and dependable name, and Whoopi would not do. We settled on Ignacio— "Nacho" for short—a tip of the hat to Mexico, which would be the first country we would cross on our around-the-world drive.

3

Sheena stares ahead from the passenger seat in a familiar way, watching the scene unfold through the wiper-streaked windshield that somehow, after having circumnavigated the entire globe, managed to emerge without a single chip or crack.

The highways in North America are too straight. It is no wonder that drivers fall asleep at the wheel. We have just crossed a long straight bridge over a nameless body of water, and now we are driving a straight line carved out through the low trees of the Louisiana swampland. In places the roadway is supported by stilts so as to rise above the marsh. I keep a hopeful eye out for alligators, but the only wildlife I see here are the long-legged white birds that stand in the shallows and pick tadpoles with their skinny beaks. American roads are too straight because to make unnecessary curves would add cost, and it would ultimately take longer to get from one place to another. The American landscape is a pattern of straight roads in constant flux toward a state of pure efficiency. There are no unplanned features on these paved surfaces, and there are few curves to mind, so it is easy to mentally drift away.

Ahead the white lines denoting the road shoulders shoot forward like perfectly straight arrows, culminating at a single point on the horizon, laser beams shooting a distant enemy. My mind runs with the image, and then wanders off like a lost soul.

I am the commander of a futuristic army and only my van's twin laser beams can save the planet's needy children. I am three, and I have gone to work with my father without my pants, and for the first time I realize that I am too old to be in naked in public and I feel ashamed. I am driving a miniature car in a parade to celebrate the birthday of Chairman Mao, but I run out of gas, thus embarrassing myself and bringing shame upon the car's owner. I deliver strict instructions to a group of my Chinese border guard subordinates and they salute me by stomping one foot and slapping their rifles with their gloved hands.

It is no wonder people fall asleep at the wheel on American highways.

From the ramshackle border towns of Mexico to the sticky jungles of Panama, and onward to the windswept, featureless landscapes of Patagonia there was always something to keep a driver's mind occupied. Driving the routes that made up the Pan-American Highway, from Tijuana to the Straits of Magellan, had been more akin to mountain biking than driving, zigzagging across roadways to miss boulders and potholes and the places where the road had flaked off into the abyss. To drive to Tierra del Fuego was to drive a quarter of the way around the

4

globe on a forlorn power line road. Boredom is a featureless interstate, white lines converging on the horizon, but it was nearly impossible to fall asleep at the wheel on the Pan-American.

On a nondescript section of highway bordered by a concrete barrier – protection against dozing off into the swamp, surely – one front tire becomes misshapen and begins to grumble and shake as if flailing a whipping chain against the ground with each revolution. The grumbling shakes me from my Chinese border post and at once I pull over. While crossing Patagonia our tires had taken so much abuse as to give up the ghost, and they had begun popping nearly every day. I had gone to extreme measures to get us to Buenos Aires. One evening on the beach near Puerto San Julian, after slashing two tires in a day, I had used a fish hook and a length of 120 pound fishing line to stitch up a ripped sidewall. It held air until we reached a tire repair shop twenty miles away the following day. After leaving South America by ship, and after much searching, I had finally procured a new set of tires from a man in a dirty tee shirt who spoke no English, and who conveyed the virtues of my new tires through wild hand gestures and unintelligible sounds like a verbal machine gun. This tire had been through hell and back, diving in and out of bomb craters across the subcontinent of India, traversing the Himalayas, and crossing the Sahara. Now, on a boring stretch of Interstate 10 outside of New Orleans where the pavement is featureless and pancake flat and the white lines shoot the horizon like laser beams, the sidewall bulges out, the tread delaminates, and the tire finally pops.

There are millions of miles of roads on this planet, and our path had comprised a great number of them linked together to make a meandering line around the world, broken up by several stretches of ocean. Our tire popped at precisely this location as a result of a string of hastily-made and ill-advised decisions.

Our original hare-brained plan, hatched spontaneously over dinner one night, was to drive from our home in Arizona to the southern tip of Tierra del Fuego, the farthest south that it is possible to drive in the world. That was supposed to be the easy part, the warm up. After that we would ship Nacho to Asia—the hard part—and then slowly work our way around to Europe. But we had gotten a rough start to the Americas, and after six solid months of mechanical problems we found ourselves stranded in the remote mountains of Colombia for two months with a failed transmission, our motivation in shambles. Then and there we decided that if we ever made it to Tierra del Fuego—and we were pretty sure we'd never make it—then we'd treat ourselves to a rest by

5

shipping Nacho to Europe instead of Asia. But several months later when we reached the end of the continent, and failing to heed the lessons of history, we shipped Nacho to Asia anyway.

We had hit our groove and found comfort in uncertainty. We had finally recognized that the most worthwhile experiences were borne of struggle and vulnerability. The real adventure begins at wit's end, as it were. Europe would be too easy. The roads there were straight, there were rules and regulations and speed limits and health codes. The place would be too cosmopolitan, the people prim and coiffed. But of Asia we were ignorant, having neither experience nor preconceived notion. The land beyond the Pacific, an unfathomably faraway place, was filled with slack-jawed cannibals clicking their tongues, and the possibility of adventure was endless.

The heat was stifling and my shirt clung to my skin like a wet blanket as I shuffled sideways in the dark. Drops of sweat stung my eyes as I located the lock and fumbled the key into it. Stale heat oozed slowly out of the van as I cracked the door open, and it touched the side of the shipping container, creating only a twelve inch opening. I contorted and squeezed myself through the crack and into the driver's seat. After thirty six days at sea the battery was nearly dead, but the starter was able to coax just enough electrons from the battery to spin to life and weakly turn over the reluctant engine. The alternator belt squealed like a bloodthirsty banshee and I eased the transmission into reverse and slowly emerged from the shipping container into the thick air. The smell of palm trees and warm saltwater created a perfume that hung like smoke.

Sheena smiled and pinched her fists against her sides to contain her excitement. A dark-skinned man directed me to a parking spot next to a dilapidated building, and as I came to rest Nacho's odometer turned over 300,000 miles. I signed my name to a piece of paper, and then Jan and Kevin signed theirs. Their motorcycles had made the journey from Buenos Aires inside of the container with Nacho. They stood in stark contrast to us, we in our shorts and tee shirts, they in their full motorcycle gear. They inspected their bikes, which were still covered in Patagonian dust, and they pointed at new oil leaks and tested their grips in the blistering heat like ants under a magnifying glass.

The dark skinned man looked up from our paperwork and gave us the thumbs up. We gestured to the main gate of the port and looked back at him and he nodded his approval. We were finished and free to go. We started our engines and drove slowly in single file out of the port,

6

where drivers zoomed by on the wrong side of the road. Scooters were piled high with bundles of baskets, overloaded trucks trundled by, and we timidly joined the flow.

The next day it felt as if a weight had been lifted. In the early afternoon we went for a walk when the sun was high overhead, heating the humid air into a sauna that speckled our shirts with perspiration. Vines climbed from the ground into the canopy of a tree, out across the limbs, and then dangled in the air above our heads. We sat on a bench and watched people go by. A Chinese couple passed, followed by several young Muslim women. Their silk head scarves shaded their faces from the hot sun while their smooth gait and petite sandals tapped out a rhythm on the sidewalk. They floated smoothly along in their elegant silk gowns in such a way as to seem impervious to gravity.

The French say that by presenting ourselves artfully, our presence may add beauty to the world. I can only imagine that they came to this conclusion after watching Muslim women walk.

The loudspeakers atop the mosque's minarets crackled to life, and then a voice like a singing cello began its steady, melodic rendition of the call to prayer. The voice carried out over the city, *a cappella*, in an enchanting echo reminding Muslims that it was time to find a peaceful place to face Mecca and pray. We sat back and let the sound pour over us and it dawned on us just how far from home we were. We were in the Islamic world now, in Kuala Lumpur, Malaysia.

We sauntered along the sidewalk, shriveling in the heat, gulping the saturated air as though it was liquid water. Between two buildings a Hindu temple appeared, adorned with hundreds of ornate statues of mystic blue gods. From within the temple the squealing notes of a *shehnai* filled the street and the ground reverberated with the thud of a hand drum. We kicked off our sandals and walked inside to see where the music was coming from, and were met by a scene of pure jubilation. Under the central pavilion men and women were dressed to the nines. Musicians sitting on the floor belted out wild instrumentals while flower petals were thrown and little girls in saris ran through the canopy of cheerful adults. It felt like a Bollywood dance scene might break out at any moment.

We had walked into a traditional Indian wedding.

The bride and groom were dressed in elaborate outfits with headdresses, necklaces, jewels, and bright makeup. In-between trips around the shrine people showered them with flower petals and wafted candle smoke onto them, and all the while they were surrounded by smiling family and friends. We struck up a conversation with an older woman who gave her name as Raji, and she gave us the inside scoop about the bride and groom. They were from Tamil Nadu in southeastern India, but they met in Kuala Lumpur. Raji was the cheeriest person I had met since arriving in Malaysia. Everyone at the wedding was like this. The little girls ran around in their saris handing out party favors to the guests. Outside of the pavilion more guests ate curry and rice with their fingers, smiling in the sun.

Aristotle said that happiness is the meaning and the purpose of life, the whole aim and end of human existence. I can only imagine that he came to this conclusion after attending an Indian wedding.

In the late afternoon, Sheena and I hopped on the metro. As soon as Teng Tsen heard that we were in town, he called his Volkswagen club together for a proper welcome party.

I had told him that we would meet him at Sri Petaling station at 6:15, that we'd be the goofy- looking white people.

"I'm the good-looking Malaysian guy. Look out for the VW kombi!"

We emerged from the station to find Teng Tsen waiting for us in his pristine 1974 air-cooled Volkswagen bus. We loaded up and rolled out with the windows down, a cool breeze filling the bus. We took a quick detour into a residential neighborhood where Séb and Soizic tagged along in their 1966 split window VW bus. Somehow, through the tangle of Asian chaos and coincidence, we met up with the other members of the club in traffic on a busy freeway, and then slithered as one big VW snake to a roadside food stand.

Over bowls of Yong Tau Foo we told lies about our travel-related triumphs and conquests. All the while, Sheena and I had to keep pinching ourselves. Were we really in Asia? Had we really just been in South America? It already seemed a lifetime ago. This was about as different from the wild expanses of Patagonia as one could get on this planet.

We loaded up again, this time in Séb's bus, and headed out for cold drinks. In a parking lot near the freeway filled with groups of smiling young Malaysians, we crowded around tables in folding chairs. We were soon joined by more smiling faces of the Malaysia VW Club, and we threw back several glasses of ice cold tropical juice. The parking lot was packed with Beetles and buses, and our table was equally packed with fun-loving car enthusiasts. Try as we might, nobody would let us pay for anything. "When you're in our country, you are our guest!" they said.

Eleanor Roosevelt once said that happiness is not a goal; it is a byproduct. I can only imagine that she came to this conclusion after driving in an old Volkswagen bus.

For the days before Nacho arrived at the port we took a hotel in the center of Kuala Lumpur. We rose with the sun and set out for breakfast at a bustling street market near the river. At this early hour the market catered to the service industry workers who slurped bowls of spicy noodle soup before taking up brooms and hand trolleys and cooking implements. The night suppressed the humidity, and as the rays of the rising sun bounced between the buildings and onto the tin roofs of the market stalls, the wetness slowly returned, and brought with it a thickness to the air and the fragrance of chilies and bananas and tin.

The market was itself something of an urban cavern sunken deep between tall buildings. Its stalls spilled from the sidewalk into the street, turning what would have been a thoroughfare into an urban obstacle course of street food and tapestry sellers. Malaysia has three primary cultural groups—the Malay, the Chinese, and the Indians—and this market was quintessentially Chinese. This was made obvious by the Mandarin characters on the overhead flags, and by the spitting. Some Chinese spit as a means of cleansing, believing that eliminating the slimy deposits of built-up phlegm from their throats will make them healthier. Thus, especially in the early morning, Chinese gathering places become an orchestra of hacking and lurching. We spent our market mornings in flimsy plastic chairs under makeshift rusty shelters slurping the most delectable of rich and salty noodle soups, the handmade noodles smacking our lips and leaving drops of fiery chili, all underscored by a soundtrack of roaring wet lurches, like sticky flesh being dragged through rubber tubes, and then—*ptooey!*

Jan and Kevin had taken a hotel on this street, and to enter their lobby one had to duck between the snarl of outdoor kitchens and trinket stalls and enter through what seemed to be a hidden door.

We had first met them in Patagonia near the base of Mount Fitzroy, and their decision to come along with us to Asia was made in the spur of the moment. They had ridden to South America on a couple of old BMW motorcycles, and their traveling style had been rather different from ours. They traveled faster, only staying a few days in each place, and stayed in hotels every night. They traveled light, and we came to know

9

them not only by their personalities but also by what they wore every day. Kevin, the Canadian, could always be found wearing brown khaki shorts and a black fast-drying tee shirt, while Jan, the Dutchman, sported blue jeans and a sleeveless white shirt. "You're always wearing that old wifebeater shirt," we teased. We had taken an apartment together in Buenos Aires, and day after day Kevin would leave early and return late with his camera slung over his shoulder, while Jan hung around the apartment in his wifebeater shirt. We fell asleep to the murmur of Jan Skyping with his Colombian girlfriend, seven months' drive away to the north. We had become roomies, but after leaving Kuala Lumpur we would go our separate ways.

When Nacho arrived by ship we checked out of our central hotel and moved to the outskirts of Kuala Lumpur where we had been offered a place to stay in someone's house—a friend of Teng Tsen. His name was Terence, a Malaysian of Indian descent from the south Indian state of Tamil Nadu, and a part of the Tamil Volkswagen club. Terence was a Malaysian bachelor, and so each night when the brutal sun slid below the horizon and the wet blanket was lifted off of our faces, we drove out to the row of buildings bordering the highway to eat dinner. There were several places to choose from, and each night other Tamils met us for dinner of *roti* and *thali* with a Malaysian twist. I often chose the ultimate health-nut option of *roti pisang*, an Indian flat bread made by slapping sticky dough against a surface until it was as thin as paper, and then covering it in butter and throwing it onto a griddle. After adding bananas and more butter, the layers of dough were folded over and over, finally firming up into a chewy banana-filled pastry. To finish it off, it was covered in sweetened-condensed milk and served with spicy curry sauces for dipping. It is the Tamil Big Mac – what doesn't kill you makes you fatter!

The Tamils taught us how to eat curry with our fingers, and how to send messages to the waiter by folding our banana leaves. There is a system in Indian restaurants and by following it we started to feel more at home, comfortable in our surroundings because we were in the know. Upon our arrival we would head to the back of the restaurant and wash our hands in the sink. This was important because Indian food is eaten with the hands. If we ordered *thali*, the waiter would first lay down a banana leaf, and then place a large scoop of rice in the middle. He would then ladle scoops of various curries and lentils around the perimeter. To eat it, the right hand—always the right hand, never the left!—was used to mix some rice with curry and mold it into a pellet. It was then lifted to the mouth with the elbow out and thumb toward the face, whereupon the thumb was used to slide the pellet off of the fingers into the mouth. If done well it was a pretty clean way to eat, and much more satisfying that eating with silverware. This dish, costing only a dollar or two, was all-you-can-eat. To tell the waiter that we were finished and didn't want any more refills, we folded the banana leaf along its spine so that the opening away from the table edge. To tell the waiter that we were dissatisfied, which we never were, we were to fold the leaf down so that the opening was toward the table edge. Last, we would walk back to the sink, wash our hands, put some water in our mouth and slosh it around, then spit it into the sink. The meal ended with several rounds of sweet milk tea.

One night at a curry joint beside the highway, at tables spilling into the parking lot, we asked Terence and Adrian and Lavern why the Tamils and the Chinese each formed their own VW clubs in Kuala Lumpur instead of consolidating. They were all friends, and we had been introduced to Terence (a Tamil) by Teng Tsen (Chinese), although we rarely saw them together.

"We're all friends, but we travel different, *la*!" He looked like a young Michael Jackson from the Thriller days, and his face seemed more at ease when smiling than not. About seven in ten Malaysians speak English, and the Tamils had their own pidgin language combining Malay and English terms. One of the more charming quirks of the language was the tacking on of the word "la" to the end of most sentences, and peppered throughout. It was a do-all suffix and space filler which imparted a Rastafarian innocence on the speakers.

"When da weather is good, da Volkswagen clubs go road trippin', *la*, like when we went to Vietnam. But da problem with da Chinese is dey travel too fast, *la*! We take our time. An' den there's the issue of eatin', *la*. Da Chinese always want hot pot. And we don' like road trippin' with the Muslims, *la*, because dey always need to find *halal* food. Sometimes we just wanna sanwich, but they gotta keep searchin', *la*! Too much plannin'!" He looked across the table at Vijay, who had recently converted from Hinduism to Islam after falling in love with a Muslim girl. "E'cept Vijay over dere, he may be Muslim but he'll eat anythin', *la*!" He flashed his teeth and laughed, then scooped some rice and curry with his fingers and popped it into his mouth.

One afternoon, Sheena and I found ourselves standing in the wet parking lot of Studio 16 in Kuala Lumpur. A video camera was trained

11

on us as we stood in front of Lavern's hippie bus, painted like something out of a psychedelic acid trip.

"I think team Apec was totally corny. The way that the girl flung her arms around—"

"Cut! Can we roll that again? Listen, the team's name is 'Apex,' not 'Apec,'" the director said.

"Oh, okay, sorry about that. Apex? Got it."

"Three…two…one…action!"

"I think team *Apex* was totally corny. The way that the girl, like, flung her arms around and said that she was going on her honeymoon was really over the top. I definitely preferred team Maverick." Yeah! Nailed it!

Somehow, after a little more than a week in the city, we had landed on an episode of the Malaysian version of *The Apprentice*. The day had started off normally enough. I had parked Nacho in Terence's driveway and put on my VW surgeon's gloves. During our last few weeks in Argentina our water purification system had sprung a leak somewhere under the false floor. I had hinged the floor so that almost the entire water system could be easily accessed, but there was one section under the rear seat where it was inaccessible. The leak, of course, had sprung under the rear seat.

I started by removing the seat, and then went to work enlarging a pass-through in the false floor where the rear heater poked through so that I could get my hands on the connection between two tubes where a hose clamp had become loose. Around midday we got a call from Teng Tsen.

"You're going on TV tonight. Start driving to the IKEA, and someone will meet you on the freeway to show you where to go. There will be lots of Volkswagen people there, so bring Nacho. Dress business smart."

I looked at Nacho. The rear seat was missing, the heater was balanced on its side, and the battery and inverter were delicately stacked on top of one another to power the Dremel tool, which was sitting next to a half-cut hole in the floor. Tools, wires, tubing, and tape were all stacked on the counters, and various cabinets and storage boxes were all open and disheveled. Nacho wasn't going anywhere.

With Nacho down for the count, Sheena and I put on our only clean clothes.

"Hey Sheena, what does 'business smart' mean?"

"I don't know."

"Do you think these sandals are business smart?"

"Uh, probably not. Maybe you should wear your running shoes."

Once we were business smart in our jeans and semi-clean, slightly wrinkled shirts and tennis shoes, we hopped in Lavern's hippie bus and lurched and sputtered onto the freeway.

Sure enough, as we approached the IKEA, Stephen—of the Chinese VW club—waited for us on the side of the freeway, and then pulled out in front of us to lead the way to Studio 16. When we arrived the parking lot was full of old Volkswagen Beetles. We parked and were led to some tents where the cast and crew were eating Indian food. We settled in, filled our plates, and sat around looking business smart near a group of portable tents in the parking lot. Just then it began to rain, and soon the rain became torrential.

While we ate, sheltered by the tents, an Indian woman who seemed to be a production assistant brought us up to speed. For this episode of *The Apprentice*, two teams had created marketing campaigns to promote the new Volkswagen Beetle. We would be in the audience, and would watch the teams present their commercials to some executives from Volkswagen. Among the VW representatives was Simon, the lead designer of the new Beetle.

The production assistant poked her head out of the studio door and over the sound of the torrential rain told us to get ready. We would walk into the studio in single file with the cameras rolling, and then sit down. My television debut! Should I strut, or maybe do more of a saunter? Should I smile? No, smiling makes people seem submissive. I would look straight ahead, dead-eyed like a catwalk fashion model. Yeah, that would look awesome. Oh man, this was going to be great! I'm going on TV! I'm going on TV!

Just then the awning above me reached its water-holding capacity and buckled, sending several gallons of rain water directly on top of me. Everyone stopped what they were doing and looked at me. I felt like Carrie after the bucket of pig's blood had ruined her prom glory. My eyes looked left, twitched to the right, and then left again. My face still held a relic of a grin on it from when I was thinking about how awesome I would look when I walked in like a catwalk fashion model, but the grin had turned into a strained grimace. My matted hair stuck to my forehead and my business smart shirt clung to me like a bag of pudding.

"Umm, I think it'll dry in time," someone whispered sympathetically.

"All right everyone, enter on THREE...TWO...ONE..." The production assistant poked her head out the door, and then disappeared. The first person walked in, then the second and third, and then I was standing in front of the door. I looked around to see who wanted to go next, but everyone looked back at me expectantly. I clasped the door handle in my clammy, wet hand and pulled the door open. My waterlogged business smart tennis shoes sloshed and burped as I walked down the aisle, staring blankly ahead like an emotionless catwalk fashion model. I went to the front row, swiveled, and splashed down into a chair.

"Pssst!" It was the production assistant. "You can't sit there. That's where the client sits!" she whispered.

Oh damn. The proverbial catwalk model had twisted his proverbial ankle and proverbially fallen off of the catwalk into the crowd. I slowly stood up, looking as cool and business smart as possible, and sloshed and burped my way back into the second row where Sheena sat patiently waiting for me to stop making an ass of myself.

The two competing teams took turns standing in front of first a new yellow Beetle, and then a new black Beetle, performing the commercials they had created. After about an hour the teams had finished performing, we had finished our requisite audience applause and laughter shots, and it was time to leave. Everyone stood up and started filing out the doors when the production assistant pulled Sheena and me aside.

"You two! Would you stay behind so we can shoot some additional material with you?" she asked.

"Of course," we said. Aha! I must have nailed the dead-eyed catwalk fashion model impersonation after all! My television debut was going great! We walked out of the screening room, trailing a cloud of evaporating storm runoff and wet sock vapor.

Back in the parking lot, the director asked us to stand in front of Lavern's bus and tell him what we thought about each team's performance. After explaining how corny we thought Team Apex was, the director had one more request.

"Okay, listen. Now we want you to look into the camera and say 'You qualify, Beetle up!' Can you do that?" We were supposed to point at the camera with both fingers when we said "you qualify," and then transition to two thumbs up when we said "Beetle up." And all this after I had just finished reprimanding Team Apex for being corny.

"All right, action!"

"You qualify, Beetle up!" we echoed.

"Cut! You were pointing while she was doing the thumbs up. Can we roll it again? Pointing first, then thumbs. Action!"

"You qualify, Beetle up!" we repeated.

"Wait, wait, I messed up again," Sheena cried. "I pointed, but my thumbs were up at the same time like little guns. Let's do it again."

"Okay, two…one…action!"

"You qualify, Beetle up!"

The last time everything went perfectly. We were in synch like a well-practiced boyband, our fingers pointed in harmony to the rolling camera, and then deftly transitioned to the thumbs-up position before the backdrop of our cheesy smiling faces. Our television debut. We could only hope that the footage would be lost in a building fire, never to see the light of day.

There was one thing that initially dismayed me about Terence's house, and about Malaysia in general.

"Terence, there's no toilet paper, *la*!" I had taken to throwing *la* in here and there so as to fit in with the population, but despite my linguistic adaptations, my towering 6'3" stature and white face gave away my foreignness. As did my aversion to—if I may be so crass—wiping my ass with my hand.

I had always known that in Asia it was bad form to touch someone or eat with your left hand, a sign of disrespect and bad sanitation, because the left hand is used for wiping one's ass. In my mind I had always just figured that Asians were particularly sensitive about the mechanics of personal hygiene, or that some archaic custom of dynastic sanitary chivalry had survived the ages and manifested itself as this strange abandonment of one entire extremity.

But when I walked into Terence's bathroom on that first day and stared confusedly at the setup, it finally dawned on me. There was a toilet, and next to it a rubber tube attached to a garden spigot coming out of the wall. Like a housecat with limited cognitive ability I stared doe-eyed at the toilet, then at the tube, then at the toilet. No toilet paper holder? I thought for a long time, and finally all of the evidence fell into place like the climax in a Law and Order episode.

By Jove, I've got it! It *is* unsanitary to eat with the left hand!

By thorough investigation and deductive reasoning I was able to ascertain that these rubber tubes I'd observed everywhere were to be held and aimed by the right hand while the bare left hand did the scrubbing. It made perfect sense! Why had it taken me twenty-nine years to understand this simple concept? Finkle *is* Einhorn! Einhorn *is* Finkle!

These rubber tubes were vile, and were to be avoided at any expense! What's worse was the fact that most Asian public toilets didn't have any soap! I shared my findings with Sheena and we began religiously carrying toilet paper with us at all times, and we carefully watched where our food servers were placing their left hands.

We had only been in Asia for a couple of weeks, and hadn't yet given in to doing things the Asian way. Each time I entered a bathroom I eyed the vile rubber tube with an instinctive distrust. I calculated angles and imagined the misuses and overspray, and I clenched the wad of toilet paper in my pocket like a safety blanket.

On the day before we left Terence's house to embark on our maiden Asian voyage aboard Nacho down the coast toward Singapore, Sheena and I walked toward the highway where there was a little mall. We had taken to using the mall for internet access since Terence didn't have access at his house. We settled in at a small café and soon enough I felt a rumble in my belly, an effect of last night's *roti pisang*.

"Sheena, I'm off to the bathroom. Wish me luck." She looked up from her computer and gave me a stern nod, and I was on my way. I passed the hardware store filled with Chinese tools and the fashion store selling Indian saris and strappy sandals, and soon arrived at the bathroom in a back hallway.

Western toilets are a rare thing in Asia, and are usually only found in modern homes. Public toilets invariably have squat toilets: simple porcelain dishes inlayed in the floor with anti-slip foot platforms, and this one was no different. The floor around the squat toilet was all wet, and a vile, discolored red rubber tube was stretched across the wet floor and its end rested on the bottom of the porcelain bowl. I suppressed a gag reflex and moved the tube out of the way with my foot. There was a red bucket underneath a garden spigot to be used for flushing.

After doing my business I decided to introduce a bit of Western flare to this backwater by creating my very own flush toilet. I would use the vile bum sprayer to do the flushing instead of filling and pouring the red bucket of water into the bowl. I positioned my right foot on a tiny patch of dry floor and used my left foot to scoot the tip of the foul tube so that it pointed at an angle into the side of the toilet bowl. This, I calculated, would provide just the right degree of swirl so as to emulate the flushing mechanics of a proper Western toilet. I checked my work, and once satisfied, I reached over and turned the faucet handle to full blast.

I am an engineer, and I graduated with an emphasis in fluid dynamics, but enough time away from academia had evidently turned my brain to mush, because what happened next caught me completely by surprise. A split second after turning the handle the red bum sprayer tube came to life like a whipping sea serpent. The force of the water being pushed through the hose turned it into an out-of-control rocket ship. I lurched backward to escape the whipping torrent of water but there was no safe place in the tiny bathroom stall. I closed my eyes and flailed my arms to try to stop the barrage of filthy water, but it was hopeless. The serpent hissed and whipped and slashed the walls with its fecal water ray. I lunged through the flood and turned off the faucet. My eyes were pinched shut and I dared not open them for fear of exposing them to this flood of poison eye drops. I wiped my soaking face with the back of my damp sleeve, horrified. I tumbled out of the stall and fell onto the counter, and scrubbed my face and arms until they were pink and raw.

Walking back through the mall there was no way anyone could have guessed what had happened. It was too foolish. I had tried to beat the game by circumventing the rules, and Asia had won. The whipping toilet snake had won.

I lowered my drenched body into the plastic chair next to Sheena and let out a pathetic whimper. My hair poked out where the violent stream had caught it.

"What in the hell happened to you, boy?!"

I explained what had happened, my eyes downcast and ashamed, and told her that I had learned my lesson and was ready to abandon my Western ways.

2

Route 5 to Singapore

Brad

The depth of my knowledge about Singapore up until our arrival had been gathered from the news in the 1990's, and from reading Paul Theroux books. I knew that the entire structure and inner workings of the city-state were conceived by one person, a sort of Wizard of Oz deciding what would fly and what wouldn't. I knew that the laws there were so strict, and the punishments so severe, that there was virtually no crime. Chewing gum was illegal, but prostitution was allowed, and vandalizing cars would get your ass repeatedly caned with a bamboo switch. The special insert that the border agent slipped into our passports summed up the essence of the city's low crime rates:

Warning: death to drug traffickers under Singapore law

You cross the border into Singapore with a dime bag and they straight up kill you. And they're old school about it—their method of choice is hanging. I shuddered at the thought of the unmarked Ziploc bag in Sheena's backpack containing generic pain killers. *I swear! These aren't drugs!*

Bill Clinton stood up for Michael Fay after he vandalized a bunch of cars and was arrested, and I was pretty sure that Barack would get my back if an international painkiller incident were to arise. Of course, even with Bill Clinton begging for leniency, Michael Fay still had to grab his ankles and feel the full stinging force of Singaporean law.

Sheena and I sat quietly on the bus as we entered Singapore, trying not to break any laws. Yes, the bus. As it turns out, it's illegal to drive a foreign vehicle into Singapore if it is outfitted with a bed or cooking facilities. First potential caning incident: dodged. An unusually high number of things are illegal in Singapore, and it's a costly place.

If you wanted to own a car in Singapore, you must first buy a permit, good for ten years, for $75,000. After that, you must buy a new car, and you would pay 200-300% tax on it for the privilege. You would then be free to drive your $150,000 Toyota Camry around for the next ten years before you'd be legally obliged to sell it back to the government for a few peanuts and then buy another new car and another permit.

We got off of the bus at the Queen Street Station and let our noses lead us to the nearest food hawker stands in Little India. Southeast Asia is a wonderland of cheap, delicious street food, and we were told that Singapore would be a concentrated paradise in this regard. We quickly found a vast collection of hawker stands not on the street, but in a giant food court on the ground floor of a mall.

The city-state of Singapore has 250 malls, and each of these malls has a bustling collection of food hawkers arranged in food courts, selling cheap and delicious food. For a couple of dollars one can stuff oneself on his choice of Chinese, Malay, or Indian food. For each of the four days we spent there we would walk to a food court when we got hungry, scout out a stall with tasty looking food, and commence gorging ourselves. The experience usually left us in a food coma with the sweet burn of chilies on our lips and the smell of curry excreting from our sweat glands. But not every time.

One evening, after having enjoyed a nice plate of spicy noodles and a bowl of clay pot soup, we wandered around looking for a dessert stand. There was only one, so we sat down. Sheena ordered tapioca, while I asked for the grass jelly cocktail. You heard right. Grass jelly cocktail. I foolishly assumed it was a reverse-euphemism for something tasty, so I ordered and waited.

Sheena took delivery of an appetizing chunk of steamed cassava root bathed in coconut milk, while mine consisted of a pile of shaved ice covered in stringy goo and some pieces of fruit cocktail.

"It can't actually be grass," I assured Sheena. "It's probably some kind of confection that looks like grass." She looked at me with worry in her eyes. I wore a confident smile, but behind the façade I was frightened.

First bite: oh yeah, that's not sweet. No sir, this is actually grass. Grass jelly is indeed jelly made out of grass clippings. Neither sweet, nor tasty. Boy, the shaved ice really makes it a lot worse than it needs to be. Who dreamt this up?

"Mmm. Grassy," I said, a piece of long grass hanging out the corner of my mouth, and caught up in the scruff of my four-day beard. Sheena recoiled and made a gruesome frown.

"You have gooey grass all over your face."

I managed to eat half of the bowl, hoping that at some point I would break through an invisible culinary barrier, emerging into a kind of understanding with my grass jelly cocktail. It never happened, and I stopped more for Sheena's benefit than my own so that she would stop dry heaving every time I scooped a giant spoonful of slimy, icy lawn clippings into my mouth.

On our penultimate night in Kuala Lumpur, Terence had brought us out for a crab dinner with his sister Margaret, who was visiting for the weekend from Singapore. When at last we left the city and had made our way down Malaysia's West coast to the city-state at the tip of the peninsula, we were invited by Margaret to stay with her in Singapore. This was perfect, since our home on wheels had been declared illegal.

Margaret, her Belgian husband Bruno, and their two children lived in a nice condominium complex set back in the trees off of a main thoroughfare, as was the living arrangement of many of Singapore's middle class. Their neighbors were Italian and British and Chinese. There are relatively few native Singaporeans in Singapore, its status as a great place to do business having diluted their numbers. It had become the ultimate international melting pot.

Most families in Singapore employ a maid, and Margaret and Bruno were no different. Not to have a maid, Bruno told us one afternoon over tea, was to be considered lower class. Their maid was named Wei, a happy smiling girl of twenty eight who hailed from Burma, and lived in a small closet under the stairwell in the kitchen.

"I don't like having a maid," Bruno had confided. "There's something about it that just doesn't seem right." His face was pained, and he picked his words carefully so as to convey the moral contradictions that he struggled with. "To me, this feels like slavery. I mean, yes, we're providing a job for Wei, and it pays very well compared to what she could earn back in Burma, but she isn't free. We try to be friendly and treat her like a part of the family, but at the same time she knows that she has to do whatever we tell her or else she will get sent back to Burma. She is allowed to live in Singapore because we sponsor her, and if she loses this job, she will go back to a very hard life. That's not freedom. She is our slave, and I hate that, because we are expected to have a maid in order to be accepted." He, like others I'd spoken to, were torn about life in Singapore. It was a city with a clean and fresh face, but under the skin it was suffocating.

One evening I sat in the kitchen with Wei while she prepared food for Margaret's kids. I asked her about Burma and her past, and was surprised to learn that she held a degree in chemistry, and supported two children back home, whom she was unable to visit. She worked in Singapore because there was no opportunity in Burma, and she had left so that her children could have a better life.

On our last night in Singapore, Margaret and her friend Jeannie, a native Singaporean, invited Sheena and me out to the red light district to try durian fruit. We had heard that durian only smelled like rotting flesh, but that it tasted rich and delicious. There was only one way to find out.

We loaded up in Margaret's car and drove to the red light district, finding an illegal parking spot directly across the street from a street corner stand piled with thousands and thousands of enormous spiky durians. From across the street, the smell pressed itself into my nose like a three hundred pound messy-pants wrestler sitting directly on my face. Margaret smiled giddily and said that she loved the smell, but I had a feeling that she must be bluffing. I reminded her that the previous day she had scolded Bruno for bringing a durian-flavored muffin into the house.

"Yes I like the smell, but I don't want my house smelling like that. That would be disgusting, *la!*" Margaret was a walking, smiling, giggling contradiction.

We sat down at a table near the sidewalk and Margaret and Jeannie walked over to seek out the best durians. This was, after all, to be our durian devirginization, so it had to be special. They came back satisfied and smiling, a durian salesman following close behind with not one but three fetid, stinking spiky balls. He set them on the table and gave each one several whacks with a large knife, exposing the yellowish, putrid fleshy seeds inside. They reminded me of the bulbous growths attached to an orangutan's hindquarters, an image that didn't help to redeem the fruit of its atrocious smell.

We each took up a fleshy ball in our hand and Sheena and I looked to our hosts for guidance. Without hesitation they devoured the flesh, smiling and rolling their eyes in ecstasy. Sheena and I looked at each other, and then started in.

At that moment, I knew what it was to have a rotten, decomposing skunk carcass inside of my mouth. The smell was akin to being stuck in a small cardboard box with no air to breathe except for hot, humid flatulence pumped into the box through a warm, semi-decomposed pork bung. But the taste, the taste was something

21

unspeakable, something extraterrestrial. It was a collection of rotting animal carcasses tossed into a boiling pit toilet, and then distilled into a soft paste, which we voluntarily placed into our mouths.

Sheena bit one seed, nearly wretched, and told out hosts that she would be unable to continue. I wanted to understand how people could willingly go out of their way to eat this, so for the sake of anthropology I forced myself to eat the flesh of five or six enormous seeds. It never got any easier, and my throat twitched with each putrid mouthful.

Afterwards, looking for a way to rid ourselves of the oily decomposed flesh that coated our tongues (Margaret and Jeannie were still giddy and smiling), we grabbed a table on a busy corner in the red light district and ordered Chinese food from a heavyset Chinese woman wearing too much makeup and a dress several sizes too small. All around us old men openly dined with their hookers, while young girls in tight dresses walked around the tables like sharks looking for prey. I, with my three lady friends, quickly established myself as the restaurant's alpha male and was not approached by any hookers.

With Jeannie's local knowledge and encouragement, we ordered a giant bowl of frog legs in black sauce. Why we were still listening to Jeannie's culinary advice after the durian incident was a mystery, but the frog turned out to be quite tasty and we happily devoured the meat off of every tiny bone. Margaret, however, found the very idea of frog legs to be utterly revolting. With every frog leg, I watched from the corner of my eye as her face turned gray and the corners of her mouth turned down. It was sweet revenge.

Singapore is a melting pot of cultures and contradictions, and we left town having made new friends from all reaches of the globe. We had wandered through exotic barrios, eaten mouth watering ethnic food, and admired the city's modern architecture. And although we had escaped without having to endure a bamboo cane to the bare buttocks, we had unexpectedly endured a far worse punishment.

"Durian," our French friend Séb would later tell us, "is like a poo in the mouth." And so it was that we rode the bus back to Malaysia with our heads held high and a faint hint of poo on our breath.

The sound of jungle insects reverberated through the dense, humid night air and the sea beyond the grassy slope made no sound at all. A slow loris crept along an overhead electrical wire strung between a tall wooden pole and the cinderblock hut where a woman cooked rice and noodles for the few jungle people who lived around these parts. The loris, looking half koala bear and half sloth, stopped midway across the wire to give us a wide-eyed stare, and then continued on its way, grabbing a low hanging branch, and disappearing into the jungle.

"Anda selalu makan yang sama!" I had seen Hairi's face turn serious just before he yelled the string of incomprehensible gibberish. He raised his hand and brought it down toward his son.

"Setiap kali hamburger, hamburger, hamburger!" Hairi's hand landed softly on his son's head, and then gently ruffled his hair. His serious face turned soft and he let out a laugh. Hairi's wife, Nora, grinned widely from beneath her headscarf.

"My son," he said, "he always order the same thing. Hamburger, hamburger, hamburger!" He laughed, and his son smiled at us from beneath his mop of messed up black hair. A dab of ketchup stuck to the corner of his mouth.

A couple of days prior, while heading up Malaysia's East coast, I had studied a Google Map of the area searching for a place to camp. In the low quality image I could make out a small finger of land extending from the jungle with what appeared to be a white beach on one side. We decided to aim in the general direction of the peninsula and see if we could somehow drive there.

As we neared the supposed beach spot, we turned off of the main highway and started driving on small roads toward the ocean. Several times we came to dead ends, and several times I hopped out to ask for directions from non-English-speaking shopkeepers.

"Beach?" I would ask, to which they would confusedly say, "Beats? Beats! Beats?" and bobble their heads around. I took this as a positive sign, and continued driving. Eventually we found our way onto the peninsula and onto a rough dirt road that wound into the jungle. When we finally emerged from the dark undergrowth, we were on a white sandy beach in a hidden bay.

In the shade of a palm tree, a man sanded the side of a rundown fiberglass boat.

"I am Hairi," he said. "This is my home." He pointed to a canvas tent in a meadow at the edge of the jungle. Behind the tent, the meadow curved up into steep embankments covered in tightly packed vines, trunks, and leaves. In front of his tent the dense foliage opened up to reveal a white sand beach with an unimpeded view of several small islands. He reminded me of Robinson Crusoe, marooned out here all alone on the edge of civilization.

We positioned Nacho parallel to the beach so that out of our sliding door we would also have a commanding view of the beach and the islands. The setting was serene and beautiful, and as we settled in for the evening we saw a flashlight approaching our door.

"You eat dinner?" It was Hairi. "My family go to town, you come?" Without hesitation we jumped into his dilapidated car, squeezing into the backseat with his two boys. From their CD player, Alvin and the Chipmunks' rendition of "You Had a Bad Day" filled the car. Nora habitually smiled while their kids stared at us in silence. A rare cool breeze brushed my face through the open window as we wound and bounced along the jungle track.

At the cinderblock eatery we sat down at a plastic table outside, and then a teenage girl came out and set a smoldering egg carton in the grass beside our table. "Smoke keep the mosquitoes away," Hairi explained with a smile. He mimicked killing a mosquito on his arm by slapping it, and then he laughed. The smoke swirled around, Nora smiled, and the boys stared at us. Sheena asked Hairi how they were able to sleep when it was so hot and humid. "We open all windows in tent." he said.

That night while we slept in Nacho I drifted in and out of sleep. Suddenly my eyes snapped open and I gasped for air. I felt as though I were being water-boarded in some secret CIA prison camp. I rolled over and pressed my face against the window screen, gasping for a breath of fresh air. It never came, and I dizzily rolled onto my back, breathing belabored, hot breaths of thick water vapor. The mattress and my pillow were soaked with sweat. I laid on my back for what seemed like an eternity, our small oscillating fan pushing the watery air over our bodies. I hoped I would adapt quickly to the stagnant heat and humidity of the jungle.

The next evening, over another meal of ramen noodles and rice at the cinder block restaurant, Hairi talked about life in the jungle and about Muslim traditions. I told him that I was jealous of the way Muslims got to wear comfortable silk pajamas to the mosque on Fridays.

"If I wear my pajamas in public, people just think I'm lost or homeless," I said.

He told us about Mecca, and how every Muslim dreams of making a pilgrimage there. "Have you ever been to Mecca?" I asked.

"I have not gone. Not *yet*," he said, emphasizing the word *yet*, and then smiled broadly. "This my dream, so I will go one day. My dreams are coming true."

"One day," he said, "I was working on the beach. I see big yacht out near island, so I say, 'okay, I go see.' I borrow small boat and I row. I row a long time, and I get to yacht. The man on yacht come out, and he from Scotland. He sail boat here, all the way from Scotland!" His eyes glistened in the dim light from the restaurant's bare light bulb. A swirl of moths and mosquitoes whirled around and smacked the bulb, casting fleeting shadows.

"The man tell me to come onto boat, so I do," he continued. "We talk, and I ask him how he able to come here on boat when it so far away. And he tell me, 'Hairi, if you want to be like me, you can be like me.' He tell me, 'make a list of one hundred dreams. Everybody have dreams, and if you write them down on a list, your dreams come true. And after your one hundred dreams come true, you write a new list of one hundred more dreams.'"

It seemed a little superstitious to me, but I listened on skeptically.

"So I go home and I think about what the Scottish man say. I say okay, I find a pencil and a paper, and I write down my dreams. One, two, three, four—I write down 100 dreams. I hang up my dreams by my bed, and I start to look at it every day." Hairi paused, placed his hand on his knee, and lowered his head. He then stared at us and continued, slowly.

"You know what happen?" he said. "I see that list every day and I start thinking about my dreams. This list make me think, to remember. My first dream is I want to have own boat. But we don't have so much money, so I go and I find old boat with hole in it. Owner don't know how to fix boat, so I learn how to make fiberglass repair, and I fix boat! Now I have boat!"

He was visibly excited by this, and I suppose there was something exciting in this key he'd discovered. By thinking often about his goals he could more readily realize them with fewer resources when opportunities presented themselves. But it seemed like a small victory. Hairi continued.

"Next, I have dream of being diver. But to become diver, it cost 3,000 Ringgit! I do not have 3,000 Ringgit, so I look for other way. I find resort that have diving school, so I try to get job there. I think, if I can work at resort, maybe I can learn to dive. I work hard, and they hire me to wash dishes. So I work, and I ask how I can learn to dive. They say for workers at resort they have dive class for 25 Ringgit. So I take class. I become diver, and resort hire me to bring clients diving!"

By now Hairi was beaming, and Nora smiled proudly at her husband for being so resourceful.

"Next, I have dream to swim with whale shark," he said. He hummed the tune to Jaws, smiled, and continued. "So one day after we dive with clients, we taking the boat back to resort and we see big whale sharks! So big! We all jump in water and we swim with them. I touch them, I touch the big sharks with my hand!" He mimicked the touch as though he were stroking a beautiful woman's hair.

"My big dream," Hairi continued, "was to touch a battleship. Since I was a boy in school I like these big battleships. But the closest battleship is in Hawaii! How do I do it?" By now, Hairi's eyebrows were raised, as though there was no possible way.

"So," Hairi continued, "I ask at resort, and I find out Star Cruise Lines hiring workers for cruise ships. I ask for job, and they hire me to clean up on ship. My ship go from Kuala Lumpur to Manila, Philippines and back. One day in Manila, there a Star Lines ship that go to Hawaii, so I find someone who work on that ship, and I ask if he want to trade me. He say yes! So I take ship to Hawaii! When the ship get there, they tell us, 'Okay, you have two days before ship leave. You can go explore.' So I get off ship, and I go to harbor where battleship is parked." Hairi slowed down as if savoring every word. "I walk to battleship, and I go to the side. I place my hand on it, like this." He placed his left hand on the inside of his right elbow, a gesture of respect, and pretended to touch the ship with his right hand. He touched the imaginary ship for a long time, as if reliving the moment.

"My dreams are coming true." He ended his story and sat there with a big grin on his face next to his son, who had long since finished his hamburger. Nora looked at him admiringly, as if he had just saved his entire family from a burning bus. And Sheena and I looked at him admiringly, too.

Here was a man with very few resources, who lived in a tent in the jungle. Yet he had obtained his own boat, had become a scuba diver, had swum with whale sharks, and had traveled across the ocean to another country to see an icon that he'd only read about in books.

The next morning, Nora invited us over to the tent for a breakfast of traditional Malaysian pancakes with sprinkled sugar, and a plastic pitcher of black coffee. For a family living in their conditions, I imagined this special occasion must have been difficult to pull together. We all gathered around the outdoor wooden table and dug into the delicious food as the sounds of birds and insects echoed around the meadow. A dog bolted out of the jungle, followed closely by an angry monkey. Hairi yelled at the monkey and Sheena and I laughed.

"Wait here," Hairi said, and then disappeared into his tent. He emerged carrying a comfortable-looking Malaysian shirt, which he called a *baju melayu*, and a traditional plaid wraparound sarong. He smiled and handed them to me. "These are for you. So you can dress comfortably on Fridays like Muslims." He asked me to stand, and then showed me how to wrap it in the traditional way.

He turned and went back into his tent. He emerged a minute later with a rose-print dress and blouse, and handed them to Sheena.

"Nora made these by hand. We want you to have them," he said, and then handed them to Sheena. We had been humbled. We made a quick assessment of things we could offer them, and decided on a fresh jar of *dulce de leche* from Argentina.

For a moment I considered what an adventure it would be if we changed our plans and drove Hairi to Mecca. It would be the ultimate gift, the realization of his wildest dreams, and an amazing experience. It really would have been something, but I let the impulse pass. He'll make it there eventually; he'll just have to wait until it pops up next on his list.

3

The Route 3 East Coast Road

Sheena

After leaving Hairi's jungle outpost, it felt strange to be back in civilization. Young people loitered near the seawall of a small city we'd come to, enjoying the breeze and eating take-away from the bustling outdoor market just a parking lot away. Down below, a mess of boulders formed a wave break. Cats pounced between the rocks, unhindered by their strangely mangled tails; some were stumps, others crooked, and a few had ends like lollipops. I had voiced my sadness about these cats a week earlier, and was glad to have been told that it was simply a genetic defect found in Asian cats, not some sadistic sport carried out by knife-wielding youths.

Past the boulders, the tide was way out, exposing a wasteland of puddles and sticky, shin- deep mud. Two Muslim girls, around twelve years of age, sat on the boulders of the wave break singing along to the streaming music on their phone. One girl casually tossed a rock between her hands, and finally lofted it into the mud. The girls exploded in a fit of giggles as the rock splashed into the mud, unexpectedly speckling their faces and their silky hijabs with mud. We smiled at their reactions while our gaze shifted ahead.

"Look at that poor fish flopping in the mud!" Brad said.

A rather ugly fish, grey like the mud with spiky fins, was so far from the water that there was no chance it would survive its own negligence. Soon the mud plain was alive with movement, and I realized that there were hundreds of these fish flopping in the mud. Could they all have ignored their natural instinct to follow the shifting tides back out to sea? And then I noticed something even more surprising: using their pectoral fins, these fish were actually walking! I clearly knew nothing.

I later learned that this fish, called a mudskipper, deliberately stays behind when the tide goes out, hiding in seaweed and tidal pools until the coast is clear. At this point they begin their double life on land, retreating every so often to their muddy burrows to stay wet, and defending their territory by catapulting their muscular bodies up in the air in animated brawls with other skippers.

Eventually the sky darkened and we were forced to leave our rocky rest spot. We wandered down the coast to the glowing canopy of an evening food market.

This was one of the most rewarding aspects of Malaysia: diving into street food markets, never knowing just what we'd find. Depending on our location, the options can vary widely based on the mix of the three main ethnic groups in Malaysia. Down one street, a market will cater to the Chinese community. Head down another and there may be *halal* food for the Muslims, or perhaps *mamuk*, a cuisine that has resulted from the intermarriage of migrating Indian Muslims and Malay women.

Our options were endless, but we gravitated toward *mamuk*. Clearly Indian in flavor and technique, but only found in Malaysia, *roti chanai* is the most common of *mamuk* foods. A skinny Tamil man with a moustache and a tank top—and it is always this man—kneads, folds, oils, tosses and finally fries the dough on a griddle. It is somehow both stretchy and flaky, and is served on a circular metal tray with a few sides of spicy chutney and lentils.

While Brad usually ordered some variation of *roti*, I opted for *thosai*, a crepe made from a mixture of rice flour and black dhal, left to ferment overnight and then cooked on the griddle. We washed down every meal with a couple of rounds of *teh tarek*, literally, "pulled tea," made with sweetened-condensed milk and poured back and forth between two containers arm's length apart to mix and froth it. The higher the pull, the thicker the froth. It is an artist's process, worth ordering if only to watch it being made.

When we weren't eating food of Indian or Chinese influence, our Malay food was *nasi,* a variable rice dish. Malay food is not complete without a healthy portion of noodles or rice, and ordering a meal without them is like ordering a sandwich without the bread. It may sound boring by contrast, but the combination of ingredients, flavors, and techniques mean that these dishes never get old.

One hot afternoon I stopped by a small cart and pointed to an egg. It was all I wanted, but before I could blink an eye, the vendor had twirled a piece of parchment paper into a cone shape, filled it with rice, fried peanuts, dried anchovies, a cucumber slice, a dollop of spicy bean paste, and a hardboiled egg on top. He folded the parchment down over the top like a lid and handed it to me.

To drive through Malaysia is to blaze a trail from one great market stall meal to another, and this night would be no different. After sitting and watching the Muslim girls splash themselves with mud, and the cats searching for lizards among boulder piles, and the walking fish chasing each other across the mud flats, Brad and I sat down for dinner in front of an illuminated market stall in the parking lot set back from the muddy coast. Tonight we would feast on satay cooked over a charcoal fire, served with spicy peanut sauce, cucumber slices, and tightly packed cubes of sticky rice. We washed our sticky fingers with hot water from a communal kettle, and then finished the evening by sampling an array of pink fluffy muffins and crispy pancakes oozing with crushed peanuts and chocolate.

We returned to the waterfront with full bellies, found Nacho, and said goodnight to the cats and the walking fish. We would need our rest, because tomorrow there would be more stops to discover on Malaysia's food trail.

4

Route 3 to Terengganu

Brad

We passed the days slowly meandering northward along the east coast of the Malaysian peninsula. The two-lane road carried us past banana plantations and sections of dense jungle, a repetition of leafy vines and bamboo, and cinderblock and tin villages. It was election time and the popularity of the blue party could be measured against that of the red party by a comparative observation of colored flags flittering at the roadsides. Sheena's window was down, but mine was closed and I cursed the Argentinean thief who'd broken it six months prior. Unable to find a replacement window in Argentina, I'd had two panes of shatterproof glass placed into the window frame and adhered together with silicone. It kept wind and water out, but it was a curse in this suffocating humid heat. Without air-flow and without air conditioning, driving through the Malaysian jungle was nearly unbearable. I practiced suppressing the feelings of hot, claustrophobic panic by breathing rhythmically and focusing on my heart rate. Eventually I would get used to it—that was the reason we removed our air conditioner in the first place. By altering the environment to seem more comfortable, it's hard to ever get used to it. But air-flow was necessary, and every day in this hot jungle I cursed that anonymous window-breaking *pendejo* a half a world away.

We entered a nondescript seaside village just like many others we'd passed throughout the day, regarding the stick huts and colorful banners siding the roads. Suddenly a car raced up beside us in the oncoming lane and the two dark-skinned men inside wildly motioned for me to roll down my window. I held my hands palm up and shrugged my shoulders, unable to roll my window down. I thought to myself, "that Argentinean *pendejo*." They motioned to the roadside. We've always held that in general, people are good, so we obliged and pulled over to see what they wanted.

"Hey guys, nice van!" The men had jumped out of their car and were walking quickly toward Sheena's window. "My friends and I are doing some video production here. You should come to our house and hang out for a while."

There were few rules to this game, but one of them was that you should never turn down an invitation, so we agreed. We did a u-turn and followed the men back in the direction we'd come until we arrived at a wooden hut, where we parked in a dirt lot.

Inside the hut there were a couple of other young Malaysian men looking at a laptop. The driver of the car introduced us to the others and said that they had noticed us on account of our van and figured we weren't from around there. They were, they explained, producing a surf video to be filmed entirely in Malaysia.

"Nobody thinks of Malaysia as a surf destination. Everyone goes to Indo instead. The surf in Indo is more consistent, but we have great surfing here, too. You just have to know where to find it and when." They explained that they'd been traveling all over Malaysia for six months, discovering new surf spots that nobody knew about because no surfers had ever bothered going there. "We've even found some offshore spots that get a pretty big swell," they said. They were compiling their footage, and were going to release their surf video in the hope of attracting surfers to their peninsula. Outside the hut, tiny waves softly lapped the shore.

"I guess this place isn't one of the secret spots," I said.

"Not now, but last week it was huge!"

The conversation came to a lull and Sheena and I stood up and prepared to leave. As we walked out into the dirt lot the guys mentioned that they were having a beach barbecue that night with some friends, and that we should come. "It's just beyond the point over there," one of them said, gesturing with his chin toward a sandy bar extending from the beach a half-mile away.

That evening when it got dark, after setting up camp in a small clearing next to a clump of trees just up from the beach outside of town, we walked barefoot onto the beach and headed toward the point. The sand was cool under our feet and tide pools had formed in a few places. Little crabs scurried away sideways as we passed, and the low glow of the moon and the bare bulbs of the sleepy village behind us illuminated the way. Around the point we saw the lights of a hut supported on stilts, and a few people wandered about or lounged on chairs.

When we arrived we introduced ourselves to the others: a few Malaysian surfers and boat drivers. The hut was actually a bar that had been closed down for the group's private party. We drank coke and ate barbecued fish while we chatted with our new friends. We met Shuhaimy, a Muslim man who lived down the coast on a hidden cove, and he offered us a place to stay on his property.

"I built my house on the best surf beach in Malaysia. You see, most Malaysians keep a row of trees between their houses and the beach for protection from storms, but I cut down the trees in front of my house so I could see the surf. From the beach it looks like I am the only house. Come there this weekend. I will feed you and you can go snorkeling." We told him we surely would.

We grabbed a couple of beers and walked out on the deck above the sand. A cool sea breeze floated in from the water and made the temperature perfect. Sheena and I sat there in the dark, the quiet rhythm of jungle drums floating out from a pair of speakers, and we watched the reflection of the moonlight in the hypnotic, lapping waves. Just then a white bodiless tank top traversed our line of sight and approached the bar from the empty beach below. We had forgotten that a world existed outside of our tranquil beach bar, and we watched the figure approach. I sipped my beer and slowly turned to Sheena as the figure reached the halo of light cast on the sand.

"Is that Jan?" I caught his attention by waving my arm. "Jan! I'd recognize that old wifebeater shirt anywhere!" He paused and let it sink in, and then walked quickly over to us.

"I can't believe it!" he said. "You still recognize my wifebeater!" It had been three weeks since we'd parted ways in Kuala Lumpur and had gone off in different directions, but here we were, at a barbecue on a random beach on the South China Sea.

"How did you manage to hear about this barbecue?" I asked. There were only a handful of people there, and it was a private affair. "We just sort of stumbled upon it ourselves."

"Actually I have no idea where I am! I was just walking along the beach thinking and I saw some lights, so I came to see what it was."

It was comforting to see Jan again. In Asia we were out of our element and he represented a link to our past life in South America. We wondered how he was holding up, and he seemed a little bit torn about his decision to come to Asia. He and Kevin had recognized that, after

33

having ridden from Canada to Argentina together, their traveling styles had become disparate. Kevin preferred to stay in one place for a long time and take photos, or fall into a groove. Jan, on the other hand liked meandering, seeing where the winds would take him. But the winds had slowed down upon reaching Asia.

"My bike is having some troubles, and I'm starting to feel as if I'm just wandering aimlessly." He was working on getting Karina, who we all referred to as his "Latin lover," out to Thailand for a visit, but beyond that he wasn't sure what to do. He seemed disheartened. "I've been thinking about going home sooner than I had planned. I can go back into my practice as a tax lawyer."

We'd found that emotional highs and lows were a part of this kind of travel, and I guessed that he was going through one of those inevitable troughs. But he seemed content, not like he was sulking. It just seemed to me that it was the wrong time to quit with so much left to do.

"Jan, by complete random chance you're eating grilled fish at a beach barbecue in Malaysia with your friends you met in Argentina, and tomorrow you'll ride away through the jungle on your motorcycle without a care in the world. These things won't happen when you're a tax lawyer in Holland."

Jan had a pensive face, and when he smiled his forehead and eyes didn't wrinkle. He could be smiling or frowning, but you would only know by looking at his mouth. Now his mouth seemed to convey a sense of amusement. "Yes, but at a point you just don't care anymore, and that's when you know it's time to go home. Some people get lost out here and they never go back, but that's not me. I enjoy being a tax lawyer. I also enjoy traveling. But when traveling loses its appeal, I might as well be a tax lawyer."

I saw his point, and he was only putting into words what we had always known. We'd met a few people on the road who had left home half a decade or a decade before, and seemed plagued by the same monotony that had likely pushed them out the door in the first place. Eventually we humans can adapt to any situation and it becomes normal. It had occurred to me that people always wonder what it would be like to be someone else: Bill Gates, Brad Pitt, David Beckham. But in the end those people enjoy the same average number of endorphins rushing through their bloodstreams as the rest of us. The trick is to make an endorphin-inducing change and ride it until it levels out, and then make another change.

We bid Jan farewell and in the morning made our own geographical change. We would go back the way we'd come to spend the weekend at Shuhaimy's beach, and then we'd resume our northward trajectory before parking Nacho and trying on our sea legs for a taste of the island life—toes in the sand, a good book, and smooth sailing with soft waves lapping at the bow of our boat.

5

Water Taxi to Kuala Besut

Brad

With every wave that crashed over the bow, our small boat took on more water. The panic on our young captain's face shattered any hope that we would make it out of this tropical depression without a miracle, and my brain wouldn't stop humming the theme from Gilligan's Island. I wondered how the brain could have a sense of humor when it knows that this will surely be the end. I knew it in my bones, the woman who sloshed around in the saltwater at our feet knew it, and the two sobbing girls who clung to their belongings next to us knew it. But my brain kept humming along.

Just sit right back and you'll hear a tale,
A tale of a fateful trip
That started from this tropic port
Aboard this tiny ship...

Sheena and I sat on the beach with our duffel bags and waited. We had been on Perhentian Island for three days of relaxation and white sand beaches, and it was time to get back to the mainland. By mid-afternoon we would be reunited with Nacho so that we could continue our northward trajectory up Malaysia's East coast. Our instructions were to wait on the beach for the eight-person water taxi that would take us on a 45-minute jaunt back to the mainland.

When a small, motorized canoe approached, Sheena and I climbed aboard, and were joined by a young couple from England. The canoe sputtered back to life, reversed, and then spun around to bring us toward the waiting water taxi.

The water taxi was wooden and rickety with a few plank bench seats and a makeshift awning to block the sun during the crossing to Kuala Besut. A small outboard motor hung from the back, and several rags, wires, tools, and a car battery littered the floor of the boat near the

36

engine. The boat's captain was a young Malaysian man in his early twenties, obnoxiously indifferent, and having a wisp of hair fashionably poking out from above his forehead like Billy Idol. He looked more like a DJ than a boat captain.

Once onboard, we put our bags on the floor and waited. We asked the driver a few questions, but found his command of our native tongue to be only slightly better than our command of his. Soon, another boat approached and two French girls came aboard and sat down next to Sheena and me on the rearmost bench seat.

The captain fired up the engine and sped off toward Perhentian's larger island, and as we approached a bay dotted with small hotels, he killed the engine and we waited again. As we waited our boat slowly rotated in the water and I saw that the eastern sky was pitch black from the horizon to the heavens.

I got Sheena's attention and motioned toward the approaching storm. "I sure hope we don't get caught in the likes of that," I said. The Englishman and his girlfriend overheard and looked up to see. The French girls were getting impatient.

"What are we waiting for?!" one of them scolded. The captain squinted and searched the beach with his eyes. "We wait," he said. The girls hunched over and complained to one another in French.

The wall of black steadily approached, and then all at once our boat began to pitch and tilt as a blast of wind hit us from the East. The strength of the squall in front of the storm suggested that it was fierce and moving fast. Within a minute big, heavy drops exploded into the ocean around us as though someone were pouring buckets of steel marbles from the clouds. With each drop, a small burst of seawater exploded into the air, which the wind carried across the surface of the water, giving the ocean the look of a blizzard blowing across tundra. The awning on our boat did little to protect us from the sideways rain, and what water was collected on top of it drained into the boat.

"Let's go!" one of the French girls screamed.

Just then, out of the rain came another motorized canoe carrying a man and a woman in their mid-twenties. When they reached us, they rolled their soaked backpacks aboard and stepped onto our boat. They were a German couple, and I immediately took a liking to them. The French girls gave off an air of superficiality and self-righteousness, while the English backpackers seemed standoffish and disinterested. But the Germans wore smiles despite being soaked to the bone. They greeted everyone, took their seats, and smiled at each other.

By now the black clouds had enveloped us, and the rain and wind had intensified. We could no longer see either one of the islands, and the visibility had been reduced to a mere 20 meters.

"Okay, let's GO!" the French girls shouted in unison. The boatman fired up the engine and sped off into the storm.

Sheena and I crouched down, hugged our legs and hid in the draft of the English couple to stay out of the wind and rain. As soon as we had moved beyond the protective shield of the islands, staying dry became impossible. The wind whipped the waves into sloshing six-foot peaks, and the ocean peeled off in layers, drenching us. I pulled my sunglasses over my eyes to block the continuous barrage of salt water.

A terrible feeling began to come over me like a heavy, wet blanket. I lifted my head and looked around. In all directions there was nothing but whipping water and towering waves, which seemed to be hitting us from all sides. Our boat was nothing more than a wooden shell with a couple of benches, and the wind and waves tossed it about like a toy. Driving into this storm had been a bad decision. I turned around to look at our captain for the first time.

The young boatman was crouching behind the wheel, soaked from head to toe, his Billy Idol hair long since flattened into a dark smear across the tight creases in his forehead. His face was a portrait of pure fear. He squinted and jerked his gaze around in all directions, trying to see into the dense wall of water that surrounded us. I had to look away.

I couldn't believe what was happening. The boat rode sideways up a tall vertical face, and I had to press both hands against the side of the boat to keep myself from falling over the edge. I looked back at the boy captain and saw that he was starting to panic. He frantically looked around, wiping the salt water from his eyes with his trembling hand. His mouth was slightly agape, and the corners of his mouth were turned down.

The Englishman noticed that our engine speed was becoming erratic, and he turned around. The boat began to pulse and weave as the captain continued to lose his bearings.

"What's he doing?" the Englishman barked. "Doesn't he know where we're going?"

By now everyone had stopped trying to protect themselves from the wind and rain, and we all stared expectantly at the captain.

"Excuse me," the German man said in a stern, loud voice, "do you know the direction to land?" The boatman stopped searching the narrow ring of visibility around our boat and his wide eyes stared at the

German. The look on his face was one of alarm. He helplessly shrugged his shoulders and shook his head. He slowed the motor and began turning the boat in tight circles. He had panicked, and in doing so, we had become disoriented and could no longer remember in which direction we'd been traveling before.

At that moment, 30 minutes into what was supposed to be a 45-minute water taxi ride, we realized that we were hopelessly lost at sea.

The German man, recognizing that this probably wouldn't end well, stood up and began grabbing life vests from the netting beneath the bimini top and passed them around. "Does everyone who wants one have one?" He had to yell to be heard over the wind, the crashing waves, and the sputtering motor.

After donning our life vests, I took another look around the boat. To our right, the two French girls had their heads down and eyes closed, sobbing into their duffel bags. A barrage of waves crashed over the sides of our boat, and somehow the German girl ended up on the ground at our feet, sloshing around in the saltwater, crying inconsolably. I put my hand on the girl's shoulder and held her against my leg for stability, and Sheena tried to convince her that everything would be okay.

"How can everything be okay?" she sobbed. "The captain is looking around like he doesn't know where we are." The way that she sobbed the words describing our situation made it all the worse. "I'm so scared. The storm is so strong, but our boat is so small!" She remained at our feet, hiding from the reality outside of our boat.

Another wave crested our bow, and the captain realized that we were beginning to sink. He abandoned the controls, and I looked back to see the sea level only a few inches below the rear edge of the boat.

He jumped back and crammed his hands into the water under the rear bench seat near the car battery. He produced a piece of garden hose attached to a small pump, and positioned the hose so that it would evacuate the water out of the boat. He fumbled with the pump's bare wires and pressed one of them onto the negative battery terminal. When he pressed the other wire onto the positive terminal, his body jolted violently. He had been electrocuted, and he whipped his hand back and forth as if it were on fire as he pulled himself back to the wheel. I watched the end of the hose, but the pump never came to life.

As time went on, our situation continued to get more serious. The storm was becoming more intense, and the captain was becoming more and more erratic. Sheena and I had been looking for buoys and trying to find ways to help the captain, but everyone else seemed to be waiting for a miracle. Finally, Sheena had had enough.

"Hey!" She yelled. "The captain is lost, so we need to try to figure out where we are. There were buoys out here on the way out, so help us look for them!" The Englishman and the German started looking around, while the French girls continued sobbing. The German girl had long since gone hysterical, and remained pinned to my leg.

From the peak of each wave the boat repeatedly slid sideways down a ten-foot wall of water before riding up the next wave. Without warning, the German man flung himself forward, onto the floor of the boat.

"Balance boat! Balance boat!" the captain wailed. When the German had moved, the boat's balance had been disrupted and we began listing heavily to one side. "Just wait!" The German yelled. A minute later he pulled himself back onto his seat and thrust his hand into the air. "Look what I found! I remembered this! It is a compass!" he hollered. From the boat there came a collective cheer, and he passed it to the captain.

The captain looked at the device, turning it over in his hand while trying to keep the boat upright. He held it close to his eye, but it was becoming clear that he had never used a compass before. As a water taxi driver, his navigation had been totally visual. He handed it back to the German and told him to point him in the direction of shore.

As the minutes ticked by and the daylight continued to wane, we began to wonder whether the first hour of our trip had been spent driving toward or away from shore. We continued to scour the area around our boat for clues. Finally, at the two-hour mark, we found one.

"Are those pillars?" Sheena yelled, excitedly. We all looked but could see nothing. "Look! Over there! I see some pillars in the water!"

The captain steered left, and soon we saw a fisherman's net draped between several steel poles. We weren't out of the woods, but at least we were somewhere near civilization! Our spirits started to lift, and after a few more minutes of motoring, it came.

"Land! I see land!" It was the Englishman, and he could hardly contain himself. He bounced around and spun in his seat. "Wooooooo! Do you see it?!"

From the fog a faint outline of limestone hills began to emerge. We had done it! Even if we capsized now, I reasoned, we could probably swim to shore. We continued motoring, and as the shore came into view about a quarter of a mile away, there was no sign of our port in either direction. The captain steered northward, but soon we crossed into a shipping lane. It was the shipping lane entering Kota Baru; we had drifted over twenty miles off course, and were nearly in Thailand.

Realizing where we were, the captain began to panic again. He was overdue in Kuala Besut, and had a lot of distance to cover before nightfall. He flipped the boat around and began a high-speed blast southward along the coast, parallel to the tall, rough waves. Our boat repeatedly became airborne, crashing down in the trough of each wave. Now that our captain had regained his confidence and was trying to save face, we seemed to be in even greater danger than before.

"Excuse me!" the German yelled. "I think I speak for everyone when I say that we want you to drive to shore right now. We will find a road and we will hitchhike! Please, take us to the shore!" But his pleas fell on deaf ears. Dropping a load of soaked and frightened passengers off on a remote beach so that they could hitchhike to the port was a surefire way to get himself fired, so he stayed the course. We blasted south, taking warm blasts of tropical seawater to the face with each crashing wave.

Finally, just as evening had settled in on Malaysia's east coast, we gained sight of the sea wall at Kuala Besut. The German girl, still sobbing, fell into her boyfriend's arms and began apologizing. She turned to us and explained, still sobbing, "Coming here was my birthday gift to him. I'm so sorry." The two of them hugged a while longer, and then he held his compass over his head like a gold medal. "Best five Euro I ever spent!" he cheered.

When finally at long last we passed through the opening in the port's wave break, the boat stopped rocking. The captain slowed the engine, the German girl reclaimed her seat, and the French girls stared blankly ahead. Everything was going to be okay, but somewhere deep inside of my sick brain, I wished I could have seen where this whole Gilligan's Island thing would have gone.

At the northern end of Malaysia, just below the Thai border, which we had nearly crossed in the storm aboard the S.S. Minnow, the land rose steadily skyward to the hill stations of the Cameron Highlands. The road climbed from the sticky jungle into the cool mist and the trees gave way to rolling tea plantations where hunched-over Indians filled large sacks with tea leaves.

We had driven around the circumference of Malaysia over the course of a month, and had resigned ourselves to the sweltering heat. At first we found that we couldn't fall asleep in the stagnant, wet air, so we had improvised our own survival methods. Each morning we would place four cans of beer in Nacho's freezer. At night we would bring the cans up to bed and lean one on each side of our necks so as to cool our blood as it passed close to the surface through our jugular veins. In this way we found that we could drop our body temperature just enough to be able to fall asleep, but if we failed to fall asleep before the cans warmed up, then we spent the night tossing and turning on the sweat-soaked mattress. Before crossing into Thailand, we decided to head to the Cameron Highlands for a brief respite from the heat.

On the eve of my birthday, Sheena and I walked along the main drag in the hill station of Kampung Raja. An Indian restaurant had set up several folding tables on the sidewalk, and as we passed, something caught my eye.

"Hey, I would recognize that wifebeater shirt anywhere!" It was Jan, sitting at one of the tables eating curry in his trademark white tank top. We sat, and over cups of pulled milk tea he told us that he had climbed into the highlands in a rainstorm, and his bike had started misfiring. Eventually the engine died, and he had done some minor tinkering to try to understand what had happened. Once the engine dried out, it started back up, but he had finally lost faith in his bike. We chatted for a while longer, regaled him with our dramatic tale of being lost at sea, and then went our separate ways.

When we left the Cameron Highlands heading west, the road sliced back and forth through tea fields, and with each curling switchback the air became tangibly thicker. The hills gave way to jutting limestone spires whose sheer walls gave them the look of vine-draped ships rising out of the jungle, sailing westward to the Andaman Sea.

6

Route 6 to Penang

Sheena

"It's all about trust. And when it comes to monkeys, I have none."

—Anthony Bourdain

I should have learned my lesson weeks ago. It was early in the morning and Brad and I were strolling down a sleepy street in Cherating on Malaysia's east coast. Several kitten-sized baby monkeys suddenly caught our eyes as they swung in the trees and pulled each other's tails. I wanted to squeeze their little cheeks and rock them in my arms, so we began to cross the street. We didn't make it very far. A massive mother monkey came flying out of the canopy like a bat out of hell, charging at us and screaming hysterically. We attempted to sprint away with lightning speed, but without our morning coffee we stumbled away clumsily as if fleeing from Alfred Hitchcock's birds. When we were no longer deemed a threat, we slowed down and had a good laugh, dumbstruck by our own naiveté.

Now, after descending from the highlands, we decided to make one final stop on the island of Penang before crossing into Thailand. Penang is different from the rest of Malaysia in that it retained its British identity following its independence from British colonial rule in the 1950s. Today Penang exemplifies multi-ethnicity: colonial buildings from the English back up to Chinese neighborhoods, and the Hindu customs of migrant Indian workers mingle with traditional Malay culture.

To reach Penang we crossed the Strait of Malacca on a thirteen-kilometer bridge. On the island, dense jungles, waterfalls, and fruit and spice orchards butted up against fishing villages and beaches. Once over the bridge, we veered away from Penang's main city, Georgetown, and headed down the shores along the strait.

The maddening traffic and chaos of the city dissipated with each curve of the road and soon we were rolling through dense jungle hills and small one-street villages. We explored random dirt roads in search of a worthy campsite, but found nothing. We followed the main road for over an hour until it came to an end. We were left wondering what to do next when, through the trees, we noticed a picture-perfect quiet ocean inlet dotted with colorful fishing boats and one massive tree shading a beach. We squeezed under the tree and had just enough room to pop Nacho's rooftop tent. We slept the night away next to a happy pack of lounging street dogs.

The next day we climbed the side of a mountain into the interior on a winding road sheltered by jungle. We stopped next to a pile of coconut husks near a strip of roadside vendors. Bags of banana chips, bottles of coconut oil, and fragrant packs of cinnamon, star anise, nutmeg seeds, pepper, and clove dotted the covered tables at the roadside. We climbed over boulders to follow a stream into the jungle, and came across a clear pool with a waterfall cascading into it, where we lounged in the sun for a while before heading back to resume our drive.

On our way back to Nacho, Brad led me to a cage where a family of four monkeys lived next to a vendor stall. The parents sat in the center, bored and uninterested in us, picking nits from each other's fur. The babies catapulted off the cage walls, full of energy, rambunctious and completely out of control. I leaned forward to touch one of the babies' hands. It reached out and wrapped its little hand around my index finger. I stared at its delicate little fingernails and imagined it was a human baby.

My train of thought, which by now had meandered from baby monkeys to my future babies, was suddenly cut short. I felt myself being yanked forward, like my hair was being sucked into the propeller of a motorboat. My eyes were pointed to the ground and I couldn't see what was going on, but I could hear the alarming scream of an angry monkey. The crazed mother tightened her grip on my hair. I tried to display submissiveness by allowing my body to go limp while leaning forward to reduce the tension. Brad, seeing that I was one swipe away from having monkey nails in my face, pulled me away in one quick motion. The mother retained in her wrinkled little hand a fistful of my hair.

I was humiliated. As I peered back at the monkeys, head burning, I watched as my hair was distributed amongst the four. They twisted it between their fingers, studied it closely, wrapped their tongues around it, and then ate it.

By lunchtime we closed the loop of the island, ending in Georgetown. And here lay the reason why we really came to Penang. Anthony Bourdain: No Reservations—my all time favorite travel documentary—had visited Georgetown just one year prior. It was a surefire endorsement that we would find something good to eat.

The essence of the show is this: a famous New York chef-turned-author-turned-television host travels to wild and faraway places, discovering the best of exotic cuisine and culture. It is packed with food erotica; unfamiliar faces, steam billowing from pot-belly pots at hawker stands, alleyways with twisted jumbles of lights hanging from above, heaping piles of pork, everything garnished with hot chilies or exotic sauces. I freaking love it.

When we lived in Flagstaff, we often watched these shows at night. They were a source of entertainment, but also of inspiration, pushing us forward, keeping us focused on our goal to travel the world. We wanted to go to these places, too.

I was curious what Anthony Bourdain had thought of his visit. Here's what he had to say:

"I feel inexorably attached to Malaysia for many reasons, but one of them is that I got there early in my career as a traveler, wasn't really ready for it, and was changed by the place. It seduced and overwhelmed me at the same time. The smells and colors and flavors—the look and sound of the place, the at times impenetrable mix of Indian, Malay and Chinese cultures—it fucked me all up...Lots of people, lots of food, lots of cats. The cats are a good sign."

I too have been left with an overwhelming excitement from Malaysia. The major joy of my experience, Malaysia having been my first taste of Asia, is that every sensation is intensified. Everything is more exciting and more intriguing. You feel like you are never going to get used to it and never shake the butterflies from your stomach. It is a wonderful feeling.

Georgetown didn't disappoint. We spent most of the afternoon in Chinese neighborhoods filled with antique stores, electronics, key makers, and quiet alleyways where the locals slouched on their patios. At the Sky Hotel on Chulai Street, a smiling old Chinese man worked behind his food stand organizing and cutting strips of pork and duck. We sat down at a plastic table in the open-air dining area, which consumed the ground floor of the building. A woman set two drinks on the table and then the old man delivered our lunch: two plates of white rice, topped with sautéed greens and barbecued, honey-sweetened pork. The combination of hearty greens and simple rice, with gooey, crispy, succulent pork was life altering. It haunted my thoughts for days.

7

Phetkasem Road
to Krabi

Brad

At the town of Krabi, in the southwest corner of Thailand just above the border with Malaysia, the tall limestone ships that ply the inland jungles, draped in vines and slicing through the sky with their tree masts, spilled out into the Andaman Sea like a stone armada. The town sits on a toe of land surrounded on three sides by green rivers that spill into the sea. Thai men waited along the river shores aboard narrow boats fitted with automobile engines that are rigged up to have propellers at the end of a long tail, which they dipped into the water on a fulcrum. They waited in the shade of their boat canopies for passengers who wished to explore the limestone karst formations along the river.

We took a room in a small guesthouse set back a few streets from the beach, and at equal distance to the largest river. While in South America we rarely used hotels because it was easier and more comfortable to camp. But in Asia the population density is high, rendering good campsites harder to find, and the stifling heat turns airy guesthouses into welcome pit stops. Thus, in the early period of adaptation to the environment, we took a room in a guesthouse about once per week for the luxury of air conditioning and the ability to starfish on the bed.

The difference between Malaysia and Thailand was clear from the moment we crossed the border. It was something akin to crossing from the United States to Mexico; the roads in Thailand were slightly rougher, narrower and curvier, and the drivers were a little bit wilder. And while Malaysia, a Muslim country, practiced strict modesty, Thailand was a free-for-all.

One evening, we attended the Ms. Krabi Pageant, which was a beauty pageant sponsored by the local Lion's Club chapter, where scantily-clad drag queens competed for the honor of the town's representative man-lady. As we walked home through an open-air food market near the riverbank, I noticed something familiar.

"Hey, I'd recognize that wifebeater shirt anywhere!"

Jan leaned back in his chair and smiled, opening his arms wide in a welcoming gesture.

"I'm stalking Nacho!" Jan said, his mouth still half full of pad Thai. Every time we coincided with Jan on the road—at the beach barbecue in Terengganu, in the Cameron Highlands, and now here in Krabi—I thought about the book *The Celestine Prophecy*, which I read in High school. The author suggests that when people repeatedly run into each other by coincidence, it is because they have something important to tell each other. I wondered what this man in his wifebeater shirt had to tell us. We pushed him for information, hoping that he would lead us to great treasure or wisdom. But in the end we only learned that he had decided to go home after Thailand, and that he expected a visit from his Latin Lover in Chiang Mai. Acknowledging this, and wondering what good lessons he was hiding from us, we said our goodbyes.

In the morning we awoke and dressed quickly. For a change of pace we decided to put someone else in charge of our day, so we signed up to take a tour of the limestone karst islands dotting the Andaman Sea: the stone armada. We arrived at the prearranged street corner just in time for the white tour van to pick us up.

Gonzalo was from Argentina. We could tell he was a good guy just by looking at him—it was something about the way he carried himself. When we found out he was from Argentina, it only solidified what we already knew: that he was a really good guy.

We asked him where he was from as soon as he sat down next to us in the white tour van.

"Argentina," he replied in the Latino accent of The Most Interesting Man in the World. "A town called Mendoza."

I knew he was a good guy, Sheena and I collectively thought.

For the next fifteen minutes, all the way from Krabi town to Ao Nang, we all excitedly reminisced about Argentina: empanadas, Christina de Kirchner and her downward spiraling economy, *parrillas*, blood sausage, dirty money, banditos, wine, and wide open spaces. By the time the van dropped the three of us off in a dirt lot near the ocean, we'd made ourselves more than a little hungry. From a dirty little shack in the parking lot we purchased some Cup o' Noodles, extra spicy, and ate them while longing for thick cuts of steak washed down with smooth Mendoza wine.

After close to an hour, a man told us to walk down a dirt track, which led to a skinny pier jutting into the sea. A small wooden long-tail boat awaited our arrival, and then shakily transported us to a waiting tour boat moored in the bay for a sunset snorkeling tour.

Once aboard the boat we were joined by a dozen or more tourists all ready to get their feet wet with some snorkeling action. Given that we were to be cruising around and in between several of southern Thailand's spectacular limestone islands, we quickly bolted to the open-air upper deck to secure ourselves the best seats in the house: a few plastic lawn chairs situated at the bow. We waited for the hoards of other passengers to crowd in behind us, but it never happened. For some inexplicable reason, every last one of them decided to pack themselves together in the below decks like sardines where they could safely observe the world-class scenery and towering limestone cliffs from between the fiberglass pillars supporting the viewing deck above.

The boat rumbled to life, and slipped away northward along the coastline. Soon we approached a group of islands jutting straight out of the water like teeth. The boat cut between them while we stared in awe. The driver killed the motor just off the shore of two islands connected by a shallow sandbar. A rickety boat sputtered toward our vessel to ferry passengers to the islands. Gonzalo looked off of the side of the upper deck.

"Do you think the water is deep enough to jump in?" he asked.

It was hard to tell; several coral heads dotted the sandy bottom, and the small waves messed with our depth perception.

"Only one way to find out," I said. And before we knew it, he had flung himself over the edge and had disappeared into the water below.

"It's all right!" he yelled as he came to the surface.

I swung my legs over the railing and leapt. Sheena, less danger seeking, walked down the stairs and safely lowered herself into the water. Just then, a skinny, spotty English kid with bad posture, whom I'd noticed earlier, appeared above the rail.

"Wow, it's really fah down theh. Is the wootah ceauld?" he asked. I assured him that in fact the water was really quite warm. It felt like a big bathtub.

"No, it con't be! It's prubbly ceauld! It's seau ceauld, you must be jeauking!" And with that, the spotty English kid plugged his nose, closed his eyes, and fell awkwardly through the air and into the lukewarm water below.

While the rickety boat loaded the other passengers to take them ashore, Sheena, Gonzalo, and I decided to swim instead. It hadn't looked all that far, but after what seemed like an eternity of slogging through the water with the inefficiency of drowning cattle, we soon enough fatigued. The water became shallow and I could see that the bottom was littered with dead coral and sea urchins, whose poisonous spines came uncomfortably close to our tiredly kicking feet.

Just before succumbing to fatigue and drowning, we reached the shore. The next forty five minutes proved an amusing study in Asian sociology; amid all of the available sandy spots in the Andaman Sea, dozens of us had ended up on one skinny sandbar, sitting in knee deep hot water wearing rubber masks and snorkels, surrounded by dead coral and leafy detritus floating about in the water. It was what the hip kids might call a snorkeling fail. We happily boarded the rickety boat and left the island.

Once aboard the main vessel we continued our trajectory up the coast. The captain's assistant excitedly pointed out "Chicken Rock," which was a rock that looked like a chicken's head. It is rather strange to consider the things in nature that people tend to find interesting. On a nerve-shattering bus ride to Machu Picchu, a drive that took us through canyons and Andean mountain passes, our driver pointed out all of the natural features that looked man-made. There were mountains that looked like statues of Virgin Maries, eagles, and faces. Here in Thailand, our guides pointed to rocks that looked like crocodiles, heads, elephants, and Buddhas. To some, it seems, nature is only interesting if it looks like something carved by man—a most anthropocentric view. I scoffed at Chicken Rock as it passed portside.

Finally we reached the romantic climax of the sunset snorkeling tour: the sunset beach barbeque. We disembarked on a small island and made our way to the table on the beach where tin foil-wrapped fish and a pot of rice awaited. The barbecue had apparently happened at a different place and time, but we were here to reap the rewards. We took a couple of big plates of cold fish and rice, Sheena put her sarong on the sand, and the three of us enjoyed the scenery as the sun plunged to the horizon next to a picturesque limestone tooth jutting out of the sea.

Once the sun had plunged beyond the horizon and our cold fish and rice had been devoured, it was time to head back. We boarded the boat and began weaving back through the islands from whence we came. But the crew had one more surprise in store.

"Okay everybody, listen to me," the captain's assistant announced. "Now it very dark. In fifteen minute we go snorkeling with phosphorescent plankton. Yes, that right, you swim with plankton. Fifteen minute." And with that, she retired to her seat. This was going to be great!

The boat approached a limestone wall undercut by millennia of lapping waves, and the captain cut the engine. Several of us donned our snorkels and masks and made our way to the back of the boat. We all stood there, peering into the pitch-black ocean, waiting for someone to go first. Just then, something appeared in the water.

"What the hell was that?" a rather rotund man asked. There appeared to be two large plastic shopping bags swimming around right where we were supposed to be experiencing the phosphorescent plankton. The captain quickly put his foot into the water and kicked one of them, trying to move it away. Only then did I realize that he was attempting to move two seriously large jellyfish aside so that we could frolic in the water. Jellyfish. In the water. Suddenly, seeing phosphorescent plankton wasn't on the menu anymore.

The captain, satisfied that he had rid the water of the deadly floating human-killers, turned back toward us and smiled. "You can see phosphorescent plankton," he said, timidly.

Hell no I'm not, I thought. Just then, the spotty English boy stepped onto the swimming platform and jumped in. *What the?! That little twerp?*

He put his head down and slowly wriggled toward the cliff wall. We all stared at him, waiting for his body to convulse and then sink to the bottom in a state of jellyfish shock, but instead he raised his head and spoke.

"Wow! Thehs loads of 'em. When oy swing moy ahm 'round, the wootah lights up wiv all 'ease bright buggahs." I couldn't believe it. This guy? The spotty English boy? Whereas a couple of hours ago he seemed like such a pansy, now he was swimming through a swarm of jellyfish, waving his arm about like Luke Skywalker's glowing sword.

Damnation, I thought. If he can do it, I simply must!

I took a quick survey of the immediate area around the boat and saw no jellyfish, so I leapt. It was a simple leap, but it felt as if I were jumping to my death. The warm water enveloped me and I immediately got the heebie jeebies. But the spotty English boy was in the water too, so I was forced to feign a sense of calm. I put my head down and began paddling toward the cliff wall. I didn't have to go far before I was lost in a trance.

I stared down into the black abyss below me, unable to see a damn thing except infinite darkness. The thought of all of the creatures that must be surrounding me, and the untold depth of the ocean below scared the bejeezus out of me. But when I swiped my arm through the water in front of me, the whole place lit up like a fireworks show. I became mesmerized, swiping the water left and right, and as I did, stars were born right before my eyes, whirling in eddies around my hands in 3D. The harder I swiped, the more intensely the plankton lit up. It was like I was flying through outer space at warp speed. I forgot about the deadly jellyfish closing in on me, and about the scary sea creatures below, and the untold depths that divers would have to dive to retrieve my body after I was finally stung to death by a straight jacket of stringy tentacles.

Sheena, obviously finding me irresistible in the way I was waving my arms around like a schoolboy, daintily lowered herself into the water and joined me in my Star Wars warp speed fantasy world. Together we floundered like disoriented Klingons, breathing belabored breaths through our snorkels like Darth Vader, until we sensed that the others were becoming bored back on the boat.

After fifteen minutes or so the spotty English boy headed back, and Sheena and I returned to the boat to reclaim our seats next to Gonzalo, whose fear of death by stinging had kept him high and dry.

"Entonces," Gonzalo said, "cómo fue?"

"Vale la pena" was all I could come up with. *Worth it*. And at that we motored southward.

8

Phetkasem Road
to Khao Sok

Brad

"Jungle trekking, yeah!" Sheena was visibly excited on the morning of our ill-fated jungle trek.

She'd picked up a new pair of trekking boots after we left Argentina, and now walked in circles in the parking lot of Thailand's Khao Sok National Park, stealing glances at her fancy footwear as I finished loading up the backpack. Rain jackets, water filter, bug repellent? Check. Bathing suits and water? Check. Canned tuna (curry flavor), rice crackers, bananas? Check.

"I heard they have wild elephants here," Sheena reported, energetically bouncing around in her boots. "And you know what?" she continued. "I also heard they have rare barking deer!" Her eyes looked like they were about to pop out of her head. If the wild elephants didn't get me excited, those rare barking deer surely would!

We finished loading up our things and set off across the bridge, leaving our jungle encampment behind. The sun was already high overhead, evidence of our perpetual difficulty in getting out of bed on time, and our tendency to lollygag and engage in a lengthy coffee and breakfast routine. It didn't take long before we found ourselves trudging through a dense thicket of bamboo.

"How are your new boots feeling?"

"Really good!"

Sheena kept the trail in her peripheral vision while scouring the surrounding jungle for any sign of a rare barking deer.

"What was that sound?" She would say.

"It was a bird."

"How do you know it wasn't a rare barking deer?"

"Sheena, it was a bird."

By the time we had passed the first three or four scenic offshoots to the main trail, each leading to a swimming hole or small waterfall, the sun had turned the jungle into a sauna. The temperature soared and the stifling, syrupy air strangled our lungs with every breath. The jungle morphed from dense bamboo thickets to a tight tangle of vines and trees. A barking deer? Possible. But there was no way that a wild elephant could live in this mess.

Our goal for the day was to reach the end of the trail, which terminated at the seventh waterfall. After the sixth, the trail shot straight up and over a series of steep ridges. We could no longer walk; instead we were forced to scramble by holding onto roots and vines. We climbed on, drenched in sweat, stained by mud, and nauseous from the heat.

"I think we should turn back," Sheena said as we topped the final ridge. "The trail is too steep. We still have to come back through this."

Having walked close to five miles through the dank jungle, giving up so close to our destination didn't seem right. Besides, what if there was a rare barking deer out there somewhere? We reluctantly descended the far side of the ridge on a worsening trail. The sound of a waterfall intermingled with the rumble of thunder from the swelling clouds overhead.

When we finally reached the bottom of the ridge we lowered ourselves off of a tall rock ledge onto the rocky shore of the river. Before us a waterfall cascaded gracefully into a large pool surrounded by enormous boulders. We spotted a flat rock and made our way out to it for our celebratory lunch of curried tuna and crackers.

Shortly after situating ourselves around our fancy lunch items, we heard a distant hum. Sheena nimbly shoveled scoops of zesty fish into her mouth as I fumbled with the crumbling rice crackers. I had barely gotten my can of curried tuna open when the distant hum grew into a buzz and presented itself to us as a large swarm of angry bees.

"All you have to do is hold still," Sheena confidently announced. I tried this, but the tickle of tiny wings brushing my face and body got the better of me and I started to freak out.

"God, they're everywhere!" I shrieked. Sheena sat there, apparently of less interest to the bees. "I need to get in the water!" I said, gasping, and proceeded to hurriedly whip off my clothes and throw them onto the rocks. The bees temporarily followed my clothing, saturated with my apparently tasty perspiration. The bees quickly lost interest in my clothes, and one bolted back at me and stung me on the back. I yelped, and then leapt from the rock into the chilly water.

I paddled away from the rocks toward the center of the pool. I could see Sheena holding very still on the rock. I paddled over to the waterfall and sat underneath its flow, letting the heavy water massage my shoulders. Everything was going to be okay.

Just then I heard Sheena's signature squeal, so I looked up. She stood atop the rock, frantically making hand gestures toward me like a Navy landing signal officer. The only difference was that Sheena's hand signals bore no resemblance to anything remotely comprehensible. She seemed to be making a sock puppet with one hand, while she pinched at the air in random flailing motions with the other hand. I yelled that I didn't understand, at which she successfully signaled that I was a dolt. Next, she raised both arms and did what appeared to be "jazz hands," and then looked all around and pretended to pick up random scattered objects with chopsticks. I had no idea what she intended to say. Finally she started whipping at the air and ran away into the jungle.

As she disappeared into the trees I heard her scream "Bees!" The jungle closed up behind her and she was gone. A new curtain of fear drew over me; the situation had worsened, and I would have to go fill my backpack and put on my boots amid a swarm of killer bees.

I timidly swam toward the rocks, and when I got close I could see a dark cloud of winged bodies around my things. If I expected to get out of there alive, I would have to be Indiana Jones about it. I jumped out of the water and ran into the bee cloud, whisking the bees off of my saturated tee shirt. I picked up the shirt and began violently whipping it about like a helicopter blade, or a Ninja Turtle nunchuk. The bees backed away from me, and the ones that didn't got their asses chopped with my whipping shirt. I could hold them off—for now—but I had to figure out how to accomplish my tasks while my favored hand was being used as an anti-bee weapon.

With my left hand I dumped my curried tuna over the edge of the rock, hoping to create a diversion. It had no effect on the bees, so I started clumsily putting my clothes into my backpack while I whipped the air and my torso with my sweaty shirt like some kind of masochist.

When at last I had sufficiently repacked my bag, I hastily jammed my feet into my heavy trekking boots. I pulled the laces tight, but was unable to tie them with one hand, and then lowered my head, upped the tempo of my nunchuk action, and bolted. The bees followed me.

I ran through underbrush and thorny trees, trying to evade the bees, and finally came to the rock ledge that we'd lowered ourselves down earlier. I stopped whipping for a moment and ran at the ledge full speed, somehow making it to the top by imitating a loose approximation of parkour in my unlaced trekking boots. When I hit the trail, I bolted uphill as fast as I could scramble over the roots and rocks until I'd reached the top of the ridge.

Sheena was nowhere to be seen. It had been close to fifteen minutes since we were separated.

Maybe she continued down the trail, I thought. *But why would she do that?* The bees had long since turned around, and there would be no reason for her to go farther. I opted to continue down the other side.

I slipped and stumbled my way down the far side of the ridge, and finally reached the bottom, where the next ridge began, but still no Sheena. *What the hell?* There was no way she would have hiked so far without me. At that point I could see two possibilities: she had either continued even farther than I had already gone, or she had fallen off of the trail while running from the bees. Maybe her parkour skills weren't as fine-tuned as mine, and she had fallen into the river while climbing the rock ledge.

I decided the first step would be to yell at the top of my lungs, which I did, for five or ten minutes. I alternated between eardrum-busting whistling and yelling her name, but there was no response. "What the hell?" I kept saying aloud. The sun was getting low in the sky and the jungle was becoming dark.

Finally, just as I was about to turn around and scramble back over the ridge to the killer bees to look for her, I heard a familiar sound.

"Tee hee! Here I am, honey!"

"What?! Where have you been? I've been worried sick about you! I thought you were unconscious and that the bees got you! What is wrong with you? Didn't you hear me yelling?!"

"Well, you see," she said, in a voice that made the situation seem much less serious, "I ran away into the jungle and went really far, and then I waited for you. After ten minutes the bees were still hunting me and I started to get really mad at you for making me wait so long. I was like *'What? No he DIT-INT,'* but then I realized that I didn't recognize anything. I finally walked back and saw that I wasn't even on the trail. Woopsies! So then I came this way and here you are!"

I could hardly be mad at her. When you think someone has perished, and then you realize that they actually haven't, you can really only be relieved. But we weren't out of the woods yet! Literally, we weren't out of the woods yet.

The clouds had continued to build overhead, and the thunder was becoming louder. The last thing we needed was to be stuck out here on these slippery mud ridges in a downpour. We swiveled our hips wildly from side to side as we speed-walked through the jungle on the trail.

"Sheena, hold up," I said, "I need to tie my shoes." The situation had been so tense that I hadn't realized that my boots were still untied and I wasn't wearing my shirt. I pulled the soaked tee shirt over my head, retrieved some socks from my bag, and laced up my boots. The speed-walking recommenced.

With about a mile left to go before reaching camp, I looked down at my swim trunks and could hardly believe my eyes. My right leg appeared to have been shot, and my shorts were drenched in blood.

"What the hell happened to you, boy?" Sheena shrieked.

I shakily slid my pant leg up to reveal two seeping wounds. I wiped the blood away, but the flow immediately resumed. Sheena's face turned white, but there was nothing we could do. We continued walking while I held pressure on my bullet wound.

Finally, at long last we reached the bridge, crossed it, and found Nacho alone in our camp. We started to drop our things on the ground in exhaustion when I looked at Sheena's shorts. She noticed the disgusted look on my face and looked down. A stream of dried blood was caked on her leg.

"Ohmygod…I think I'm going to be sick," she gasped. She quickly ran out of sight to investigate what the heck was going on. When she returned several minutes later, she was holding a bloody garment.

"Look what was stuck to my clothes," she said, holding out her hand. In it, a swollen leech was nestled in the fabric. That explained what had gotten me as well. We retrieved our stainless steel salt grinder filled with pink Peruvian rock salt from the Andes, and proceeded to cover that mo-fo with dash after dash of fine rock salt until it disintegrated into bloody shreds.

We gathered some fresh clothes, a few band-aids, some Benadryl and soap, and prepared for a shower. We could wash off the blood and I could coat my bee sting with antihistamine, but it would be a very long time before we would feel the urge to go jungle trekking again. And the rare barking deer? Those rare barking deer can bite me.

9

Phetkasem Road
to Prachuap Khiri Khan

Sheena

A man we met in Thailand told me that a good massage is the right of every Thai person – an essential part of daily life. Walking down the street in Pratchuap Khiri Khan, we were drawn to a sign advertising just that and decided we had nothing to lose in trying it out. The sign had a cartoon sketch of a woman on her stomach with her back arched painfully high as her arms were pulled backward by a pony-tailed woman kneeling behind her. It seemed painful, but both characters had serene smiles painted on their faces.

At seeing the price, we were sold. For only five dollars an hour, we couldn't afford not to get massages. Brad and I stepped inside where we were welcomed by a cheerful lady in her fifties. She made a quick phone call and by the time my feet had been soaked and scrubbed, another younger woman appeared on a red scooter, beads of sweat on her face, eager to get to work.

I followed the younger woman around a bookshelf that partitioned her massage room from the street. She flipped on two oscillating fans and I lowered myself onto a hard mattress on the floor. I quickly realized that the Western interpretation of a massage did not apply here. I repeatedly teetered on the verge of laughing or crying, unable to believe this woman's power. She used not only her hands, but also the weight of her entire body applied through her knees, elbows, feet and toes.

She twisted me into a pretzel, bounced on top of me, and pulled my fingers and toes until they snapped like popped bubble gum. She sat in front of me and, using one leg as an anchor, pressed her toes into my upper hamstrings. She dug her heel deep into the crevice of my inner thigh and crotch, with each stroke pushed a little harder and a little longer. It was agonizingly painful, but in some way glorious. Finally I was able to lay my head on a pillow that rested on her lap. This began pleasantly, but soon she dug deeper and found each knot in my back, twanging on them like guitar strings as I held my breath, trying not to wail in pain.

In the end she melted my pain away by rubbing my temples and eyebrows, and scratching my head.

Prachuap Khiri Khan sits at Thailand's narrowest point, where only eight miles separate the Thai coastline from the Burmese border. We had arrived on a busy road filled with tiny trucks stacked high with tremendous loads of produce.

In the back of one of these trucks a net had covered a teetering pile of coconuts. Atop the pile there sat two workers and a gnarly-looking monkey, trained in the fine art of pulling coconuts. The monkey looked bored and tired, uninterested by the commanding view from the top. Farther up the road, we had stopped to buy banana chips and a full tank of gas, only to realize that we were short on cash by nearly the entire sum of the bill. But it was no problem. A cheerful gas station attendant loaded Brad on the back of his scooter and took him down the road to a nearby ATM machine, leaving me behind with Nacho as collateral.

In Prachuap Khiri Khan, a leisurely walk down the beach made it evident that this village was far more focused on fishing than tourism. It was unpretentious and intriguing, and had historical significance. During World War II it had been the site of the first invasion by Japanese troops along the Gulf Coast. Its picturesque bay of tropical blue water was dotted with bobbing wooden trawler boats, bobbing like corks in a bathtub.

A congregation of fishing boats unloaded their bounty in plastic crates containing the day's catch. Brown-skinned Burmese and Thai men waded back and forth between the shore and the bobbing boats, carrying crates of fat juicy fish atop their heads. We watched a local man purchase a crate of fish, and then a little boy went to work sorting the contents of the bin into piles of good fish and damaged, unsellable ones. The remaining bins were moved from the beach to the road by an assembly line of workers. The workers shielded their bodies from the sun, fully covering their arms, legs, and faces. They wore long sleeved shirts, pants, and wide brimmed hats with a flap of extended fabric reaching down and around their necks and tied under their chins.

At midday the boardwalk was not filled with strolling people, but rather with trays made of framed metal fencing, which rested against the cement wall. Atop each of the trays, neat rows of squid and bits of fish were left to dry in the sun. Across the street, the town's residents napped through the hottest hours of the day. They snoozed on raised platforms with thatched roofs, the Asian equivalent of the Western patio, less the lawn chairs, table and umbrella, listening to the peaceful sound of lapping waves.

In the evening, we wandered into a busy restaurant on the waterfront where, earlier in the day, the trays of fish had dried in the sun. Being so close to Burma, the town was rich with Burmese influence. The girls who ran the restaurant were from Burma, in fact, as evidenced by the *thanakha* cream smeared on their cheeks. After an exchange of hand charades between our giggling Burmese waitress and ourselves, we succeeded in ordering a few random dishes from the menu.

We didn't know what we had ordered, and when the waitress emerged, she delivered a spicy seafood salad and a plate of deep fried silver whiting fish with green mango salsa. The spicy seafood salad, called *yam ta-lair,* was exceptional – a perfect balance of sweet and spicy, made of shrimp, squid, octopus, and mussels, mixed with green onion, coriander, and celery leaves, and soaked in a spicy lime sauce. I was skeptical of the deep fried silver whiting. The plate contained a few dozen bite-sized fish, butterflied and fried, with ribs and spine intact. I quickly decided that this was going to be a throwaway dish – way too much work for such little reward; the thought of sorting out needle-sized fish bones in my mouth was unappealing. I stared at the dish in frustration, but Brad went for it, dipping the little fish bodies in the mango salsa and popping them into his mouth whole. I eventually did the same, and soon, like the Thai massage poster from earlier in the day, we both melted into our chairs, serene smiles painted on our faces.

One of the great pleasures of travel is the discovery of places through food. One can tell a lot about a place—its priorities, its pace of life, the strength of its culture—by observing the eating habits of its people. A culture of wine, bread, cheese, and cured meat implies an appreciation for things that take time, and that require both precision and an artistic hand. Such a food culture did not rise out of struggle. A place with simple dishes of high-energy staples—rice with steamed manioc or potato, soup, and small cuts of meat—these are the foods of peasants. Bland food feeds those at extreme latitudes or in cold climates, while spicy foods are equatorial or desert foods. Colonial rule often leaves in its wake a taste for tea or baguettes. Food defines cultures, and for this reason, wherever I went I was drawn to markets.

I don't think I had ever been to a market while traveling that had everything I was looking for, but at the same time, every market I'd been to had something that I'd never seen before. As frustrating as that may have been sometimes, that was the beauty of them. They were regional and seasonal, with a continually changing mix of produce, flavors, spices, textiles and faces. I always had the overwhelming desire to go to every stall, upturn every bag of unknown content, unwrap every banana leaf to reveal its insides, and sample every fruit and vegetable. My senses were overwhelmed in the way that I imagined they must be for a child going to Disneyland for the first time. Even if I had nothing to buy, I still wanted to go merely for the visual exploration. It was an opportunity to interact with the locals, to take their pulse, and to observe their daily routine and way of life.

It should come as no surprise then, that given my absolute love for these places, I often planned a particular route to coincide with them. This was usually my little secret until we arrived within the vicinity, leaving Brad little chance to invent an emergency diversion.

It just so happened that we were to arrive in Bangkok on a Saturday, and it just so happened to be the same day on which a number of weekend floating markets were taking place. We steered Nacho to Bang Noi, which had been attracting Thailand's river-dwellers for more than a hundred years. With the building of roads, the market nearly died off but was recently revived by the government, keen to hold onto its traditions.

Upon entering the shop houses next to the river, I saw local women sitting on the sidewalk with their blankets laid out, proudly displaying their produce for the day. This was the most authentic part of the market, with old-fashioned commerce being carried out between the locals. As we walked to the water's edge I braced myself, expecting to see something extraordinary: perhaps a swarm of colorful boats, women with cone hats, or maybe a pig or two being transferred from one boat to another. I wanted to see those things, yet all I saw was the murky brown water of the canal and bunches of hyacinth floating by.

Hyacinths are a huge problem in Southeast Asia, growing so quickly that they clog the canals and impede the flow of water. It is actually some peoples' job to remove the hyacinth from the waterways by cutting them at their roots and letting them float away. Nowadays much of it is collected, dried, and made into the latest and greatest in new trendy woven furniture.

Instead of a true floating market, we had come upon a simple marketplace on the river. Lining the canal there were old wooden shop houses filled with cute cafés and restaurants, souvenir shops, handicraft stores, and produce stands. It was all very pleasant, despite its misleading name. We entered and split up quickly. Brad was drawn to a small café overlooking the river where a Thai man played a guitar, and I continued on, strangely overwhelmed by the uncanny laid-back atmosphere of the market. And so, while Brad shared a table with a few locals and enjoyed a beer, I went searching for unique foods.

One woman roasted tightly wrapped tubes of banana cakes on her charcoal grill while another sold pairs of neatly arranged fish in bamboo bowls. A woman pinched off silver dollar sized pieces of rice flour dough, placed them in a pan, patted them down, and gently flipped them until they were lightly brown. She layered the stretchy pancakes between sheets of plastic wrap until her sister, working the second half of the process, topped them generously with crushed peanuts, brown sugar, and sesame seeds. She then rolled them into bite-sized wraps, stacked them neatly in pyramids, and placed them into small origami banana leaf trays. They were sweet and nutty – perfect alongside the complimentary shot glass of green tea.

I continued walking, eventually crossing over a bridge that led to the other side of the water. Young Thai men racing their long-tail boats, oblivious to their own noise, broke the silence in the air intermittently. Each time they passed through the canal, the green water sloshed back and forth between the buildings and conversations paused briefly until the people of the market could hear the sound of their own voices again.

After making the rounds, I found Brad at the café. On our way out we passed a stand where a sweet-looking couple made pork steamed-rice parcels. The wrinkly little dumplings were made using a method I had never seen before. It began with a thin pastry mix poured onto a small round surface and quickly covered with a metal cone-shaped lid. In less than a minute, the dough had turned from transparent to opaque, and a dollop of sweet pork filling was added to the center. Using two spatulas the stretchy dough was pulled and twisted over the meat topping. After showing me the technique, they handed me their spatulas and I added a few deformed dumplings to their collection.

We headed back to Nacho and drove a few miles south to the enormous Amphawa Floating Market. There was clearly no way we'd make it through in the few hours we had left, for thousands of vendors clung to the elevated banks of the half-mile-long canal. This seemed to be the floating market of choice for Bangkok residents, and surprisingly, we didn't see another Western face there. The whole atmosphere was reminiscent of a bygone time; the steps that led down to the canal were packed like bleachers with Thais eating seafood. All eyes were on the cooks who floated in the boats below, splitting their time between preparing and handing food to people, and cooking on their grills. We ordered grilled squid and pad Thai and sat there on the banks, just two individuals observing a crazy maze of food and people.

10

Route 323
to Kanchanaburi

Brad

My mom and brother had arrived some time before Christmas in 2003, our first visitors during our year of living abroad in Wales. We loaded their belongings in the trunk of our tiny red Kia Mentor. Our first stop would be Stonehenge, but only barely, after cheating death on England's winding, icy backroads at night with malfunctioning headlights. The ensuing two weeks are best remembered as a string of days in which my poor mother endured pure torture as a passenger on a 2,000-mile winter road trip through Europe with three juvenile ruffians.

Ten years later, and against her better judgment, my mom again stepped from the tarmac and into our road-tripping machine. It was one o'clock in the morning, and Bangkok's lingering nighttime heat threatened to melt the soles off of our shoes as we walked from the terminal to the parking lot where Nacho awaited. My mom is a smart lady, yet how soon she forgot the lessons of history.

In the morning we walked from our guesthouse along Samsen Road, past the frippery shops and tee shirt hawkers on Khao San Road, and past the row of meat-on-a-stick vendors. Since sidewalks in Bangkok are generally used for motorcycle parking, store displays, storage, food preparation, and public urination, we walked in the blistering sun on the side of the blistering hot roadway. By now, having been in Southeast Asia for a considerable amount of time, Sheena and I had grown somewhat accustomed to the heat and humidity. I turned to look at my mom and realized that she was nearly dead, fast approaching the point at which her blood cells would turn into lifeless bits of sand.

"Oh...look," she faintly whispered, "there's a 7-Eleven. Let's...cool off."

Bangkok is home to more than 3,900 7-Eleven stores, each of them spewing unregulated cold air into their clean interiors like little oases of freshness. Without these, my mom would be dead.

We eventually arrived at the Grand Palace and were turned away by angry security guards. They bit their thumbs at our tastelessness; both my mom and I were exposing our knees, which is an unspeakable atrocity inside the walls of a tourist attraction of such grandeur. We retreated to the sidewalk where innumerable fly-by-night vendors rented cheap elephant-covered gypsy pants to us foreign heathens. I saw this as an opportunity to school my mother in the fine art of negotiation.

"Four dollars?!" I ranted. "I shan't pay a farthing more than three dollars! Mom, walk away…they have to see you walking away."

We procured some ugly rented pants at my aggressively negotiated rate, and we entered the palace.

Having long since suffered from a condition that I call "wat burnout," Sheena and I walked around the complex looking at the painted gold buildings with a sense of boredom. My mom looked enthused, but after a few minutes I realized that she too might have reached "wat burnout" stage far sooner than anticipated, undoubtedly fueled by the setting-in of her heat stroke. We looked at statues of Buddhas, admired the gold trim adorning the buildings, and took lots of photos, despite our condition.

Back on the street I returned my rented pants, while my mom decided to keep hers and forfeit her deposit. "These will make great pajamas," she said. After over an hour without air conditioning, her tongue began to swell and become rigid. Later, while eating lunch in an outdoor, non-air-conditioned establishment, I told her to stay away from air conditioning if she ever wanted to adapt to the weather. She didn't complain. Sheena spied a splash of heat rash on my mom's leg, which my mom dismissed with a smile, saying, "It's nothing!" I came to the realization that I was torturing my mother.

I was eager to show Mom the Thai countryside, so we hit the road to Kanchanaburi – the place of World War II fame where prison camp labor was used to build a railroad bridge over the Kwai River on its trajectory to Burma. She had seen the film *The Bridge on the River Kwai* when she was eight years old, and was elated to see it in the flesh. The very bridge!

After two hours of driving out of Bangkok, it seemed we were still in Bangkok. The countryside never materialized, and instead, those two hours were spent driving through industrial sprawl. We reached

Kanchanaburi as I tried to reassure her that yes, in fact, there are undeveloped parts of Thailand. We were pleased to find that Kanchanaburi maintained its small town charm, despite being attached to Bangkok by a gray industrial umbilical cord.

For two days my mom tried to remember the whistling song from the River Kwai movie. We walked. She tried to remember.

"I think it's *twéet twēet, twéet twuh twéet...* no, that's not right."

Each day seemed hotter than the last, but we ignored it to the best of our abilities. We found the bridge, we walked across it, we visited the museum, and as night fell we all enjoyed the miracle of the five-dollar, hour-long Thai massage. We all changed into the provided comfy pants and shirts, lay down on the floor mats, and proceeded to take severe punishment from the muscular Thai Army girls masquerading as massage therapists. My girl also happened to be a sumo wrestler. She wrenched on me so hard that she made herself grunt, and on two occasions elicited whimpering cries of pain from me, requiring me to tap out or else be left paralyzed.

We finally found a copy of the film and watched it. Of course! It's *twéet twēet... twēet twéet twÉet twÉÉt twÉÉt twéet.* We were so pumped about it that we actually booked seats on the train, now affectionately known as the Thai-Burma Death Railway, and spent the next day snaking into the hills, then slowly snaking back out of them.

We took a day to drive into the mountains and visited a waterfall to prove to my mom that the existence of Thai countryside isn't just propaganda that I dreamed up. The mountain trail was marked by a ten acre parking lot lined with food hawkers and souvenir shops, from which a paved path led to several pools and waterfalls. For some reason the place was packed with Russian tourists, but we were able to shake most of them by walking to the farthest waterfall from the parking lot, perhaps two miles away.

The swimming was beautiful. Flesh-cleaning (carnivorous) fish tickled (chomped) our feet and legs, and we had a nice time experiencing Thailand's nature. To our delight, we returned to Nacho without having picked up any bloodsucking leeches.

When I was a kid, I remember sitting in the passenger seat of my mom's Camry as we drove over the top tier of the new 2-tiered overpass linking Loop 202 to Interstate 17 in Phoenix. Just as we reached the zenith of the overpass, my mom cracked. She ducked her head below the level of the windshield, clasped the steering wheel in a death grip, and started yelling "Oh my God! Oh my God!" This was the day we came to fully appreciate—and believe in—my mom's fear of heights. By now I had forgotten all about it, a fact that came back to haunt me. Or more appropriately, to haunt her.

In Ayutthaya, our final stop on mom's visit, I had the great idea of taking her on a tour of the old city. Not on an air-conditioned bus, or even in Nacho, but on bicycles. And not on nice bicycles, but on bicycles that were so rickety and in disrepair as to be lent to us free of charge by an actual business.

Sheena led the way, heading west, and then curving north to follow the riverbank. It quickly became evident that to cross the river we would have to temporarily cut onto the freeway and take the bridge. I looked at my mom, her shirt soaking wet and her skin flushed from heat stroke.

We cut right, waited for a break in the heavy freeway traffic, and then precariously joined the narrow lane for our trip across the high bridge. Sheena continued to lead the way, followed by Mom, and I brought up the rear. My mom's seat had by now slipped down and her derailleur was stuck in a hard gear, making her pedal stroke slow, shaky, and powerless. As we reached the zenith of the bridge I noticed that her head was ducked down, her arms tense. Passing cars whizzed by, heat radiated from the pavement, and my mom fought through heat stroke and acrophobia while piloting, with quivering hands, the scrap heap of a bike I'd placed her on.

Amid this calamity, a crystal clear thought entered my mind: Brad, you're a bad person and if there is a hell, you're probably going to end up there. But she should have learned the lessons of history.

11

Soi Lat Pra Khao 14

Brad

While driving through Colombia on the Pan-American portion of our drive a year earlier, our transmission failed. We had been driving up a dirt road in the middle of the faraway mountains when Nacho voided his bowels in the middle of the road and gave up. A man in a pickup truck towed us to a tiny mountain village where a deranged mechanic further incapacitated poor Nacho, without our knowledge, rendering us really, really stuck. We had lurked in by cover of darkness, stolen Nacho away from the mechanic, and deposited him on a farm, cracking the side mirror on the farm's rear gate. We had found neither favorable nor legal options for getting our transmission working, so we flew home, bought a used transmission, cleaned it up so it looked new, created a fake receipt for it in Photoshop, packed it into a suitcase, and brought it onto a plane as checked baggage. Upon our arrival, the ever-so-thorough Columbian customs officers detained us for three days, and released us upon the payment of a hefty tax. After porting the transmission to the farm in the back of the farmer's truck, I spent two weeks fixing Nacho, which brought our total stranded fiasco time to two months.

Then, after all of that pain and suffering and hardship and money, our new transmission leaked from its drive flange. My lips formed into a sad rainbow, my eyes pinched shut, drool seeped from the corner of my mouth, and I fell to my knees while feebly punching the air before crumpling into the fetal position and sobbing like a pants-wetting kindergartener. The leak persisted for the next ten months through South America, across the Pacific to Malaysia, and into Thailand.

It also came to pass that in Argentina, a bad man with a crowbar had burglarized Nacho, and many important things were stolen. He even broke Sheena's treasured walking stick, recently collected from the shores of Lago Tromen, a lake that will only live on in our minds because the

68

bad man also stole the camera that contained all of the pictures of Lago Tromen. I was reminded of the bad man every day thereafter, especially the really hot days, because it turned out to be impossible to replace my broken window with the correct window glass, rendering me unable to roll down my window. This became especially unappreciated after arriving in Southeast Asia, because Nacho didn't have an air conditioner. Not being able to roll down my window in such stifling heat and humidity had caused my brain to begin to disintegrate from jungle rot.

So when we arrived in Bangkok I declared to Sheena, "All right, I'm putting my foot down!" Sheena knew me well as a maker of frivolous declarations, so she paid no immediate attention. However, my seriousness was hard to ignore when she found herself sitting in the waiting room of a garage in a Bangkok suburb surrounded by Volkswagen vans, including Nacho. Now Sheena knew I was serious. My foot was down, and it would stay down until I had a non-leaky transmission, a window capable of one-dimensional translation, and a usable side mirror.

When we had left Terence's house in Kuala Lumpur, he had put us in touch with a wily group of Volkswagen lovers in Bangkok. The group had pulled together a great welcome party containing more than a dozen vans like Nacho to meet us when we arrived, and then proceeded to take us out to daily lunches and nightly dinners. We made fast friends with them, the Thais being a fun-loving, likeable people. When they heard that we needed work done to Nacho to fix damage incurred in South America, Pat and Gak stepped up to the plate, discussing amongst themselves the virtues of the various VW shops in the city, before settling on the best option.

One morning we met up with Gak, and we followed him as he drove his split window VW bus, very slowly, through Bangkok traffic until we arrived at the mechanic's garage. He ordered pizza and had it delivered, and then we waited.

Given my deep mistrust of local mechanics, a sentiment well-earned by trial and error during the first year of our drive, my immediate feeling when turning Nacho over to the hands of others was one of deep nervousness and stomach discomfort. The mechanics that Pat and Gak chose were an intrepid team of young Thai men, and they displayed their worthiness by immediately locating a new window and side mirror, and successfully replacing the old with the new. Next, Nacho was hoisted on a lift and made airborne. The intrepid Thai mechanics dispersed and quickly returned with—and this seemed a real miracle after what we'd come to expect—all of the correct tools. They had a triple square bit for my beloved CV bolts, circlip pliers, and even the big cylindrical tool used to remove the axle flanges. They deftly removed the axle, noting that both of my CV boots were ripped, which they later replaced with spares from our roof box full of spare parts. They then removed the leaky drive flange, only to find that the main sealing o-ring was cut in half. And seeing as how the leak began on day one, I surmised that it was cut in half when I bought it, which made me quite angry indeed. But the mechanics had the right part on hand to fix it, so my anger was forgotten, and we all left for the evening to let the guys finish up.

It was about time. After only sixteen months on the road, we had finally managed to find a shop that used the right tools and knew what the hell they were doing. I also asked them to replace one of Nacho's upper control arm bushings, which had disintegrated in Ecuador and had been clanking around ever since. Driving away from the shop was like being born again.

With Nacho in tip top shape, and I use that term loosely, we were free to sit around in Bangkok traffic, meet with our new friends for lunch, sit in Bangkok traffic, hang out with our new friends over long and delicious dinners, sit in Bangkok traffic, and meet up with the entirety of Bangkok's Vanagon-owning Volkswagen community in front of the King Rama V monument. We gave everyone tours of Nacho's water purification system, hot water generation abilities, interior remodel, and I performed a barely-legal demonstration of Nacho's onboard shower.

On one of our very last days in the city before heading back out on the road, I found myself sitting in traffic. It was another marathon jam. I hadn't moved but a few feet in forty-five minutes, when whom should I see but a traffic cop approaching on foot. He reached my window, which I had proudly rolled down, and I attempted small talk before realizing that he spoke no English. After some polite smiles and hand waving, he began to insist that I had made some kind of traffic violation. He seemed to be saying that I had run a red light.

"But I've been sitting here for forty five minutes," I said, which didn't matter since he spoke no English.

"Kai jai tai doo mai wai kai!" he insisted.

He pointed to a picture of a driver's license on his clipboard, so I reached for the ashtray where I keep one of my many *extra* driver's licenses. To my shock and horror, the license was missing. I made a mental note to reprimand Sheena for moving my unlawful decoy license, and I regretfully pulled my real one from under the dash mat. He placed it in his ticket book and pointed to his clipboard, which contained several lines of cryptic Thai script. He read it to me, slowly and loudly so that I would understand.

"RAI MAI JAI...KWAI MOO GAI..." he went on for an eternity, and finally pointed to where it said "1,000." I deduced that he was going to write me a ticket for 1,000 Baht, or around thirty-five dollars.

"But sir," I said, uselessly, "I haven't done anything wrong. I literally haven't moved in forty-five minutes!" We went back and forth like this for at least fifteen or twenty minutes, and at every opportunity I attempted to convince him to give me my license back so that I wouldn't have anything to lose. Finally, through much frustration, charades, and incomprehensible jibber jabber, I convinced him to trade my license for a 1,000 Baht bill, which I was pretty sure he promised to hold onto while I followed him to the police station. He walked to his motorcycle and made a tunnel through the traffic, through which I followed him.

Several minutes later, after a number of close calls and nearly losing him in traffic, he stopped at a main intersection and got off his bike to stop traffic so that I could pull out. As I pulled into traffic, he signaled that he'd catch up. It should have come as no surprise that I never saw him or my 1,000 Baht again.

It is true that I was duped by a Bangkok motorcycle cop, and in doing so I had shamed my family and lost my reputation for being a stone-cold cop-tricker. But at the end of the day Nacho's transmission ceased to leak, I could see out of my side mirror, I could hang my arm out the window, and our front suspension probably wouldn't fall off. In the grand scheme of things, we'd won.

12

Asian Highway 1
to Mae Sot

Sheena

It's no secret that I have an undying love for Anthony Bourdain, host of *No Reservations*. While we were traveling through Malaysia, he launched a new show on CNN called *Parts Unknown*. He said that he accepted the offer because it would gain him access to places that American television cameras rarely get to visit. And where in the world, given this newfound access, did he choose to debut the new show? Burma.

Bourdain said, "If we had come a year earlier, we would have been deported. Almost overnight, people there were free to say what they wanted. Press restrictions had been lifted. That was an extraordinary thing to witness."

I thought about this particular episode as Brad and I skirted the Thai–Burmese border. Besides Anthony's show on Burma, the only other footage I had ever seen of the country was from a documentary called *Burma VJ*, which followed the disturbing protests in 2007 against the Burmese military regime. The smuggled footage clearly displayed the people's frustration with their government's censorship and dictatorial oppression.

When we arrived at the border, Burma was already in the midst of rampant change. Censorship had been lifted to a large extent in much of the country, and talks had begun about opening the borders for the first time in half a century. Despite the country's claim of having open borders, at the time of our arrival it was still not possible to travel more than a few miles beyond the border by foot, and it was not at all possible to bring Nacho in. Travel within the country is still highly restricted; the government has designated specific zones as "tourist appropriate," leaving the remainder of the country absolutely off-limits to the wandering eye of the foreigner. For us, given the restrictions to certain provinces and our inability to take Nacho across the border, driving through the country to reach India, as we had hoped to do, would be impossible.

While we couldn't get into Burma, we could get pretty close. We drove to the border town of Mae Sot, the main point of entry for more than 180,000 Burmese refugees who had fled into Thailand to live and work. These circumstances, as unpleasant as they may be, created a mix of faces and cultures unlike anything we had seen in Thailand.

Bobo was a handsome Burmese man with deep brown eyes, a wide jawbone and black tattoos that ran up his forearms and crept under his sleeves. Ma Yae, a Burmese woman, stood at his side as we prepared to depart for the market. Her shiny black hair rested at her shoulders, and she was as cute as a button in her red collared shirt sprinkled with Mickey Mouse faces. In less than a week she would return to Burma to attend her sister's wedding.

We followed Bobo and Ma Yae on foot to the fork in the road, and turned right toward the Burmese market. They had agreed to give us a cooking class, and step number one was hunting down the ingredients. Given the time of morning, the market was in full swing. As we moved from the outer streets inward, the paths became a challenging obstacle course. The locals were smooth and fluid, weaving in and out and around each other. Bikes and motorcycles sputtered by, women carried platters of fruit on top of their heads, and others crouched down next to their buckets of eels, fish, and frogs. Bins of steamed roaches sat next to mangoes, fried worms, and bags of rice. Under the overhanging roofs, packets of spices and prepackaged goods hung from strings, and eggplants the size of peas were scattered about the tables. There were wing beans in bamboo baskets, bundles of holy basil, and everything else imaginable and otherwise. A colorful variety of people worked the stands: men in cone hats, Indo-Burmese Muslim men in plaid sarongs, Karen tribal women, and Burmese natives with their faces brushed in circular swirls, stripes, and speckles of yellowish-white *thanaka* cream.

When half the morning had passed, we stopped for intermission at a traditional Burmese tea shop. It was an atmospheric place: loud, busy, and filled with tiny tables and chairs. When we settled in, we were served a complimentary pot of plain green tea, always free and always bottomless at a Burmese tea shop. Next, we ordered vegetable *samosas,* flaky pastries, and a round of *lapae yea,* a black tea mixed with a heavy dose of sweetened condensed milk that sinks to the bottom of the cup like a thick white custard, sweet like candy and delicious.

As we made our way out of the market, we watched a woman prepare a collection of betel leaves on her chalky tabletop. Brad had read about this very thing in a Paul Theroux book. The author had admitted to his hatred of the habit, complaining that the users were constantly spitting red juice everywhere. We were intrigued by this woman, who spread a calcium paste to the leaves, and then coved them in a sticky goop. Next, she opened up a half-dozen calcium-smeared containers and sprinkled their contents on top of the leaves: whole cardamom seeds, clove, *catechu*, slices of betel nut and some other unfamiliar ingredients. She finally folded them over into little bundles and handed them to us.

"If you start to feel dizzy after a minute or two, please stop and spit it out. Do not swallow it." Bobo clearly wanted to avoid any unfavorable international health incidents. "Place the whole thing in your mouth. Chew on it and spit it out once you've released all of the juices and flavors from the inside. And please, if you start to feel dizzy, *spit it out!*"

Brad and I each had one and so did Ma Yae. She also took one to go, which was wrapped tightly and secured with a rubber band, for later. We all stuffed the leafy bundles into our mouths and began to crush and squeeze them between our cheeks and teeth. The flavor was that of a leaf filled with toothpaste and a hint of Indian spices. Just one was enough for us.

In the afternoon we returned to Bobo and Ma Yae's place and prepared a beautiful meal of potato dumplings, Mandalay noodle salad, Karen pumpkin curry, and lime basil juice. We learned new preparations and cooking techniques, savoring the results and our good luck.

I had made one last special request of Bobo for our Burmese cooking experience. I had read that Burma was one of the only countries in the world where people not only drink tea but also eat the leaves. They eat them either in a pickled tea leaf salad, or served in the center of a shallow dish—also pickled—along with fried garlic, peas, peanuts, toasted sesame, dried shrimp, preserved shredded ginger, and fried shredded coconut. I was eager to try the tea leaf salad, and Bobo was willing to show me how to make it. We rehydrated some pickled tea leaves, crushed them in the pestle and mortar, and then tossed them with tomatoes, cabbage, fried nuts, and seeds. The resulting flavor was something entirely new and wonderful. The tea leaves were pungent and spicy, mixing perfectly with the crunchy nuts and mild vegetables.

We enjoyed our meal at a picnic table in a leafy courtyard. It was peaceful and serene, and everything just felt good. It was a perfect afternoon. I wondered what would come of Mae Sot in the future. I asked Bobo what the community was like here, and if most people knew each other. His response surprised me.

"No, I do not recognize most of the faces here. People are always coming and going. This isn't really anyone's home. Now that things are getting better in Burma, many of the NGOs in town are starting to disappear. People are even starting to return home."

On one hand it was a little sad to think Mae Sot was changing so quickly, but more than anything it made me happy. People deserve to live with their families, to live in peace, to know their neighbors, and to enjoy a good meal within their own country.

13

Route 105 to Mae Chaem

Brad

Brigit and Bret lived in a modest house on Grand Canyon Avenue. A few bicycles adorned the front porch, which overlooked the street and a front garden filled with mint, strawberries, lemongrass, and a peach tree. Brigit was the most fashionable of all of the scientists at work, always looking like she'd just stepped out of a scene in *The Great Gatsby* before ducking into the lab to analyze compounds in the mass spectrometer. Sometimes I'd swing by the house on my way to work to pick her up on our vintage Vespa, wearing the leather shoes I bought in Italy. She wore a scarf to fend off the morning chill, and we'd zip away in a Euro-inspired carpool to work in the lumberjack mountain town of Flagstaff, Arizona.

Bret had a friendly smile, a firm handshake, and a knack for crafting lemon squares that could change your life; confections that made you question everything you ever knew about food, joy, religion, and the universe. Brigit and Bret comprised twenty two percent of our weekly dinner club. The Helders, the Franklins, and Josh filled out the rest.

As we drifted through the mountains along the Burmese border in northern Thailand, Sheena and I were lost in a reverie. Sometimes when we drove, it was nice to let our minds wander, and when they wandered, they often went back home. When we passed someone riding a Vespa with her scarf whipping in the wind, I wondered what Brigit and Bret were doing at that particular instant. With our windows down, the mountain air wafted through the van just like it did back in Flagstaff. A song flowed from the stereo speakers, drowning out the low moan of our engine. A banjo riff brought me back two years in an instant to our beloved group of friends with whom we had shared our weekly dinners. It was Josh who had played the banjo.

Curtis, Mike, and Josh were roommates. Curtis and Mike were brothers, hailing from Michigan. The first things you noticed about them were their maniacal smiles, and the fact that despite being two years apart, they looked just like twins. Josh was from Maryland, had a compact frame and great posture, and red hair. He played the banjo with reckless abandon and was in love with Tammy. We were all engineers at W. L. Gore & Associates, better known for their magical expanded polytetrafluoroethylene membrane called Gore-Tex. That's how we came to know Curtis and Mike and Josh.

After a couple of days spent exploring the small border town of Mae Sot, Sheena and I pointed Nacho northward and began snaking through the mountains along Thailand's border with Burma. For the first time in a very long time the air was fresh and cool. I held my arm out the window and let the breeze wash over it. As we rounded a bend we began to see indigenous people lining the roadside. Some carried baskets, while others pushed bicycles or walked with their children. In the meadow to the left of the road the jungle gave way to a thick tangle of makeshift wooden huts built on stilts with roofs made out of leaves. Food was being unloaded from a large truck. We peered through the trees and into the tangle of muddy paths between the homes, clothes drying on lines, women in vibrant sarongs tending to their children or cooking. A small boy rode his bicycle in circles in a clearing, carrying his little brother on the back, and when he noticed I was watching, he laughed and rode faster. This was a Burmese refugee camp.

When Burma gained independence in 1948, many of the hill tribes attempted to break away to form their own independent country. When the military took control of Burma, they violently quelled these attempts by burning over 3,000 villages and attacking the minority tribes. Since then, over 700,000 indigenous people have fled the country, and many live in a series of nine refugee camps in northern Thailand. This was one of them. Many of the people living at this camp had been here for twenty years, and a new generation was now being born in the camp, never having known a normal life.

In America, one doesn't have to throw the stone very far to hit someone who is angrily ranting about some unthinkable atrocity being carried out beneath our very noses. The Republicans are killing health care! The Democrats want to take our guns! Marriage is between a man and a woman! The President is a Muslim! Breastfeeding in public is a crime against humanity! Driving through the refugee camp made us think about how embarrassingly frivolous most of our problems are.

The previous day, while talking to a Burmese man, the topic of health care had come up. He had described how expensive procedures are relative to the income of the population, and how most low income Burmese don't even understand the concept of health insurance. I found myself getting ready to say, "Oh yes, it's similar in the United States," but then I caught myself. Truthfully, I have no business complaining about health care to a Burmese refugee. In fact, very few of us have any business complaining about much of anything at all. Sometimes you just have to talk to someone who has fled his homeland due to legitimate fear of personal harm to put things into perspective.

In the late afternoon we turned off of the main road in search of a camping place. Our map showed a winding appendage of a road taking off into the mountains and coming to a dead end, so we took it. The road pitched up at around a 25% grade, testing Nacho's climbing legs. At the top of the mountain, the road turned downward and descended the far side through the jungle with equal steepness, whereupon we came across a small indigenous village. We wove our way slowly past wooden huts built on stilts with roofs thatched in dry leaves, just like in the refugee camp. Indigenous women walked along the road in tribal clothing, corncob pipes hanging from the corners of their mouths. We followed the road a few hundred meters to its end, where a meandering stream emerged from the wide, dark mouth of an enormous limestone cavern.

We crossed the river on foot and entered the cave. As daylight disappeared behind us we passed a group of local teens sitting in a circle in the sand next to the river in the dark. We explored for a half an hour, and reemerged from the cave into a torrential rainstorm. The view from the mouth of the cave—the backdrop of a river winding into the jungle obscured by rain—was unreal. Night settled on our camp as the bugs and frogs bellowed out a symphony from the natural amphitheater surrounding our van and heavy rain drops tapped out a rhythm on Nacho's roof.

Sheena never had rhythm. We all intrinsically knew it, but had never spoken about it or assigned a label to it. It had been right there before our eyes the whole time, but it was Josh who had finally brought it to light. One evening after dinner at Curtis, Mike, and Josh's house, already having eaten dessert but not wanting to leave, our hosts broke out their instruments. Josh was already well versed in the banjo, while Mike and Curtis were learning to play the guitar and bass, respectively. They frequently played songs for us, and we took to calling them "The

House Band," mostly because they all lived in a house, and they were a band.

On this occasion, The House Band wanted audience interaction, and as we settled onto the couches in the living room, Mike handed out the auxiliary instruments. Sheena and I were to play the egg shakers, which were basically little plastic eggs full of beads. Mike showed us an example of how to keep the background rhythm going with the shakers, and then picked up his guitar. The House Band began its rendition of *Wagon Wheel*, and Sheena and I began shaking our eggs.

"Whoa, whoa," Josh said, stopping mid-verse. His voice had a gentle frankness. "What was that?" He was looking at Sheena.

"Umm...I'm shaking the egg," Sheena said, timidly.

"Sheena, look. When we play the song, you go *'chick-a-chak, chick-a-chak, chick-a-chak'*, got it? Easy, just a simple up and down motion."

"Okay, I'll make the egg go *'chick-a-chak'*," Sheena, said.

The House Band restarted its rendition of *Wagon Wheel*, and on our cue we began shaking. Sheena might as well have started the couch on fire.

"Okay, everybody stop. Wait, wait, wait – stop. Now Sheena, you're supposed to be going *'chick-a-chak, chick-a-chak'*, but instead you're going *'chick-chick-chick-ch-ch-ch-ch-chak'*, do you see?" He was speaking with the kind tone that a father might use to address his disappointment of a child.

"I'm sorry, I don't have any rhythm," she said, and then surrendered her weapon of musical destruction.

Shortly before we left on our drive, The House Band dissolved. Curtis and Mike traded Flagstaff for Denver, moving there within a few months of one another. Brigit and Bret left a short time later for the chill and fog and high culture of San Francisco. Josh had decided to move back East to study infectious diseases and to marry Tammy. We gave him a stethoscope as a going away present on his very last dinner club night. We didn't want him to leave, even though we knew that we, ourselves, would be leaving in due time.

In the morning, Sheena and I were startled awake. The sun peeked through the window of Nacho's pop top tent, and when my eyes focused I could see a herd of water buffalo right outside of our van rolling around in the mud puddles left by the previous night's storm. Two or three buffaloes rolled around, legs in the air, radiating pure bovine joy as the muddy water coated their skin, and then they moved aside and make way for the next bathers. It occurred to me that it was a Thursday morning, and that most of my friends would be waking up to a very different agenda on this day. I rolled onto my back, inhaled the fragrant morning air, and thought about how lucky we were to be able to go to sleep near an indigenous village at the mouth of a cave in Thailand, to wake up to bathing water buffaloes, to drive through refugee camps and freely drive out of them.

We packed our camp, fired up the engine and made our way back toward the small village. Cool air filled the van, indigenous women smoked their pipes, a banjo riff floated from our stereo, and I thought to myself, *I wonder what Josh is doing?*

14

Unmarked Road
to Ban Huai Seau

Brad

On a Tuesday afternoon Sheena and I boarded Nacho and set off in search of a human zoo. "A human zoo," you say? It must be so, for it said so in our guidebook.

> *The villages are often derided as human zoos, and there are certainly elements of this, but we find them more like bizarre rural markets, with the women earning much of their money by selling tacky souvenirs and drinks.*

The villages that the guidebook referred to are Kayan Burmese refugee camps in the hills outside of Mae Hong Son, just a few kilometers away from Burma on the Thailand side. Tourists refer to the Kayan people as "longneck tribes," because the women have unusually long necks adorned with stacked brass rings.

The women's necks aren't actually stretched, as most people believe. Rather, by adding rings over time their collarbones and upper ribs begin to tilt downward, giving the illusion of a longer neck – a sign of beauty and tribal identity in Kayan culture. In a quickly modernizing Asia where Abercrombie & Fitch has largely replaced tribal sarongs, it is amazing that such customs still exist. But not everyone seems to appreciate this fact. Still, our guidebook found the villages pitiable.

> *The Kayan we've talked to claim to be happy with their current situation, but the stateless position they share with all Burmese refugees is nothing to be envied.*

There is a distinct subset of backpackers out there who revere travel guidebooks as holy testaments. If it's not in the book, then it doesn't exist. And if it is in there, then it must be true.

"Hi, I'm Tyler. Nice to meet you Brad and—what was it? Sheila? I left the States like eight weeks ago. Too much white sugar and corn syrup. I trained as an elephant mahout when I was in Thailand and I kayaked down the Mekong and only ate raw vegan food. I'm a pescatarian, but I'm cleansing with my guru. Did I mention I'm a trained elephant mahout? You're from where? I don't believe in homes, and neither does my guru. I may never go back to the States. Did I mention I live on a dollar a day? Oh, by the way, do you have anything I can eat? What? You went to a longneck village? I would never go to one. I basically think of them as human zoos."

In the weeks after going to the Kayan village of Ban Huai Seau Tao, we told six people about it. And six times we heard, "Longneck village? Those places are human zoos." It's a shame to come across travelers who are open-minded enough to seek out worldly experiences, but then fail to use those experiences to cultivate their own original thoughts.

From Mae Hong Son we followed a stream through a densely wooded forest. After the third or fourth stream crossing, we saw a couple of elephants leashed to trees in the shade to graze and drink from the stream; elephants in this remote corner of Thailand are still used as field animals to haul loads or pull plows, much in the same way that water buffalo or cows are used elsewhere. Finally we arrived at the Kayan village and parked just outside. Before being allowed to enter on foot, we were asked to pay a few dollars to support the village—another thing that gets backpackers all riled up ("It's a human zoo!")

There are several Burmese refugee camps along the border, and most of them deliver a relatively low standard of living. By restoring their dying cultural customs, the Kayan have created a means of generating their own revenue, and by doing so have improved their standard of living relative to the other camps, reducing their reliance on outside aid.

We paid up and walked into the village. After crossing a stream on a small bridge, we came to the main thoroughfare in town: a small walking path between thatched huts. The village was very small, and there were a couple dozen shops set up on the path, each tended by one or two Kayan women. More than half of the women wore traditional brass rings around their necks, and all of them wore their tribe's traditional vibrant sarongs, woven tops, and colorful scarves.

The most popular items for sale were hand woven sarongs and scarves. Many of the women sat on wooden benches inside of their huts weaving on looms stretched between their waists and wooden posts.

Each sarong takes several days to complete, and the prices were surprisingly fair – only a few dollars each. Four or five tourists meandered around the shops, giving the place the feel of, gosh, what would I call it? A crowded strip mall? An international airport? No, that's not right. Oh, of course! A human zoo!

We left the main walkway and headed up the hill to where Italian missionaries had long ago built a catholic church in an effort to save these villagers from their sinful, tribal ways. Based on the condition of the church and the traditional feel of the village, it would appear as though the mission had failed. But the numbers say otherwise. Two thirds of Kayan villagers have given up their spirituality and now identify as Roman Catholics.

The Burmese government also made attempts to quell Kayan traditions in order to look more modern by encouraging the villagers to stop wearing their traditional neck coils, and many villagers obliged. Even more young Kayan removed their coils to fit in with modern society after fleeing to Thailand. The odds are stacked against the Kayan and their customs, but for now it's pleasing to see the old traditions kicking and struggling to stay afloat in a quickly modernizing world.

Before leaving the village we bought a couple of cold drinks and enjoyed them in the shade of a tamarind tree. Sitting there with a cold drink in hand, the sun's intense rays filtered by the fair leaves of the tamarind, I thought I felt something. *What is this feeling?* I wondered. I retrieved our guidebook from my backpack and consulted the index to see what it was, but I found no mention of tamarind trees or cold drinks. I placed the book back in my pack and zipped it up. *Must have been nothing.*

15

Chiang Mai Ring Road

Sheena

We gathered around the table covered by a cloth imprinted with cappuccino cups and fluffy croissants. I would have imagined that we were somewhere in Italy, but the dishes in the center of the table gave it away. They were cooked with basil, ginger, *galanga*, chili paste, lemongrass, and plenty of fish sauce. I had survived my introductory course in Thai home cooking under the watchful and experienced eye of Karn's mother, Nid.

Had I pulled all of the legs off of the prawns? Did I rip the lime leaves correctly? Did I crush the chilies well enough with the pestle and mortar? I nervously executed the steps as instructed as we prepped dinner together in her kitchen.

We had met Karn just a few days prior through an introduction from Pat and Gak in Bangkok. We had met up with Karn near the stacked brick wall of the old moat, whose once clean lines had morphed over the centuries into horizontal spines of drooping waves that wrapped around the old city in Chiang Mai. From there we followed him back to his house where we would stay for a few days to experience life in northern Thailand from a local's perspective.

On the first evening we made our way to the neighborhood market to pick up items for an impromptu picnic. We followed Karn's old blue and white bus as it bounced down a dirt road ahead of us, eventually pulling off and parking on the banks of a quaint pond. We rolled out bamboo mats on the ground for an evening of food discovery: homemade sausage and sticky rice, fish coconut soufflé in banana leaf bowls, roe-stuffed crab heads, fried pork skin, eggplant curry, purple mangosteen, and red rambutans.

"I'm always watching television," Karn said between bites of curry. "But it is okay, because it is my job!" Karn is a translator, and it is his job to watch television and translate the words into Thai subtitles. "Not too long ago I finished translating *The Bachelor,* but now I'm doing the *Martha Stewart Show.*" Despite being the man behind the curtain of some of the top American TV shows in Thailand—a pretty big deal!—he was nonchalant about his secret celebrity status. "I know everything about Martha Stewart. Did you know that every dish on her show is her favorite?" Doing his best Martha impersonation he cried out, "Oh my! This apple pie is just *my favorite!* This blueberry tart is just *my favorite!* This chocolate chip recipe is my all time *faaavorite!*"

The following evening in Chiang Mai's hip downtown district, a bartender crafted drinks for us from the inside of a rusty blue and white Volkswagen bus that had been converted into a bar. In addition to our mysterious blue cocktails, we snacked on typical Thai bar food. You know, the usual sampling of raw peanuts, kebabs, fried crickets, and bamboo worms. These bugs seemed tame compared to my last run-in with edible bugs.

Just a week ago, we had visited at a roadside restaurant outside of the mountain town of Pai in search of *lahp koo-a,* a typical regional dish. The restaurant's owner had been honored to serve us his local specialty appetizers, on the house: a bowl of hideous, gigantic bugs accompanied by a bowl of red dipping sauce. They had reminded me of some mutated version of a roach or cicada, having eyes the size of beads and legs like strands of thick wire. Their lower bodies were hollow and crispy and they stared at us with their dead eyes. The locals had very enthusiastically encouraged us to try them, all the while chanting the virtues of their prized bugs to us in unintelligible Thai gibberish.

For some unknown reason, on that day in Pai, I had been feeling more adventurous than usual. Anyway, I just didn't know how to refuse the kind offering. The restaurant owner would have been so disappointed in us. The locals had popped the bugs into their mouths like Skittles, shrugged their shoulders, and asked us *why don't you try?* I had picked one up and held it at eye level. I had examined its shiny black glazed eyes, its tentacles, its mandible, wondering where they had found it. Had it been scurrying about in the grass, or under an upturned log? Had it been resident, or in the midst of a seasonal migration to another land when it had been captured? That day, as I closed my eyes, I had envisioned Kit Kat bars and peanut brittle, and then I ate it. Brad told me then that he'd never kiss me again.

Now, back at the bus bar in Chiang Mai, the locals around us chomped the bugs like Skittles, shrugged their shoulders, and asked us *why don't you try?* And so I went for it. Once again, I held the bugs up at eye level and questioned how they came to be nestled atop this fine layer of faux grass on my foam tray. I thought again of Kit Kat bars and peanut brittle, and then ate the bugs. I ate them this time, though, for the sheer comedy in knowing that Brad would be forced to follow suit. The crickets were palatable, like little citrus-infused burnt bits left in the bottom of a pan. The worms were, however, gag-inducing: little collapsing sponges that squirted foul juices with each chew. Was it worth it just to watch Brad's face? Yes, yes it was.

Besides the bugs, we also tried some other local dishes while we were in Chiang Mai. There was *Kow Soy*; egg noodles in a spicy coconut broth, topped with crispy noodles, and served with a dish of lime, pickled cabbage, and red onion. I'm not like Martha Stewart and I don't claim to love every dish, but this was out-of-this-world amazing. In all of Asia so far, it was truly one of my favorites.

I had mentioned to Karn that I had wanted to take a cooking class while in Chiang Mai, and he made short work of my request. "It is no problem. My Mom will show you how to make Thai food."

We followed Karn's wife, Yui, as she scoured the neighborhood market, grabbing bags of minced pork, basil, lemongrass, and chilies. She picked out the prettiest blue prawns in the seafood section, while the rest of us stood around, entranced by the dozens of miniature fans with strings tied to the blades, whipping around just above the surface of the food to keep the flies away.

Back at the house we got underway. Having been the translator for Martha Stewart, Karn was well prepared for his role as translator for our very own cross-cultural cooking experience.

"Today we are making three things: steamed eggs, tom yam soup, and a basil stir fry. These are all quick and easy dishes, but the first thing we do is make rice. It is the base for every meal in Thailand. After that, we will make my Mom's steamed eggs. This is a very popular recipe but every household has their own version."

After we loaded up the massive rice cooker, we began on the eggs. Nid walked me through the steps as we mixed egg and water, rehydrated dried shrimp and mushrooms, added pork, onions, shallots and seasoning, and then gave it all a good beating. We placed the mixture in a bowl on the steaming rack above a covered pot of boiling water.

Moving around the kitchen was quick and easy, and it reminded me a little of our tiny house back home in Flagstaff. One wall of Nid's kitchen featured a long countertop, while the other had a tabletop stove shielded on three sides by aluminum. Underneath the stove there sat an exposed propane tank, and on the other counter sat a bin of cooking ingredients, a sink, and a rice cooker. Homes in Thailand don't have built-in kitchens, but rather a place to set a portable propane stove and ample counter space for food preparation. Many apartments don't have kitchens at all, due to the fact that most people in the big cities eat the street food because it is so cheap and convenient.

As the eggs steamed, Nid wandered outside and came back with a dozen freshly picked kaffir lime leaves for the tom yam soup. We made a broth of lemongrass, kaffir leaves, chilies, *galanga,* and lime juice and let it simmer. We prepared the prawns, pulling off their shells, snapping their heads, breaking their legs, and slicing their backs to devein. We added the prawns and a few handfuls of strangely shaped straw mushrooms for just a few minutes before turning off the heat.

Our last dish of the evening was a pork and basil leaf stir-fry. It was simple: a quick stir-fry of onion, garlic, pork, and a heaping mound of basil. The flavor was delightful – the meat provided a rich depth of flavor while the holy basil added a sharp, mentholated aroma and taste.

And so there we were, gathered around a table that was covered with a vinyl tablecloth, sporting pictures of cappuccino cups and fluffy croissants. Grandma held baby Phuphing while the family's French bulldog spread its body against the cool tiled floor.

"In a Thai home, all dishes are communal," Karn said, scooping rice onto each of our plates. "This is how we do it." He held his fork with his left hand and his big spoon in his right. "You just push a little rice onto your spoon with your fork. The fork is only a tool for moving food. We don't eat with it. Get some rice on your spoon, and then, from the dishes in the center, just scoop a little soup or curry onto your spoon. One scoop at a time."

One scoop at a time? One scoop at a time?! I then understood how Thai people stayed so thin!

Using my fork, I nuzzled a little rice onto my spoon and then lowered it down into the communal bowl of tom yam soup. This was the first bite in our very own slow-food revolution. The dishes were all wonderful, but I went away with a new special place in my heart for those steamed eggs. Dare I say, a new favorite?

16

Route 11 to Sukhothai

Brad

It all started with a little bump.

"What on Earth was that?" Sheena asked, wide-eyed and alarmed. "Just a little bump," I said reassuringly.

As dictated by Murphy's Law, we had driven 92 kilometers into a 100 kilometer diversion off of Thailand's northwestern mountain circuit that would have taken us to a high mountaintop campsite next to a glistening lake, when suddenly the road turned up at an unusually steep grade. Rounding the bend and seeing the road going straight up, we knew it was over before it began. I gunned it, we slowed, I kept the pedal on the floor, we slowed more, I feathered the clutch, and then the engine died.

"Bloody hell." Just a few days prior we'd come within ten kilometers of the highest point in Thailand before we were forced to turn around for lack of power. Nacho weighed in at a portly 5,800 pounds while our engine packed only a 92 horsepower punch. That's a morbidly obese man on a child's scooter.

Now with the engine stalled on the unusually steep grade, and without engine power to boost our brakes, I wouldn't be able to hold Nacho there on the hill for long, so I slowly guided us backwards until we came to a small side road. I wedged Nacho up onto the small side road, which took off at an unusually steep grade, and started the back-and-forth motion of a thirty-six-point turn. At long last I pulled onto the road in the other direction, but when I did, the steepness of the side road exceeded our exit angle, and our exhaust pipe and rear bumper slammed into the ground.

"Probably nothing!" I said as we carried on. I made a mental note to check that out later. Two days later I finally remembered to look at it. I found that we'd dented the bumper a little, and the exhaust pipe looked fine. When the exhaust pipe fell off the next day, it became clear that, in fact, the exhaust pipe was not fine.

All right, no exhaust pipe. The muffler was still there, so seemingly the only difference was that exhaust gases would come out of the side of the van instead of being diverted backwards. We carried on through Chiang Mai, and drove a few hundred kilometers south to the town of Sukhothai where we imagined ourselves passing our days strolling among ancient temple ruins.

"The idle's a bit erratic," I told Sheena. "I'm going in for a closer look." We had checked into a guesthouse, and that's where I left Sheena as I walked to an adjacent field where I had left Nacho to see why he was misbehaving. I removed everything from the back and popped the engine lid for a closer look.

Lots of dirt, little bit of oil – normal.

Throttle position switch still clicks – good to go.

No loose connections, no broken hoses – sweet action.

A big charred ball of wires stuck to the exhaust heat shield? Hmmm.

My mind went into analytical mode, recounting the possibilities. *Oh yes. I see. Oh, of course. That's bad.* Soon enough I'd realized why engineers invented exhaust pipes in the first place. Whenever we sat still at an idle, the heat from our muffler had been wafting straight up into the engine compartment rather than being diverted safely out the back. This had caused the heat shield to become red hot, which in turn melted our main engine wiring harness, which was inexplicably strung right across the heat shield. I picked it up and inspected it, but it was obvious that all of the wires had melted and shorted together, causing all fourteen of them to become one big charred mess. It's a miracle Nacho didn't burst into flames, as this charred ball sat directly under our brittle plastic, semi-leaky fuel rail – a 1984 original.

I hopped on a little girl's bike that I found at the guesthouse, and pedaled it to the nearest home building supply store, where I purchased thirty meters of monofilament wire. Not exactly the right stuff, but one can't be picky when one's engine is in shambles and one's wife is contentedly sitting in her comfortable guesthouse, unaware that she might have reason to be discontented.

And that's the story of how I came to be sitting in a hot field in Sukhothai for the whole day rewiring our entire engine. Thank goodness for multimeters and beer.

Being that we were still on Earth, and thus still under the constant pull of gravity and Murphy's law, it started to rain just as I was finishing up. And boy did it rain. And rain. And rain. I opted to save the test drive for the next morning, when we would be able to jet out of town to explore the nearby temple ruins.

When morning rolled around we loaded Nacho up and crossed our fingers. I turned the key, and to our collective delight Nacho whimpered to life, stuttered, nearly died, and then resumed an unhealthy idle fluttering between 800 and 1,500 RPM. Yes! Back to normal!

I threw it in reverse and pressed the gas. Rather than moving backwards, as expected, we traveled straight down, approximately eight inches, into the ground, which was unexpected.

As it turned out, the heavy rain had turned our field into something of a soil crème brûlée. The slightest movement of our tires had caused us to break through the crispy top layer and sink into the clay custard below. Out came the sand ladders, and out came the shovel.

Damn you, Murphy!

The white guy with the tiny shovel caused quite a sensation, and soon we had a small audience of old Thai ladies and seemingly helpless backpackers from the guesthouse, who must have forgotten that it is customary to offer help when a fellow countryman finds himself stuck in the mud.

After several nearly successful tries, which saw our tires slipping deeper and deeper into the custard, two of the little old Thai ladies decided that we would not be successful without their help. They sprang into action, throwing bits of debris into our tire holes—making the able-bodied backpackers look terribly lazy—and then motioned for me to fire it up. I delicately put it in reverse and slowly released the clutch. Seeing little promise of success, the little old Thai ladies started pushing. The bigger of the two pushed on the front bumper, while the smaller one, weighing in at around 75 pounds, placed her hand on my door handle and pulled with all of her might.

Slowly Nacho crept backwards, and soon I was crawling out of the quagmire, trying not to run over the skinny old lady who still held tight to my door handle. Success! The backpackers went back to their coconut waters and their books, the old ladies helped us wash off our sand ladders in their well, and soon we were on our way to the welder to get a new exhaust pipe.

What a cluster. And to think it all started with a little bump.

17

Thai-Lao Friendship Bridge
to Vientiane

Sheena

Brad sat comfortably on a cushion with his back facing the Mekong, and as the minutes ticked by his face slowly darkened to a silhouette of black. The sky was smeared with the most brilliant blues, and the dark clouds seemed to sit on an invisible sheet of glass. We rested there along the Mekong River, on one of the many balconies that hung from the side of Chiang Khan's traditional timber houses. On the far shore, Laotian fishermen wearing cone hats crept along the cattails in narrow dugout canoes.

I was thrilled to be there, and it felt as though I were sitting next to a celebrity, because the Mekong is just that. This flow had originated on the Tibetan Plateau in China, picking up trickles and streams from glaciers in the Himalayas, steadily becoming more turbulent as it picked up volume, until it became this swirling, churning brown torrent before us.

As the sun set, the fishermen made their way back to their respective shores: the southerners to the Thai side, and the northerners to the Laos side. The two sides of the river represent two uniquely different worlds, cultures, and faces.

Brad hummed the lyrics of *Mekong* by The Refreshments, an Arizona band whose sounds often graced the interior of Nacho as we roamed the globe, and he ordered a beer.

Barkeep, Another Mekong please
Yes of course you can keep the change
A new glass here for this new friend of mine
Forgive me I forgot your name

Now that we were within striking distance of Laos, it was decision time. We could cross into Laos at the Friendship Bridge only an hour away, or follow the Mekong for another couple hundred miles south in Thailand. Thailand had been good to us, delivering more mountains, elephants, temples, spicy food, beaches and amazing people than we could have asked for. But we felt that persistent nagging for new adventure.

By morning we had made up our minds. We made a quick stop for lunch at a roadside rice noodle stand, and then crossed the river toward Vientiane. It was capital city time. As drivers of—by Asian standards—a gigantic monster truck, driving in busy capital cities was one of our least favorite activities.

We made our preparations and readied ourselves for the chaos. I paused the music and cleared the emergency break of jammed books and water bottles just in case. Brad tightened his grip on the wheel, preparing to swerve around dogs and children and motorcycles if the need were to arise.

But it never arose. In fact, Vientiane was the anti-big-city: a rural outpost compared to Bangkok or Kuala Lumpur.

We passed Patuxai, the city's war monument, and then all of a sudden were cruising down the capital's main avenue. It was strangely peaceful. We could hardly believe that this was the country's capital. There was even Laotian-style on-street parking; we did as the locals do and launched Nacho onto the pedestrian sidewalk and then killed the engine, coming to rest in a tilted sidewalk-straddle, which gave the impression that we had parked there on accident. It was a perfect Laotian parking job.

Upon our arrival we phoned Pepe; another friend of Pat, Gak, and Teng Tsen; who quickly found us in the un-crowded city. This was the standard operating procedure in Asia; we were passed around like foster children among friends of friends, who were always happy to host us and give us a glimpse of their culture.

Pepe was from Thailand, had married a Laotian woman, had a child, and had lived in Laos for over twenty years. He introduced us to his young son, who wasted no time in renaming his dad's 1960's VW bus *Nacholine* after being introduced to our van. Despite Pepe's insistence that their van was also male, the boy wouldn't budge. Brad went through the motions of giving a tour of the van, but when he switched on the water purification system, smoke mysteriously wafted up from under our floorboards. We soon discovered that the controller for our UV water purifier had entered self-destruct mode, which was timely, given our trajectory into cholera territory.

92

The guys talked mechanics for most of the afternoon, and when dinner rolled around, Pepe led us to a Vietnamese joint. Despite the capital's petite size, its international food scene was bustling: Laotian, Vietnamese, Chinese, Indian, and—because Laos was a former French colony—ample French food. Street stands served up French-Laotian fusion: crusty baguettes bulging with cucumber, meat, pickles, radishes, green papaya, meat pâté, sweet chile sauce, spicy hot sauce, cilantro, and spring onions.

Since we'd never tried Vietnamese food, we dropped in on Pepe's favorite hole-in-the-wall and let him do the ordering. Servers filled our table with fried spring rolls, sausages, a plate heaping with vegetables and herbs, rice noodles, and rice paper wrappers with an array of dipping sauces.

"Watch carefully," Pepe said as he pulled a sheet of rice paper from under the lettuce stack and cupped it in his hand. He then placed a piece of lettuce over the rice paper.

"Always cover the rice paper with lettuce. That way it won't dry out and fall apart. Next take one piece of everything on the plate. A slice of cucumber, some bean sprouts, a little bit of rice noodles, basil, mint, cilantro, some bitter herbs, and a bit of sauce. And last, add a slice of sausage or fried spring roll if you want."

While he talked I built my own supersized wrap.

"Now you put the entire thing in your mouth. That way you will get all of the flavors in one bite."

I squeezed my lettuce wrap to condense it down to something marginally ladylike, and then stuffed it into my mouth in one great bite. I was in heaven. This was what I had been looking for. The mix of flavors was intensely fresh with just the right amount of sweetness and spice, and to top it off, the scene around me was something entirely new: men eating lettuce wraps. I couldn't ask for anything more. Nothing turns an ordinary man into a total beefcake like a lettuce wrap in hand.

For the next few days, with umbrellas in hand, we explored Vientiane. It had the temples, the gold stupas, the night market, and river walk, much like the other side, but life felt markedly different on this side of the river. The women all wore traditional sarongs paired with collared blouses and high heels. This was the national dress code, and it was required for most office jobs. The result was a unified adherence to tradition. The people of Vientiane seemed happy.

On our final evening, Pepe took us to a fancy Laotian restaurant where, he said, government diplomats take their high profile visitors. At the front of the restaurant, a small stage was set up where a male college student played a traditional Laotian wind instrument made of a double row of bamboo-like reeds. Girls with porcelain faces and cone-shaped buns atop their heads performed the national folk dance, extending their arms and legs in deliberate movements while their hands swayed back and forth, their fingers arched back towards their wrists.

Pepe said that for Laotian and Thai dancers, the ability to arch the fingers backwards is an important symbol of experience and ability. Dancers start training at a young age, attempting to mold their finger bones to gain prominence later in life. As a result, many dancers are extraordinarily elastic and able to extend their fingers backward almost to the wrist. The young dancers and musicians at the restaurant were all students at a local music school, practicing here as part of their program. At the end of each dance, the girls would bow and then quickly race off in a fit of giggles.

While we watched the girls dance, we ate sticky rice – a staple served with nearly every meal in Laos. This translates into a consumption of 240 pounds of rice per year, per person! In comparison, the average American consumes just twenty pounds of rice per year.

Pepe demonstrated the proper way to eat sticky rice. He pulled a chunk of rice from the clumped mass housed in a bamboo container, and held it between his fingers. "Before eating sticky rice you must squeeze it between your fingers," he said. While he talked, he continued to squeeze and pinch. "Many foreigners don't do this correctly. Some of them eat it with a fork!" His face was pure disgust as he said this. "They don't understand that the more you squeeze, the better the sticky rice will taste. When it reaches the right consistency you dip it into your curry or soup."

I pulled off a chunk of the sticky rice.

Without going into my history of disliking rice, I will simply say that I didn't believe that kneading this bland hunk of goo between my fingers would make me like it any more. But I followed procedure, pinching and kneading until it eventually became a featureless ball of white putty. It was moist and chewy and, I will admit, delicious.

In the evening we left the restaurant and returned to our urban campsite along the banks of the Mekong River, right across the street from the Grand Hotel. A few steps away, a long row of clothing vendors had set up for the night market. People walked around selling snacks, while mobile pedicurists carried their manicure tools, stools, and shallow tubs for washing feet, ready to start scrubbing with the wave of a hand. The late Chris Farley created a stigma around living in a van down by the river with his *Saturday Night Live* character, the motivational speaker named Matt Foley. But on that night, sleeping down by the shores of the Mekong before a backdrop of Vientiane, we happily drifted off to sleep knowing that we'd done Mr. Foley proud.

18

Sisavangvong Road

Brad

A moist jungle haze had settled over our camp like a warm blanket, and the heavy air asphyxiated me awake. I roused Sheena, swung my legs over the sleeping ledge, and lowered myself into Nacho's compact living room. Already the sounds of the temple and the town filled the air. Monks chatted with one another, street touts advertised their wares, and pale-skinned tourists smelling of sunscreen and bug spray fended off obnoxious tuk-tuk drivers.

"Hey you mister! You want tuk-tuk? You go waterfall, go see elephants? Mister! Tuk-tuk?"

The sun beat down on me as I walked to the line of huts where the monks lived, perched atop stilts behind the temple. We had hoped to rise in time to see a procession of monks walking through town collecting food in their alms bowls, but we had overslept. I blinked several long blinks to let my pupils adjust to the sunlight as I walked.

"Excuse me," I called out, "do you speak English?" The monk standing in the doorway shook his head and pointed inside. He went back into the house and emerged with another.

"Yes?" the second monk said shyly, as he adjusted his orange robe. He looked to be about eighteen years old.

"We're ready to go. Do you have the keys to the gate?" He disappeared into the house and emerged with a ring with a couple dozen old keys. He trotted down the wooden stairs and fell in step beside me as we walked back to the gate enclosing the temple grounds.

We had arrived in Luang Prabang the previous day around lunchtime, with plenty of daylight left to secure a suitable campsite. Finding a place to camp on a daily basis should have been simple, until one considered the state of camping in Southeast Asia.

In South America we had been spoiled by the ubiquity of camping options. Most nights we slept in the wild near rivers or rock outcroppings or deserted vistas. Over the course of our final five-and-a-half months in South America, we'd spent only one night in a hotel. One night in a hotel to one hundred and sixty-five nights of camping.

In Southeast Asia, however, finding places to camp had not been easy. What undeveloped land there was usually remained undeveloped either because it was covered by impenetrable jungle, it was too steep to walk on, or because it was thought to contain unexploded land mines. Camping had often taken the form of finding a suitable parking place in a low-traffic area where we could draw the curtains and imagine being surrounded by nature.

After an hours-long search for a suitable camp spot in Luang Prabang we came up empty handed. We asked at hotels, hostels, and shops to see if we could stay overnight in their parking areas, but were refused. We drove endlessly up and down the outlying roads looking for anything resembling privacy. Nothing. But there *was* something. When we had first arrived in Luang Prabang I had suggested it, but Sheena outright refused. Only after reaching the point of exhaustion, she relented.

"Fine," she sighed, "we can try to camp at the temple." Back in Bangkok, Pat had given us the idea. He said that monks will never turn down a traveler in need, and I was fully prepared to exploit this Buddhist loophole.

We drove to the temple smack-dab in the center of town, found some monks, asked about camping, explained what camping was by drawing pictures, were invited to come chant with them, gained permission to camp, drove into of the temple grounds, popped the tent, and drank a beer. I had forgotten to ask if drinking beer in the temple grounds was acceptable, so I enjoyed my beer with curtains drawn.

"Do you mind if I try the key?" I asked. The young monk had worked his way through all two-dozen keys, but none would open the gate's lock. The sun had long since cleared the trees and now bore down on us from the cloudless sky. *The poor guy doesn't know how to use a key*, I thought to myself. He handed me the ring of keys and I started trying them in the lock. *Nope. Nope. Not that one. Nope.* I worked through all of them and stated with the utmost authority to the young monk that indeed, none of these keys matched this lock.

The boy retreated to his hut. A minute later, he returned with an older monk, one who had been there longer and had more knowledge of keys. The older monk took the ring of keys and proceeded to try each one. When he had finished, he started over at the beginning and tried each one again, but with more twisting force. I watched him as he applied all of his strength to each key, and I hoped that none of them would break off in the lock.

By now a crowd of monks had formed around us. The foreigners were trapped in the temple, and that was something to see. Whoever had locked the gate the night before had misplaced the key, but the monks weren't ready to accept defeat. They worked diligently and with good humor to find the right key for the job. A third monk, even older than the first two, decided that the problem was not with the key, but with lack of experience. He took hold of the key ring and went through it twice, testing each key and turning it with great force before conceding that, in fact, the proper key was missing.

The foreigners are patient, but the sun is high and the day is getting hot. How long will the foreigners remain calm? We must get them out of here before it's too late!

A young monk, acting on orders from an older one, ran behind a building and returned with a fist-sized rock. He began feebly smacking the lock with the puny stone, an action that caused the gate to ring out like a temple bell with each awkward swing. His aim was sloppy and he occasionally hit his fingers on the gate.

"Hold on," I said, but nobody understood me on account of the fact that I spoke English and they spoke Laotian. I held up my hands like a traffic cop until the boy stopped smashing his fingers, and then I walked over to Nacho.

"What's going on?" Sheena asked. I informed her that they'd lost the key, and that I was going to have to coordinate a jailbreak. I opened the ammo can that I had bolted to Nacho's front bumper and pulled out the switchblade hack saw that I had picked up at the Home Depot back in Phoenix, but hadn't yet found occasion to use. The monks were excited by this, and motioned for me to give it to the oldest, wisest monk to try.

The wise old monk began timidly sawing at the lock, but his efforts were fruitless. The blade repeatedly slipped off of the shiny chrome surface of the lock's shackle. After a while I took over. After getting halfway through the shackle I stepped aside and handed the saw to a young monk so that he could own the glory of finishing the job. Finally, after several of us were covered in sweat, the blade passed through the shackle.

In the movies, this is the point where the lock victoriously falls open and we make our escape. But in Laos, escape scenes unfold much more slowly. Despite the shackle being cut, the lock still inexplicably refused to open. The young monk picked up his fist-sized stone and continued feebly smacking the lock. I made traffic cop hands and retreated to Nacho, returning with a large crescent wrench.

"Stand back!" I said, and everyone suddenly understood English. I fitted the jaws of the wrench around the lock's body and leaned my weight on the handle until the shackle had twisted out of the way. The monks cheered as the lock came free of the gate, and the young rock-wielding monk hopped with joy, enthusiastically dropped his rock, and slid the gate open.

At this point I would normally parade around and give everyone celebratory chest bumps and bottom slaps, but being that we were guests in a Buddhist temple, I restrained myself and thanked each of the monks in turn by pressing my hands together in front of my face and discreetly bowing my head while repeating one of the few Laotian words I knew—"*kopchai...kopchai...kopchai...*" The monks smiled and walked together back into their huts.

We had won the battle, but there was still a war to fight. Our first night in Luang Prabang was behind us, but we had several to go. I could see the defeat in Sheena's eyes before any words were said. While she was usually very picky about our camp spots, she already knew that there weren't any places meeting her strict criteria in Luang Prabang. It would be up to my less discriminating eye to choose a suitable spot, and I quickly found one: a parking space wedged between obnoxious tuk-tuk drivers on the tourist street that runs along the banks of the Mekong. I triumphantly backed Nacho into place while explaining to Sheena that she simply needed to lower her standards.

In the course of driving from Vientiane to Luang Prabang, we had spent a couple of days winding through a particularly steep and twisty set of mountains. They were the type of mountains that are typical of old Chinese paintings: steep and rugged, with shrouds of mist rising and falling through green river canyons—which made sense, since we were by then very close to the Chinese border in a mountain range that extended into Yunnan province. We had rounded a bend and seen that atop one of the peaks a motor home was parked, and, imagining that it must belong to a French family (by now we were very experienced in guessing nationalities based on vehicle), we drove to it and introduced ourselves. The motor home had indeed belonged to a French family, the

Lassaras. We made fast friends with the parents, Benoit and Aude, and were most enchanted by their four fine children: Jeanne, Blanche, Alexandre, and Emma. We had known beforehand that there would be four children, for nearly all of the traveling French have four children. Before we knew it we were sharing dinner in the motor home, camping together at the lookout point, and being served morning coffee by Blanche, the eight-year-old, with a commanding view over mountain ridges cascading southward. We had parted ways several days before we arrived in Luang Prabang.

As it turned out, our new French friends also ended up in Luang Prabang, and had chosen a similarly questionable campsite just down the street from us in a parallel parking spot. We convened outside of their camper for a picnic dinner on the bank overlooking the Mekong, and then the children ran wild through the trees on the bank while we sat in lawn chairs watching dugout canoes coasting down the river in the fading light. Afterwards, we strolled back to Nacho, our path illuminated by streetlights; the tuk-tuks had long since gone home and the street was ours.

After our visit, we opened Nacho's rear door, set up the shower, and took turns washing off the day's sweat under the cool, refreshing water. We were close to the town center, but outside of the shower we imagined rock outcroppings, deserted vistas, and solitude.

19

Unmarked Track
Along the Nam Ou

Brad

I wiped the perspiration from my face, lugged my backpack onto my lap and opened Nacho's sliding door. Out of the corner of my eye I noticed our GPS tracker in the center console. It had a button which, when pressed, would update an online map showing our location. As an afterthought I picked it up and pressed the button. Dead batteries. I changed the batteries, pressed the button again and waited until the green light blinked, indicating that the signal had gone through.

The sun shone brightly overhead as we left the tiny collection of grass huts known as Nong Kiao on a dirt track following the riverbank. Above us the mountains hissed with the sound of jungle heat, while below us the swollen river whispered and whooshed around the rocks and bushes that lined the banks. As we walked away from the van, our GPS tracker silently went haywire, sending a rogue message into space where it was reflected by a satellite and passed back to Earth. Seconds later the message was relayed through a server and dispersed to a list of emergency contacts. The message was abrupt, ominous.

Brad and Sheena need help. This message was sent because they pressed the "SOS" button on their GPS tracker.

Device Name: Drive Nacho Drive

Latitude: 20.57012

Longitude: 102.61716

Unbeknownst to us, within minutes, a response had arrived in our email inbox. It was from Sheena's father, one of our emergency contacts.

"WHAT IS GOING ON?"

We walked on, none the wiser, into the wilderness. Cicadas buzzed in the trees while a dugout canoe silently floated past on the Nam Ou.

The dirt track rose and fell as it passed over ridges and dry creeks extending like fingers from the mountain to touch the ribbon of water. The jungle thicket to our right soon dissipated, replaced by bare hillsides planted with corn and beans and rice paddies. Simple thatched huts dotted the bare hills, providing a place for farmers to escape the tormenting sun. To our left the river carried on, opaque with suspended mud that would eventually mix into the flow of the Mekong.

**

The S.O.S. message transmitted six times in a row, one minute apart, before the signal went silent. Having heard nothing from us after the S.O.S., Sheena's father quickly sprung into action. It was early morning in Arizona when he found himself launching an international rescue mission. He first called my mother to bring her up to speed, and then tried to contact SPOT, the company that manufactured the GPS tracker, for guidance. After much searching, he eventually found a phone number for the company, but no human existed on the other end – only a robot slinging cheerful automated messages repeating mantras of how great the SPOT tracker is.

Unable to speak to a human, he gave up and decided to try the State Department – a place widely rumored to employ actual humans. He also posted the text of our S.O.S. message to social media to get the word out.

**

After an hour of walking we saw the first signs of civilization. A dilapidated hut obscured by dense trees, a fence concealing a garden and a shed, a simple schoolhouse. We rounded a corner onto a straight section of road where we could make out the figures of several small children in the track. It didn't take long for them to notice us; only a handful of people would pass through the village all day. Suddenly the children transformed into wild animals. Their legs were sprinting towards us before their bodies knew what was happening. Sheena and I stopped in our tracks, uncertain how to react.

In the final few meters before the children reached us, they simultaneously threw their hands out, palms turned skyward. They gasped for air and panted wildly, but their eyes were big and hopeful and full of excitement, their hands unwavering.

"Hello pen! Hello pen!" they shouted. *Pen?* We hesitated, and one of the little girls mimicked writing on the palm of her hand. "Hello PEN!" she shouted, smiling and hopeful. We showed them that we didn't have any pens, or anything useful for that matter. Unable to comprehend why foreigners would be walking in the wilderness without pens, a few of them persisted.

"Hello...pen?"

Finally they realized that we must have been very unlucky foreigners who indeed traveled without pens. They stood in front of us, hands behind their backs, silent. The girls swayed back and forth looking at their feet, tracing out shapes in the dust with their bare toes. A small boy stood in the back of the group with his head cocked to one side, staring at us with squinty eyes. He must have been wondering how we could have been so foolish as to leave home without any pens.

Suddenly one girl broke rank and ran into the weeds at the side of the dirt track, and the rest followed. They frantically grabbed at the weeds, and a minute later emerged with handfuls of flowers. They consolidated the flowers into a bouquet and the girl in charge handed them to Sheena with a shy smile. The poor foreigners. At least now they have some flowers.

The children fell in step behind us, matching our strides while giggling and smiling. After a few minutes they stopped in the road and waved goodbye to us, yelling over one another the parting chant of the milk-face:

"Bye! Bye! Bye! Bye!"

***

It didn't take long to get a representative from the US State Department on the phone. Within minutes, Sheena's dad was patched through to the US Embassy in Vientiane, the capital of Laos. The representative took down the coordinates and then typed them into his computer.

"They're way up in the mountains in a place called Nong Kiao," the man from the Embassy said, "we don't have anybody up there." He explained that our last known location was in a tiny village way off the grid, and that the closest police station was nearly a day's drive away over bad roads. He told Sheena's dad to hang tight, and that he would mount a search and rescue mission from within Laos.

* * *

We made our way down the exposed dirt track under the heat-lamp sun that left patches of dry salt on our shirts. Around a bend in the road a man rested in the shade of a rubber tree next to a makeshift wooden shelter that housed a pile of freshly picked pineapples. We placed our order and the man picked up his machete and cut off several enormous leaves from a nearby tree. He used one leaf to clean off the blade of his machete, and then placed the rest of them on the ground to form a clean work surface. He set a pineapple on the leaf mat and proceeded to slice it into edible chunks before wrapping one leaf into a to-go container. We paid him the equivalent of twenty-five cents and continued on our way, fresh pineapple juice dripping from our leafy satchel, and down our arms and chins.

A short while later we ducked into a grove of lime trees and found our way down to a shady place where a tree had fallen on the riverbank. We found the flat parts of the downed tree where it was most comfortable to sit, retrieved the tuna and crackers from the pack, and drained the oil from the tuna can into a gopher hole. A small team of ants crawled onto my shoe, over my toes, and down the other side into the powdery dust. In the river a dugout canoe with a small outboard motor slowly worked its way upstream. The canoe slowed as it came to a narrowing in the river where the water velocity increased, then regained its speed and disappeared around a bend.

* * *

It was nearly midday when the representative from the State Department in Vientiane started making calls. He called every police station in the capital to sound the alarm about the American couple in the mountains that had dropped off the radar after sounding an S.O.S. alarm. He was a diligent man, and he knew that people were counting on him to bring the couple back safely. And he might have launched a successful rescue party if Laotian police were the hard-working type. But as it turned out, the State Department representative was unable to locate

104

a single on-duty police officer in the entire capital city. By late afternoon the effort had gone nowhere.

***

When we passed the pineapple man on our way back, he was chatting with a tiny, dirty villager carrying a backpack. The pineapple man waved at us and then said something to the tiny man and pointed toward us. The tiny man grinned a big toothy grin, trotted over, and began walking with us.

"Mugulubglub boggily rai chap moo gulai!" the man said. I noticed that his eyes were a little glazed over.

I spoke slowly and clearly in hopes that it would help him understand my language, which he clearly didn't speak. "We do not speak Lao. We speak English. I do not understand what you are saying."

"Grubai! Ha! Wulai buggarudai cruap gai!" No language barrier would stand in this man's way.

"I am sorry," I continued, even more slowly than the first time, "I do not understand the words that are coming out of your mouth."

"Ha! Willynu rug moo kwai bloo roomai!" He spoke quickly with grand gestures of hand and body, as if retelling a very exciting story. He continued on for what seemed like ages as we walked, occasionally glancing my way for a reaction, to which I would respond with droopy eyebrows, or a smile, or with raised eyebrows depending on the reaction that I guessed his story warranted based on his facial expression. Occasionally I interrupted him mid-sentence.

"Sir!" I would interject, "I have no idea what you're saying!"

The tiny man didn't care. Whatever he was on prohibited him from realizing that the words coming out of my mouth were of a different language than the words coming out of his, so he filled the minutes with nonstop jibber jabber. I decided the man just needed someone to talk to, so I joined the game.

"Kuan ton prai muglai ekkamai loo boo crap–"

"Wait a minute! Did you say airplane? I thought you might have said–"

"Doo da bai kumai–"

"I'm sorry, but your airplane story reminded me of a tale of my own. Do you know how these bamboo trees came to be here? Well let me tell you sir, and please make yourself comfortable, for my tale is a long one. The length of my story will indeed remind you of times in your life when you wished that things had gone differently. Like the time–"

"Gooba dai prai!"

"Tanning leather? Well why didn't you just say so! The first step to tanning leather is to obtain a hide. Now this is the tricky part, for animals with suitable hides for tanning are often quite mean and hard to kill…"

The kilometers ticked by in this manner—him speaking in gibberish, and me interrupting him to tell my own meandering made-up stories—until we reached the village of the children, whereupon the tiny stoned man became distracted and stopped walking long enough for us to make our escape. A half an hour later he passed us by on the back of someone's motor scooter. As he passed he tried finishing his story.

"Goo moo bannnnnntaaaaaiiiii–"

When we got back to Nong Kiao it was late and we were exhausted from the relentless sun. We spied our tiny friend sitting in a ditch beside the bridge over the Nam Ou, so we walked to a small kiosk and bought him a lemon soda. We delivered the soda to him (he didn't remember who we were and was very confused at his great fortune) and made our way back to where Nacho was parked. After showering, I opened the computer to check my email.

What I found upon connecting to the outside world was nothing short of a Mongolian Charlie Foxtrot.

It didn't take long to suspect the SPOT tracker as the cause of this mess, and a quick inspection of the device verified our suspicions. The plastic safety cover protecting the S.O.S. button was still firmly in place, ruling out an accident on our part. The green message light, which should have stopped blinking hours before, was still blinking, and I was unable to power off the device without removing the batteries. I sent off several quick emails to family and then I called Sheena's dad.

"I'm glad to hear from you," he said. It was the understatement of the century. He sounded pretty flustered, and I explained what had happened. "You should call your mom," he said. I hung up the phone and rang my mom on Skype.

"Uh, mom?"

"OH MY GOD, ARE YOU OKAY?!" She was audibly upset, to put it mildly. "Oh my GOD I'm so glad you're okay! My sister is here and she's been trying to keep me calm."

I explained that our GPS tracker had malfunctioned, and that we found this whole affair rather surprising. She finally calmed down and suggested that I write a strongly worded letter to SPOT, the company that made the device. Sheena's dad was two steps ahead of us, and had already written a detailed incident report with suggestions about how to improve their system for future situations of a similar nature. Four days later a robot replied to his email, verifying that, in fact, no humans actually work at SPOT.

20

Route 7 to Phonsavan

Sheena

In the distance the dirt road split, with the worn down, dusty ridges of dried mud veering off at angles. The fluttering orange bundle on the back of the motorcycle taxi veered left. I pointed ahead and motioned to Brad to follow. "If we keep that monk within sight, we'll find the temple."

The red dirt road leading out of Phonsavan was smooth and fast, but given Laos's prolific livestock population, we had to remain on guard for suicidal cows and sleeping dogs. The monsoon skies were moody and it was anybody's guess when the dark clouds would burst like water balloons, showering water upon the radiant green rice paddies.

As expected, the monk led us directly to the temple and hence to our destination. The temple acted as a parking area for one of the mysterious collections of ancient vessels known as the Plain of Jars. A big red sign sponsored by an NGO provided some information about the area; in 2005, 6,863 pieces of scrap metal and 22 unexploded ordinances, or UXOs, had been cleared from the area surrounding the jars. While this seemed like an awful lot of bombs in such a small area, it was nothing compared to the untold millions of them still scattered throughout the country.

After traveling to Laos and learning more about it firsthand, it became apparent that my schooling had failed to bring to light a particularly dark piece of American history: the CIA's Secret War. My country, I learned, had created a real nightmare of a scenario here; in the nine years between 1964 and 1973, the American Air Force dropped eighty million bombs on Laos, killing around 350,000 men, women, and children, and displacing a tenth of the population. I found it unbelievable that we had dropped more bombs on Laos than we had on Japan and Germany combined during World War II.

Seventeen bombs per minute, for nine straight years, rained down on innocent civilians, many of who didn't even know what America was. Of the eighty million bombs that were dropped, twenty-four million didn't even go off. This left Laos, forty years after the war, still dealing with the aftermath of America's distaste for their choice of political systems, and its unfortunate proximity to Vietnam. To this day, one hundred people die every year, 40% of whom are children, from stepping on unexploded bombs that the Americans dropped.

After driving through the mountains from the North, we arrived in Phonsavan, one of the country's most heavily bombed regions. During the war, villagers who lived there cleverly opted to spend an excruciating nine years living in the region's vast limestone cave systems. One such cave, called Vieng Xai, became a safe haven for 20,000 villagers. And if one could forget for just a moment the terrible fact that bombs were dropping from their skies like raindrops, the whole network of tunnels, kitchens, assembly rooms, schools, and sewing rooms were utterly fascinating.

The big red signs we saw all over the countryside weren't so surprising then, and we kept in mind that the areas without them were in all likelihood littered with unexploded cluster bombs.

From the temple parking lot a local man pointed to a bridge that led us through a thicket of tall bamboo branches. The bridge ended at a ridge between two rice paddies and we walked between them. These paddies were just two out of the dozens that joined together in terraces that ran down into the valley. Field workers crouched over in rows and planted rice saplings, while in the next plot over, a man up to his knees in mud pushed a tilling machine. Aside from the mechanized tiller, very little about the scene unfolding before us had changed much over the last thirty years. We watched the rice workers while they watched us. They were our entertainment and we were theirs.

Past the rice fields a small hill rose up, and at its crest it flattened into a grassy meadow dotted with mature trees. Scattered throughout the trees in the meadow we found what we had been looking for: the Plain of Jars. We wandered among the ancient stone jars, which were covered in moss, sunken into the ground, and tilted at various angles. They had been carved from rock, were open on one end, and most of them were around three or four feet tall. This site was just out there in the open, accessible for anyone to explore.

The history of the jar sites is sparse, but it is believed that they date back to the Iron Age, around 2,500 years ago. One theory has it that the jars were carved from solid rock to be used as funerary urns. It is thought that the dead were first placed in the larger jars, which were up to nine feet tall, for distillation, to ensure a gradual transformation from the earth to the spiritual world. The bodies would then be moved to the smaller vessels for cremation. All of the jars have lip rims, so it is assumed that at one time they all had lids. Since few lids have been found, they were probably made of perishable materials that did not survive the years.

Local legend has it that the jars were from the mighty king Khun Cheung, who had them made for brewing rice beer to celebrate a hard-won victory. Laos deserved that hard-won leisure: a moment to kick up its feet and get lost in a frosty rice beer, so we'll just go with the legend.

21

Route 1D to Tham Kong Lo

Brad

The announcement of the arrival of the rainy season in Laos fell on deaf ears.

"It sure seems to be raining a lot lately," Sheena would say.

"That's just orographic precipitation and the rain shadow effect, my pea," I would confidently retort.

We woke up and started driving south, and the rain continued to fall. It seemed it would never stop. Without any warning, the mud on the side of a particularly steep mountainside became saturated, then freed itself from friction's grip, and came to rest over the road—our road. We came around a bend to find a long line of cars just sitting there. I asked Nacho to stop and I walked all the way to the front of the cars to see what in God's name was going on.

And then I saw the rocks and mud and several mature trees all sprawled out across the narrow mountain roadway, and I realized what had happened. It was a dang landslide, and it made me start to question everything I ever learned about orographic precipitation and the rain shadow effect.

Initially I stood there like a wide-eyed schoolboy, sheltered from the driving rain by my purple umbrella. I stared with amazement at the enormity of the mud and detritus strewn all over the place, and then at the naked hillside devoid of trees and much of its prior landmass. And then the mud. And then the hillside. Wow! I eventually hurried back to the van and told Sheena.

"Wow! There is a hillside with nothing on it, and there is also a thick layer of mud and detritus!" She was just going to have to see for herself, for I was too excited to give a non-cryptic description.

111

We speed-walked together back to the scene, she with her orange Snoopy umbrella and me with my purple one, and watched the scene unfold. The folks on the near side of the slide stood around in the rain, looking at the mud. The folks on the far side looked on in a similar fashion.

Ironically, the first vehicle to arrive on the far side was a semi truck carrying a very large bulldozer, but I rationalized that there was something wrong with the bulldozer that would prohibit it from clearing the slide. I came to this conclusion after the bulldozer remained on the trailer, never making any attempt to clear the slide. After much nervous chatter, some brave people had ideas.

First, a man with a 4x4 Toyota Hilux fired up his truck and timidly approached the slide. He steered off the road, toward the thick vegetation separating the road from the bottomless abyss of the deep canyon below. He gunned it, slid all over the place, spun his tires, flung mud, and by the skin of his teeth managed to get his truck back onto the road before either rolling over or sliding off into oblivion.

The confidence of the people had been aroused, and a few other Hilux owners followed suit. The Hilux was a popular truck in the backcountry wilds of Laos, and with apparently good reason. Soon, a crazy bastard in a two-wheel-drive sedan tried and succeeded. I stood there for many minutes studying the approach, noting the obstacles hidden by the deep river that had formed in the right tire track, and visualizing Nacho's triumph over this seemingly insurmountable challenge.

"I can do it! Nacho can do it!" I exclaimed.

"I don't know." Sheena said. "I'm going to make a salad. Let's try after lunch." And so it was. Sheena made her salad and we sat down to a nice lunch while we watched through Nacho's window, as more and more people became brave enough to make the treacherous crossing. I wanted to get on it before my bravery waned, so we ate our fancy salads with balsamic vinegar and olive oil very quickly. All of the other cars had made the crossing now, leaving Nacho alone.

As we finished forking the final pieces of lettuce into our mouths, a young man on a farm tractor whizzed by.

"Oh joy! A young man on a farm tractor!" I exclaimed.

I touched the corner of my mouth with a napkin the way British people do, and then I walked with my purple umbrella to the edge of the slide to watch the tractor boy work his magic. Oh the utility of people under hardship! The miracle of communism, just the way Marx envisioned! By the people, for the people!

The young man on the tractor started by proving his worthiness with a bit of showboating. He worked the controls like a machinist, deftly scraping one or two tons of mud over top of the tracks that once served as the only passable route from our side to the other. Next, he pulled to the side of the road, turned the engine off, and sat there silently.

"What? Hey, why'd he stop? Sheena, do you know?" I walked over to the tractor and inspected the undercarriage. Was it broken? I took my shoes off and walked into the mud to see if the track was passable any more. It definitely wasn't.

"Bollocks, I'm going to read a book." And so we retreated to Nacho to read books. It would be thirty minutes before the young man on the tractor was content with the growing number of drivers that had collected on either side of the slide. He fired up the tractor and resumed his work while two of his associates worked their way up the line of cars. They approached Nacho, so I rolled down the window.

"Man oh man," I commented, "that guy sure is making good progress."

"Good money, good progress," the tractor man's associate said. "We want ten thousand Kip from every car."

Marx would be saddened to know that communism in Laos had failed, even despite the Vietnam war in which the evil Americans were defeated, allowing communism to thrive. But dare I say that even Marx would be at least somewhat impressed by the young man's astute planning and the entrepreneurial prowess of his cohort.

The rain continued to fall. It fell and it fell, and it covered the roadways. When it was shallow, we drove through. But when it was chest deep we had to find another way. Laos is serious about its rainy season.

Since first arriving in Laos, we had been the proverbial thorn in the side of the country's Buddhist monk population. Owing to Southeast Asia's distinct lack of camping opportunities, we'd gotten pretty creative with our campsites. Sometimes we simply camped in public parking lots (romantic), while in extremely rare cases (maybe twice), we had found a nice beach overlook or rare dirt road into a forest where we could camp. But when the search failed to yield results, we knew that we could count on the monks.

And so we did. But getting Sheena to agree to camp next to Buddhist temples was much harder than expected, and I couldn't understand why. It must have been some deep ingrained malformation in the female genome that made her feel uncomfortable whenever people knew that we were sleeping inside of our car, and it was especially strong when those people happened to be peace-loving Buddhist monks. But on occasion, when we were desperate enough, she would agree to it. The night following the landslide in the jagged Laotian mountains was one of those nights.

After descending from the mountains beyond the landslide in heavy rain, we arrived in a small village, just as evening was setting in. We asked around at a couple of huts to see if we could park for the night, but were pointed each time in the direction of a temple. Sheena wailed her disapproval at the idea, but after convincing her that it was either the temple or the side of the road, she grunted, crossed her arms, and silently agreed. I parked Nacho in the driveway of the temple, grabbed the paper from our dashboard that a Laotian man had written for us, which asked in Lao script if it was okay for us to camp there for the night, and I knocked on the monks' door.

After five or six monks read my note, each giggling a little bit and passing the note on, the paper landed in the hands of a monk who knew the English word "yes." Riding high on the sweet endorphin wave that success brings, I floated back to Nacho, hopped into the front seat, and started lying to Sheena about how charming I had been when dealing with the monks. I threw it into drive and lurched forward. Almost immediately our front wheels disappeared straight into a hidden mud trench, and our bumper slammed to the ground.

While no villagers had been visible before, our state of distress seemed to have been broadcast into every bamboo hut in the area, and within minutes we were surrounded by curious onlookers. I circled the van, cursing our bad luck so close to our final destination. I decided the solution would involve our trusty jack, so I got that out and started jacking up one front corner. Soon the villagers swarmed the van, each making suggestions to me in Lao, which I didn't understand. I jacked the van, villagers dug in the mud and collected pieces of wood and rock, and soon Nacho's front wheels were supported by terra firma. I fired up the engine, and to the choir of incomprehensible shouting, I drove forward.

Now Nacho's front and rear wheels straddled the trench, and I figured it best to use our steel bridging ladders to create a bridge for the rear wheels to drive across the trench. I began to get out of the van.

"Ooga bing dang booga!" The villagers shouted, signaling that I should gun it and stop being a pansy.

"But I should use my bridging ladders, yes?" I suggested.

"Dang ooga bing dang booga!" they shouted, again signaling for me to stop being such a sally girl. Did they know something I didn't? I looked at the holes I'd just escaped from and they looked deep like bomb-blast craters. The villagers pointed to the holes, told me to man up, and signaled for me to gun it.

So I gunned it. The first thing I felt was slow forward motion, then I felt the soil give way under the van, and then the rear bumper land solidly on the ground. Should have used the bridging ladders.

Monks joined the entourage and we again jacked, dug, and shoved trash under tires. I gunned it, nothing happened, the entire village pushed, I gunned it again, and still nothing happened. Finally a 4x4 truck found its way to the temple, we attached a tow-rope, the truck burned its tires, I burned my clutch, but nothing. Finally, adding village-pushing power to the towing force, we managed to get loose and drive into the temple grounds. We profusely thanked the villagers, saw them off, and parked for the night.

As we parked, the monks streamed out of the temple, picked up two wheelbarrows and an array of shovels, and went to work filling the bomb blast craters I had created in their driveway. I grabbed my shovel and joined the effort. Buddhist monks are happy people, always smiling, but I have to believe that they must have thought that we were a huge pain in the ass. We finished filling the holes, the monks smiled at us, and they retreated.

Later on, one monk returned to the van carrying a cell phone. I came out of the van and he handed me the phone.

"Hello?" I said into the receiver.

"Yes, hello, I am the monk's friend. He wanted me to ask you what you want them to make you for dinner."

"Oh, please, nothing. They've done enough. We're just passing through and we have our own food."

"Do you need bedding? A place to sleep? They can do anything for you."

I told the man on the phone that we were totally self sufficient, and that we appreciated the help they'd already given us. All the while I wondered how, after having been such a pain in the ass, they could extend such unwarranted kindness towards us.

In the morning there was a knock on our door, and outside we could hear someone yelling "Hello! Hello!" I opened the door to find a monk carrying a warm bowl of tapioca and corn porridge. They had made us breakfast. He asked if we wanted any coffee, made sure we had everything we needed, and then we watched him walk through the steady rain, back to his room.

22

Route 33A to Kep

Brad

One day, in a Dairy Queen near Sheena's parents' house, a strange thing happened and we found ourselves sitting adjacent to the booth occupied by Alice Cooper. Several years later, in a place very much unlike a Dairy Queen, we once again found ourselves in the company of creative greatness. This time it was in Cambodia, in the tiny seaside village of Kep. But first, Alice Cooper.

"Oh…my…God, lookovertherequick—it's Alice Cooper!" I was screaming and whispering at the same time. I had long since passed through the gates of puberty, but was nonetheless taking a risk; if my voice had cracked at any point while scream-whispering then I would have inadvertently screamed the information mere feet from the celebrity himself, rendering my sighting not only non-secretive, but outright embarrassing.

"Oh wow," my mom whispered back. "I can't believe it…now, which one is she?" I flopped my head around wildly as if it were attached to a neck of rubber and then stared deeply into her eyes so as not to be misunderstood. I spoke loudly enough so that Sheena could also hear, just in case she, too, lacked this basic knowledge, but not so loudly as to allow Mr. Cooper to overhear. "Alice Cooper is Freddy Mercury's long lost scary cousin."

"Freddy who?" It was no use. She took it on good faith that Alice Cooper was a big deal, and without any warning stood up and started walking over to his table. *What?! No! You can't just show up uninvited!* It was too late.

"Hello," she said, bending down right in the man's face. "Are you Alice Cooper?"

117

"Yes I am," he said, Oreo Blizzard in hand. His wife and kids stared at my mom. This had probably never happened before. At least not since Wayne's World.

"I just wanted to tell you that you have a very beautiful family." And with that he thanked her and went back to eating his Blizzard.

Having spent the last several months socked in by mountains and jungle, we'd had enough and decided it was time for the sea. We drove southward until we could drive no more, whereupon the road curved from south to east, and to our right the angry sea lashed the shore with dark, frothy wavelets. The road became narrow and winding, and to our left a mountain grew up out of the jungle creating a bulbous jungle-covered peninsula. On the far end of the peninsula we arrived in the small town of Kep. Signs advertised fresh crab, and the water's edge was lined with thatched cabanas. This would do. Oh yes, this would do.

Just outside of town, beyond the last row of cabanas, we came upon a grassy area shaded by the outstretched branches of a very old tree. We situated Nacho twenty feet from the sea wall so that our sliding door opened to the ocean. The sound of lapping waves made the rest of the world inaudible and the faint hint of ocean spray did nothing to help the small rust spots starting to form around Nacho's window frames. Awning, lawn chairs, table, drinks. We sipped our adult beverages from our very own roving beachfront resort and let the tension from the road seep out the soles of our feet as the sun plunged into the horizon and set the sky ablaze.

In the morning as we laid in bed listening to the waves lapping the shore, we heard someone get into a car, which had parked next to us at some uncivilized hour during the night.

Reer reer reer...reer reer reer...reer reer reer...

"Engine's not getting any gas," I mumbled to Sheena, still half asleep. The driver tried for several minutes, but the engine never fired. "He'll drain his battery."

Reer...reer...click-click-click.

I looked out of my screen window and saw the driver walking away from the car toward the road.

We got up and made breakfast, and in doing so realized that we were almost out of coffee. When breakfast was over we opened all of Nacho's doors and windows, and started roasting a batch of coffee over the stove in a pot, as we had been doing ever since Colombia. Just as the beans were getting into a nice rolling first crack, the driver and his compañero returned to the car to try to get it going. Above the sound of cracking coffee beans I could hear the failure.

Reer...reer...reer...click-click-click.

Pretty soon the two men came around to find us; Sheena greeted them and then they started talking to me.

"Not now amigos," I said, brandishing a wooden spoon and trying to keep the beans from burning. "Give me ten minutes!"

When I emerged from the van, the two men were sitting in their dead car waiting for me.

"It is dead," one of them said, pointing to the battery under his open hood. I gave the engine a quick once-over and then told them what I had deduced while lying in bed that morning.

"Your engine isn't getting any gas." They stared at me, confused, then sprang into action and removed the battery. Once the battery was free they brought it over to Nacho and asked if I could charge it. I figured, what the hell, and charged it for a couple of minutes and gave it back. Within a few cranks it was dead again.

"You guys are out of gas." Finally one of them left to go get some gas.

While the younger of the two was out getting gas, we began talking with the other. His name was Prom, and he told us that he split his time between Phnom Penh and Kep. He had a wife and a kid, preferred the city to the country, and—wait—what?!

"I'm a movie star here in Cambodia."

"You're a what, now?"

"I'm a movie star. Have you seen the movie *My Family, My Heart?*"

"No. But it sure sounds good. Tell me more."

He went on to describe what the film was about, and proudly boasted that he played the lead role, a bad boy obsessed with money.

"So do people in Cambodia recognize you on the street?"

"Yes, especially in Phnom Penh. That's why I never go out unless I'm wearing a pollution mask and sunglasses."

"Can I touch you?"

"Yes."

The following day, Prom swung by our campsite with his wife, a thin and shy young woman with a great big smile, and their two sons. We hopped in their car and headed for the interior of the peninsula where a friend of his operated a butterfly farm on the land owned by an elderly and wealthy out-of-town German fellow. We frolicked with butterflies for a while before climbing to the top floor of the tall three story house, which was designed and constructed out of natural materials by Prom's friend, putting us above the jungle canopy. From behind the house, two

119

ridges fanned out on either side of the property, creating a shallow canyon that emptied into the sea. From our vantage point the ridges perfectly framed a view down the valley to the ocean, perhaps a mile away. We welcomed in the evening from our deck chairs, watching the ocean turn from green to dark blue to black, and then it was time to go. Probably a typical evening for a Cambodian movie star, we figured.

On the way back, we rolled along the base of the mountain for a while before stopping beside a roadside shack where an old woman served bowls of rice noodles from a giant cauldron.

"So, is this okay?" Prom seemed worried that we wouldn't like it. "I don't know if you're worried about…eating clean food." White people are always fretting about cleanliness, sure, but it was clear that I had forgotten to tell him about my obsession with third world street food.

"Prom, there is nothing that you could do to this food that would make us not want to eat it."

"Okay, it's just that some tourists are worried about getting sick."

The following evening we opted for a picnic dinner at our ocean side campsite. We spent the afternoon preparing food and setting up a nice picnic area next to the sea wall, and then I decided to go explore the interesting boat launch just a short distance from our camp. It comprised two elevated concrete ramps that extended out into the sea before slanting downward and into the water. I couldn't be sure if the intent was to drive on it, as doing so would constitute a suicide attempt by most measures, and that's why I found it interesting.

I coolly strolled out onto one of the narrow concrete beams above the water. I pulled my sunglasses down over my eyes, slid my hands into my pockets, and daydreamed about starring as the bad boy in my very own Cambodian bad-boy flick. As I reached the high tide mark, the slanted ramp became covered in razor sharp barnacles. *La-dee-da*. I walked on. A moment later, nearer the low tide mark, I placed my sandaled foot on a green slimy mess of bio-growth, and my foot immediately squirted out from under me like a bar of wet soap in a men's prison shower. I did the splits, a thing that feels terrible to a grown man having long since passed through the gates of puberty, and began sliding on my side toward the angry green ocean only a couple of feet away. Just before reaching the water, however, the friction between the razor-sharp barnacles and my doughy white skin was enough to stop my downward trajectory, sparing me from a painful and watery dip. I whimpered, frowning, afraid, and dripping blood from my hand and ankle as I inched my way back up the dangerous barnacled plank to safety.

120

The picnic dinner went off much more pleasantly than my evening stroll had. We set out the Burmese pumpkin curry—a recipe given to us by Bobo and Ma Yae consisting of fresh vegetables, cucumber salad and fresh fish—and ate it as the cool air poured over the sea wall. The faint salty mist made the air feel charged. We chatted about life in America, and then switched to the far more interesting topic of life in Cambodia. Prom recounted his experiences in film and in business. Like many others we've met in developing countries, he longed to visit America, but found it impossible to come up with the money to do so given the low value of Cambodia's currency.

In the days that followed we relaxed at our camp by day, while by night we hung out with Prom and his wife, exploring the best seaside restaurants, dessert spots, and scooting around the small town in his little white Toyota. On our final night we sat around a table at a seaside restaurant sipping drinks. By now his shy wife had really opened up, and we felt as though we were hanging out with old friends. For the first two days we didn't think that she could speak English, but now she was easily conversing, laughing, and playfully harassing Prom. When they dropped us off for the final time we were sad to say goodbye.

In the morning we awoke early and began breaking down our camp. The village was quiet, and the coastal road was without cars except for one vehicle parked on the roadside far off in the distance. We ground some fresh coffee and prepared it in our small stovetop espresso maker, then sat on the sea wall to drink it. Finally, as the morning wore into day, we fired up Nacho and rolled out. As we made our way down the coastal road, we could see that the parked car from earlier that morning looked familiar. As we drew closer we could see that it was a small white Toyota. I rolled up next to it and lowered my window.

"Prom, I didn't expect to see you so soon."

"I know. I've been here all morning." He looked really happy to see us. "I was headed to the gas station and I ran out of gas. Now my battery is dead." It was déjà vu.

After a friendly haranguing and a quick lesson about internal combustion engines, we put some of our spare gas into his tank, and then said goodbye for good. But what can a common man such as I say to a cultural icon such as this that he hasn't heard a million times already?

"Take care of yourself, Prom."

And then I remembered my mother and Alice Cooper, and added, "You have a very beautiful family."

23

Street 217 to
the Killing Fields

Brad

There is a high school in downtown Phnom Penh known as S21, but it is no longer used as a school on account of the blackness that fell upon it in the 1970's. We wound our way through streets and alleyways, and when we saw the rusted razor wire atop the school's perimeter wall, we knew that we'd arrived.

In 1975, following the Vietnam War, a ravenous group of idealistic youths descended upon Cambodia's capital, commanded by their leader, Pol Pot. They believed that Buddhist Cambodia should abandon its capitalism and embrace fundamental communism by whatever means necessary. They called their party the Khmer Rouge.

The unsuspecting capital quickly fell, and within days, all of Phnom Penh's inhabitants had been forcefully evacuated from the city and marched into the countryside to do communal labor. Soon the entire country had been overtaken; the borders were sealed, businesses were closed, and the population was forced into manual labor camps.

The first order of business for the Khmer Rouge was to carry out a process of brainwashing, and to eliminate anyone with an education. Anyone who had been to college, who could speak a foreign language, who had worked as a professional, and who wore glasses was silently removed from the work camps. Furthermore, anyone suspected of dissent was silently taken away. Nobody knew where the people were taken, but day after day families were broken up and nobody quite knew if or when they themselves would be carted off.

Since education was no longer necessary, the Khmer Rouge turned S21 into an interrogation facility. Whenever someone was suspected of harboring feelings of dissent against the party, he or she was

122

brought there. The purpose for being taken to S21 was never explained to the subjects, and initially they went along without suspicion. When they entered the school, each person was photographed and documented. When we arrived, the photographs of each person who had passed through S21 were displayed on boards and walls in several of the classrooms in chronological order. The earliest photographs depicted happy people, eager and wide eyed in the same way that we had come to know modern Cambodians.

After being photographed, people were chained together and made to lie face down for days on end in classrooms-turned-holding cells while they awaited interrogation for made-up crimes. Dozens more classrooms were segmented into prison cells by crude brick walls.

The real terror began as subjects were brought in for interrogation. Men, women, children, and the elderly were asked to confess to crimes that they didn't commit. When they refused, the torture began. We walked from room to room in the school as pictorial scenes of medieval torture unfolded before us. Fingers and toes were lopped off with diagonal cutters, arms and legs were broken with clubs or farming implements, teeth were pulled out or smashed in, and they had a special table for water-boarding. Some of the people were hung upside down from a large wooden structure in the school's courtyard and lowered face-first into water tanks repeatedly for hours on end.

If subjects admitted to the accusations, they were made to write confessions, and then they were executed on the spot or else sent to death camps in the countryside. If they refused to admit guilt, they were simply beaten and tortured until they died. As the population began to suspect the reality of what was happening at S21, the faces of the incoming subjects reflected the horror of what was coming.

Within four years, 17,000 people were interrogated at S21. Only 12 survived.

Thirty-five years after the nightmare ended, very little had changed at S21. As we walked from one classroom to another, we found metal bed frames to which prisoners had been chained and beaten. Photographs on the walls showed bludgeoned bodies still chained to the beds, suspended over coagulated pools of blood. The tile floor in each classroom was permanently stained with blood.

After a harrowing and emotional morning at S21, we got into Nacho and drove toward the killing field on Phnom Penh's outskirts. It was to the killing fields where the Khmer Rouge sent the educated, the dissenters, and the falsely accused to be done away with. 20,000 mass graves have since been discovered, but most are inaccessible, still surrounded by live land mines placed there by the Khmer Rouge.

The killing field is a vast expanse of land, which is now completely covered by mass graves. We walked into the area and were met by a scene of dozens of partially excavated pits. Around the complex small shrines held bones, skulls, clothing, teeth, and other remembrances of the thousands who died there. When it rains, bones continually push up to the surface and can be seen everywhere—even in the middle of the walking paths. As we strolled through the peaceful landscape, we could feel the bones of the dead through the soles of our sandals like pebbles on a trail.

There was a large tree near the center of the killing field that was decorated with small bracelets, and to the side of it there was an excavated pit grave. When the Khmer Rouge fell and this killing field was discovered, this tree was found covered in dried blood, hair, and scraps of skull bone and brain. Excavators began digging next to the tree, and made a horrifying discovery: this tree was used to kill babies and small children. The babies were held by their feet and swung into the tree to smash their heads, and then their lifeless bodies were tossed into the pit. It was one of the most disturbing things I've ever seen: a testament to the lows to which humans are capable of sinking.

Executions at the dozens of pits around the area were carried out in a similarly disturbing fashion. Prisoners arrived in trucks blindfolded, and were led to the pits. They were lined up and one by one they were pushed to their knees at the edge of the hole in the ground. The executioners were ordinary Cambodians, forced to do this task lest they themselves be killed, and executions were carried out twenty-four hours per day without stopping. Lacking guns or other weapons, they were forced to use more rudimentary implements. From the leaves of the surrounding palm trees they created cutting tools, and when the prisoner knelt by the pit, the executioner would first saw the jagged edge of the palm stem across his throat so that he would be unable to scream. Next, they would swing a farm tool such as a hoe, a hammer, or a shovel against the back of the person's head, killing them. As one dead body fell into the pit, the next person took his place.

Prisoners who were brought to the killing fields were told that they were going to new work camps. Fearing that the people waiting in the nearby barracks would prematurely learn of their impending fate, the Khmer Rouge played communist party songs at ear-splitting volumes over loudspeakers throughout the fields at all hours of day and night, powered by loud diesel generators. They couldn't hear their countrymen dying only a few meters from where they sat crammed against their brothers, sisters, parents and neighbors.

In other cases, prisoners were made to dig large pits, and then were made to stand in them while they were buried alive. Khmer Rouge leadership decided that out of the country's over seven million people, it only needed two million to build its communist utopia. To the others, it broadcasted over the radio: "To keep you is no benefit, to destroy you is no loss."

After several hours of walking sullenly around the fields, we made our way to the Buddhist stupa built in remembrance of those who died there. The stupa comprised a clear glass building that contained over 5,000 of the skulls found at the site. We stared at the stacks of skulls, each bearing a hole from a hammer, a crack from a machete, or missing teeth that had been smashed out. *How could this happen—again?*

Pol Pot and the Khmer Rouge carried out genocide against its own people from 1975 to1978. In those four years, an estimated 2.5 million people were murdered—over 30% of the country's population.

Finally, in 1979 help arrived from the North. Vietnamese troops entered Cambodia and defeated the Khmer Rouge, sending their leaders fleeing into the jungle. The Vietnamese assisted Cambodia in forming a new government, and the healing process finally began. But despite the reprehensible atrocities carried out by Pol Pot and the Khmer Rouge, politics intervened and denied Cambodians dignity and closure.

America was fresh out of the Vietnam War, and having lost the war, still harbored ill will toward Vietnam. America and its allies thusly refused to recognize Cambodia's new government because the Vietnamese had implemented it. Instead, Pol Pot's Khmer Rouge was officially recognized as Cambodia's ruling government, and the party was subsequently offered a place in the U.N. For years to come, western governments gave substantial aid money to the Khmer Rouge—the jungle-hiding murderers—to aid in rebuilding the country. The money was used not to rebuild Cambodia, but to ensure the survival of the Khmer Rouge. America and the United Nations continued to recognize and support the party up until 1993.

And what of Pol Pot, Cambodia's Hitler? He eventually came out of hiding and went on to live comfortably in his own home until he died in 1998 of natural causes at the age of 73. He was never tried for any crimes.

Our stop at Phnom Penh had been an educational experience, and for the second country in a row we found our history to be laced with ugly and embarrassing episodes that had escaped our school curriculum. In Cambodia we had failed to act when aid was truly needed, unable to swallow our pride, and in doing so had allowed an oppressive genocidal regime to maintain power for fifteen years too long. We in America like to think of our country as an unwavering model of decency, goodness, and humanitarianism. We are the world's police; we take out the bad guys and replace them with good. These experiences were necessary to fill in some of the gaps in our global education and help us form a more complete picture of our role and our place in the world. What an education it's been.

24

Cambodia National Highway 6 to Siem Reap

Brad

In Cambodia's west-central jungles lay the ruins of an ancient Khmer kingdom, at the center of which sits the impressive site of Angkor Wat. There are uncountable ruins of palaces, temples, and royal buildings immediately surrounding Angkor Wat, but it was an outpost an hour away to the northeast that initially caught our attention. We had heard stories of ruins still covered by dense overgrowth – a look into the past, back to what the ruins would have looked like before their uncovering by archaeologists, and a place to be discovered by the rays of sunlight seeping through dense vines that hang from centuries old strangler fig trees.

As the road signs indicated Siem Reap thirty miles ahead, we swung Nacho onto a tiny side road that wound through rice paddies and villages toward the North. Soon the villages dissipated and the countryside became a patchwork of jungle and rice paddies, and then we arrived at Beng Mealea.

In the afternoon, a lone bus departed just as we arrived, and then we had the whole place to ourselves. We found a spot right next to the highly decorated stone promenade leading to the entrance of the complex, and declared a campsite for ourselves.

With limited time before sunset, we decided to wait until the morning to explore the ruins. Instead, we locked our doors and walked farther into the jungle on the muddy dirt road on which we'd arrived. The road wound its way through a tangle of vines, past rice paddies and a few stick huts, before splitting into two smaller tracks. At the fork in the road we noticed a trail heading into the jungle. We had been warned that thousands of unexploded land mines still littered this jungle, but we assumed that if we stayed on a worn footpath then we should be safe. After all, wouldn't a previous walker have set them off if there were any? We entered the dark undergrowth.

The trail wound its way through the trees for a while, and we soon noticed some half-buried, hand-carved stonework protruding from the jungle floor. As we continued on through the dense foliage, more and more stone carvings were noticeable under cover of vines and half buried in the mud. Suddenly the trail hooked to the left, and we found ourselves on an unexcavated stone thoroughfare of some kind, lined on both sides by intricate carved statues of seven-headed snakes, ferns, and round columns.

We imagined what it must have felt like to be among the first discoverers of Angkor Wat – to have walked in this jungle, and to have stumbled upon fragments of an ancient civilization.

We followed the thoroughfare farther and its condition continually improved until through the trees we could see an enormous stone wall, partially toppled by the swollen root of a strangler fig. It turned out we had accidentally found our way to an ancient road used to access the complex of Beng Mealea from a different direction.

We carried on in the evening's fading light, alone in the crumbling ruins. We walked among walls decorated with intricate carvings, through enormous arches adorned with snakes and elephants, and we stepped over enormous stone blocks dislodged by roots that had toppled onto the jungle floor. After a brief survey of the complex, we circled around to the front and found our way back to Nacho for the night.

In the morning we awoke early. We wanted to be inside of the complex when the first rays of sunlight permeated the jungle canopy and cast columns of light on the ruined walls. At 5:30 we walked down the stone promenade toward the ruins, wiping the sleep from our eyes. Soon, a small disheveled girl and her disheveled friend joined us in stride.

"One dolla chia?"

She was so cute and tiny, and spoke in such a funny little chipmunk voice. She stared up at us and put her hand out, and then repeated herself.

"One dolla chia?"

"Hi there little lady. You sure are cute!"

"One dolla chia?"

Her tiny mouth took the shape of an upside down horseshoe and she made her voice crack as though she were about to cry.

"One dolla...chia?" she repeated, dragging the last word out for drama and following it up with a sniffle. It became clear that someone—probably her parents—had taught her how to ask foreigners for money. She had taken "one dollar each," and without a basis for the English language had transposed the sounds to "one dolla chia," which sounds exceptionally cute when coming from the mouth of a tiny Cambodian chipmunk girl.

But when it comes to giving away free money to perfectly able-bodied beggars, regardless of body mass, age, gender, or voice pitch, I am heartless and cutthroat.

"One dolla chia? Are you crazy?!"

"(sniff)...One...(whimper)...dolla chia? (whimper, sniff)"

"If I gave you one dolla chia, and then gave one dolla chia to every kid who asked, I would very quickly run out of money. Don't your parents feed you?"

"One dolla chia?"

"You go back to your parents and tell them that they should feel ashamed of themselves for sending you out here to beg. You should be out acting like a kid."

The girl continued to follow us around for ten or fifteen more minutes as we entered the ruins and crawled all over the giant carved blocks that had been strewn about by the strangler figs. She finally gave up and disappeared.

A few minutes later, tiny children began appearing on top of the tall walls of the ruins. They walked about with ease, oblivious to the deadly drops to either side, and they jumped from stone to stone over deep crevasses and over vines. They wore no shoes, and were as agile as monkeys. They were the children of the nearby stick huts, and rather than go to school they roamed around the ancient ruins in packs.

As Sheena and I walked along an elevated stone walkway midway up one of the enormous walls, the pack of children approached from the opposite direction. They marched toward us in single file, and when they reached us they flung themselves like lemmings, one by one, off of the wall to the hard ground below. One Dolla Chia was the last one in the pack, and before flinging herself off of the wall she glared deep into my eyes and gave me a colossal stink eye.

The ruins were like something that time forgot. A tall, thick protective wall surrounded the complex, and inside there was a huge collection of rooms, covered hallways, an underground corridor, and various walls covered with elaborate inscriptions. Giant trees filled the open spaces, and many of the structures were topped by giant strangler figs, named for their creeping roots that seem to strangle the ruins below them, and which grow through the walls and then swell up over time, toppling entire walls and columns.

By 9:00 in the morning we had explored the whole complex; we had been there for the first rays of light seeping through the canopy, and in the absence of other people, we had seen the place much in the same condition as when it was discovered.

On the walkway heading out of the complex toward Nacho, we passed by the first group of tourists for the day. And out of the woodwork came One Dolla Chia.

25

Vithei Charles du Gaulle to Angkor Wat

Sheena

"It is of such extraordinary construction that it is not possible to describe it with a pen, particularly since it is like no other building in the world. It has towers and decoration and all of the refinements which the human genius can conceive of."

-Antonio de Madalena, 1586, one of the first Westerners to visit Angkor Wat

Angkor Wat is Southeast Asia's biggest attraction, drawing throngs of people across the Thai border onto Cambodia's rough and dusty red dirt roads, or by air to Siem Reap. I was excited to see what all of the fuss was about, but I also wondered if this Buddhist temple was truly as worthwhile as everyone said it was. In the backs of our minds we remembered the hype followed by the slight anticlimax of Machu Picchu much earlier in the drive, and we hoped that this would be different. It was to be our last destination before circling back to Thailand to inventory the rations and plan our westward assault. I hoped to leave Southeast Asia with a bang.

We rolled into Siem Reap under a roasting midday sun and quickly decided we weren't ready to explore the ruins. Instead we embraced the town's tourist infrastructure by cooling off under the air conditioner at a Swensen's ice cream shop. Soon the clouds moved in and sheets of rain temporarily extinguished the intense heat outside.

I left Brad behind with his ice cream and his book, and moved on to Siem Reap's covered market. There was an authentic section of the market where the locals did their shopping for fruits and vegetables, meat, and household goods. Then there was the tourist market, a maze of aisles with loud vendors slinging replicas of Angkor Wat, Buddha statues, wooden elephants, and silk scarves. After a half an hour I was finished. If I had even so much as turned my head, an explosion of activity would erupt from the vendors.

"Lady! Lady! What you want? You want scarf? Real silk! Oh so nice! What you want? How much you pay me? I give you good price! Good price for you! Lady! Lady!" I disappointed the enterprising hawkers by buying nothing more than some black sticky rice and tomatoes, and then we left Siem Reap to seek out a campsite for the night.

Just before nightfall, a local official granted us permission to camp in a clearing next to a rural road near the entrance to a rarely visited ruin. I started on dinner and Brad set up camp, snapping our front window curtain in place and spreading our new bamboo mat in front of the door like a welcome mat. This was going to be one of those perfect nights: a peaceful camp in a quiet clearing. Midway through dinner preparations the official returned and peered in at us from outside.

"I am sorry, but I was misinformed. You cannot stay here. It is not safe. Please, you must leave now."

We pleaded with him, telling him that we would happily accept the risk, but he held fast to his decision. We had found that in Asia, we were fine as long as no official types saw us. But if anyone of authority knew we were sleeping in our car in their jurisdiction, they asked us to leave so as not to be responsible for us. A crime against a foreigner on their watch? Rather than chance it they would usually tell us to leave, using the catch-all explanation that it was not safe. We continued cooking and contemplated where to go next. We always avoided trying to find a place to camp after the sun went down; it was hard enough in the light, and we usually ended up in dubious situations as a result of not being able to see. We decided to see if the official would let it go, but he returned twenty minutes later, looking anxious and a little upset. We figured he must have asked someone higher up in the chain of command and had been given orders not to let us stay, and by staying we had put him in a delicate situation. But this man was a good Buddhist, so rather than raise his voice he proposed to help. "Please, if you follow me I will show you a safe place."

Our procrastination paid off. While Brad followed him down the winding road, I held our half-cooked meal over the stove so that it wouldn't spill. The man wound through the countryside and stopped a while later in front of a Buddhist temple.

Brad walked inside, and emerged a few minutes later giving the thumbs-up. It only took a moment for the entire community of orange-robed monks to crowd into the space in front of our sliding door. While our dinner simmered on the stovetop we talked for a long time, and the conversation meandered all over the place.

A few of the younger boys were dressed in street clothes. The head monk spoke English, and told us that the temple also took in orphaned children and let them train to become monks. We played a game of age guessing, and they all agreed that their favorite actor was Jet Li. We asked them to describe the daily life of a Buddhist monk in Cambodia.

"Every day we wake up at four o'clock to pray. Then we walk around and collect food from the people in the village. We combine all of this food into a big pot and stir it up, and then distribute it amongst ourselves. It is our only meal of the day. We never eat after eleven o'clock, but we can have soda or juice. After that we study again and in the evening we pray."

After they left, we fell asleep to the beautiful melody of monks chanting and crickets chirping.

In the morning, the crickets had stopped but the mesmerizing hum emanating from the temple gave the illusion that the chanting had gone on all night. After breakfast the head monk—a man of about thirty with short, black hair and round eyes—greeted us and apologized for having chanted so late into the night, and again so early in the morning.

He was surprised when we told him that we loved it. It was the kind of surreal night that, as elderly people, we may look back on it and wonder if we had fabricated aspects of our youth which could not have possibly been real.

We dedicated the day to discovering Angkor Thom, the last capital city of the Khmer Empire, and the second most popular set of ruins in the area. It was built in the late twelfth century and remained the capital until the Khmer kingdom fell in 1609.

To enter the ancient capital, we drove Nacho through a massive city wall via an incredible thirty-six foot tall gate, which was topped by a gigantic stone face that looked down on us. The look seemed to tell us we should not be allowed to enter. This was the same gate through which war horses, men returning from battle, and the King had passed. We followed a perfectly straight road to the center of the grounds to the capital's iconic temple, known as the *Bayon*.

The walls surrounding the temple were adorned with shadowy bas-reliefs of battles, scenes of daily life, and pictographic legends. Beyond the walls, covered stone corridors brought us to steep stairs that led to an elevated stone court within the temple spires. Carved stone windows framed rooms like works of art, and every flat surface boasted carvings of stone goddesses. We climbed more stairs to the temple's second level and enjoyed a commanding view of the surrounding forest and ruins. We were surrounded on all sides by fifty-four imposing stone pillars, each topped by giant carved heads with faces on all four sides. The effect was to depict supervision at all times by the watchful eyes of 106 giant carved faces, each bearing a likeness to the ancient Khmer king. We sought refuge from the abusive, scorching heat in stone alleyways and under protruding stone edifices, but we never escaped the scrutiny of the King.

Angkor Wat is the world's largest religious monument, and for its age it is immaculately preserved. The complex of temples comprising the Khmer kingdom had been largely abandoned after the fall of the empire, and for centuries it was known only to local jungle-dwelling Khmers. In the mid-1800's Western missionaries were startled to find what was essentially a lost city covered up by jungle, a complex more than twice the size of Manhattan. The pearl at its center is Angkor Wat, the prominent temple surrounded by a perfectly square moat.

While many Khmer temples were built to honor the ruling kings of the time, Angkor Wat by contrast was built to honor the god Vishnu, although it was used as the final resting place for King Suryavarman. It faces west, the direction representing death in Hindu cosmology. Its foundation was built to symbolize the mythic Mount Meru, while its five inter-nested walls represented a chain of mountains. The square moat surrounding the temple represented the cosmic ocean.

We entered Angkor Wat by crossing the six hundred foot wide moat on a stone bridge, buckled in places and strewn with giant stone blocks. The bridge continued beyond the moat and delivered us through the first set of walls. The five million tons of sandstone used to construct the Angkor complex was carried from a quarry twenty-five miles away, suggesting that with six hundred elephants and 300,000 workers, anything is possible.

As with Angkor Thom, we passed through a number of galleries adorned with bas-relief walls. The carved panels stretched for nearly a half a mile, telling stories of the empire like ancient comic books. It was easy to identify the carvings that had been touched countless times: an elephant's head or a woman's breast, polished black and shiny like marble.

Farther into the temple, the epic tale in bas-relief ended and the theme changed. Every wall and pillar was decorated with carvings of seductive goddesses. Buddha statues sat cross-legged between pillars— remnants of the kingdom's migration from Hinduism to Buddhism. Some carvings were unfinished, and I could see where the outlines of figures had been scratched into flat surfaces, but they were never carved out. Despite its grandiose form and long period of use, Angkor Wat was never entirely finished.

We left the temple and found a peaceful place under a canopy of trees, where we ate a picnic lunch outside of Nacho's sliding door. A family of monkeys noticed us and congregated around our chairs, hoping for a banana or for a stray scrap of food to drop. Brad sipped a midday coffee while carrying on a one-sided conversation with the father monkey sitting directly in front of him. But the monkey stared over Brad's shoulder and picked his nose – a slap in the face to any speaker.

At last we made our way to Ta Prohm, one of the only temples in the Angkor complex (Beng Mealea was another) where the jungle trees had essentially been left alone, and were in the process of swallowing up the temples' stones. It wasn't hard to imagine *Tomb Raider*'s Lara Croft or Indiana Jones running about through the ruins (parts of both were shot here). Strangler fig roots tangled through corridors and around columns, blocking throughways, while the giant trees themselves perched precariously atop walls, engulfing entire buildings.

When at last, after several days of exploring the old kingdom ruins, we loaded up and took to the highway with a sense of completeness. We had arrived in Southeast Asia over four months prior, and had covered as much ground as we had been able. We had been denied entry into China and Vietnam on account of driving our own car, and Burma's borders were still sealed by its secretive government. But within the bounds of those political barriers we had drawn loops and squiggles all over the map, discovering places and people and food. Angkor Wat had been a perfect capstone, and so we filled up the gas tank, rolled down our windows, and headed west toward Bangkok.

26

Sukhumvit Soi 62

Brad

Back in Argentina when we made the decision to deliver ourselves to Southeast Asia with our van, we sort of already knew that we would be trapped there. To the South and East it is all ocean. Burma lies to the West, and their borders had been sealed for a half-century prior to our arrival, and they weren't going to make any exceptions for us. We later verified this by driving to a tiny Burmese border crossing in northwestern Thailand, and were stopped there by the Burmese military. We asked very nicely if they would let us into their country, using our best charisma, but they slowly shook their heads and pointed us back to Thailand. To the North there is China. To cross China in one's own foreign-registered vehicle, it is necessary to jump through a great number of hoops. One must secure the requisite government permits, obtain a Chinese driver's license, register the vehicle in China, and hire a private, government-approved guide to ensure adherence to a strict, pre-approved route and schedule. We started going down the path to do this. We asked for permission to drive from Laos to Nepal, and then from Nepal to Kyrgyzstan by way of China. For this, we were instructed to pay a smidge over $16,000. We had a good laugh, and then we got angry, and then we got spiteful, and then we screamed profanities at the Chinese government through our computer screen whilst wagging our middle fingers at the realization that we were, for sure, stuck.

But there is always a way. Though it would be a great pain in the neck, we decided to return to Bangkok to ship Nacho to India, the land that lies beyond Burma. But before doing so, we would make the very best of our situation. We would go out with a bang! One night in Bangkok? Hell no! We promptly drove from Cambodia to Bangkok and rented an apartment. We were going to need our rest before flinging ourselves hopelessly into the most chaotic place on Earth.

136

We hit the streets on an apartment search, and settled on the second one we looked at; a spacious, clean unit on the fourth floor of an apartment building on Sukhumvit Soi 62. The kitchen window overlooked the building's front garden, while the bedroom window looked onto a pharmaceutical factory. From our bedroom we could see the factory's giant sign displaying an enormous hypodermic needle. It was charming. We were greeted as we came and went through our building's lobby by Innie, a bubbly, charming girl with narrow glasses and squinting eyes, and Wasan, a young man whose face bore a permanent smile and whose demeanor could best be described as flamboyant.

We settled into our apartment and parked Nacho in the lot next to the pharmaceutical factory. We had been steadily working on a book about our drive from Arizona to Argentina, and we made it a goal to complete the book and send it off for publishing before we left for India. Aside from that, our primary goal for our five-week stay was to let Bangkok do the driving and see where it took us.

On the day after our arrival, our next-door neighbor, a Japanese boy of twenty-five who had just moved in, was hit by a car in the crosswalk in front of the apartment building and killed. In the evening I heard sirens, and looked out of the kitchen window to see an ambulance out front. We would later find out that it had taken the ambulance over an hour to reach the scene due to the overwhelming density of Bangkok traffic, and the fact that nobody moves over for emergency vehicles. He had bled to death while a man held his head and people looked on helplessly.

We walked by the scene of the accident every day on our sojourns to the Bang Chak sky train station on Sukhumvit road, and when we walked to the street market each day for dinner. Cooking is prohibited inside of many Bangkok apartments, including ours, and most do not come with built-in kitchens. Nobody seemed to mind much; it was cheaper and easier for one to buy pre-cooked food from the city's ubiquitous street markets than it was to cook for oneself. A typical meal at the street market would cost around one or two dollars and was far tastier than anything money could find in a Thai restaurant back in America, so every day we walked to the sprawling maze of outdoor food stalls at the end of our street and bought our dinner. On those walks, we observed the rotation of offerings that people from the neighborhood left on the sidewalk at the scene of the accident: a plate of rice, a flower, candles, and fruit. Despite having known the boy, Innie and Wasan never talked about it. When we brought up the accident to them, they remained upbeat, saying a couple of words of regret ("Thai drivers don't stop for pedestrians, you must be very careful.") before changing the subject and wishing us a good day or asking us where we were off to.

Being back in Bangkok gave us the opportunity to tend to the relationships that we had cultivated during our first visit, and allowed us to forge new friendships. As time went on, our social lives became split between two disparate circles of friends. There were the expatriates—Italians and British and one American, all having relocated to Bangkok to work—and then there were the Thais, most of whom we had met through the Volkswagen community, but who grew to include others as well. It was nice to spend time with the expats, to have some remembrance of the West, but we spent most of our free time with our Thai friends, and above all, Pat.

I had mentioned to Pat several times since arriving in Thailand that Nacho was underpowered, and that our engine was reaching the end of its life. By the time we had reached Tierra del Fuego at the southern tip of Argentina, our engine's idle had begun to surf more severely than usual—that is, it was unable to find the right mix of fuel to oxygen, and so the engine had begun to go crazy like a border collie in captivity. At rest, the engine would repeatedly cycle between 800 and 2,000 revolutions per minute, and Sheena would sit in the passenger seat and imitate the sound so as not to go crazy herself, rocking back and forth like a deranged person in the padded captivity of an insane asylum.

"Reer...REER...reer...REER...reer...REER..."

"Sheena, get a hold of yourself! Come on now, my love, snap out of it!"

"Reer...REER...reer..."

Normally I would make some adjustments, or else replace a temperature sensor to fix the problem. But after a while, the problem became irreparable; the throttle body had become too worn out to control the air flowing through its various gaps. We had idle-surfed our way to Buenos Aires, and then from Kuala Lumpur to the farthest reaches of Southeast Asia.

I had sought reassurance about our engine's health in online forums, but what I found didn't put my mind at ease. "These engines are great—they'll last upwards of 190,000 miles!" they said. Having over 200,000 miles since its last rebuild, Nacho had the heart of a smoking octogenarian.

In northern Thailand alone there were two occasions when the roads proved too steep for us to drive up and we were unable to proceed, despite the fact that they were paved roads. We had to retreat and find other ways to our destinations. This had happened several times in the Americas as well, and we began to feel nervous for our safety as the Himalayas loomed closer. It had become clear that Nacho's nearly 6,000-pound beer gut was no match for our 95 horsepower smoking octogenarian engine.

"I know a garage that can help you get Fat Nacho back in shape," Pat said one night over street food. "Do you know why Thai people so much smarter than American people? Because every Volkswagen van in Thailand have Subaru engine—except one, and that belong to Fat Gak!" he laughed hysterically and pointed to Gak, who shrugged his shoulders and smiled. Gak had the reserved face of a wise man and he measured his words before he let them go. On the other hand, Pat was always the center of attention, always ready with something witty to say. Every day, be it a workday or weekend, he wore the same camouflage cargo shorts and a tee shirt. I had first spoken to him on the phone from the Thai-Malaysia border, and found that he had the most interesting voice. He spoke in a slightly higher pitch than I had expected, and the way that he pronounced words—enunciating tonal changes, dragging out his vowels, and emphasizing his Rs—gave his words the color of Skittles and the shape of rainbows.

Of all of the people we met in Asia, Pat was the most passionate about cars; he had Thailand's biggest collection of classic Volkswagens (sixteen cars). His family was further testament to his obsession; his wife's name is Benz, and he has two sons, Porsche and Bayerische Motoren Werke, or "BMW" for short. If there was anyone we should listen to about Nacho's issues, it was Pat.

Pat explained that nearly every water-cooled Volkswagen van in Thailand had undergone a Subaru engine conversion, and that one mechanic on the outskirts of Bangkok had done most of them. The engines came on a ship from Japan, he said, and could be bought in the sprawling autoparts district in an outlying industrial area. For very little money, and in no time at all, Nacho could be given a new heart. I mentioned the protection from danger that a new engine would afford, and then looked to Sheena for feedback. She hemmed and hawed for a minute, and then made me agree to use Nacho as my daily driver for the next twenty years, and then she agreed. I gave Pat the go-ahead, and he arranged everything.

Within a couple of days I was driving through Bangkok, following Pat's car toward the autoparts district. The autoparts district is a rambling maze of tight streets, perhaps fifteen square blocks, containing nothing but salvaged autoparts. When we arrived, it seemed like a chaotic jumble of industrial tin buildings covered in grease and littered with stacks of metal where auto dismantlers separated cars into their individual components to be sold. Each street had its specialty, and each shop featured only one thing. There were shops selling only horns, or Kia body panels, or Nissan exhausts, or Ford transmissions. Pat steered me first to a small hut on the edge of the district where an elderly woman served us a quick lunch of soup containing cubes of gelatinous congealed pig's blood ("This soup make you hairy chest!")

When we had finished eating, we steered Nacho into the heart of the district on a narrow street lined with metal scraps and stacked car chassis, and squeezed in between parked cars in front of the shop that sold only Subaru engines. I grabbed my compression tester and we approached the open garage door, inside of which there must have been a hundred and fifty engines stacked atop one another.

Two Thai men picked out a couple of engines with a forklift and set them on the side of the street near Nacho. One of the men attached a garden hose to the coolant system, placed a tube into a bottle of gas, filled the engine with oil, and then jumped the starter with a screwdriver. It purred to life and I checked the compression of one, and then the other. I wrote the numbers down on a notepad, and when we had finished, I pointed to the second engine and gave them the thumbs up. It had good, even compression, and only 62,000 miles under its belt.

I paid one of the men the equivalent of eight hundred dollars and the forklift driver carefully maneuvered the arm in front of Nacho's sliding door. The engine swung precariously from a chain as the driver used the controls to square it up to the opening in the side of the van. The men had placed a car tire on our living room floor to set the engine on. Just then the sky opened up and the autoparts district was engulfed in a torrential downpour. Water immediately gushed from the middle of our rain gutter directly into the van, drenching our wood floor, and the operation that had started smoothly quickly became tense. With one hand I tried to divert the flow of water away from our floor, while the other hand kept the car tire from moving.

"Watch the cabinets! A little higher! Okay, set it down!" The men didn't speak any English, so I might as well have been yelling Shel Silverstein poems.

"Did you hear about Ticklish Tom? He got tickled by his mom! Wiggled and giggled and fell on the floor! Laughed and rolled right out the door!"

Pat had already set everything up with the garage, so all we had to do was drive there and drop off Nacho. We strapped the engine down and I made it a point to be especially careful on Bangkok's crazy motorways. An accident of almost any magnitude would result in me being tossed around with a loose engine inside of the cab.

Soonthorn Garage was thirty miles from our apartment, but Pat assured me that it was the best place for the job. The owner specialized in Volkswagen-to-Subaru engine conversions, and had already done around fifty of them. We would leave Nacho there for ten days and the mechanic would do the rest, and it would be cheap. Whereas the same swap back in America would have cost between $12,000 and $18,000, we were told that this would only set us back around $3,000. After a string of terrible experiences with local mechanics in Latin America, I had my doubts. Sure it was cheap, but what of the workmanship? Would this be a beer can and bubble gum job? Pat gave me his assurance, so I parked Nacho in Soonthorn's dirt lot next to several other vans and I handed over the keys.

A couple of days later, Pat picked me up at our apartment and drove me out to the garage to check on the progress. The mechanic had removed our poor old engine and we found it in the middle of the floor next to its replacement. The old engine looked like a dead hobo tangled up in a fishing net, while the new engine looked like a freshly manufactured Kalashnikov killing machine. Still, I found myself sitting and staring at the old engine, remembering all we'd been through. I'd pretty much replaced or fixed everything on that old engine. I knew it inside and out. I could almost hear its surfing idle.

REER...reer...REER...reer...

I left the mechanic with a new set of head gaskets and other assorted parts and seals that I'd ordered from the States so that our engine would be totally fresh and Himalaya-ready. I handed him a new clutch throwout bearing, took one last look, and then we retreated back to Bangkok in Pat's Syncro.

Back in the city, Sheena and I stuck to our routine of writing in the mornings, and then heading out for lunch when the street carts rolled up to feed the factory workers next door. In the afternoons there was more writing, and then in the evenings we would head out to explore the city. It was monsoon season, so the stifling heat that we had experienced on our first pass through Bangkok was gone, replaced by warm, cloudy days and cool nights. Most days we would catch the train at Bang Chak station and take it into the center of town. We attended an Italian Film Festival, or we went to the mall to look at million dollar cars at the Bentley or Lamborghini dealerships. We ate the most amazing food like it was going out of style: grilled fish, curry, mango sticky rice, or spicy noodle soup in the markets, Iraqi or Egyptian food on the Arab Soi, and authentic Italian pizza served up by expatriated Italians on Thong Lo road. Bangkok had everything, and we really came to love it.

The mechanic called Pat on the tenth day and mentioned that he would need to buy a new starter, and wanted my permission to spend the money. Thinking that I knew best, I assured him that our starter was fine, and that I'd replaced it in Colombia as a part of our mass car parts smuggling operation. He begrudgingly agreed to use it, and told Pat that we could come check out Nacho's new heart.

Pat, who had acted far more generously toward us than we felt worthy of, took a third day off of work to pick me up at our apartment and drive me the thirty miles out to the garage. I again offered to pay for his gas, which he refused, and when we stopped for lunch he once again paid for my food, and there was nothing I could say about it.

When we arrived at the garage, I heard the faint purring of a smoother-than-usual baby kitten, and knew it must be Nacho with his new lease on life. I was ready to go – it was test drive time. I walked over to Nacho, hopped in, and turned the key. The starter emitted a shrieking noise like a dying hyena, and transformed into a disheartening grinding sound. I killed the engine and shot a glance at the mechanic. He squinted his eyes and shrugged his shoulders. I hit the key again and heard nothing but a light zipping noise.

As it turned out, the mechanic had known what he was talking about when he requested permission to buy a new starter. My starter had a different number of teeth than that required by the new flywheel, creating a slight mismatch. The old starter succeeded in a few starts, but then the shaft of the starter finally sheared off.

On the way back to our apartment—a trip which typically took more than an hour due to traffic—and after having been turned down yet again when I offered to give Pat some gas money, I decided to ask him a question that Sheena and I had been wondering about. From the moment we arrived in Bangkok, whenever we were with Thai friends they never let us pay for anything. Night after night they took us out, often to expensive restaurants, and they always paid. Pat had organized an engine swap on my behalf, and had taken three days off of work to help me pick out an engine, or to drive me the sixty miles round-trip to check on the progress at the garage. He picked us up on weekends and brought us around the city for cultural experiences, to eat strange foods at his favorite places, to look at the tables full of battery-powered gyrating dildos and sex toys in one of the strangest street markets we'd ever been to, or to meet his parents, who presented us with gifts of homegrown honey. Finally, as the air conditioner pushed cold air and we waited for traffic to inch along the motorway, I popped the question that had been bugging us.

"Pat, why are you so nice to us?" He continued smiling, and then stumbled for a minute, trying to figure out where to start. He spoke matter-of-factly, shaping each Skittle-colored word into a rainbow, and drawing out each vowel and overcompensating for each R.

"Here in Thailand, we are Buddhist people. And because I am Buddhist I feel very lucky that you and Sheena found me. You are traveling the whole world, and there are so many places that you could have gone, but you came to Thailand and met me. I am very lucky, because I believe that you and I were friends in a past life, and that you must have done something very important for me. Maybe you saved my life. Now you were sent here so that I can pay you back." And then he added, "So you cannot pay for my gas!"

I tried to think of something to say, but it was the ultimate trump card. Now that we were on the topic of Buddhism, I asked him to explain everything to me, to deliver his worldview. After five months in Asia I had lots of questions, and I asked them indiscriminately. I asked him about monks ("Every good Thai boy is sent off to be a monk for a short time, but I never was."), about the ubiquitous transgendered people we'd seen all over Thailand ("We call them lady-boys, and every person in Thailand is fine with them. You can spot a lady-boy by looking at their calf muscles."), and about death. I mentioned that our neighbor was killed in the street in front of our apartment, but that the Thai people in our community had seemed to forget about it immediately.

"Those people did not forget about the boy. You must understand that as Buddhists, we do not see death in the same way that you do. We believe that when a person dies, he is only moving on to a different body. Of course we are sad when someone close to us dies, but only because we will miss being with them. If my mother dies, I will be sad because I will remember the times that we were together, but I will also be happy because I will know that she lives on. When that Japanese boy died, Thai people believed that he moved on to a different body, so they will not grieve for him."

Pat was unable to take the following day off of work because he had to attend some meetings at the publishing company that his family operated. But something as flippant as work would not deter Pat. I took a taxi to a specified spot on the side of the motorway, where Pat's company van picked me up on its way to work. I waited at Pat's office in one of the spare conference rooms until he was finished with his meeting. Afterward we loaded up into the van, along with several of the company workers, and Pat instructed the driver to make a long detour to the Soonthorn garage. We arrived around lunchtime, so the driver piloted the van to a food stall down the road from the garage for a lunch of fried rice and congealed pig's blood soup. Everyone was in good spirits, and nobody seemed to mind the little field trip into the countryside. At last the time had come, and the van dropped me off before speeding off to bring Pat and the workers to their next meeting.

I walked to the garage and found Nacho ready to go. I turned the key and the engine spun to life, and then it assumed a low purr like a resting housecat. In fact, the engine idled so silently that from the driver's seat it was impossible to tell if the engine was even running. No vibration, no sound; it was perfectly balanced and perfectly tuned. The only evidence of life was the engine speed reading on the tachometer. To add icing to the cake, we had nearly doubled our power and torque, and improved our fuel economy while we were at it. I paid the mechanic the bargain price of $2,400, and it was finished.

Driving it was like dreaming after years of restless sleep. When I pulled out of the driveway it was clear that things had changed. Stepping on the gas no longer produced a delayed, slow acceleration, but rather a sharp and powerful forward jump. I pulled onto the country road in front of Soonthorn and gunned it. The van accelerated in the way that I imagined a real, grown-up car must. I could feel myself pressing back into the seat from the acceleration. On the motorway back to Bangkok I pressed the accelerator and effortlessly reached 80 miles per hour. Outside the window factories and bridges and temples whizzed by, and I recognized that I had fallen in love with Thailand.

27

Bangkok Roads

Brad

One thing we came to appreciate about our Asian friends was their ability to coerce us into doing unusual activities that we would have otherwise never done. Their subtle trickery was achieved through nonchalance and a sprinkling of urgency, like the time that Teng Tsen made us appear on The Apprentice, unclean, unshaven, and in my case, in desperate need of a haircut.

We should have recognized the signs that something was fishy when Pat called us one Saturday morning as we lounged around our Bangkok apartment.

"Hi Brad. Are you guys busy today?" (Testing the waters.)

"I'm wearing my underwear, and planned to do so until dinnertime. Why, what's up?" (Naïveté.)

"There's a classic car show today. Do you guys want to go with me?" (Trickery, coercion.)

"Sure, we'll go. Let me find my pants!" (Fell for it.)

"All right, meet me at the National Museum. You might see a couple of people in Volkswagens." (Lies, all lies.)

After winding through Bangkok in heavy traffic, we find our way to the National museum. The casual manner in which Pat mentioned this opportunity had given us a false sense of calm. We turned into the National Museum and slammed on the brakes. Something smelled fishy.

There weren't many Volkswagens around, but there were dozens of shiny classic cars: Bentleys, Rolls Royces, MGs, and Porsches. A small boy walked by wearing some kind of 1920's pantaloon shorts with suspenders and a driving cap. His outfit, incidentally, was a perfect match to the 1920's roadster that he had arrived in.

Seeing our confusion, a young man—one of Pat's accomplices—approached.

"Hi Brad and Sheena! You can park over there. My name is Kaeg. No Sheena, that's not how you say it. No, it's not *Keg* either. Look, just call me Samurai. I think it's easier for westerners to pronounce. Follow me, I'll show you where to register and get your number plate."

Samurai pointed to a parking space in between a classic Austin Healey and a Rolls Royce, and he was dead serious. The cars were so shiny that as I passed by I could see my reflection in the paint, and I looked like a total sucker. A sucker driving a mud-coated van with a rusty steel box hanging on its bumper.

Since arriving in back in Thailand, we hadn't found the time to wash Nacho. This meant that our white paint was invisible under various layers of brown Cambodian mud, applied as if to a Jackson Pollock canvas over weeks of driving on sloppy roads across Cambodia.

Sheena wanted to hide. She pleaded for me to take her home where she could crawl under the covers of our fluffy white bed, but it was too late. All of the drivers and their families stood around a flagpole and we listened to the King's Anthem, and then someone took official photographs of the classic car drivers, ourselves included. People took pictures of the cars, and Nacho succeeded in ruining all of the photos. We were ushered back to our cars and we took to the street, a big classic car train winding through Bangkok traffic—a classic car train with a fat, brown, 1984 caboose with a rusty box bolted on the back.

We drove out of the city and found our way to a temple in the countryside. Pat innocently joined the rally driving his Volkswagen Syncro Doka as if nothing were amiss. As if he weren't taking the mickey out of poor, muddy, slightly ugly Nacho.

"Hi Brad and Sheena, you made it!"

"Yeah, here we are. Now, when you said that we were going to a car show, you might have forgotten to mention that we were *in* the car show."

"What? Hey, do you know how to grease a CV joint?" An underhanded subject change, no doubt. He knew that I had a penchant for working on CV joints in parking lots. While I got under way, Sheena was snatched away by Samurai.

"Hello Sheena! Come with me, I'll give you a tour."

And with that, Sheena was whisked away for a tour of the temple, where she would spend the next ten minutes looking at sacred things, eating coconut ice cream, and buying little Buddha idols. Pat handed me paper towels to wipe the foul-smelling grease from my arms, and he correctly guessed that I preferred this to looking at temples.

146

Nacho ruined several more photographs and then it was time to move on to the next stop. I still felt uneasy about sullying the show's clean image.

"Pat, so, this is a classic car rally, right?"

"Yes! Are you having a good time?"

"Yes, it's wonderful, but do you think that we really belong here? I mean Nacho is from 1984."

"Oh look, everyone is leaving!"

Before we knew it we had parked at another location and were climbing into a double-decker London bus, which was going to take us to lunch. Our new friend Sim was snapping photos and I was minding my own business when all of a sudden an electrical wire shot out of nowhere and its trajectory promised to decapitate Sim from behind. My head-ducking reflex was faster than my verbal warning reflex, and I only managed to warn Sim about the wire after he'd been clotheslined by it.

Moments later, while I was observing the young boy in pantaloon shorts, my world temporarily went black when a stationary tree branch collided with my temple. Double-decker busing in Thailand is not for faint-hearted or the elderly. We finally wised up and put a little more emphasis on safety. We passed under several more low power lines, but this time we had appointed a powerline carrier to walk the length of the bus carrying the dangerous wires in his bare hands. Safety first!

At lunch, a troop of highly decorated dancing children entertained us over tea and an elaborate Thai buffet. As was becoming a theme, we rounded out our meal with even more coconut ice cream, much to Sheena's delight. Before we knew it we were back on the bus, then back in our cars, and then jetting off to an automobile museum containing the extensive collection of one eccentric collector.

Back in the city, the final stop of the day brought us to a university. We all parked in a long line and went inside where another buffet had been erected, which was divided into separate sections to represent the food from each region of Thailand. We gorged ourselves on more food, demarcating each course with coconut ice cream served inside of coconut shells—again, much to Sheena's delight. Students from the university's fine arts department took the stage and performed a traditional Thai dance.

And then it was time for the awards ceremony.

The awards ceremony?

The awards ceremony. We listened to a barrage, many minutes long, of incomprehensible Thai jabbering, listening for our names. Each person went to the stage to collect his certificate of participation, and then I heard it.

"Ching hodai chang dee doh—Brad and Sheena—dingo chan—semi-ugly Volkswagen."

I accepted our award for ruining all of the classic car club's photos, then I forgot to bow to my gracious host, and walked off the stage, where I proceeded to the coconut ice cream stand to lose myself in more substance abuse.

Moments later, as I whipped my tongue across my chin trying to mop up a few stray drops of coconut cream, Pat approached.

"Hi Brad! I see you really like the coconut ice cream." He paused for a moment, and then continued. "You're going on TV in four minutes." And with that, he turned and began walking away.

"Pat! Huh?!" By now I'd forgotten about the ice cream on my chin and I fired off a barrage of questions as I trailed behind him.

"On TV? But why? Do you know what kind of show? Is it, like, local or national?" I didn't even know where to start. Three minutes.

"Do you see that guy over there who looks like Elvis Presley? Every person in Thailand knows who he is. You are going on his show. It is the most famous car show in Thailand." I shot a worried look over to Sheena, my unfailing moral supporter—the woman who stands by my side through thick and thin.

"Leave me out of this!" she wailed, and then turned her back on me.

Before I knew what was happening, I was standing next to Elvis Presley—who goes by the name Sheeva—answering questions about our world trip. I could still smell the coconut ice cream on my own breath, and out of the corner of my eye I saw Sheena with a smug look on her face, and she was eating—could it be? A fresh coconut full of ice cream! The scheming weasel!

"Problems? Oh yes, we've had many problems…"

I sure hope the coconut ice cream lady is still open when this is over…

"In Colombia our transmission failed…"

If she got the last coconut, I swear to God…

"Our brakes failed, our wheel bearings failed…"

Is that? No! The coconut lady! Where are you going?!

When the interview wrapped up, we stood around talking to Sheeva as dusk settled in. He was passionate about classic cars and had that larger-than-life style typical of television personalities. He flipped through photos on his phone, showing us the cars he had designed and built himself. The Chevy that he drove to the event was of his own

148

design. While he was talking, he thought of something and his eyes lit up. He opened the back door to his truck and rummaged around for a minute, finally emerging with a bottle of his namesake rum, Sheeva WOP – WOP being an acronym for World of Peace, not a derogatory wartime slur for an Italian person. We happily added the Sheeva WOP to Nacho's onboard mini bar.

As night settled on the parking lot, the rest of the car club had already gone home. The only people remaining were Sheeva and his camera guys, Pat with his wife and son, Sim, the curator of the Jesada car museum, Sheena, and me. As we began to part ways, Sheeva told us to wait. He ran to his Chevy, opened the door, and grabbed the dream catcher that hung from his rearview mirror; we later learned from watching his show that this dream catcher was a part of his brand persona, appearing in his show's intro clips. He presented the dream catcher to us and wished us luck on our trip.

Just before we all headed our separate ways, the curator of the Jesada museum shared some exciting news with us.

"We are so happy to have you in Bangkok," he began "and as you know, next week is the Queen's birthday." True, true, we did know that. Go on. "So the Jesada Museum would like to invite you and Sheena to drive a historic miniature car from the museum in the Queen's birthday parade." My first instinct was to shoot a glance at Pat to see if he had anything to do with this. *No*, I thought to myself, *Pat wouldn't have given us that much notice.*

28

Sukhumvit Road
to Laem Chabang

Brad

It was a bright morning in Bangkok, and a beam of light reflected in just such a way from the rooftop of the pharmaceutical factory as to awaken me from my bear-like hibernation. We had been living in the apartment on Sukhumvit Soi 62 for a month, and we had finally accomplished everything that we had set out to accomplish in Bangkok; Nacho had received a new engine, we finished our book and sent it off to be published, we cultivated a community of friends, and we began to see Bangkok through residents' eyes.

The previous evening after dinner on the Arab Soi we had wandered the back alleys past shops selling spices and fabric, past the Iraqi restaurant and rows of turban-clad men loitering around *shisha* pipes. We crossed Sukhumvit road on a pedestrian bridge with a view of the city, and then stood there for a long time watching people and cars go by before the backdrop of the city that now felt so familiar. We could imagine living long term in Bangkok, despite the fact that we had always considered ourselves small-town mountain-loving people. But at the same time, we had started to feel the itch to move on. We still had a long way to drive.

Our apartment was situated only five minutes from Bangkok Port, but we received word from our shipping agent that our container loading process had been moved to Laem Chabang Port, one hundred kilometers away. Our shipping agents, being overly friendly Thai people, offered to drive out to the port with us to load Nacho into a shipping container, and then give us a ride back to our apartment. But when Gak caught word of this, he simply wouldn't have it. If anyone were to give us a ride back from the port, it would be him. We informed our shipping agent, and followed Gak to Laem Chabang in his classic 1960's VW bus.

When we arrived in Laem Chabang, the people from our shipping company who would guide us through the loading process met us for lunch, and then we all rolled out to the port together. We paused at the port entry while our agent went inside to get clearance, and then everyone crammed into Nacho to drive into the container yard together. When we got there the container was open and waiting. I slowly and ceremoniously drove Nacho inside. It felt like we had been in Asia for an eternity. We had learned a lot since arriving from South America, and putting Nacho onto a container ship felt more like a capstone than the next step in a journey.

Our shipping agents got uncharacteristically caught up in the moment, and although we had only just met, they took photos of us, of Nacho, and of each other. It was a far cry from our first shipping experience, in which we endured fourteen days of unhelpful people and logistical hell in order to transport Nacho the two hundred miles from Panama to Colombia. Thai people, we realized, lived life joyously.

Sheena and I finished bidding ado to Nacho, and then loaded into Gak's bus to head back to Bangkok. Gak had insisted that he was a better candidate than our shipping agent to bring us back to the city, and this was his time to prove it. We cruised to the gas station and bought a couple of Cokes. A good start, a solid effort. It was late in the afternoon when we turned off of the main highway and headed toward the ocean.

We wound through several small beachside communities to an overlook above the beach town of Chon Buri, and then carried onward, toward the fishing wharves on the outskirts of Bangkok city. We found our way onto one of the docks and drove the bus out to the end where the dock workers were shucking clams. The happy workers dressed in threadbare tee shirts and shorts and plastic flip-flops welcomed us, and told us they were from Burma. Several people collected the shucked clam meat, while others placed the shells in bags to be sold and ground down into bulk calcium carbonate.

The work looked terribly difficult, and we knew that they only received modest compensation for their hard work. During our time in Southeast Asia we had met numerous Burmese laborers, and had learned that immigrants from Burma typically performed the low-pay manual labor and servant work for the surrounding countries of greater wealth, much like the undocumented Latin-American immigrants in the United States. The difference in Thailand was the much lower pay, and the often-extreme working conditions that laborers endured. Still, the Burmese keep on smiling, and they still managed to send much of their meager income home to support their families.

After forty-five minutes with the Burmese clam shuckers, the sun began to set and they called it a day. Despite their inability to speak Thai or English, we managed to carry on a lengthy conversation of charades and guesswork, and came away with the impression that they were a happy people. We left them on the dock, sitting in a group smiling.

On our last night in Bangkok, Gak and Pat planned one final dinner at the city's supposed best hole-in-the-wall restaurant, which was highly renowned for its pad Thai and fresh-squeezed orange juice.

It didn't take long to verify that the orange juice claim was legitimate; Sheena and I had to suppress moans of ecstasy as we sipped it through thick straws. The pad Thai was amazing, and came wrapped in a little package of fried egg – a nice touch. It felt good to be together with these people. After so many months in Asia, Pat and Gak had become our extended family, and it would be tough to leave them behind. Pat kept us laughing with his quirky explanations of Thai social antics, explaining that in Thailand it is not considered rude to tell someone that they look fat.

"Why would it be strange?" he asked, innocently. "They already know they're fat." He seemed really baffled by the idea that the topic would be treated delicately.

"Yes, but aren't there Thai people who are trying to shed some pounds, who might be self-conscious about their weight?"

"Of course there are people who want to lose weight, but they still know they are fat. It is normal!"

"Even women?"

"Yes, women can be fat, too."

Pat turned to Gak and told him that he was fat.

"Hey Fat Gak, do you only eat and never shit? Ha! See?"

Gak smiled and laughed, shaking his head. We all had a good laugh while feeling a little insensitive and politically incorrect.

As a going away present, Pat gave us the Thai license plate off of his Syncro, and presented us with the first copy of the book that we had finished writing in our Sukhumvit apartment, which he printed through his family's publishing company. We had asked him to write a message on our dedications page, and he wrote a page-long letter to us in Thai script in order to fully express himself. "You can read it after you learn to speak Thai," he said, but then read it aloud to us. His words were the distillation of all of the kindness and friendship we had come to know from our Thai friends, and I noticed that Sheena was crying by the time he reached the end.

Gak brought his own copy, which he had bought online, and asked us to write a message of our own. We couldn't seem to express our feelings as eloquently as Pat had, but did our best nonetheless. And with that, we left. After half a year in Southeast Asia, it was time to move on – away from our new comfort zone, and straight into the unfamiliar madness of India.

Hairi and his family stand before their tent home on a hidden beach on Malaysia's east coast.

A line of Volkswagen vans materializes at the King Rama V monument to welcome Nacho to Bangkok.

Pat jokes with onlookers while sitting in an antique miniature car about Brad's uncanny height as a result of all of the GMO American corn that he eats.

In the mountains of northern Thailand, a boy passes on his way to the fields; in this region, Elephants are still used as draft animals.

Two boys ride in circles in a clearing within a Burmese refugee camp on Thailand's border with Burma. Beyond the hill lies their forbidden homeland.

Having been officially denied entry to Burma, we drive to a remote outpost on the Thai-Burma border to see if there is any way that the guards can be swayed. They can't be.

Brad describes the intricacies of chocolate-chip pancake preparation to a crazy Laotian man who has emerged from the jungle. Meanwhile, an international missing persons case unfolds and an unnecessary rescue mission is botched.

Laotian workers plant rice in paddies, and risk stepping on unexploded landmines dropped by American planes during the Vietnam War.

Sheena does her daily shopping routine at a typical Laotian street market in Luang Prabang. This is the way most of the world buys its food.

"Wow! There is a hillside with nothing on it, and there is also a thick layer of mud and detritus!" A landslide during monsoon season halts Nacho's progress through the mountains of Laos.

Shortly after bypassing the landslide, Brad creates a mess of the driveway leading into a Laotian Buddhist monastery where he and Sheena will camp for the night.

Buddhist monasteries become surefire campgrounds while crossing Southeast Asia. This time, near Angkor Wat.

Brad and Sheena look around to see if anyone will stop them from driving into Angkor Thom, but nobody does. They put on their Indiana Jones hats and keep on going.

In Bangkok, Nacho undergoes a Subaru engine transplant. The new engine is safely tied down onto a tire in Nacho's living room for the lengthy trip to the garage.

Brad is yanked away from the coconut ice cream lady to be interviewed on television by Sheeva—or Thai Elvis.

A group of Burmese clam shuckers is more than happy to have an audience as they separate the meat from the shells by hand. Each burlap sack (right) full of shells fetches about one dollar.

Part 2

Subcontinental Drifting

29

Purasawalkam High Road

Brad

Our plane landed in Chennai in the dark, and we emerged from the airport into a tumultuous mess of bodies. Touts hurried from passenger to passenger trying to round up business for the taxis. Swept up in the chaos, we found ourselves cramming into the back of an old Ambassador with a velour headliner and ornamental drapes hanging above the windshield. The driver gunned it and we heaved into a thick torrent of box trucks and taxis and motorcycles. We fought the urge to fall asleep aboard this Indian death rocket while we listened to our cab mates: a couple of idealistic young hippies who were on their way to becoming enlightened and certified as ayurvedic healers at a meditation retreat with their internet yoga guru.

One hour later we were deposited in front the Hotel Melody, a ramshackle heap of brick and mortar that we had booked in a hurry online in order to receive our Indian visas, and which looked nothing like the pictures. Nothing about it seemed "quaint and inviting." The cab driver did his best to cheat us out of more than the agreed fare, but we stood our ground and he drove away with the hippies and their guitar.

The hotel owner was kind, and walked us to our room—a mosquito-infested, moldy, dank hole in the corner of the dilapidated building. The beds were hard and clammy, and the air stank of deep, pungent body odor. It was as if the humidity in the room, which soaked the walls and sheets, was not water, but rather a fine mist of rank armpit juice. Throughout the first night I would repeatedly wake up gagging, as though a big sweaty Indian man were smothering my face with his sour, repulsive underarm. This was a rude awakening after five weeks spent in our fluffy white Bangkok apartment; we weren't in Kansas anymore.

In the morning I dragged Sheena along to a corner store that sold incense sticks, and I burned them continuously the following evening to try to mask the body odor. Our room had neither mosquito nets nor window screens, so we slept with the windows closed to fend off dengue fever. The room quickly filled with incense smoke, making it hard to breathe, but every time I awoke I was relieved to be asphyxiated by hippie-smelling smoke rather than by a big, wet Indian armpit. When our booking expired in the morning, we hastily moved to a slightly less repulsive hotel.

Out on the street, Chennai could be described as no less than a complete and brutal assault on the senses. There were no in-betweens. The traffic was suicidal and unforgiving, every car continually blasting its eardrum-splitting aftermarket horn. The roadsides, alleys, and street corners were ankle-deep in rotting trash, and the gutters were filled with a black sludge formed by a concoction of human and animal excrement mixed with stagnant water, urine and dust. The sidewalks were unusable, filled with parked motorcycles, shop inventory, or else replaced by deep crevasses filled with black goo.

There was never a time that the place didn't smell. It fluctuated depending on location, so walking in a straight line brought a rainbow of odors ranging from decomposing garbage, to mutton *briyani*, to burning plastic, to *chana masala*, to cow poop, to the overwhelming wet odor of copious amounts of human piss baking in the sun. But it never smelled like nothing.

Cows roamed the streets, rested in busy intersections, shat on sidewalks, and swallowed plastic bags like they were weeds while dining on the trash heaps that filled every nook and cranny of the city.

But amid all of the slime and stench and ear-splitting noise, Chennai had a saving grace: it was fascinating. We had found a place with more color and life than any place we had ever been. Men with wooden staffs and white robes hobbled down the middle of the street, beautiful sari-clad women traveled in packs, people in cars honked incessantly at one another, but waited patiently as enormous cows sauntered along in front of them.

One night we were awoken from our sleep in the middle of the night by the sound of drums and eerie horns outside. We jumped out of bed and ran downstairs and into the street to see what was going on at such an hour. When we emerged into the empty street, we found a group of men carrying a giant statue of Ganesh, the elephant-headed god, down the middle of the street. A band of musicians marched in front while women twirled around, flapping their vibrantly colored saris in the night air. A shirtless man walked up to us and handed us some sweet *pongol* in

166

cups, and then the procession left us behind. We ate our *pongol* on the street in our pajamas, then sauntered back upstairs and fell back asleep. It was as if it was all part of a dream.

Eating in Chennai was like realizing that our tongues had been sheathed in a protective coating all along, and then removing it to taste food for the first time. Each day we emerged from our guesthouse and found our way to one of the hole-in-the-wall restaurants lining the chaotic streets. Sometimes it was simple, as in the case of the boy who served mutton *briyani* into a page from the day's newspaper. We would pay him the equivalent of fifty cents and then stand on the sidewalk eating it with our hands out of the newspaper. Other times we sat inside sweltering restaurants while fans pushed the humid air around, and we gorged ourselves on mouthwatering curries and south Indian specialties like *dosa, idli, puri*, or the all-you-can-eat south Indian *thali*. We ate always with our hands—but only the right hand, as my early attempts to hold my *naan* with my left hand caused other diners to stare at me and laugh. We drank masala tea, served in steel cups and poured back and forth at full arm extension between the cup and its deep saucer in order to mix and cool it before drinking. The most expensive entrée on any menu hovered around a dollar or two.

And then there were the people. People-watching in Chennai became our favorite pastime while we waited for Nacho to arrive at the port. Each day we emerged from the guesthouse with the camera, in search of people. Four shops down, there was a hole-in-the-wall where men sat around a crude machine. One man cranked a large wheel while another sat on the ground sharpening knives and scissors against a spinning piece of stone. Seeing my camera, they invited me inside, told me the story of how Gandhi used to spin thread for his own clothes, and then they let me take a series of photos. Next door the young man with his giant cook pot asked me to photograph him serving up some *briyani* into a steel bowl, and then offered me lunch. On the next block, we peered into an open gate where a young girl in her school uniform watched the boys exercise in the yard before class. When we turned to leave, a beautiful woman who was seated on the curb asked me to take her picture. And down the block the story continued.

But the fact that we were intriguing to strangers was both a blessing and a curse. One afternoon we walked from our guesthouse to the beach. Along the way we met a homeless family, and we made small talk with charades. They were thrilled when we wanted to take their photo, and excitedly handed Sheena their bare-bottomed baby for the occasion. Arriving at the beach, we walked a hundred meters across the sand where mobile popcorn stands were painstakingly dragged through the deep sand, young Muslim and Hindu couples strolled, and people huddled in the shade of the dozens of abandoned wooden carts dotting the sand. As we strolled, young groups of boys began approaching us. They would ask us where we were from, and then quickly ask for our photo. They had no interest in me; the bottom line was that they wanted their photo taken with Sheena. We found it a little disconcerting, and were later told that young Indian men and boys like to take photos of themselves with white girls so that they can post them on Facebook and claim that they have a white girlfriend. The constant photographing may have been a small annoyance at first, but when we reached the waterfront we couldn't walk more than twenty feet without being stopped by a different group of boys wanting their photo taken with the white people.

After becoming quickly overwhelmed, we retreated toward the street. In doing so, we found ourselves behind a bunch of abandoned shacks, and soon a dodgy looking man fell in step behind us. We could tell he was there, but thought nothing of it at first. A short while later we passed a trash heap, and the man bent over and picked up an empty glass bottle. He fell back in step and got closer to us and we could feel him burning holes in the back of our heads with his eyes. Sheena stopped and turned to me.

"I'm feeling uncomfortable," she said.

"Got it. Let's go," I said. We turned around and walked past the man with the bottle, and as we passed him he angrily threw the bottle at a shack and it burst into pieces. We speed-walked out of there and made our way back to the guesthouse feeling a little exhausted, and a little jaded.

Our first impressions of India were that it was too loud, too stinky, there are too many beggars and touts, the traffic was the worst we had ever experienced, and some of its men had a tendency to be inappropriate. But on the other hand, it was possibly the most interesting place we had ever been, everybody was interesting to look at, and some of its people had a tendency to be very kind. It was going to be a fascinating place, if not more than a little overwhelming.

30

Triplicane High Road

Brad

Nacho arrived in Chennai Port aboard a mighty container ship after having floated from Bangkok to Singapore, and then across the Indian Ocean to India's central-East coast. The logical procession of events would have had Nacho unloaded from the ship so that we could have been on our way, but in India logic has no place.

Our shipping agents were right on top of things, having delivered our *Carnet de Passages*—a sort of passport for Nacho—to the customs agent for processing. But the first day went by with no action. And then the second and third day. And then four, five, six, and seven. Every time our shipping agent asked the customs agent if he had done his job yet, he said, "tomorrow."

Meanwhile, Sheena and I transitioned from being amused by India to feeling under siege by India. Day after day we renewed our room in the guesthouse on Triplicane Road, and made our sojourns into the city for what can be euphemistically called "cultural experiences" to the chorus of cars honking, cows eating trash, and people staring at us.

After our first trip to the beach we realized that beachcombing wasn't any longer in the cards for us on account of our status as extraterrestrials and the constant pestering that that brings. Our walks in the city became one-hour jaunts—expeditions, really—into frenzied and overwhelming territory filled with aggressive touts and beggars. Our white faces marked us not as people, but as walking money, causing everything to cost double and people's hands to magically open, palm up. These outings required immense mental preparations, and were followed by evening bouts of PTSD.

One evening I took a picture of some children dancing, and then offered them two rupees in thanks. They snatched the rupees, and I was immediately mauled by at least a dozen street kids who poured out of the

169

woodwork like angry wolves in a bad horror film. They hung onto my clothing and limbs while I tried to escape, demanding more money. In my struggle to get away, during which time Sheena and I lost each other, I was dragged into an ankle-deep gutter filled with fecal goo, wearing only my sandals. I barely kept myself from concurrently barfing and slaughtering the children, and the event was infuriating enough to send me into a two- day funk. As the days passed and these events began to multiply, we became jaded, and I only partially emerged from my funk.

All the while, cars honked, cows ate trash, and people stared.

One day a new face appeared at the hotel – that of Tatjana, a petite twenty-something German girl with blond hair and blue eyes. It seemed to us that Tatjana never left the guesthouse, a fact verified by Tatjana herself when we invited her out to lunch.

"I haven't left the guesthouse in two days," she said as we entered the restaurant a few doors down from our home base. On her first day she had attempted to walk to the beach, just as we had, but upon exiting the guesthouse, twenty Indian men surrounded her and proceeded to grope her body while one man tried kissing her neck as she walked. She looked to passersby for help, but everyone simply watched like slack-jawed spectators at a cricket match. She retreated to her room and refused to leave, subsisting on granola bars that she brought from Germany. We wondered how she would cope during her planned six-month stay in India.

On the morning of the eighth waiting day, ten days after we had arrived in Chennai, I called our shipping agent. I could tell he was disappointed, but he told me to hire a cab and come by the office anyway. When I arrived, two of the agents got in the cab with me and told the driver how to get to the customs office.

As we approached the customs office, they explained to me that the customs agent was purposely ignoring us day after day, most likely expecting a bribe to get him to do his job. By bringing me along, they hoped to force his hand. I was to be used as a sacrificial lamb in a fight against corruption and ineptitude. Our plan seemed destined to succeed.

When we got to the customs office, our shipping agent entered first and then grabbed my arm and pushed me into a chair in front of the customs agent. The agent was in his late twenties and appeared to be in a state of repose. He put down his newspaper when I sat down.

"This is a foreigner," our agent began, "and he has been waiting for four days to get his car from the port [a gross understatement]. He is foreign. We would simply like for you to process the foreigner's paperwork." He repeatedly placed emphasis on my foreignness, perhaps so that I would be felt sorry for. It didn't at first have the desired effect.

"Who do you think you are?!" the customs man began, addressing our shipping agent. "Do you think that you can pressure me? I have superiority! I am your superior! Besides, it's after 4:00, so it is impossible to process this today." This was the part where the angry chief nonchalantly slices off the sacrificial lamb's head. I closed my eyes and waited. It hadn't worked.

"Yes of course, you are my superior, sir," our agent said, backpedaling a little bit. He had to play the game, and he had to play it with British imperial mannerisms. "I wouldn't dare pressure you, as I am merely a shipping agent and you are a customs agent. I simply wish for you to accompany us to the port so that we can help this foreigner get on his way."

The customs agent settled down a little as the praise was lavished on him, and he finally reclined in his chair. He had saved face, and waited a few moments before continuing. I stroked my doughy soft neck with my hand.

"I will accompany you to the port, but only because of my graciousness. It is my decision, do you understand? This has nothing to do with your demands."

"Of course, sir," our man said.

Awkwardly, I was to share the back seat of the cab with the customs agent on the hour-long journey to the port. I put on my cheery face and used the hour to make friends and bring him up to speed on our trip. I knew that a customs approval in India could get ugly fast, so having the agent on our team would be critical. We arrived at the port and found Nacho's container.

I climbed inside, fired up the engine, and backed Nacho out for inspection. I stood there looking dopy with an innocent smile on my face. This was intentional. After a cursory glance around the outside, it was time for the interior inspection. Nacho was supposed to be completely empty, as our *Carnet des Passages* only covered importation of the van and a few choice accessories.

"Ready to have a look inside?" I said cheerily, and then slid the door open to reveal our treasure trove of undocumented belongings. "Here she is, surfboard, clothes, this is a toilet, shoes..." I smiled at the agent and shoved my hands into my pockets like a bumpkin, and then stepped aside.

He looked dumbfounded. He checked the list of approved accessories, and then peered inside again. He turned to someone and whispered, "None of this is on the Carnet." I pretended not to hear. He looked over at me and I smiled. After a few minutes he gave me the motion to close the door, and we were done.

But it wasn't over. No, this was India, and in India it is never that easy. I drove Nacho back into the container, whereupon it was re-sealed, and then a truck moved it a few rows over, where we would come back for it the following day.

The next day, after a couple hours of paperwork, it was time for the grand finale. We opened the container, and prepared to remove Nacho. The moment that the doors were opened, people emerged from the woodwork and surrounded the container to watch. We had started to notice that gawking was something of a theme of India. All work at the port seemed to cease, and I emerged to the blank stares of a dozen dead-eyed onlookers.

I had noticed a small pool of brake fluid under one of the rear wheels, so I decided to stop just outside the port to investigate. Sheena and I drove out from the container yard and found a small, empty parking lot where I could work. I decided to start by checking my tire pressure, and I hunched down next to one rear wheel. Nothing out of the ordinary.

When I stood up to move to the next wheel I was shocked to find more than a dozen Indian men surrounding me, staring. I stared back, confused. Where had these people come from? This place was like the Twilight Zone. I walked over to the next wheel and the mob silently followed me, staring, as if witnessing for the very first time how man makes fire. I hunched down at the second tire, and the mob stood directly over me, straining to see the tire pressure but never speaking. They followed me around to each tire, and then waited in Nacho's doorway as I found my tool kit. I crouched at the rear wheel, and the men stood over me silently. Occasionally I looked up or waved, but they stared back at me as if I were an alien. When I had finished I stood up, hot, sweaty, dirty, and hungry.

From the car, Sheena handed me a portion of *briyani* wrapped in newspaper, and I stood in the middle of the mob of men and opened it. They stared at me. I stared back. They said nothing. I said nothing. I scarfed down the *briyani* with my hands, all the while being watched intently only inches from my face by the slack-jawed mob. I played their awkward game.

172

When I was done I looked around, turned, and got back into the car as awkwardly as possible.

"Bradley, please don't set up the GPS right now," she pleaded. "Let's just go down the road a little."

I agreed, and we merged onto the congested, dusty street. A hundred meters away, where there were clearly no people around, I pulled over and started dialing in our destination on the GPS. I leaned forward to search the map for our guesthouse, and after a few seconds something didn't feel right. It was the feeling as if someone were standing right behind me. I paused, and turned my head. Inside of my window, right behind my head, three Indian men stared intently at the GPS.

We were officially in India with our own vehicle. A place with no concept of personal space, where traffic is dizzying and dangerous, and where we were literally regarded as alien creatures. A place where Sheena couldn't be left alone, where we would always have to be on our guard. Perhaps to the greatest extent so far, we felt very far from home. We rolled on, eager to leave town. Meanwhile, the cars honked, the cows ate trash, and the people stared.

31

Indian Highway 49 to Mahabalipuram

Sheena

India, we quickly learned, was not going to be a cake-walk. It didn't take long for the realization to set in that any hope of finding personal space or blending in with the masses was unrealistic. Over the two years preceding our arrival in India we had grown accustomed to feeling like foreigners, but in India we suddenly felt like extraterrestrials.

Chennai had been a serious eye-opener. It was a crazy concoction of everything beautiful and ugly in the world, and I had seen a transformation take place in me while we were there. The most peculiar things began to seem normal after just two weeks: men sleeping in their rickshaws at night, cows lounging on busy city streets, random nighttime parades, women in saris, everybody staring, Hindu rituals, and the segregation of men and women. Chennai had been brutally alive and its energy was hypnotizing.

But the city had drained me, and I knew it was time to leave when I had begun to see our hotel's elevator as my secret getaway closet. It was a manual elevator, and once inside the cage I would close the double set of metal caged doors, press the button for the third floor, and then relish in my seven seconds of personal bliss. Nobody could see me, and I couldn't see anybody. Indian tunes would begin mid-song and a blast of cold air would explode from the ceiling fan, temporarily extinguishing the feeling that I was being baked alive.

When the day came to depart from Chennai, I was in an emotional quagmire – excited yes, but more than anything, I was hesitant. Was I really ready for this? It had been almost two months since we had done any real overlanding, and it had begun to feel foreign to me,

174

like we had forgotten how to survive. And India? What a place to have forgotten how to survive!

We left the gates of the Chennai port at three in the afternoon. It was far too late to begin our first drive in India, but we certainly weren't going back to Chennai. There was absolutely no way. We turned south and started driving, and a few hours later we pulled up to the police station in the coastal holy town of Mahabalipuram in the dark.

"Here goes nothing," Brad said, and then he disappeared into the station while I patrolled Nacho. I felt at peace. The streets were pleasantly quiet and no one had discovered us yet. I recalled the day's events in my mind while Brad worked his magic with the police.

"Good evening, sir. My wife and I are driving a campervan and are looking for a safe place to park for the night. Is there a place nearby?"

"Oh no! It is not possible. Very dangerous! You must stay in a hotel."

Brad wasn't having any more Indian hotels. "I'm sorry, but that's not possible. Our car is our home. What about in the police parking lot?"

They didn't have a parking lot, as evidenced by the police cars that lined the side of the dilapidated road in front of the station. "Impossible. You can't sleep on the street. It is too dangerous."

"Oh no, is it really dangerous?" Brad asked. He put on his worried face and began his act. "I don't know what we're going to do. It's so late." He pointed outside to the van. "I think we will have to camp right there on the street tonight. Good place?"

The policeman pondered what to do with this stubborn foreigner who refused to stay in a hotel, and then picked up his phone and placed a call. After a few minutes, he hung up the receiver and addressed Brad.

"I have called my friend. He is the manager of Sthala Sayana Perumal Temple and he says it is okay. You can camp at the temple. When you get there ask for Santhanam."

We only had to venture a few minutes to find the 600-year-old temple, and Santhanam was waiting for us outside. I liked him instantly, and after two weeks in India, he felt like the first real person we had met. He looked at us with curious eyes but not like we were aliens.

"If you need anything, call me. We have a guard here at night so it is safe." We both felt grateful. He was proud of his temple. "I am the manager at this temple. Before me, my father was the manager, and before my father, it was his father. Please I want to show you inside. It is dedicated to the reclining Lord Vishnu."

We followed him inside the dark temple—by now it was late at night, making the experience seem like a dream—and he led us to the shrine of Lord Vishnu where we were greeted by Gopal Krishna, the temple priest. He looked like an exotic character from the National Geographic. He wore a white *lungi* and decorated his forehead with a series of painted lines: a vertical red one down the center and two other white lines that merged at the ridge of his nose. We talked with him for some time and I came to like him just as much as Santhanam.

"Welcome to India, Sheena and Brad," he said, and then dipped his finger in a red paste and marked our foreheads with *tikka* dots. On our way out I stopped to listen to two men play their horns in the temple's inner courtyard. Their melody echoed through the building and instantly brought me back to the Indian wedding we had stumbled upon back in Kuala Lumpur. It was the same song.

We parked Nacho in the middle of the temple's dirt courtyard, surrounded by the ancient buildings. During that first night, I awoke and peered out of our rooftop tent window. Visible in the full moonlight were dozens of cows sleeping in a circle around Nacho. They were the town's cows, which plied the city streets by day, dining on anything remotely edible and wreaking havoc on traffic. At night, this was their peaceful domain. It felt so surreal, to be sleeping in the center of a circle of holy cattle under a full moon in a temple, although in the morning we noticed that one of the cows had eaten the corner of our bamboo mat, which somewhat lessened our appreciation of them.

We awoke the next morning to a frenzy of activity around Nacho. The temple was bustling with worshipers and we were in the middle of it. "Can't we just stay in Nacho all day?" I suggested. I was still having India stage fright, and being inside of Nacho with the curtains pulled shut was our only sanctuary. Unfortunately it didn't take long for our sanctuary to become stiflingly hot and muggy under the south Indian sun. We opened the sliding door to a sea of colorful saris and curious eyes. Gopal Krishna was waiting to greet us into the day. "Brad and Sheena! Good morning!"

I learned quickly that Mahabalipuram was not some secret find, but indeed a World Heritage Site, and with good reason. The town sits amid granite hills and boulders, and the surrounding rocks are littered with carved stone monuments dating back to the years around 500 AD. Just outside the temple we stood face to face with the world's largest bas-relief etched into the side of a boulder. It depicted a scene of Hindu mythology that springs to life during the rainy season when the cleft in

176

the rock, representing the Ganges River, flows with water and drains into a stone pool at the boulder's base. All throughout the surrounding hills were other boulders scraped and sculpted into shrines and caves and stone columns, their walls covered in stories of Hindu mythology. It was spectacular, and we purposely lost ourselves in the boulders to enjoy some solitude. An Indian man found us and began following us through the ruins.

"To your right you will see a carving depicting an offering to Lord Vishn–" Brad and I exchanged looks and then cut him off.

"Sorry but we don't want a tour guide." The man acted hurt.

"I am not a tour guide. I'm a student, and I have a shop that sells rock sculptures."

"Sorry we're not interested."

"Please come to my shop."

"No we aren't shopping. We just want to walk." The rock seller left, but was almost immediately replaced by another rock seller, and then another. We had been warned that in Indian culture it is not normal to approach strangers for the purpose of making friends or offering help, and that if someone approached us to offer unsolicited help, it was probably out of their own entrepreneurial interest. So far we had found that to be true, and it took great effort not to become jaded.

Beyond the top of a ridge, where a granite slab sloped downward into a grassy field, we came across Krishna's Butter Ball – a comical name for a giant round boulder, precariously balanced on the slope, looking as if it might roll away at any moment. We continued on through the maze of boulders, passing billy goats that hopped carelessly on the sides of boulders, and scores of monkeys that bounced and jumped to their daytime hideouts. We walked on, and then hid under cover of a leafy tree as the weather changed and it began to rain.

We walked to the beach, where we bought coconuts from a man with a machete, and we drank the water inside. In the late afternoon we returned to Nacho, where, on the other side of the van, a homeless family had set up shop for the day. Before we had a chance to retreat to our sanctuary, the homeless children bombarded us with their palms upward, pinching their fingers together.

"Money! Money! Money!"

We distracted them with games and Brad taught them how to play Stingbee, a hand-slapping game, which caused them to erupt into fits of laughter. It was his underhanded way of beating the parents at their own game, while adding some joy to the children's lives; a joy their parents had failed to deliver. Soon, however, their mother saw that they had made no money and screamed at them to return. She gave us the stink-eye and we returned the look. The children quickly returned after some coaching, looking even more desperate.

"Money?"

We coerced them into playing more Stingbee, which further induced fits of laughter—just what these kids needed, we thought—and then retreated into Nacho.

The next morning Santhanam invited us into his house for coffee. His house was just outside the temple walls, set back from the street and tucked between two buildings. He saw us from inside and excitedly waved us into the inner courtyard of his home. The courtyard was surrounded on all sides by pillars and doors, and the walls were decorated with posters of Hindu gods and goddesses. A giant tree and a deep, wide well dominated the back garden.

He pointed us toward his bedroom. "Please take a seat." He turned on the ceiling fan and left to make us coffee. He came back carrying a tin tray with three cups of coffee. "The shops in town do not make such good coffee. That is why I wanted you to come here. You are the first guests I have ever had in my home."

Given his role as the temple keeper, and the fact that most visitors came and went without staying long, it must have been difficult for him to build relationships with outsiders. We felt honored to be his guests, and we could tell that he was very proud. A few hours later as we prepared to leave, Santhanam presented us with a few unexpected gifts: a set of postcards of India, another set featuring only Mahabalipuram, a yellow felted Hindu necklace, and a small framed photo of Ganesha. "You must put this in your van. Ganesha is the god of travel and he will protect you on your journey. Please do call me in the future. You are now my friends." We placed the picture inside and hung the yellow felt necklace from our rearview mirror.

We were fortunate to have met Santhanam when we did. While he had no way of knowing it, we had met him at the perfect time. He had shown us a different side of India, one that we both needed to see. We all walked together back to the temple. We started Nacho and prepared to leave, when Gopal Krishna emerged from the temple.

"Good morning Brad and Sheena! It has been a pleasure to have you at the temple the last few days. I wish you the happiest of journeys!"

And with that we were off. Maybe India wouldn't be so bad after all.

32

Auroville Main Road
to Sadhana Forest

Brad

By the time we reached Pondicherry, we really had our system down. We would drive into town and ask at the police station where it would be safe to camp. Following a series of high profile rape cases in India, including cases involving camping foreigners, it wasn't any place to mess around. I'm a squeamish person, after all, and my nightmares often involve the dropping of soap in prison showers.

But in Pondicherry, our camping system would have to wait. Our India guidebook said that Pondicherry was "a little pocket of France in Tamil Nadu." Oh? Upon entering town we expected to see a parade of dapperly dressed androgynous artists carrying baguettes on their antique bicycles, but the truth fell short of the high bar set by our frog-eating friends of Gaul. I hadn't recalled Paris having been quite as loud, so full of street cows, or having sidewalks so extensively decorated with discarded garbage. We wound our way into the city center, distinguished from the rest of the city by two streets having pastel-colored buildings – what our guidebook must have been stretching to call "a little pocket of France."

We wanted two things in Pondicherry: a safe place to sleep, and some French food, as would be expected from a little pocket of France. We found a restaurant with a French name, and then conducted a culinary experiment whose outcome unambiguously concluded that pastel-colored paint does not a French restaurant make. Indeed, ratatouille should not be ordered unless it is either prepared by a loveable cartoon rat, or by a person with generations of finely aged, hickory-smoked camembert cheese coursing through their veins, and has a last name in which at least 30% of the letters are silent.

179

As we sipped our après food lemon soda, the gods decided to spontaneously punish some group of sinners somewhere by flooding Pondicherry. The rain came down just as described in that biblical story about the flood, and before anyone could even begin to think about saving any animals, the city was under water. But a simple flood would not deter me—I was on a mission to avoid a rape-y camping experience, and went out with my umbrella to find the police station on foot while Sheena read her coming-of-age princess novella in the van, which was by that point nearly submerged.

I scoured the city amid the shin-deep sewer, and was passed from one police station to the next. As it turned out, the police of Pondicherry became quite busy with traffic issues when the city spontaneously flooded, and the needs of worried American car-sleepers were rightly ignored. Eventually I was directed to the main police station, and over an hour after my walk began, I emerged, prune-legged and successful. Our camp would be within the cramped and flooded courtyard of the downtown Pondicherry police station. I returned to the van, which was by then under water, and told Sheena the great news.

As the rains continued to fall and Pondicherry sank deeper under water and ever closer to a state of emergency, we did what any sane person would do. We sought out the deepest waters and watched cars try to pass through them. Just as we arrived, whom else should we miraculously run into but our German friend Tatjana from the Chennai guesthouse, along with a protective male chaperone. We caught up for old times' sake, recounting the events of the few days since we'd last seen each other, while standing knee-deep in the street's gray water.

After Tatjana left, we watched with carnage-hungry eyes as cars, motorcycles, rickshaws, and bicycles attempted to ford the dangerous standing water. From my younger years spent playing Oregon Trail on the computer, I knew that this could be very dangerous. We lost a lot of good Zekes fording rivers back then. And if fording the river didn't get them, you could bet that cholera was waiting just around the bend.

At just about the point where we were ready to call it a day and retreat to the police compound for the night, we noticed two wide-eyed, idealistic-looking western hippie types approaching on their underpowered scooter. This should be good, we thought, and waited in anticipation. To our dismay they stayed upright, but just as they reached the deepest part, their little one cylinder engine aspirated some water and died. They pulled it to higher ground where they were met by hoards of well-meaning Indian men, who also happened to be clueless about motorcycle mechanics.

Indian man after Indian man grabbed the bike, twisted the throttle, and kicked the engine until fatigue got the better of them. After a while it was determined that the bike would never run again, and the idealistic-looking western hippies seemed hopeless. At this, I walked over and told the couple that their bike had aspirated some water, and that they'd have to dry out the cylinder before it would start. This produced blank stares, so we walked the bike over to Nacho where I removed the spark plug and cranked a small typhoon out of the cylinder, then set it to dry out.

While we waited, it became dark. And when it became dark, our new friends became worried. They talked in whispers, and the outlook seemed bad. They didn't trust the bike and didn't want to ride it so far at night, what with the prowlers and all. Sheena and I looked at each other for a split second and just as soon came to the collective conclusion that wherever they were going was better than the flooded police compound.

"Look," I said, "we'll take you home. You can come back tomorrow to pick up your bike." At this they became wide-eyed and idealistic again, and loaded into Nacho.

"All right amigos, where are we going this evening?" I asked.

"To Auroville," Ivy said. Ivy was an American from California who had decided to move to India to live on a hippie commune, and had ended up in Auroville, where she met Alex of Latvia. They had become the best of friends before their ill-fated scooter ride into Pondy.

"I have no idea where that is," I said.

"It's like, north. Or maybe, east."

"Oh, I assure you it isn't east, as we're on the east coast. Do you know how far? Or what road?"

"It's on the road that goes north, I think," Ivy instructed.

To summarize, we drove for a long time through the city, a trip that didn't seem familiar to either Alex or Ivy. Later we ended up on a northern highway, after which we turned west for a prolonged sojourn through the woods on a back road, which later placed us on a southern highway. A while later we were on a steadily diminishing dirt road, made muddy by the biblical rain, and finally we arrived at the Sadhana Forest, a sort of hippie commune on the fringe of another hippie commune, whose goal was to reforest Tamil Nadu's desertified plains, using idealistic western volunteer power, or some such.

181

We parked in the pitch-blackness outside of the commune, and walked through the dense foliage into what was turning into a very strange evening indeed. We entered an enormous circular bamboo hut where a couple dozen people sat around on mats. When we entered, Ivy called everyone's attention and introduced us.

"Excuse me, everybody, I have an announcement." And then it was silent. "This is Brad and Sheena. They saved us today in Pondy."

"Hi Brad and Sheena," said the collective voice.

We sat on the floor and chatted with Alex and Ivy, and then with a family from the Netherlands. Next it was a man from Spain, and then a Swedish couple. Everyone had come there to get away from his or her boring life for a while. Accountants, grocery clerks, students, psychiatrists. Some had been there three months, some for ten years. A small collection of children played on a rope swing at the center of the bamboo hut. A man plucked a guitar, and people were engrossed in conversation. An African-looking girl, very slightly too old to be running around naked, ran around naked. Everyone seemed carefree.

Someone stood up and announced that it was mealtime, and a few people walked around handing out plates filled with food made from the crops that they had grown. Before we were allowed to eat, a small boy stood up and rang a bell, and then said some kind of chant, followed by a moment of silence—by now it was all becoming a ritualistic blur—and then we all ate. Someone else came around and picked up the plates.

Everyone there had a job, and was on rotation. Some cooked, while others watched the kids in the garden during the day. Some planted trees, while others dug holes around the expansive property. One girl enthusiastically told us she was on alarm duty. This meant that in the early morning it was her job to walk from hut to hut singing songs to people in order to wake them up: a human alarm clock. Each morning and night they sat in a circle and ate communal meals. In the evenings they sat in circles and took turns singing songs to each other, or telling stories for entertainment. There was no electricity except in the main dining hut, and they were their own entertainment. They were all vegans.

We would never survive there, we decided. If not for the isolation from society, or the veganism, then because we're both too embarrassed to sing in public. Behind dreams involving soap-dropping, dreams involving public singing are my second worst nightmare.

"Okay everybody, dance party!" It was Ivy, and she was ready to kick it. She would be leaving to go back to America in a week's time, and she wanted to put on one final dance party in the dining hut as her last hurrah. The lights went out and her laptop conducted techno dance tracks to a solar-powered speaker system. And just like that, the whole place was up and dancing, carelessly, dreadlocks flinging around, arms flailing, bodies gyrating. Dancing is my third worst nightmare. I would never survive there.

A day that had started out so typically, that was destined to end so unromantically in a flooded police compound, had turned into this. The beautiful result of a natural disaster combined with equal doses of hippie idealism, poor judgment, and bravery.

33

Indian Highway 49
to Kerala

Sheena

Over the course of a few days we crossed the subcontinent from the Indian Ocean westward to the Arabian Sea. We left Pondicherry, first stopping in Madurai where temple-goers celebrated the birthday of the elephant god Ganesh, and then to the hill station of Munnar to escape the south Indian heat. The ground rose from the desert plains like exaggerated goose bumps until we were in the middle of a Van Gogh painting with fluffy clouds and Assam tea fields manicured in rows of stripes and swirls. The air smelled of freshly cut tea leaves and at five thousand feet it was actually cold. I strutted around, stricken with happiness in my sweater while Brad removed Nacho's starter and reshaped its mounting surface with a file to address some starting issues we'd been having.

I loved everything I saw, and I even loved the things I couldn't see. We had parked in front of an empty resort, and the next morning the security guard reported that a wild elephant had ambled right down the street past Nacho while we slept. While this excited me, I was told that the villagers seriously feared the wild elephants. Over the course of the last few months, six villagers had been thrown like toys by the wild elephants and then trampled to death in the tea fields.

Munnar provided a refreshing introduction to the state of Kerala, and we left through the mountains to the west, dropping down in elevation until we were back at sea level at Kerala's famed backwaters, a coconut-strewn spider web of waterways that fringe the Arabian Coast. It was said to be something like an Indian Venice amid overhanging palms.

We stationed ourselves in the city of Kochi, a sprawling place that still retained its pockets of Portuguese and English architecture, ancient mosques, and old colonial churches. Its coast was lined with six hundred year old cantilevered Chinese fishing nets, cashew sellers, spice traders and everything in-between. We found a guesthouse in Fort Kochi, the city's historic center, where all sorts of fun things were going on. When we left our guesthouse on the first morning for a backwaters tour, a film crew was filming a scene for an Indian television drama on the street right where Nacho was parked. Half of the crew was staring at Nacho, while the other half was working on the scene in which a beautiful Indian girl in a sundress was staged outside of a café, waiting for her boyfriend. She looked down at her watch impatiently. Moments later her beefcake arrived on his motorcycle and she threw on her helmet, put on her best pouty lips, and stormed toward the motorcycle. The director yelled, "cut!" and angrily yelled at the girl for having put her helmet on backwards.

We rode in a van for an hour to where the backwaters tour was to begin, and it dropped us off next to a small roadside stand. We bought some water and then loaded onto a big lacquered wooden boat, its platform lined with big wicker chairs. We picked two chairs at the front and settled in for the ride.

Our captain stood proudly at the front of the boat, a slender aging man with guitar string muscles and a white moustache. He clenched a long polished bamboo pole in his hands, and after all of the passengers had boarded, he let the pole fall through his hands until it hit the river bottom. He leaned against it and walked it along the side of the boat, and we slowly crept forward. Each time the man reached the end of his platform he pulled the bamboo from the water and repeated the steps. It went like this for over an hour.

Eventually the boatman stopped the vessel and we climbed out, transitioning into a canoe that cut down one of the many tiny backwater arteries. We passed by the doorsteps of rural homes, stopping here and there to visit a spice plantation or watch demonstrations of local toddy tapping—the cultivation of a mild local hooch made from fermented coconut sap—or the making of coir, a kind of handmade coconut husk rope.

The backwaters tour gave us a glimpse into India's tranquil side, and we met some nice people, such as a young Keralan lawyer who invited us to drive south to his family's house for *Onam*.

Everyone was talking about *Onam*, a festival specific to Kerala. It was to be a celebration of the mythical King Mahabali, and is Kerala's biggest festival of the year. The air was electric with excitement, and everyone was happy. The celebration would amount to ten days of food and family, wherein the Keralans would decorate their doorsteps with flower arrangements and make elaborate meals consisting of forty or fifty different dishes.

We very much wanted to experience *Onam*, but Brad and I had been itching to continue northward, so we passed on the offer to join our new friend and his family for the holiday. We hit the road the day before the main celebration, crunching and smashing Nacho on our way out of town on India's terrible roads. After six hours of frustration, Brad pulled over. We couldn't believe that the road we were following could be considered a main highway. It was just dirt and potholes, followed by more dirt and deeper potholes.

We studied our GPS in search of a shortcut, but none existed. Just before we pulled back on the road, an elegant-looking forty-or-fifty-something couple approached our window. They asked the standard questions.

"Where are you going? Where are you from?"

We told them that we were just passing through, which prompted looks of confusion.

"But tomorrow is *Onam*! It is the biggest holiday and our town has the best celebration. The other towns are not as good."

I decided to keep quiet and not mention that by evening we would be out of Kerala, and thus out of *Onam* territory altogether.

"You must stay here for *Onam*." They waved at us to follow them. "Come to outhouse and stay. You can have *Onam* with our family tomorrow."

Brad and I looked at each other and felt that we just couldn't. There was still time to drive a few more hours and we were dead-set on putting down tracks. It would be a shame to stop now. We declined their offer and said goodbye, and then pulled back on the road. I almost immediately regretted what we had just done. These were the exact experiences we were looking for, after all.

I asked Brad to turn around and he reluctantly flipped a U-turn, but we were too late. We drove back and forth, looking up and down streets, but we couldn't find the couple.

Brad looked bummed. "You know, now that I think about it, going to that couple's house for *Onam* would have been really fun." We decided that we had to stop making such stupid decisions for the sake of staying on our imaginary schedule.

The next day *Onam* festivities were in full swing. Elephants marched down the street and people screamed with excitement in the backs of trucks. It was fun watching everyone, but I still felt sorry about our decision. We made a quick stop for lunch and left the restaurant feeling pregnant with food babies. As we sat in Nacho, ready to leave, two men appeared on a motorcycle and pulled up to my window. They asked the standard questions.

"Where you going? Where you from?"

We told them that we were just passing through.

"You come our house! *Onam!*"

I glanced at Brad for just a moment and then shouted, "Yes!" They laughed in surprise and called home to report that they were bringing home two Americans. We couldn't believe our luck.

We followed our new friends: two Indian truck drivers who worked in Saudi Arabia, one of whom spoke elementary English, and the other who spoke none. We didn't have any idea where we were going, and as the time passed and we bumped down continually diminishing dirt roads into the middle of the jungle, we started to question our decision. Was this smart? We crossed through tropical fields of banana and coconut palms, and finally reached their home. The men's wives were waiting outside for us, and they led us inside to a sofa where the women rolled a small card table out in front us and served us tea. We were foreigners, after all, and foreigners eat at tables. The men sat Indian-style on the spotless tile floor in front of us.

The women retreated to the kitchen while we drank tea with the men and learned more about their work. They were brothers, and found that they could make decent money, by Indian standards, by going to the Arab world to work. They had been long distance truck drivers in Kuwait, Iraq, and Saudi Arabia. They would work in those places for nine months straight, and then would come home for three months around the holiday season. This time they had come home from Saudi Arabia.

The women emerged from the kitchen and arranged banana leaves in front of each of us, and then served the food from pots: goat and vegetable curries, spiced chutney, *papad*, and a massive portion of Kerala's thick local rice variety. We ate on the card table while the men ate on the ground, happy to have learned the proper way to eat with our hands from Terence and the other Tamils back in Kuala Lumpur.

We encouraged the women to eat with us, but they insisted on standing by and topping up our leaves as the food disappeared. There seemed to be a language barrier standing in the way of effective communication, and when we had emptied our plates and tried to refuse seconds, we were misunderstood and the women topped up our banana leaves with enough food to constitute another full meal. When we were finished they cleared our table and served themselves. The food was delicious, and we would have been a lot more comfortable had we not just finished impregnating ourselves with those oversized food babies at the Indian restaurant.

Dessert came out next: an *Onam* specialty called *payasam* made of brown molasses, coconut milk and spices garnished with cashews and raisins. I absolutely loved it and the woman who had served it could tell, so she brought me another serving. My first food baby had eaten my second and third food babies, and now I was pouring a sugary dessert all over its head. I looked at Brad, and could see that his belly skin was stretched like a drum over his food baby triplets. A few minutes later the husband grabbed his machete and began sawing coconuts down from his tree.

His wife looked surprised and delightedly proclaimed, "First!"

The man explained that it was the first time he had cut coconuts from his tree. He messily chiseled the tops off of two coconuts, splashing their contents all over the place, and presented them to us, his face dripping with coconut water from the unpracticed effort.

To finish off the evening, the family led us down the street to a relative's home where we ate more *payasam* and drank coconut water. By then we felt like the gluttonous man from the movie *Seven*, who had been forced to eat canned spaghetti until his stomach exploded. Finally, after hours of face stuffing, we managed to convey to our hosts that we were too full to put anything else in our mouths. At this, they gave us things that could be taken on the road to eat later. One of the cousins was an experienced coconut-cutter, and quickly shimmied his body fifteen feet up a palm tree until he reached a cluster of coconuts, and commenced to let them fall with the well-practiced swings of his machete.

We left with warmth in our hearts and several food babies in each of our bellies, plus several coconuts stacked on our back seat to keep the feeling going. As we drove away we breathed carefully in short, painful breaths, and made a pact.

"New rule," I said. "We will never turn down an invitation."

I touched my food baby with a mother's love and looked at Brad.

"Deal," he said, and then winced. I think his food baby had kicked him.

34

Route 63 to Hampi Bazaar

Sheena

Back in Mahabalipuram, when we had gone to Santhanam's house for coffee, I had brought along my India map and asked for his advice on the must-see destinations in south India. While we sipped our coffee he had worked through the map, highlighting several places that I had never heard of.

"The Thillai Natarajah temple is there, dedicated to Nataraja, Shiva, the Dancer of the Universe…"

He had continued to highlight cities scattered throughout the region, each one chosen for their temple-centric highlights. This had made sense to us, as his role as keeper of a temple meant that all of his travels had been for the purpose of visiting other temples. When he had highlighted his last selection, he looked me in the eye.

"Hampi. You must go there." He put the cap back on the highlighter. "It was the capital of the last great Hindu empire in our history. There is a temple there called the Virupaksha, dedicated to Shiva. It's also the land of monkey gods."

Did he say monkey gods? It was settled, he had me at monkey gods.

Later on, Brad had looked at me with crazed eyes and reminded me of his burnout on temples, which had occurred sometime way back in Guatemala or so, solidifying my hunch that he would never survive Santhanam's pilgrimage route. Brad had decided that, for each of the world's religions, if you had seen one temple, you had seen them all.

Now Hampi piqued my interest, and for different reasons, Brad's too. He envisioned camping among the granite-boulder-strewn hills and I, in addition to camping, was intrigued by its ancient temples and palaces. The village of Hampi sits on the 14th century ruins of Vijaynagar,

190

described as one of the most beautiful medieval cities in the world in its time, and whose people specialized in the cotton, precious stone, and spice trades.

We rolled into town around midday and surveyed the area. Goal number one was to find a campsite that was both scenic and far enough away from anything so that we would be invisible to the locals, thus preventing the inevitable gawking that would occur if we were to be found. We located what looked like a potential camping jackpot on the GPS and wasted no time in pointing Nacho in its direction.

One of the most exhausting things about overlanding, especially in Asia, was finding places to sleep. Some days it took ten minutes, while other days it took hours, and sometimes—more often than not in India—we ended up camping at shoddy petrol stations, lined up out front alongside a half dozen semi trucks.

To find the area that we had pinpointed on the GPS, we would have to pass through property owned by a holy ashram. In our attempt to do so, we were denied entrance by a wise man. Two hours later, still attempting to find another way to the secluded road, I was ready to rip my hair out and offer it to the monkey gods in exchange for a little help. We gave up and began searching for an alternative.

"Hey what about that road?" Brad asked. "It looks promising don't you think?" I glanced down the dirt road and saw neither buildings nor people – only trees and rocks. Could it be? Seclusion in India?

We cut down the narrow dirt road and it squiggled along the curves of a natural canal. To our right the land dropped down to an expansive area of compact agricultural land full of banana trees.

"Monkeys!" I shrieked, mostly out of fear, but also somewhat out of amusement. It was a species I hadn't seen; they were gorgeous with long tails, beautiful grey coats, and faces so black I could hardly make out their features. Langur monkeys, I later found out. They were both amazing and terrifying at the same time. I pictured them ripping my hair out, and I shuddered.

Brad looked surprised as he swiped the GPS with his finger. "Hey this is that road I was trying to find! Somehow we ended up on the other end of it." We came around a corner and were all at once engulfed in a herd of a few hundred goats. The shepherd worked the livestock around us and then stared wide-eyed through my window. He stood on his toes and peered back at our living quarters and then back at us and held out his upturned hand.

"Money?"

If it weren't for fear of legal repercussion, Brad would have surely flipped out by then and wrung someone's neck, but instead he resorted to angry gestures and private rants, bubbling and stewing with disappointment.

Shortly after the begging shepherd narrowly escaped Brad's wrath, the road widened enough for us to pull over before it narrowed back to one lane. This spot may not have looked like much, but being that it was not a petrol station, there weren't any people in sight, and there was running water nearby, it was the best campsite we had found in our first month in India. There was no doubt in our minds that the gawkers would find us sooner or later, but we were elated. We opened up our sliding door to a view of a hillside scattered with granite boulders, and we breathed sighs of relief. In the distance silhouettes of columned temples topped boulder-studded hills.

In the morning we awoke to the eerie sound of meowing peacocks in the bushes and workers driving tractors past us to the banana fields. Back in town we filled our bellies with *idli*, a south Indian breakfast made of steamed rice and lentils, served with at tomato chutney called *sambar*. We rented two cruisers and pedaled into the countryside.

Hampi was fascinating, and unique in overdeveloped India. The small town was more or less constrained to a few blocks in a valley near the river, and a complex of ruins extended out like overspray into the surrounding hills. We couldn't go a hundred feet without seeing some sort of ruin. A mix of granite boulders and giant hand-cut granite bricks were used to form walls along the road, and old temples provided a look into the past, their floors dotted with worn pits from the grinding of grain. Other ruins sported artistic bas-relief carvings on their walls; one depicted a strange battle scene involving an elephant ripping someone's legs off.

Hampi had its own battle roaring on as well. While it is a UNESCO World Heritage site, its managing authority had struggled to meet its conservation requirements due to locals continuing to use the ruins. Villagers still grazed their livestock among the temple grounds, and occasionally we came across families who had claimed the old stone ruins as their own, conducting their lives in small communities of stone temple dwellings. Attempts at maintaining the ruins in a UNESCO-worthy manner were futile; at one of the ruins we watched a group of several women slowly working their way around an expansive grassy landscape, mowing the grass with small knives, and setting each clipping of grass into an ever-growing pile.

Like every great empire, this one, too, came to an end. It was conquered in the 1500's by marauding Muslims, pillaged for many months, and left abandoned. Most buildings were destroyed but many were left intact. The nearby Queen's Bath was a "royal pleasure complex" built for the King and his wives. Balconies and verandas surrounded a central pool that once overflowed with fragrant flowers and perfume-infused water. It was nice to imagine a place in India where such peace and luxury once existed.

On our way back to Nacho we cut along the Tungabhadra River – the most gorgeous river we had seen in all of India. Its appearance gave the impression that it may have still been capable of supporting aquatic life; most rivers we had encountered in India were garbage dumps, and seemed dead from the unmetered dumping of raw sewage from river towns. This one was something out of a fairy tale, with turquoise-blue water and boulder-strewn banks. We rode our bikes along a cobblestone path that was built in the 1500's to protect the town from flooding. The path turned too rough for our cruisers so we parked the bikes and continued on foot. Eventually the embankment ended and we walked to the river's edge. Far downstream I could see several temples carved from rock, but where we stood held the most intrigue. Flat boulders sat partially submerged in the water and dozens of *lingas*, the phallic symbol of Lord Shiva, were carved into the granite surfaces. Indian tourists continued down the path to the far temples, a woman washed her clothes at the water's edge while monkeys played on the rocks, and round teacup boats waited to be rented. We didn't make it to the temple, but instead sat on the bank and talked for over an hour to a young man from Hyderabad.

Hampi was to be our final destination in south India. There were a number of reasons for our decision to get out, among them the fact that we felt exhausted, and couldn't seem to recover. But above all, we craved the mountains and we knew that if we drove straight north we would end up at the world's grandest mountain range: the Himalayas. We figured that if all went well, in two or three days we would be crossing the border to Nepal.

35

Indian National Highway 7
to Varanasi

Brad

The distance from Hampi to the Nepalese border is 2,200 kilometers, approximately the distance from Phoenix to Seattle. Our plan was to drive to Nepal for the short trekking season, and then return to India later to explore the North.

"It's only 2,200 kilometers," I reassuringly reported to Sheena. "We'll be yodeling in the Himalayas in three days, tops." Stupid, stupid, stupid. If we had the power of premonition we would still have Lennon, the Pontiac Aztec would never have seen the light of day, and I would have retained the will to live. But we don't, and so we began the drive across India, blindly walking straight into the field of rakes.

We left Hampi on roads having a medium number of potholes, which was annoying, and which were crisscrossed by a greater than average number of speed bumps, which was also annoying. For half of the day we pushed the limits of the road, which is to say that we crawled along at a three-legged turtle's pace.

"Says here we'll reach National Highway 7 by around lunchtime," I said, swiping our GPS with my finger. Sheena shot me a look as if to say, *you'd better hope so, you sonofabitch, or you've cuddled your last cuddle.* By lunchtime we reached National Highway 7, just as expertly predicted, whereupon we stopped at a humble roadside shack for lunch and were shocked when an Austrian-registered overlanding truck pulled up next to us carrying none other than our soon-to-be road tripping buddies, Regina and David—the first and only other foreign drivers we'd met in India. Suckers.

After lunch we parted ways, Nacho being überly faster than David and Regina's truck on open highways, and we hoped to meet again. Several minutes later everything went to hell, a milestone recognized by virtue of National Highway 7 changing from a four lane proper highway into a two lane wasteland matched only in dishevelment by the streets of Hiroshima circa 1945. As we sailed off of the end of the pavement and into the rubble field, Nacho's oil pan smashed against the edge of a bomb crater. I pulled over to check that the oil pan hadn't split—it hadn't—and we continued on our way, albeit at a snail's pace, crawling all over both lanes to reduce the impact of falling into the holes formerly known as road. David and Regina soon passed us.

As the hours ticked by, my wits began to falter. The highway was a parade of overloaded trucks with inventive paint jobs which, every few kilometers, piled up behind and then overtook their comrades who had sustained broken axles or had rolled over—those poor impatient souls who drove too fast through the crater field. The driving conditions deteriorated throughout the day, and the scant driving skills possessed by the nation's motorists evaporated altogether. Cars drove on the wrong side of the road, even when a center divider was present, and trucks and motorcycles entered the roadway without signaling or even looking first, causing me to repeatedly slam on the brakes and think very bad thoughts.

On a particularly straight and excessively potholed section of road on which we crept along at around 10 kilometers-per-hour, we happened upon a motorcycle cop heading in our direction. He passed us, and upon seeing our white faces, his pupils turned to dollar signs. He flipped around, rode up next to Sheena's window, and attempted not to fall over at such a low rate of speed. He pointed to the roadside, prompting me to let out a stifled laugh—not a funny laugh, but a laugh that let anyone within earshot know that this road had taken away my desire to live, and with it any care of what would happen to me if I lost control and hacked up an Indian motorcycle cop with my Bear Grylls edition machete.

"Well hello good officer, it's a wonderfully wonderful day out here on your amazing National Highway 7, now don't you agree?" A fluent English speaker would match this to my tone and realize that I was a man with no fear, a desperate man. A suicide bomber. He didn't speak English, save for a few choice words.

"You license."

"Why yes of course I have a license. And good for you for checking. Is there anything else I can do for you?"

"You license!"

"Now, as you'll recall, I just explained to you that I indeed do have a license. If you think I'm going to give it to you, well then you're terribly mistaken."

"She license," he said, pointing to Sheena.

"This pretty little lady here is my passenger. And as you're well aware, passengers aren't required to have licenses. Isn't that about right?" This was easy enough, but I wanted so badly to punch this man in his big, dumb, mustachioed face.

"She license. She license!" He was clearly getting mad.

"Me driver...she passenger...see? Me drive. She sit there and read book. No need license for read book. Understandy?"

"One thousand Rupee," he demanded.

"Excuse me? Why?"

"One thousand Rupee!"

"I don't think so. Leave us alone." And at that he gave up and walked back to his bike without another word. Corruption. It might explain how Central India's primary north-south corridor had been allowed to fall to ruins.

As evening neared and I dangled at the end of my desperate rope, having completed only 300 kilometers of slow and painful crawling, we saw a group of Indian men staring at something on the edge of the road much in the same way that they usually gather around and stare at us. As we passed we saw a car with its hood smashed in and a crumpled motorcycle in the road, its rider hunched over but alive, sitting in a pool of blood. Nobody did anything; the spectators just stood and stared.

Distracted by the scene we launched into another crater, smashing our oil pan for the umpteenth time. As darkness fell we found a petrol station, pulled into a corner, and cried ourselves to sleep.

Early morning coffee and oatmeal prepared us for another twelve hours of battle. I tied up our full trash bag and walked to the petrol station attendant to see where I might throw it away, at which he motioned with his thumb to toss it over the wall. I said I'd rather not, but he enthusiastically encouraged me to pitch it over the wall; it's the Indian System, he assured me. Instead I secured the bag to the front bumper and we departed into the post-apocalyptic mine field known as National Highway 7.

Around lunchtime, while passing through a central Indian forest, we smashed our oil pan for the bazillionth time while abruptly dropping into a coffin-sized hole in the road, so I again pulled over to inspect it for splits. The formerly perfect rectangular prism had by now become a piece of mutant cauliflower, and had long since developed a leak around the crushed-in oil drain plug. I checked the oil level—a half-quart low—and topped it up, got back in the van, and turned the key. The engine refused to start.

Reer reer reer...reer reer reer...reer reer reer...

"Fork!"

"Oh my!" Sheena said under her breath. I don't usually swear, so she knew this must be serious. And it was, after all, since this was a new engine for which I had virtually no spare parts, no experience, and no shop manual. I thought about it a little more.

"Fork, FORK!" I said, smacking the dashboard with my hand. Could I have added too much oil? Could the air filter be plugged from the endless kilometers of this dirt road incomprehensibly called a highway? I got out, crawled under the van, and readied myself to empty a half-quart of oil out of the drain plug. I slowly unscrewed it, and before I knew it hot oil was pouring all over my hands and I couldn't stop it.

"What the FORK!" I scream-whispered as my delicate hand skin began to melt. Stupid, stupid, stupid! I only had one quart of oil left with which to replenish this Exxon-Valdez! Just when all hope seemed lost I fumbled the plug back in, stopping the flow of molten lava. Soon enough, as always happens in India, a group of men emerged from the woodwork and formed a tight huddle around me as I wiped my scorched hands on an old tee shirt, removed the air filter, and went to work removing the thick mud from its creases.

While I worked, Sheena tidied up the house under the supervision of a deranged Indian man who continually stared at her with mean creeper eyes. She collected several empty plastic bottles and tucked them into the trash bag on the front bumper, an act which enraged the creepy man. He disgustedly followed her, grabbed the plastic bottles out of the trash, and flung them into the trees, and then stared at her like a deranged and infuriated maniac. Who does this woman think she is, coming into our country and exercising environmental consciousness?

Just as I put the finishing touches on the air filter, who should arrive but David and Regina. They had stopped in Hyderabad to have their motorcycle rack welded after a legally-blind Indian driver had driven full-speed into them while they sat in a turn lane. They weren't convinced that the welder knew what he was doing, so they carried on. I told them we'd catch up in the evening, and saw them on their way. As they left, Sheena ran over and informed me that we urgently had to leave, right this second, just throw your tools into the car and get us the hell out of here now! The creepy littering man was getting belligerent, and in her assessment we were now in a state of grave danger.

I threw everything inside, rubbed the Iranian prayer beads that hung from our rearview mirror, and turned the key. Salvation! Nacho roared to life and we sped away, at roughly 10 kilometers-per-hour, from the threatening gaze of the backwoods Indian creeper, undoubtedly mere seconds before he would have tried something foolish and caused me to turn my torque wrench into a weapon.

We soon stopped at another petrol station for a fill-up. I carried our trash bag over to the attendant and was again encouraged to throw it over the wall, which both enraged and flabbergasted me. *They live in piles of garbage, and yet they still encourage littering.* I returned to Nacho, secured the garbage to the front bumper, and slammed the door.

"Am I out of my forking mind for wanting to responsibly dispose of this garbage?!" Sheena nervously twisted and pulled out a little bit of her hair, I seethed with rage, and we drove back toward the minefield, slamming our oil pan on a concrete ledge as we pulled back onto India's National Highway 7.

"Fuh-huh-HORK!"

Every morning on our trans-India drive started out the same; we awoke from fitful sleep by our talking alarm clock to the suffocating weight of reality pressing down on our chests. It was a terrible feeling, as if we had accidentally burned down the house with the entire family inside. We were damned to this fate, and there was nothing we could do to change it. After oatmeal and coffee we would tidy Nacho's insides and then pull away from our petrol station camp spot to rejoin the decaying ruins of National Highway 7.

From our captains' chairs we would catch the "golden hour" in full effect—that is, the window of time in the morning when the sun casts its golden rays upon the dozens of Indians publicly shitting on the highway, an act they carried out as candidly as they brushed their teeth with frayed sticks, stared at foreigners, or tossed giant bags of garbage over walls. Hugging their legs they watched cars go by while decorating the road with hundreds of runny little piles of poo. Sometimes they congregated in small groups to converse while communally crapping and watching us smash our oil pan on dilapidated chunks of highway.

On the third day, while approaching a small village on a rare but short stretch of pavement, we were captured on a police camera— certainly the only police camera in India—traveling at an excessively fast 48 kilometers-per-hour in a 40 zone. That's five miles per hour over the speed limit, for the metrically challenged. I was stopped, given an official ticket, and fined eight dollars for speeding on the only section of National Highway 7 where it is actually possible to speed. It was the first speeding ticket I had ever received in my life, which was ironic since I had never driven so many consecutive hours *under* the speed limit in my life. Just as we prepared to leave, a boy on a scooter put in a feeble attempt to escape after being told to stop. This enraged the officer, who took chase on foot. When the officer finally caught the assailant he very professionally punched him in the head.

In the evening we coincidentally caught up with David and Regina at a dirty roadside thatched hut where truckers sat on cots watching an absurdly loud television. We huddled on a cot and I leaned back against a wooden post, placing my head squarely in the middle of a gigantic spider lair tended by at least one, and probably more, giant squishy-butted arachnids. My flailing arms uncontrollably swiped the sticky spider net from my head and I looked up to see thousands—no, hundreds of thousands—of gargantuan plump spiders infesting the restaurant's thatched roof, only a couple of feet overhead. This prompted us to move outside into the dirt parking area to eat our gruel.

David and Regina had become similarly disheveled and overwhelmed by the roads and the mindlessness of the people who used them, and had likewise been driven to the use of profanity to express their thoughts.

"They call this a forking highway? This is India's forking National Highway forking system?! And did you see the dead motorcyclist?" We told him that we hadn't. "A couple of kilometers back, he was hit by a car and was just lying there dead in the middle of the road with a crowd of Indian men staring at him."

The next morning, against all conceivable odds, the road conditions worsened. What was once a bomb-blasted crater field had been reduced to a dirt track dotted with plateaus of sharp protruding tarmac, and at last into several bottomless ruts in the earth filled with deep, sludgy mud and rocks.

Within a couple of hours we reached a solid line of unmoving trucks. Our reconnaissance man, David, snapped into action and discovered that a six-foot-deep pit in the road had filled up with sludge after the previous night's rain, and had become an impassible, chest-deep pool. The trucks had no choice but to wait for it to dry out—yes, to wait for a swimming pool of mud to evaporate—before they could pass. Just a common nuisance, much like the ones faced daily on the primary national highways of the world's other leading economic superpowers.

I was just about to explain to Sheena how India could go fork itself, when I noticed David talking to a motorcycle rider. The rider offered to show us an alternate route, an offer that seemed dubious at best, but we had no other choice, so we followed him onto a seldom-used path leading into a rice paddy.

The rider wound us through a maze of mud paths for thirty minutes into the countryside and away from the highway. Finally he stopped, turned off his motorcycle, and sauntered over to David's window wearing a face that said, "Now you're really forked." It was swindling time. What the rider hadn't accounted for was the fact that we were happy to be swindled for his services, and he almost didn't know what to do with himself when David agreed to his first attempt at extortion of 200 Rupees ($3.25). We paid up and continued down the diminishing mud path, through several tiny villages whose residents had clearly never seen a modern motorcar, let alone milky-colored faces, and finally into a section that seemed impassible for its mud and overhanging electrical wires. Knowing that this was the only thing standing between us and freedom, we put on our Navy Seals face paint and rally hats, and a half hour later we reemerged on National Highway 7 to a flood of mixed emotions.

When evening rolled around, David and Regina called in early while we carried on into the night. We stopped and filled our gas tank to an audience of staring men, as usual, and minutes later as we bumped along the road one of them gave chase on his motorcycle in a death-defying pursuit next to my window for a good fifteen minutes trying to get me to stop so we could be Facebook friends. He gave up and we stopped to camp at a nasty petrol station at a crossroads of two nearly impassible rocky roads, one of which was National Highway 7.

The only place serving food a dark mosquito-infested cinderblock hut with stained walls and no electricity, so we accepted our fate of dengue fever and Delhi belly, and reluctantly ordered. When it was time to pay up, a boy brought us the bill, but when we tried to pay, the hut's owner decided that our white faces gave us a cheatability factor of 4.0, and the price was quadrupled. After a prolonged argument we paid his ridiculous price and tried to leave, but not before the socially retarded bastard requested that we pose with him for a Facebook photo. Later on while we slept, someone stole our bamboo mat, which had been half-eaten by a sacred cow at Santhanam's temple. Un-forking-real.

David and Regina passed us early on day four. It looked like Regina was crying in the passenger seat, but I'm quite sure she was simply having a nervous breakdown just like Sheena. A few hours later we were startled to see them bouncing back toward us over the rubble in the opposite direction. When they arrived, David rolled down his window. He was looking pretty rough.

"We came back to tell you that you probably won't make it."

"I will fight you, David. You can't make me go back." The thought of going back was more than my frail mind could handle; the closest detour was a full day in the opposite direction, and was a *secondary road*, whatever the hell that meant. I whimpered softly. This drive had killed my joy. I just wanted to go home. I wanted to sit in a cubicle, anonymously adding covers to TPS reports, for nine hours per day from there on out. Just minutes earlier I had been daydreaming about the thrill of loading Nacho onto a truck and sending him to the nearest port to get the hell out of there. I wanted to go to Afghanistan to be captured by al-Qaeda. Anything but this. And now David was standing there telling me to go back. "You can't make me!" My voice cracked.

"Well you can try, but we just tried it and almost didn't make it ourselves. The road just turns into a series of deep mud lakes." It was true that they had a 4x4 with enough clearance to drive over Nacho without high centering. But I was a desperate man.

"Turn that thing around. We're going for a swim."

The next two hours went by in a blur of desperate, adrenaline-fueled driving maneuvers through deep mud lakes, trenches, and free-falls into Nacho-sized craters. When things looked hopeless, I would think about being stuck in India and then let my survival response take over. We emerged through the whole 4x4 obstacle course by the skin of our teeth, pushing our powerful new engine to its limit and reshaping the road's high center with our oil pan.

With a quarter of the drive to Nepal still in front of us, it was time for a pit stop. When we arrived in Varanasi, we had become mental basketcases. My conversation skills had long since left me and had been replaced by Tourettic outbursts of profanity. Sheena's eyebrow-twitching had gotten out of control and she spent most of her time staring at her feet, whimpering. I scraped Nacho's side on a rickety old bus as we navigated into the city, but I didn't even flinch. I was gone.

36

The Mall Road, Varanasi

Sheena

Having reached a state that can best be described as "loss of will to live," Varanasi presented itself as a much needed intermission point; a place to stretch our legs, build back our endurance, and wash off the caked dirt plastered on our skin. We had made tentative plans to try to reconnect with David and Regina at a hotel in the city that they had picked out. We had lost contact with them early in the day, but given the state of the roads and their truck's higher clearance, we were pretty sure they would beat us there.

We threaded our way into the city during peak rush hour and soon realized that Varanasi wasn't going to let us into its heart quite so easily. It would have its pound of flesh. For the next two hours we went to battle with a few thousand other cars, taxis, rickshaws, and bicycles on a pitch dark and dusty street. Much of the road was flooded in a mysterious sludgy liquid, and all around us, despite the standstill traffic, a symphony of horns screamed like a million locusts in the night.

I rolled up my window and turned up the radio. Time crept slowly by and we crawled through the city at a glacial pace. At some point Brad looked in his rearview mirror and noticed a familiar vehicle. "You've got to be kidding me," he smiled. "David and Regina are right behind us. I guess they had a long day, too."

How on earth we ended up next to them on some random Varanasi surface street in a city of 1.1 million people was beyond me, but I found comfort in knowing there were two other crazy people undergoing the same punishment as we were. Misery does love company.

It turned out they had indeed arrived hours before us but their GPS had led them on a wild goose chase through the city, placing them squarely back where they had begun hours earlier.

"We've been driving around the city for two hours looking for this hotel!"

Together we slowly crept toward our destination. The hotel that we fought so desperately to find turned out to be a failure. The hotel tried to charge us the price of a rather costly room, even by Western standards, just to park in their parking lot. Regina and Brad put on their problem-solving hats and set off on foot down the street in search of a new location. David and I watched the vans, and as idle foreigners, we became a captive audience to a rickshaw driver who repeatedly listed the benefits of using him as our private Varanasi rickshaw driver.

"I am the fastest rickshaw driver in Varanasi! I am so fast, like a race car driver they call me."

David laughed, "If you are like a race car driver then I don't want to get anywhere near your rickshaw! I'd rather walk."

A half an hour later two silhouettes reappeared. Regina and Brad had found a place: the *Hotel de Paris*, a former British colonial palace turned chic hotel.

"We weren't even going to ask because the place looked too expensive," Regina exclaimed, "but they said it was no problem! We can camp out front in their big garden, and just rent one room for all of us to share so we can take showers."

Brad chimed in, "This hotel is something straight out of *The Shining*. No one is even staying there," he smiled.

"How are the rooms?" I asked.

"Oh just wait and see," Brad replied, cryptically.

We drove through the hotel's iron gates and circled around its beautifully manicured lawn, stopping alongside the hotel's veranda where we popped our roof tent and opened the sliding door. Our hotel room was surprisingly spacious, with the walls colored in a delicate layer of mold. The peeling carpet had been transformed into a damp and moldy sponge, from decades of dirt and moisture caked into its fibers. The last time this place was cleaned was clearly by British palace maids sometime in the 1940's.

Regina ventured into the bathroom to test the shower. She promptly stormed out of the room with a discouraged look on her face and returned with the hotel manager. "The shower doesn't even work!" she yelled in exasperation. She turned on the water and it trickled out

203

from the showerhead, one droplet at a time. The manager wanted to provide us a proper service so he unscrewed another showerhead from a neighboring room and replaced ours with a slightly less calcified one. With no shower curtain and no drain in the floor one shower was all it took to turn the entire bathroom into a sloshing pool of dirty water. But a miracle happened that night, and in just a few hours the pool of water had conveniently disappeared into the cracks of the hotel's foundation.

None of us was too bothered by our circumstances. In fact, we all felt like we were in paradise. We were clean, in a private gated area, and wouldn't have to return to National Highway 7 for at least two days. We gathered on the veranda wall next to our mobile housing units, drank a few beers, and slept away the nightmares from the previous days.

Varanasi shocked me, even after being in India for a month. It is one of the oldest, most continually inhabited cities in the world (and the oldest in India), and one of Hinduism's holiest pilgrimage sites. The city is especially important in Hindu mythology as the place where Lord Shiva stood when time began, and because of its location next to the Ganges, Hinduism's holiest river. Thousands of pilgrims arrive daily to bathe in the holy water of the Ganges, and scores of people make the pilgrimage to Varanasi every day to die. To the non-Hindu it may seem morose, but Hindus believe that dying in Varanasi and being cremated by the flames of the eternal fire allows one's soul to directly reach *nirvana,* and finally break free of the eternal cycle of birth and death.

In the morning we flagged down a rickshaw and headed to the *ghats,* which are large concrete terraces along the riverbanks. It turned out that we had arrived in Varanasi just a week after the waters had subsided from the city's worst flooding in ten years. The Ganges had risen for several days, and when it settled back down, the city's *ghats* were covered in a solid mountain of mud. The steep steps that rose up the riverbank were vital to everyday life – a public place where people bathed, washed their clothes, performed religious rituals, and burned their dead. It was also a major tourist destination, so without the *ghats,* many people cancelled their trips to Varanasi. The removal of the mud deposits would be a monstrous task, so cleanup crews decided that the best method of clearing the muck from the *ghats* was to spray it back into the water with giant hoses.

Despite the cleanup, the *ghats* were teeming with locals washing their clothes and pilgrims bathing in the water. At the top of the steps a group of Hindus were getting their heads shaved – a symbol of surrender and humility, and the first ritual performed when a pilgrim reaches their holy site.

We continued walking along the *ghats*. Boats full of pilgrims floated by, cows and goats rested on the steps, and fishermen stood in their idle boats. A naked boy herded his water buffalo out of the Ganges, and spiritual men walked to and from their temples. We approached one captivating man who let his shawl blow in the wind as he wandered down the waterfront. He didn't speak a word during our exchange, but a friendly local washing clothes nearby introduced us to him.

The back alleys of Varanasi's old town were just as interesting as the *ghats*. They were packed with people, both foreign and Indian tourists. Women scoured the sari shops looking at various prints and wandered in and out of specialty stores to buy bangles and stick-on *bindis* for their foreheads. The alleys were so narrow that small shops operated in cubbyholes cut in the walls. They were so small that the shopkeepers couldn't even stand inside. Instead, they climbed inside their cubbyholes and sat there for the remainder of the day.

Eventually we made it out to the main street where bicycle rickshaw drivers painstakingly pedaled their customers around. The heat and hard work of transporting customers this way seemed especially hard on the elderly drivers. The city was crazy, and its ceaseless activity made my head spin.

Most shocking to my western eyes was the spectacle of the Manikarnika *ghat*, better known as the "Burning *Ghat*," where the deceased are publically cremated. I felt a bit nervous about the whole thing, first because I had never seen a burning body before, and second because the ritual seemed so incredibly personal.

As we got closer to the burning *ghat*, the alley opened up into a warehouse of six-foot-tall stacked mounds of wood, and from around a corner a young child appeared to warn us, "No photos! No photos!" A man appeared and led us up a set of winding stairs to a so-called hospice that provided a viewing platform of the *ghat* below.

Beneath us the smoke billowed from ten smoldering funeral pyres, stinging our eyes. Dead bodies wrapped in red cloth were sandwiched between two layers of stacked wood and set ablaze. The fires were tended by Doms, the lowest caste in Hindu society, and the only sub-caste permitted to prepare the funeral pyre and dispose of the ashes and bone. The burning pyres were all at different stages: some were just smoldering piles of ash, while others still contained the human form. Several had been recently lit and the bodies were clearly visible as the red cloth quickly burned away and the body became slowly consumed by the fire.

We stood captivated. A man poked a charred hunk of abdomen with a stick to turn it over so that the fire could more thoroughly break it down. I turned away again and again as the wafts of smoke stung my eyes.

A hospice worker stood beside me. "For the people below, the smoke does not affect them. They've been doing this all their lives."

This ritual is only for men, first because females are considered weak, and may cry during the ceremony—which might prevent the soul from reaching *nirvana*—and also because in the past women would throw themselves into the fire to burn with their dead husbands.

The man next to me said that when a person dies, his or her body is wrapped in fabric and covered in flowers, and then carried on a wooden stretcher by the men of the family to the *ghat*. Once there, the body receives a holy bath in the Ganges and is then carried to the pyres to await an open cremation spot. Next, each family negotiates a price for the use of the eternal fire, which is said to have been burning non-stop for the last 2,500 years. During times of flooding, like the one that had just occurred, the fire is moved to higher ground. Once a family has negotiated a fee for the fire, they must procure the wood. Different types of wood cost different amounts, but a typical cost for the 300 kilograms of wood needed to burn a body is normally between $50 and $75.

Multiple cremations take place simultaneously at the Burning *Ghat*, twenty-four hours a day, 365 days a year. On average, three hundred bodies are burned there every day. The flow of pilgrims coming to Varanasi to die is relentless.

We watched as a family below approached an open pyre. The men placed their deceased family member over a pile of wood and then sprinkled the body in syrup of natural oils. Hindu custom dictates that the eldest son or the husband of the deceased is responsible for starting the fire, so from within the group an old frail man moved forward; it must have been his wife on the pyre. The men around him held him upright, and they passed a glowing torch, which his sons helped to secure in his hands. His duty was expected now. As he reached forward and touched the torch to the wood, his body became limp and he fell backward. He was caught in an instant, and within seconds was lifted like a feather off the ground and carried away.

Nearby a group of bald, white-robed men sat motionless on the top steps of the *ghats*. They were waiting for their loved ones' cremations to end, a process that can take up to six hours, depending on the person's size. In the end, all that would remain would be ash and either a pelvic bone for a female, or the ribs for a man – both of which are said to be too dense to burn completely to ash. From there the family would sprinkle the remaining bones and ash in the Ganges River, and the body would be washed away forever.

We stood motionless, still taking in what was going on down below. Men stood waist deep in the river amid the film of ash that floated on the river's surface. They made a living here, panning through the ashes at the bottom of the river in search of gold fillings and gems to sell. Alongside the men a group of water buffalo bathed, not seeming to mind the film of ash that surrounded them. They were just happy to be hidden from Varanasi's unrelenting sun.

In the evening we met up with David and Regina for a boat ride on the Ganges. Our rower had been born and bred in Varanasi, and therefore had a plethora of knowledge about the city's historical buildings and cultural ways. He rowed us up and down the shore where we saw the city from a different perspective. We revisited the burning *ghats* in the evening, and finally the Dashashwamedh *Ghat* where a nightly *Ganga Aarti* was commencing.

At the *Ganga Aarti*, hundreds of Hindu devotees and a spattering of tourists squeezed into a solid flotilla of boats bunched along the water's edge. On the steps of the *ghat* a few hundred more people encircled the ceremony that was taking place. In the center, a row of saffron-robed men performed a choreographed ritual, blowing their conch shells and waving their incense and flaming brass lamps in the air.

After a long and exhausting day, the four of us squeezed our bodies into the back of a rickshaw and headed back to the chic *Hotel de Paris*. On the way we noticed a group of men marching down the potholed road carrying a wooden stretcher. On top a body was wrapped in orange fabric. Sweat rolled down their foreheads but they didn't seem to notice. They were focused and determined to deliver their loved one to the Ganges.

37

Indian National Highway 7
to Nepal

Brad

Our time spent in Varanasi did do some good for our mental recovery. Just after leaving town, our horn's electrical contacts disintegrated and caused the steering wheel to seize up. Using nothing more than a Leatherman tool and a piece of bailing wire, I was able to reconstruct new and functional horn contacts, verifying that we were at least mentally aware, and that I still clung to my American roots. Bailing wire! 'Merica! Yee haw!

In the early afternoon we emerged from the dilapidated highway and into another featureless garbage heap of a town. We would have passed right through without incident if the villagers hadn't taken it upon themselves to build a 10-foot high brick wall right across the highway in the middle of town, which they had.

"What the fork is this? What the FORK?!"

"Fork! You have to be forking JOKING!" It was Sheena. She too had snapped and gone off the deep end. I was happy to know that I wasn't alone.

We consulted our GPS as people quickly packed themselves around Nacho to stare at us. The map seemed to show a possibility of getting around this demonstration of idiocy by taking a small track along a levy. We backtracked and found the trail; it was nothing more than a motorcycle path crisscrossed by deep channels where the levy had failed. After some time, we emerged down a steep drop-off into the middle of a small slum. The inhabitants of the slum stopped what they were doing and stared at us as we drove through their front yards and back to the so-called highway, and in doing so, we smashed our oil pan in a cataclysmic way. I got out to check it and realized that, in addition to smashing the hell out of our delicate oil pan, the impact had caused our three-inch-wide steel bumper support to sheer completely off, and now our bumper tilted backward at a thirty-degree angle. Calling once again on my American roots, I attached a ratchet strap to the bumper and secured it to the top of our rear door.

The road from there onward proved to be the worst section of the whole drive. We continued on through the wasteland at five to ten kilometers per hour—a walking pace—well into the night, desperate to get out of India. We repeatedly smashed our oil pan, but by now I had stopped checking it. Subconsciously I knew that a split oil pan would cause engine failure, which in turn would give us an excuse to quit and go home. India had broken us.

As we ascended a hill in the dark, we noticed that two semi trucks had driven off the side of the road and smashed into the forest. This seemed pretty normal, as Indian truckers couldn't keep their rigs on the road even if their lives depended on it. We'd seen at least fifty accidents since we had left Hampi. As we passed, however, we noticed that they'd taken someone with them. Underneath one of the semis was a motorcycle, and its rider was dead on the side of the road. That made three motorcycle casualties in five days.

Around midnight we found a petrol station where we would camp for the night. We were still ten kilometers from the Nepalese border: an eternity. I was covered in grime and desperate for a shower, so I squeezed myself under the nozzle of a rickety hand-pumped well in the corner of the parking lot and took a bath. Sometimes I would just look at myself and wonder, *how did it come to this?*

In the morning we set off at first light. Given that this road wasn't all that important to India—it was used only for frivolous things like international trade—it had been abandoned and overtaken by nature. We crept through craters and over enormous ridges for two hours to complete the scant ten kilometers.

We reached Raxaul, India's border town, and found our way to the customs office. We handed our *Carnet de Passages* and passports to the customs agent and watched him write out all of the information from our documents by hand, which took nearly two hours. He painstakingly inspected and reproduced the curvature of each individual letter. When he had finished, he carried all of the documents over to a decrepit photocopier and copied them, and then stapled them to the page he'd just finished reproducing by hand. I opened my mouth and almost allowed myself to bellow a string of profanities at this blatant waste of time, but thought better of it. After sixty-five solid hours of driving at an average speed of just twenty-two miles per hour, we were free.

As we prepared to leave, David and Regina arrived and walked excitedly into the office. We gathered our things and headed out the door, and just as it closed behind us I heard Regina's exasperated voice speaking to the customs man.

"Excuse me, but what is taking so long? This is a very simple task!" The corner of my mouth went up in an unfamiliar shape. For the first time in six days I was smiling.

We got in Nacho and headed North through no-man's land, lost in a swirl of dust. Motorcycles zipped in and out of our view, we bumped through deep potholes, and then we saw it. Through the dust an ornate arch appeared. It was beautiful. No, it was the most beautiful sight I'd ever seen. It was the entry to the Mountain Kingdom of Nepal.

When we crossed under the arch it was instantly quiet. No horns. No dust. No potholes. Nobody stared at us like we were in a zoo. A few people walked around smiling. *Smiling.* We parked and walked into the quaint customs house set back in a grove of gum trees. I couldn't be sure, but I could have sworn that the customs agent was wearing a white robe and glowing.

"Take a seat," he said calmly, putting down his book. "I hope you've had a good trip. Welcome to Nepal."

38

Tribhuvan Rajpath
to Kathmandu

Brad

Crossing India had been an exercise of endurance in pancake flat driving on the worst roads, with the worst drivers in the world. Upon reaching Nepal, the roads were suddenly maintained. Within a few miles of crossing the border, we began winding through foothills, and then climbing into the mountains. The terrain rapidly transitioned from low, hot plains to grassy valleys, to alpine meadows with crystal clear, meandering streams and evergreen forests. Sheena and I sat in the front seats swaying to the curves in the road, our faces cramping from the maniacal smiles plastered across our faces. Nepal was the country we had looked forward to the most when we left our driveway, and after two years of driving, we had finally made it.

"It feels like a ton of bricks has just been lifted from my chest!" Sheena exclaimed, and then made a joyous squeal. She followed it with another joyous squeal and I wondered if she would pass out.

It was the same for me, but without the joyous squeals. A sense of great pleasure and adventure had swept over us. Every jagged rock and towering tree was our best friend. Teddy bears danced in the tall grass beside the road, rainbows shot across the late afternoon sky, and a herd of unicorns sipped water from a crystal clear brook. I gave in and let out a joyous squeal of my own.

Within an hour we came to what we thought would be a shortcut to Kathmandu at a tiny crossroads, and pulled over. A police officer and a few people lingered at a bus stop, so I asked the officer about the road. He verified that it was in fact a shortcut to Kathmandu, although quite mountainous and too narrow to be used by large vehicles.

For lovers of the mountains, Nepal is heaven on Earth. In our home state of Arizona we could drive 130 miles from Phoenix to our home in Flagstaff, ascending the Mogollon Rim, which brought us from the southern deserts into the northern mountains – an elevation gain of about a vertical mile. Arizonans brag about the variety of climates that can be experienced in such a short distance as a result of the 5,000-foot elevation gain of the Mogollon Rim. In Nepal, over the same 130-mile distance, the elevation rises from 193 feet to 29,021 feet – a change of five and a half vertical miles. Nepal is quite literally the most extreme place in the world.

We took the shortcut, and before long the narrow road snaked its way onto a steep mountain spine and began spiraling into the sky. At the edge of each hairpin turn the road gave way to a sheer cliff. It was steep enough that our old engine wouldn't have been able to pull us up; the upgrade had justified our decision on the first day in the Himalayas. By the time we crossed the summit and began winding down the other side into the Kathmandu Valley, the sun had set and darkness had fallen. We picked our way along the steep, rocky one-lane road, a crumbling wall to our left, and a black abyss to our right.

When finally we emerged from the mountains and into Kathmandu, we found our way to Dhobighat, a colony on the southern end of the ring road. There aren't any residential addresses in most of Nepal, so it was impossible for us to know where we were going. Our good Nepalese friend Baroon, whom we had met back home in Flagstaff, had told us that his family would be happy to put us up when we got to Kathmandu. Thus, throughout the evening we attempted to navigate by cryptic directions delivered over the phone by Baroon's cousin, Pesal. When we got close, the all-knowing and ever-wise Pesal met us on the ring road, welcoming us with a smile and a wave. As we pulled over, he turned and led us into the maze of backstreets on foot until we arrived, finally, at his family's home. The Rai household, where Pesal lived, would be our home base in Nepal. Things were looking up.

Nepal's economy had never been strong, and in fact, it is one of the poorest countries in the world. The average worker in Nepal earned just $645 per year. Yet despite its troubles, Nepal felt rich by developing world standards. The roads were generally in decent shape, there wasn't garbage strewn everywhere, every village had toilet facilities, and most people had access to clean drinking water. Most of these things weren't even true of Nepal's richer neighbor to the south; even life expectancy was higher in Nepal. Of all of the developing countries we had visited,

Nepal's people were the happiest. And if you are happier than your neighbor, who really cares who has more money?

Nepal had endured a rough recent past, which made its widespread happiness seem even more commendable. In 2001, only a few months before 9/11, Nepal suffered its own horrible setback. Distraught over the King and Queen's disapproval of his choice of wife, the King's son stormed into a family barbecue and murdered the entire royal family, and then shot himself. This further weakened the struggling monarchy, and by 2008, after a long civil war against the violent Maoist rebels, the Nepalese Constituent Assembly formally dismantled the long-standing monarchy. What followed was a continuation of Maoist revolt and violence, a period that the people of Nepal are still attempting to put behind them. Upon our arrival, despite having signed a peace deal with the Maoists—Nepal's devious communist party—the country still hadn't agreed on a constitution and was still plagued by periodic Maoist assaults.

Over the course of our first week in Nepal, we got to know our new family: Bharat the patriarch, ever-inquisitive, reserved, and well-read; Durga, the sweet and always-smiling mother whom we came to call "Auntie Durga;" Uncle Laxman, inquisitive and always willing to join us for tea; Manika, the young and painfully shy girl from the family's village whom Bharat and Durga had taken upon themselves to educate and eventually send to nursing school; and Pesal, fresh out of the university and bound by his honor to be our trusty tour guide and confidant during our stay. The melding of our customs with those of our Nepali family was amusing, and gave Bharat endless entertainment.

In Nepal, people eat twice per day: at 10:00 in the morning and 8:00 in the evening. *Dal bhat* is served for nearly every meal, which consists of a generous helping of rice accompanied by lentils, dry vegetable curry, pickle, chutney, *papad*, and once per week, a meat curry. It should be noted that only tourists use silverware in Nepal, so we quickly adapted to the Nepali method of eating messy food properly with our hands. Bharat would occasionally stop by to harangue me about the intricacies of my food handling techniques.

"Brad," he would say, his stern face slowly panning between my plate and my hand. "What are you doing?"

"Um. I'm just eating the food, Bharat." There would be a moment of awkward silence, my gooey fingers suspended mid-air, dripping bits of *dal*-covered rice onto my jumbled pile of food.

"People will think you are very unconventional eating like this. You are eating like a savage."

"A savage? Well what do you suggest?"

At this he would describe the exact way in which a Nepali would eat, how only a little bit of each ingredient would be added to a corner of the rice, and then finely sculpted into a food pellet before being cleanly pushed off the fingers by the thumb into the mouth. Before long, I was garnering compliments and thumbs-up by old people at restaurants for having mastered "the Nepali system" of cutlery-free eating.

Knowing that Sheena and I are American, and thus accustomed to eating three meals per day, Pesal woke us up every day around 9:00—it should be noted that the recovery from our drive across India took a very long time—with a breakfast of eggs, bananas, and tea in bed. Breakfast was quickly followed by more tea, and then at 10:00 it was time for a lunch of all-you-can-eat *dal bhat*, consumed using our newly learned "Nepali system" eating method. The ensuing ten hours of foodlessness passed unnoticed on account of our morning gluttony, and in a short time we had weaned ourselves off of breakfast altogether.

In Nepal, "where guest is God," guests are customarily given the royal treatment. By convention, guests eat first and are waited on by the host, and only afterwards will the host eat. This meant that for the first few days, Sheena and I ate alone while someone from the family appeared periodically to add more food to our plates. We explained that, while we appreciated the gesture, we would very much like to eat with the family. As a compromise, Pesal ate his meals with us from then on. It was at this time that we discovered that Nepalis are much faster with their hands than we cumbersome Americans.

"Jesus H. Christ, Pesal. Are you already finished?" Our plates still contained 92% of their original ingredients as we painstakingly formed food pellets with our gooey fingers. Pesal sat patiently, his sleek hand poised on his empty plate like a freshly cleaned spider.

"Nepalis are fast eaters. I am the fastest of the fast," he said, matter-of-factly.

On occasion, Bharat would enter the kitchen to harangue me about my food handling skills and see Pesal already finished. "Pesal!" he would say, sternly.

"Yes, Uncle?"

"You should eat more slowly like these people." He would then look disapprovingly at my frighteningly mucky hands and slowly shake his head before leaving the room.

After a while, we taught Pesal some appropriate English terms to use when leaving the table while others are still eating, so that he wouldn't have to wait for us after his bouts of speed eating.

"You can take your sweet time," he would say, and then get up and leave us.

It would at first seem that eating the same thing for every meal would get old, but Durga is the best cook in Nepal, as verified by extensive field research, and each day she made variations to the side dishes. We couldn't get enough. We spent each day in a *dal bhat*-fueled happy trance, spritzed with a squirt of endorphins on account of the perfect weather and the fact that we had made it out of India alive.

We passed our days in Kathmandu eating copious amounts of *dal bhat*, drinking tea nine times per day, and visiting points of interest around the Kathmandu valley with our tireless tour guide. Pesal, always looking out for our best interest, was concerned about the legality of us driving Nacho in Nepal, as the law disallows older vehicles in an effort to curb emissions. We assured him that it was okay, but just to be safe we spent the first week exploring Kathmandu by public minibus. This proved to be what one might refer to as a "cultural experience," for better or worse. At one point I counted twenty-seven full-grown adults in our clapped-out minibus – a bus that, I will point out, was smaller than Nacho.

Bharat tracked me down every morning and afternoon, inviting me to the outdoor terrace to have talks. We sat on short wooden stools and waited for Pesal or Manika to bring us tea, and then we would stare at each other, sipping in silence. At first I felt self conscious in the silence, that perhaps he was disappointed that he hadn't been delivered a better conversationalist. He would tilt his head back and forth as if ruminating an idea, hold his breath as though her were about to speak, and then breathe again. After a while he would face me and pose the question that had been on his mind.

"So, Mr. Brad," He would say, tilting his head back and peering at me through squinting eyes. "What do you people think of the Maoists?" He used the term "you people" to refer both to Sheena and me, as well as to Americans in general. In the case of my people's view of the Maoists, I explained to him that most Americans couldn't find Nepal on a map, let alone hold an opinion about its subversive communists. Bharat hated the idea of communism, although it took a fair amount of coaxing to get him to tell me his ideas; he spoke very little, and always wanted me to do the talking.

"Bharat is always reading and thinking!" Pesal had said. I explained my thoughts on Marx and Mao, and Bharat told me that communism was the wrong answer for Nepal.

"Speaking of the Maoists," I said, "why is it that after all of the trouble they've caused, they still have so much support in Nepal?" Elections were approaching, and in the morning paper that Pesal had brought me with my hard-boiled eggs, I had read that the Maoist party still enjoyed widespread support in Nepal. He explained that the Maoists would go into remote areas where the poorest people lived, and where outside communication was limited, and promise them that under communism they could be as rich as everybody else. The very poor saw communism as a way of rising out of destitution, but given their isolation from the outside world, they weren't aware of its grand failures. Pesal later told me that Bharat had been a communist in his younger days, and had since become vehemently opposed to it.

Each morning and afternoon Bharat had a different question for me, and he would roll one question into another until I had no more information to deliver. When I asked questions of him, he gave short answers, or else ignored me altogether, and then asked me another question.

"Mr. Brad," he said one afternoon while we sipped tea on the terrace. "In what year did America give its women the right to vote?" I always tried to be as insightful as I could, but despite my best efforts I often felt as though my answers were something of a letdown. I took another sip of my tea.

"Hmm. Yes, of course, women's suffrage. Well I say, it was a very long time ago. Must have been, oh, the mid1800's? Yes, I would imagine it must have been around 1840. Don't quote me on that, but I believe it was, yes, 1840."

He leaned back and seemed to take mental notes as I spoke. His silence often caused me to ramble on until I tired myself out. He pulled one cheek back into a smile lowered his chin into his neck, creating a row of tight wrinkles on his throat, and then he spoke.

"1920."

"Excuse me?"

"You people gave your women the right to vote in 1920. It is the nineteenth amendment to your constitution."

Bharat must have thought I was such an idiot.

"Really? That seems terribly late," I said.

216

"In Nepal our women didn't vote until 1947, and in India 1949. Your women have many more rights than Nepali women." He paused and sipped his tea, and then tilted his head back and continued. "In America, men and women have equal rights?"

"Yes, they do."

"Your Hillary Clinton will be the first woman President, I think so."

"Possibly," I said.

"India had a woman president, but do you think women got more rights? Their position in society did not change. In India and Nepal, the women still do all of the work." He thought for a minute, and then let out a short giggle. He sounded like Yoda when he giggled.

"Look at me. I am retired, but Durga still works. I just sit around all day and I do nothing. But when Durga comes home from work, she is expected to cook me dinner. That is not right!"

The solution seemed obvious to me. "Well then why don't you just cook dinner while Durga is at work?"

He scrunched his brow and lowered his chin, and then laughed his Yoda laugh. "This is Nepal! What would my friends say?"

He said that it was too late for his generation, that young Nepalis would have to demand change, just as Americans had. He expected it would happen soon, since the new generation could see how it was in the West, and would want the same for themselves.

"The problem," he continued, "is that the Nepalis who would lead the movement just go away and live in other countries. It would take too much work to change Nepal, so they just go live in America or Europe instead." He shrugged his shoulders. "I told Pesal that he must stay here to take care of us, but he will probably go away, I think so. Our young people have a saying, have you heard it?" I said that I hadn't.

"They say 'American life, Japanese wife.'" He rolled his eyes, and then he scrunched his brow and explained that young people saw these as the ingredients to a perfect existence; Americans had the best lives, while Japanese women were the most loyal. If you could have an American life and a Japanese wife, you had it all.

Bharat had recently retired as principle of a public school, and so he was excited to bring us to his old school in Bhaktapur to give us a firsthand lesson in Nepali culture. We all loaded up in Nacho one day, Bharat, Pesal, Sheena and I, and made the trip to the neighboring town. On the way, while navigating traffic on Kathmandu's dusty, tumultuous ring road, a rogue public bus driver with questionable depth perception sideswiped Nacho's passenger-side mirror, and Pesal caught it in his hand from the passenger seat. I watched helplessly as the bus pulled away, and then turned to Pesal.

"American life, Japanese wife," I said, shaking my head.

"That is not the appropriate saying for this situation," he said.

The school sat atop the highest mountain in Bhaktapur, with a long view of the Kathmandu Valley. When we arrived, the new principal ushered us into the courtyard and we parked Nacho amid a throng of scurrying children in matching blue uniforms. Our arrival seemed to be much anticipated, and several of the staff ushered us into the principal's office for tea. Bharat had seemed nonchalant about bringing us to the school, but I could see that a lot of planning had gone on behind the scenes, and he had probably really hoped that we would come. We found this typical of Nepalis; they would go to great lengths to ensure our comfort or entertainment, but they would just as soon abandon all of their hard work if we felt like doing something else, and we never really knew if they had planned something until we showed up.

The staff—all women wearing matching baggy pink outfits—sat on a bench under the window and laughed as they caught up with Bharat, their former boss. They teased Pesal, who sat smilingly amongst them under the windowsill, interrupting the rays of light that descended to the carpeted floor. After tea, the teachers led us into the courtyard where Nacho was parked; a tent had been set up over a carpet to create a stage, and dozens of chairs were set up under a canopy facing it like bleachers. Students filled the chairs, and then someone turned on the music. Song after song blared at eardrum-splitting volume, while several students and some female teachers dressed in colorful outfits performed energetic traditional dances.

It was absolutely fantastic; the type of unusual experience that few visitors to Nepal are lucky enough to stumble into. By the end of the afternoon I had sacrificed Sheena to the vibrant throng of dancing teachers, and they brought her on stage to get down with the rest of the Nepali dancers. Sheena doesn't count dancing among her preferred pastimes, and therefore relies on a limited set of moves. In order to satisfy her obligation to dance, she repeated a motion of bending her knees, straightening them, and then pretending to knead bread with her hands while making fish lips. Bend-straighten-knead-fish lips-repeat. The people within her general vicinity promptly imitated her white girl dancing skills, probably assuming that they were "hip" and "up to date," and before we knew it, everybody had fish lips and was kneading bread while bouncing up and down at the knees. Right now in some bar in Kathmandu there is a new dance craze growing from the deranged seed planted by little dancing Sheena.

At the end of the day we all piled back into Nacho—with the addition of a few teachers who needed rides—and Nacho's Taxi Service coasted back down the hill to Kathmandu.

Around the end of our first week, we received an email from an acquaintance. He was a fellow writer from our home state, who had been in Nepal for over a month and had just found his way back to Kathmandu after having ridden around the Annapurna range on his mountain bike. He emailed us the name of a bar in the old kingdom of Patan and told us to meet him there. We set out with Pesal, our trusted guide, and using a combination of foot and taxi travel, found ourselves helplessly lost in the ancient back lanes of the old kingdom. Nearly an hour late and just about ready to hoof it back home, we accidentally stumbled into Mokshe Bar.

Hidden away from the disheveled ancient alleys that surrounded it, the bar was ambient and inviting, and a dozen shiny mountain bikes decorated its outdoor terrace. It was as if we had stepped into another dimension; it just happened that Commencal, a high-end European mountain bike manufacturer, was holding a new product launch there. The French owner of the bike company sat alone at a patio table while several outdoorsy-looking foreigners milled about. From within the bar I heard a voice.

"Brad! Sheena!" We turned to see Chris bounding toward us with the slight limp and the crazy eyes of someone who had just spent twelve days alone with his bike in the Himalayas. He spoke with a kind of permanent awe stamped on his face, as if he'd just seen God out there in the mountains. In many ways, he had.

"This experience has changed me, man. My life will never be the same." As we talked to him, he repeatedly came up short in trying to describe in words the kind of awe that he'd experienced out in the Himalayas. He talked disjointedly about aimless wandering, two-day climbs that terminated at impassible glaciers, and the resulting self-conversations of a crazed man with a bike in the middle of the world's highest mountains. His hair was messed up. "I've been thinking a lot about how I'm going to write about this," he said. "There's so much to say, but I don't want to come off sounding like a douchebag, you know? I mean, nobody will be able to relate to this, no matter how well I

219

describe it. It'll be a long-ass time before I can sit down and digest the last two weeks."

It was refreshing to hear this kind of speech after so much time away from home. We hadn't been around *our people* in a very long time, and we felt a twang of homesickness as he went on about bike riding, describing what was going on with our mutual friends back home, and using a crass-but-funny dialect that I only then realized is unique to certain pockets of people in the United States. But more than anything we felt a sense of aching excitement, because in a couple of short days we would be making our way west to stumble face-first into our own circumnavigation of the Annapurna range, only on foot instead of bike. For the first time since we had pondered it years before, the 150-mile trek didn't fill me with nervous dread, but rather with a feeling of warm anticipation.

39

Annapurna Trail
to Bragha

Sheena

Before we left home I had met exactly one person who had hiked in the Himalayas. That was Baroon, our dear friend whose family we were staying with in Kathmandu. I had been green with envy when he told me about his trek. Imagine! The person sitting in front of me had trekked the mountains at the top of the world, had walked around Annapurna, and had seen what I dreamed of one day seeing. Those talks had the sealed the deal. I would get there, somehow. My mind was even able to skip over the minor details, like the part about the trek around the Annapurna range being three weeks long.

When we were in India, the closer we inched toward Nepal, the more we talked about our trek. Brad had tried to be realistic and had made it clear that he thought we were incapable of finishing such a feat.

"Don't you remember what happened in Peru? We had to sleep in that guy's barn because you couldn't even walk anymore. That trek was only three days. Only three days!" he exclaimed. "You're talking about doing something that is three *weeks*!" He looked wide-eyed at me. "Do you really want to hike that long? I mean, *seriously?*"

I did remember Peru. I had cried outside of a guinea pig barn in the Andes Mountains, unable to motivate myself to take another step forward. The problem was that I had been wearing my running shoes and the weight of my pack had crushed my feet. I had reason to cry. I had been crying "uncle" for hours, but the steel pliers only gripped my feet tighter and the only way out was to sleep in someone's barn and beg a ride out of the mountains in the back of a rattletrap chicken truck.

I had learned lessons in Peru; first, that Brad would carry the food, and second, that I needed boots. With the Himalayas in mind, I bought my first pair of backpacking boots. But since buying them, I only wore them twice: first when I tried them on the store, and second on our ill-fated trek in the Thai jungle when bees and leeches attacked us.

We had desperately wanted to make it to the Himalayas, but even just a few months prior we had our doubts about whether we'd even make it to Nepal. In our minds, Nepal had been the most unattainable prize on our trip. The Kingdom in the Clouds on the direct opposite side of the globe from our home. Back home someone who had spent considerable time in Nepal told us that we would never make it, and that even if we did, we would never survive the rough roads or the rebels.

The Himalayas in a two-wheel-drive van? Please! But we had made it to Nepal after all, and that was reason enough to head out on the Annapurna circuit, one of the highest, most sought-after treks in the world. The Annapurna circuit is a 150-mile-long route that begins in the tropics and climbs nearly to the Death Zone, over one of the world's highest passes, and then spills out onto the Tibetan Plateau, all the while winding through the iconic peaks of mountaineering lore and traditional Buddhist villages on ancient salt trading routes.

It is possible to sleep in the stone huts that dot the ancient salt route, and mountain villagers serve up home-cooked meals from the wood ovens in their stone kitchens. If ever there was a trek where we didn't have to be fully self-supported, this was it.

On the morning of our departure, Auntie Durga blessed us by smearing *tikka* dots on our foreheads, and when we emerged from the house, we found that someone had given Nacho a good luck blessing for the trip ahead by placing a string of marigolds inside of our spare tire. We drove out of Kathmandu with smiles on our faces and the marigolds fluttering in the wind.

We arrived in the lakeside town of Pokhara in the afternoon, and followed a stony, potholed track around the side of the lake to a campground—the first campground we had found in Asia—and were surprised to find David and Regina there resting beside their truck. David was propped up on his elbow, basking in the sun on a longhaired fur rug on the grass His state of relaxation starkly contrasted with the state of stress and frustration that had become the norm in India. Gone were the days of Indian demolition derbies. Whereas our last shared camp had been outside of a dilapidated hotel in the middle of a human beehive, this camp was surrounded on all sides by paddies of tall golden rice stalks bowing to a soft mountain breeze.

We recovered at the camp amid the rice fields for a few days, relaxing and taking in the mountain scenery. The Pokhara Valley sits in a cleft in the Himalayas, its flat valley floor bisected by a lazy river that accumulates in the lake before continuing into the canyons below the town. Our camp was a couple of miles upstream of the lake, where rice fields filled the valley from one side to the other, beyond which the mountains shot skyward. We dropped our paddleboard into the clear river and used it to paddle up and down the valley, waving to fishermen and villagers harvesting rice. Each day we walked to the village of Pame Bazar and bought eggs and vegetables from the small shops. Brad would walk to a nearby hut and hand our milk bottle to a small boy, and then practice speaking Nepali with the other children until the boy returned with the bottle full of milk from the family's cow.

On the morning of our departure for the trek, we stuffed our packs with a four-season tent, sleeping bags, pads, cookware, a stove, lanterns, clothing, and food. Brad stubbornly insisted that, despite provisions and shelter being available from the small villages along the way, he wanted to maintain self-sufficiency.

"We don't need guesthouses. And besides, I like camping. And why did we buy this tent if we're not going to use it?"

"Yes, but remember Peru? Why make it harder than it has to be?"

"How about this," he said confidently, "I'll carry all of the camping gear. Your pack won't even be affected."

"Wait," I said, "if you carry all of the camping gear, doesn't that mean that I have to carry everything else? Isn't that twice as much as I would have carried otherwise?" He was sneaky. We went back and forth until I reluctantly agreed. He had succeeded in tricking me.

Before long, we heard the local minibus bouncing down the dirt road through the rice fields. It was invisible in the high grass, but it made its presence known by honking as it approached the stop for Pame Bazar. Brad threw the rest of the things in our bags while I stuffed the remaining contents of our fruit bowl into my boots, tied the laces together, and threw my pack over my shoulder. We took off toward the road at a trot, and I instantly snapped out of my brainwashed stupor, and I realized then that I had been tricked. My bulging pack felt like a sack of bricks. A sack of bricks I would have to transport all the way to 17,000 feet. A sack of bricks I would have to carry for three weeks!

We sat on a makeshift seat at the front of the creaking, overloaded bus for seven hours next to the driver, our feet resting atop a sack of grain, and several other sacks packed around us. Our fellow passengers were mostly mountain dwellers who had relocated to Kathmandu for work, and were headed back to their mountain villages for the upcoming holidays of *Dashain* and *Tihar*. Many would take the bus to a point, and then walk for several days to reach their remote homes. *Dashain* features heavily in animal sacrifice, and many of the riders brought goats home with them for the occasion. The goats were placed on the roof where they teetered and stumbled as we wound our way into the mountains, or in the cargo hold below the bus where they could occasionally be heard voicing their disapproval.

We, on our grain-sack-seat with a view, were the lucky ones. Half of the bus riders stood tightly packed together in the aisle, never resting over the course of the seven-hour trip. The bus driver did his best to make the drive go by faster by speeding as fast as possible around the mountain curves. He came upon an antique tractor pulling a wagon and attempted to pass it, which the tractor driver interpreted as a challenge to race. I must say I have never seen a tractor move so fast. It rocketed in and out of ditches and ruts, head to head with our bus, like a bat out of hell. Our bus driver rocketed through the same ditches and ruts, sending dust and rocks into the air. The passengers seemed nervous, but nowhere as nervous as the goats riding on the roof.

We started the Annapurna trek from the village of Bhulebhule at midday. I already felt exhausted from the bus ride and wanted to lie down on the road and take a nap, but it felt great to walk. We followed a rough dirt road alongside a crashing river for much of the day, until a trail formed, leading us through green, terraced rice fields and rustic stone villages. In front of the village huts, platters of beans, peppers, and corn dried in the sun. We made it to our first guesthouse thoroughly tired. The sun had already set and we didn't feel like setting up camp.

From my journal:

What can I say...day one kicked our butts. If ever I questioned whether I was out of shape, today confirmed it. Brad has worse problems because his fancy boots are rubbing holes right through his heels. By the end of the hike he had moleskin wrapped around his heels and every toe. At this rate we'll be out of moleskin in three days.

Brad would speak no libel of his boots. "What do you expect?" he said, "I've been wearing sandals for a year. My feet are like dough balls."

On our second day, a group of Sherpas passed us. The Sherpa porters have been carrying cargo in the Himalayas for centuries:

deliveries of food and goods for the villages inaccessible by road, and packs for trekkers who either brought too much, or preferred not to carry their own loads. A typical Sherpa can carry his own body weight in cargo for days on end in an oversized basket called a *doko*. These baskets rest against their backs and are secured with a strap that runs across the forehead, forcing the porter to lean forward and look down at the ground all day.

In the afternoon we passed a group of American and Israeli hippies, including an American girl with long, matted blond hair and a hula-hoop strapped to her bag. When we passed them they were standing in a field of ragged, well-picked-over marijuana plants, frantically attempting to fill the white plastic bags that they held in their hands, as though someone were going to come along and take all of the pot before they could pick it.

Brad's heel blisters worsened throughout the day, and he limped around like a lame dog. We made slow progress and stopped along a dry riverbed to set up camp. We had just finished staking our tent to the ground when a man from a nearby village approached and pointed to the cliff above us. We stared back and watched him play a game of charades in which he milked the air with his hands, then squatted down and covered his head with his arms. It seemed we had set up camp under a rock fall. We thanked him for potentially saving our lives, and moved our tent twenty feet outward. Sure enough, in the middle of the night we heard the meteoric *thwump* of a rock that had fallen from the cliff, landing right where we had originally placed our tent.

On the third day we ascended into a pine forest and saw our first big mountains. It was the first day of *Dashain*, Nepal's longest and most important holiday. Pesal had described it as a time when all Nepalis try to reach home to visit their families, and celebrate with large meals involving goat meat.

In the late morning we passed through a village, and happened upon a group of men butchering ten of the village's goats for the holiday. It was a rural production line; a few of the men chopped up the lower half of a goat on a wooden stump while others sorted the butchered pieces into organ and meat piles. The last man distributed the finished goods evenly among thirty-four bloody piles laid out on a blue tarp, each one to be given to a village family.

We started to gain elevation, and in the evening the cold air pressed down between the mountains. We huddled together with a Nepali family in their kitchen as they prepared our evening meal. It was a classic Nepali kitchen with a clay wood-burning stove and a wall of narrow shelves lined with cups, plates, and bowls. We drank chai and watched our hosts work through the meals that had been requested for the night. Everything was made from scratch and tonight I scored free cooking lessons. The wife sat on the ground at my feet and made dough and filling for a few orders of *momo*, one of Nepal's classic dishes of steamed dumplings stuffed with vegetables, chicken, or buffalo meat.

The next day we both limped like lame dogs. My new boots were still breaking in, and I looked just as pathetic as Brad. In a small village called Chame, we unlaced our boots and ordered lunch: a cup of local apple liquor and a heaping plateful of pan-fried potatoes, spinach, and egg. A suspended footbridge crossed the river at Chame, its cables covered in a rainbow of prayer flags that stretched in every direction. For Buddhists, prayer flags send good fortune to the world, carried by the wind. Each flag's color represents a different element: blue for the sky, white for the air, red for fire, green for water, and yellow for earth. Together they symbolize harmony, and as the old flags become tattered, they are overlapped with new flags, signifying a renewal of the cycle of life and the acceptance of change.

After lunch we begrudgingly laced up our boots and continued down the trail, which acted as a narrow barrier between the steep canyon wall and a raging river. An enormous 5,000-foot rock wall grew before us, known by the locals as *Swarga Dwari*, or Gateway to Heaven, which swept skyward like a colossal tidal wave. After passing the wall, we entered a shaded pine forest, and finally arrived at our next guesthouse in a village that looked like it had been transported straight out of frontier Alaska. The views of the mountains were once again inspirational, but I wanted to curl up into a ball and cry. My feet were in a sorry state, and the blood blisters on my little toes were so large it looked like my toenails were resting atop red pillows.

The following day things got really spectacular. We emerged from the pine forest and quickly gained elevation until we arrived in the village of Upper Pisang, which clung precariously to a steep mountainside, and whose inhabitants were nowhere to be seen. This marked the beginning of Nyesyand, a region in the rainshadow of the Annapurna range, causing it to be dry and barren and dotted with low, scraggly trees, much like southern Utah. We continued on, traversing a bare mountainside until we appeared in front of a stone wall inlayed with prayer wheels at the base of a cliff. We had the impression that we were in the middle of nowhere, but we had learned that prayer wheels were always placed just outside of villages. This was strange. I looked straight up and saw, to my dismay, prayer flags blowing in the wind far, far above us. And thus, we began our ascent.

Brad's heels were finally beginning to recuperate, and he trudged up the switchbacks as if on a Saturday afternoon stroll. At 11,000 feet, I was feeling the elevation and my legs burned with lactic acid. I felt irritated that I was struggling, and knew that the only way I would feel better would be if I emerged at the top before Brad did. At the edge of a switchback I noticed a faint trail that seemed like it must be a shortcut, so I called out and nonchalantly told Brad I was going take it.

He looked back, nodded, and continued up the trail.

I grabbed a shrub and pulled myself upward. This wasn't going to be easy. I moved in a slapdash pattern and followed any tree branch, bush, or rock that was available to assist me in my upward climb. What I failed to realize was that the landscape was slowly leading me away from the switchbacks. I only realized this ten minutes later during a brief pause to examine my next move, which led to me falling into a state of hyperventilating panic.

By the time my shaky legs rejoined the trail, I had lost track of Brad, unsure if he was above or below me. I shouted his name like a crazed person but he didn't respond. Finally I began climbing.

Ten minutes later I found him sitting on a rock ledge basking in the sun. He was smiling, "Did you get lost again?"

When we reached the top we were positively fried. We had reached Ghyara, a typical Tibetan village where the flat roof of each home provided a deck for the house above it; so steep was the mountainside on which it was built. We chose a guesthouse composed of stacked rocks, and splurged on the "big room with mountain view" for three dollars. Anywhere else in the world, this room, with its perfectly framed views of Annapurna II, III, and IV, would have cost a month's budget. But out in the Himalayas, where a family may survive on a hundred dollars in a year, we found the rooms to be only a couple of dollars, or even free if we ate dinner there.

What had once been one big room was now divided by thin plywood into three smaller rooms, ours being the biggest, and having inherited the floor-to-ceiling windows from which we could gaze upward at a wall of 25,000-foot peaks. A German couple and their Nepali friend Melina, with whom we had crossed paths several times over the preceding days, occupied one of the other rooms.

As I left our room to go downstairs to the kitchen, a new female face appeared from the other room. At first glance I thought she was naked, but then realized she was wearing skin-tone thermal tights. We said our hellos, and then I descended the rickety stairs. On the way down I passed a cheery-looking guy.

"Hey be careful," he said. "Someone could do some serious damage on these stairs!" He smiled. The two of them reminded me instantly of our old neighbors, in Flagstaff.

"Hey, where are you from?" I asked.

"Portland."

Of course. That's where our neighbors had been from.

"Sweet! My husband and I might move there when we get back home!"

"Oh really? When?"

"I don't know, maybe in a year and a half." He stared at me inquisitively.

We spent the evening exchanging stories over a thermos of masala tea. Jake and Kendra were on their honeymoon, and he had recently finished nursing school. Being that they were Pacific Northwesterners, they had foregone the tropics and honeymooned in the world's highest mountains.

The morning air inside our big room with a view was so crisp that I donned my trekking clothes over top of my pajamas. We set off to the west, passing high fields of barley and buckwheat, and saw our first herd of yaks – the long-furred, cow-like beast that doesn't simply moo, but rather emits a shrieking yell that echoes through the icy mountains. We wound through patches of juniper and quaint stone villages where women squatted, slapping yak turds into cakes and sticking them to the rock walls to dry. Hand-painted signs advertised yak yogurt, yak milk, and apple pie. We passed dirt ridges that had eroded into combs, their dry fingers splaying out at their bases to meld with the cracked ground on which we walked. By evening the trail emerged from its canyon, and continued on into a narrow valley. Within this valley sat the small village of Bragha, elevation 11,500 feet, and beyond it a theater of mountains made a megalithic backdrop. Bragha was one of two villages where it was recommended that trekkers acclimatize for a day before continuing up to Thorong La pass, and I was relieved to finally have a rest day.

In the middle of the night I was awoken by the sound of rain, and it wouldn't stop for two straight days. The next morning we cheerfully hunkered down in our guesthouse's cozy dining hall, bundled up in all of our warmest gear, pleased with ourselves for planning our rest day to coincide with bad weather. Outside, a string of trekkers trudged on, shivering from the cold and soaked to the bone.

By late afternoon, every guesthouse in the vicinity was turning trekkers away. The change in weather had put a halt to people crossing the pass, disrupting the fine balance between trekkers arriving and departing from the lodges. Porters were being pushed out of rooms and moved into tents, or else forced to sleep in the dining rooms after all the trekkers had gone to bed. And then we heard the weather report. Three feet of snow had already fallen on the high pass, and the storm was likely to continue for three more days.

40

Annapurna Trail to Ghorepani

Brad

The rain fell in Bragha for the second day and snow continued to accumulate on the pass. Information was scarce. We awaited word from the pass, but nobody had been able to get close enough to send a report. Rumors had spread that the snow was waist-deep, and that there was no end in sight. The situation had become grim; a trekker had died on the pass a week before, and the present storm had only served to drive the point that these mountains were the real deal. Our original plan had been to make a three-day diversion to Tilicho Lake, the highest lake in the world at over 16,000 feet. The mountain shelf, on which Tilicho sits just below Thorong La pass, was visible from the dining room of our lodge, and it was cloaked in white. Word soon trickled down that the trail had been closed due to avalanche danger, and the thunderous sounds of heavy slides rumbled down from the pass like the wicked gongs of a grandfather clock.

It was Kendra's turn to deal. Hearts again. I had gotten good at Hearts and Gin Rummy over the past days, and by then our new Portland friends had come to consider me a young Ted Kazyczynski when it came to card playing; cute and cuddly on the outside, but merciless and unpredictable under the hood.

"I've always liked Portland." I said. "The people are weird." Everybody nodded in agreement, studying their cards. I had been dealt a fearsome hand, and had to keep talking to keep myself from laughing out loud at how much I was about to slaughter everybody.

"But I must say, the last time I was in Portland the hipster thing kind of got on my nerves. I ordered coffee from an androgynous girl so indifferent to my existence that she almost fell asleep behind those big ugly glasses." I made a face and pretended to second-guess my hand so as to cultivate a false sense of security in my opponents. "The man who served me the coffee was dressed like a leprechaun. When that happened, I thought, well okay now, this has gone too far."

"The hipsters, they're an alien race," Kendra agreed. The rainy afternoon dragged on while we consumed thermos after thermos of milk tea. As it turned out, my good luck streak had been but a fluke, and by late afternoon my Ted Kaczynski façade had all but crumbled. I couldn't concentrate. It may have been mild carbon monoxide poisoning from the wood fire. Jake and Kendra entertained us with stories of Portland life.

"There's definitely a learning curve for new people who move to Portland. Take, for example, mushroom hunting. We take our wild mushroom hunting very seriously. Now, a while ago a new guy moved to town and asked me where my mushroom hunting spot was. Everyone just looked at him, and I was like, 'what the fuck did you just ask me?'"

Soon the other people in the room began exhibiting signs of stir craziness from being cooped up indoors. At around four in the afternoon, we witnessed the very instant when a whole group of young adults went insane. One minute they were performing card tricks and telling tales of one-upmanship, and then suddenly silence befell the group. They wordlessly huddled around one young man with an iPhone, and with the seriousness of the Dead Poets' Society, the man began reading Snow White from a file on his phone. It was terrifying. He read the whole fairy tale aloud to his friends over the course of forty-five minutes, while the rest of us shifted in our chairs and wondered just what in the hell was going on. I'm not going pretend that it couldn't have been carbon monoxide poisoning, seeing as how my ability to dominate at Hearts never did return.

"We have to get out of here," Sheena said, a hint of fear in her voice.

"Agreed. Here's what we do." Jake began. "Brad, you and I will hike to Manang on a supply mission tomorrow. We'll need more cold weather gear. The next morning we'll set out for the pass. When the snow gets deep we can take turns breaking trail." We all nodded gravely. It was a suicide mission.

That night brought a cold and fitful sleep, interrupted by bouts of wind and pelting rain on the roof. At 11,300 feet it had become difficult to fall asleep. In the morning we ate an inventive breakfast that the Nepali cooks had concocted using the meager ingredients available at these altitudes. It seemed to be some kind of pancake made of tubers.

Jake and Kendra moaned with ecstasy as they ate their tubers, and it occurred to me that alternative pancakes were probably very Portlandesque indeed.

At first light, Jake and I set off in the rain toward Manang, the district capital. The term "district capital" gives a false grandeur to the place; there are no roads leading there, meaning that supplies have to be walked for several days along a trail to reach its 1,300 inhabitants. In fact, it looked more like a collection of Indian ruins from the American West than a district capital, but for it to be any other way would be a shame. Its rugged remoteness, like that of many of the other villages along the route, made it seem as if we were arriving at some far-flung outpost in the distant past. I quizzed Jake some more about Portland as we walked, partly because Sheena and I had been considering moving there when we returned home, but mostly because the truth about Portland is far more entertaining than any other topic I could imagine.

"Sure, Portland has a huge cycling culture, but would you believe I've been run over by cars three times while riding my bike? But all that time spent in the ER is really what made me want to become a male nurse."

We reached Manang and set off on a scavenger hunt. Although Manang looks very much like an inhabited prehistoric ruin, the influx of trekkers has given rise to a great number of shops selling knock-off trekking gear.

"All right, we're going to need some ponchos and some gaiters," Jake said as we reached the first shop.

"Gaiters? Jesus." This was serious.

"It's a necessary evil, man."

"I know, I know, it's just hard to believe it's come to this."

We entered the first shop, but they had sold out of everything useful. The second and third shops, too. Things weren't looking good. The storm had caused everyone to sell out. Pretty soon we found four sets of gaiters, but it was worse than I had ever imagined.

"Excuse me, sir, but do you have any gaiters that aren't neon?"

"Gaiter. One size fit all! Also have batteries. Chocolate bar?"

"We'll take them. Better throw in these neon gloves too." If we were going to get over the pass, we were going to look completely idiotic doing it.

"Look at the bright side," Jake said. "If we go down in an avalanche it'll be easy for rescuers to find us." He had a valid point.

We raced from shop to shop looking for rain ponchos to drape over our bodies and packs, but everybody had sold out that very morning. One shop had a few left, but they were sized for children, so we continued on. When we reached the very last shop they had two ponchos left—exactly what we needed! But to our dismay, an older European couple was trying them on as we entered. We squeezed around them to speak to the shop owner.

"Excuse me, but are there any more of those?"

"Sorry, these are last two."

We backed into the corner of the store and gave the shop owner the eyebrow furrow and steely gaze that meant, *I will pay you anything you want for those ponchos*. He nodded in acknowledgement and waited for the two to make their decision. I wondered if it was bad form to start a bidding war, but decided against it. Our breathing became heavy and we tried to will the couple to put down the ponchos.

Put down the ponchos ... put down the ponchos ...

"We'll take them," the woman said. We cursed and hurried to the door, and then ran as fast as we could back to the first store that had the children's ponchos and bought two.

When we arrived back in Bragha the sun had nearly set, and the ladies were at first very excited to see us. Their joy waned as we began unpacking our bounty, and then evaporated altogether when they held up their new neon gaiters.

"You'll be easily identifiable in an avalanche," we assured them, as if this would make it more palatable. They reluctantly nodded in agreement.

The trail from Bragha passes through Manang and then climbs steadily upward toward Thorong La pass. We planned to make the approach in three stages. First we would climb to the village of Yak Kharka (literally "Yak Corral," and consisting of little else) at 13,235 feet. The next day we would climb to the lonely high-mountain outpost of Thorong Phedi, perched on the side of the steep chute below the pass at an elevation of 14,500 feet. From there we would make our attempt at the pass the following day. But there was a problem: with the pass covered in snow, we didn't know if there would be any space at the lodges. No trekkers had come from the other direction in days, so we hadn't heard anything of the conditions up the canyon. If the pass was indeed closed, then the high camps would surely be full and we'd have to retreat. Our plan was to start early and try to be among the first to arrive at Yak Kharka to snatch up a room – if there was one.

We walked though the valley and up the ridge at its far end to Manang, where the incessant rains had caused parts of the village to collapse, blocking the trail. We wound through the debris and past some small landslides, leaving the village behind and making our way into the cold, wet canyon toward Thorong La Pass.

The trail was steep, and we weren't making good time. Several other parties had the same idea about getting to Yak Kharka early. Knowing that it was nothing more than a small collection of stone huts with very limited space, we had to formulate a plan.

"I think we should send someone up the trail to secure a room," Kendra suggested. We looked around our group. Sheena and I had the heaviest packs and were both recovering from debilitating heel blisters. Kendra smiled sweetly and looked around the group, her red cheeks showing off their dimples. That would never do. We needed someone cutthroat who would be willing to scratch someone's eyes out if push came to shove. Then there was Jake.

"I say we send Jake. He has trekking poles, so he'll be the fastest." I silently noted that these trekking poles could be used as weapons. Jake agreed and quickly set off in hasty pursuit of Yak Kharka. We watched him disappear around a bend, a two-legged man made fast and four-legged by his trusty trekking sticks. The brave Portlander. Our Great White Hope.

The trek to Yak Kharka was only a couple of hours, and when we arrived, Jake was sitting on a rock wall looking happy.

"I got us two rooms!" We cheered and I glanced at his trekking poles for any sign of a struggle, but saw no indication. After checking into our rooms, the Nepali man who ran the place announced that the all of the rooms had just filled up. It was 10:30 in the morning. From our warm perch in the dining area we watched exhausted, frozen trekkers being turned away and sent back into the freezing rain. I had no idea where they went.

We spent the evening bundled up, alternating between reading and playing Hearts, and listening to anecdotes about Portland life.

"...It all started when I offered to help my buddy build a teepee on his property, and we had to find some small trees to use as poles..."

We hit the trail early for the second day in a row, walking out of camp just as the sky began to shed its blackness. I don't think I need to mention just how cold it was in the wee hours of the morning at 14,000 feet, but I will anyway. The nippy wind swept down the canyon like a frozen waterfall, and my icy nipples stabbed at my jacket like twin laser beams.

The trail left Yak Kharka and followed a narrow glacial cut in the mountains toward an amphitheater of cliff bands. Below us a ribbon of teal water snaked its way downward, carrying glacial flour to the valleys below. I scanned the mountains and ridges trying to pick out the pass, but couldn't discern a clear path anywhere. It must be a pretty steep approach, I thought. We traversed the river on suspension bridges, crossed a landslide, and then finally, around midday, caught sight of Thorong Phedi perched below a cliff band.

Thorong Phedi would not exist if not for need of a staging area before the pass. It consisted of several rows of rock barracks where trekkers could put in one final night of acclimation before attempting the pass. About two trekkers die each year crossing the pass, mostly due to pulmonary or cerebral edema. The man who had died the previous week had experienced the onset of cerebral edema, sort of a flooding of the brain, and his porters had put him on a mule in an attempt to cross the pass more quickly. But he had perished before they reached the top. Climbing too fast was ill advised, and we'd already climbed a lot for one day. We had left early in hopes of finding beds; failure to do so would have meant climbing on to High Camp at an elevation of 15,700 feet.

The good news was that the snow had inexplicably failed to materialize. The weather had been very cold and we'd had bouts of rain, but there was no accumulation at Thorong Phedi. The rumors had been exaggerated. We played Hearts and Jake told us more about Portland.

"...It's next to impossible to get paint to stick to a bamboo bicycle frame. They are very strong though. I've only broken one, and that was because I got hit by a car..."

Before long it began to snow, and as we ate our dinner, it started to accumulate. The dicey situation had been upgraded to perilous. The ladies looked admiringly at Jake and me for having secured gaiters and ponchos for everyone. It was time to mentally prepare for crossing Thorong La in waist-deep powder after all.

People seem to approach the crossing of Thorong La much in the way that they would approach the summit of Mount Everest. The 3,300-foot ascent from Thorong Phedi to the top of the pass takes just over three hours. From there it's a 5,600-foot, four-hour descent to Muktinath, where plenty of warm beds await. But for some reason, people get all Ed Viesturs about it, and set out for the pass at 3:00 in the morning. And so it came to be that we were awoken from our restless

235

sleep at 2:30 in the damned morning by testosterone-fuelled, self-motivational yells and whoops in various languages.

"Ja! Ich bin ready! Ich go auf der pass!"

"Schmeinden bounden goegenhiking!"

"Yar bruh! Shriggity shred muh fuh!"

By the time we deliriously rolled out of bed and met Jake and Kendra for breakfast at 6:00, all two hundred of our fellow trekkers had long since departed. We shared the dining room with one solitary rotund Russian man.

"So, how about these other jokers leaving at three in the morning, eh?"

"Yis. Zey leef veddy uhly." He was bundled up in what appeared to be nine layers of ill-fitting clothing, giving him the appearance of a sausage link. He waited nervously by the front door while we ate.

"Well, if there is waist deep snow up there, at least there'll be lots of people out in front of us to pack it down." Kendra looked relieved that she wouldn't have to wear her neon gaiters.

We paid our meager bill and hoisted our packs onto our shoulders, and as we did, a porter came to retrieve the Russian man. They walked out the door in front of us and made their way over to a miniature donkey.

"Oh please, don't tell me—" I knew what was coming. The porter intertwined his fingers to make a stirrup and the roly-poly Russian man thrust himself onto the poor, tiny animal. It was a horrible sight. The Russian man tilted uncomfortably to one side, hunched over with his knees bent, clearly struggling not to topple off the tiny saddle. He certainly weighed more than the donkey, and the little animal, led by the porter, struggled with each step to walk up the impossibly steep incline.

We breathed a gulp of thin, freezing air, buckled our straps, and began trudging up the pass.

The trail started off in a long set of switchbacks up the steep wall of a glacial amphitheater. A thin layer of snow had survived the night, and it became steadily thicker as we climbed. We trudged on slowly, breathing heavily. When we reached the top of the amphitheater, the pitch eased and the trail wound its way through a frozen moonscape of interwoven rocky gullies. The ground became frozen and slick, and it was hard to keep our footing.

As we crept slowly along an off-camber section of trail, the porter in front of me slipped and dropped his enormous basket of packs, pots, and pans. I hurried over to help him and noticed that he was wearing tennis shoes. I bent down to help him hoist his load onto a boulder, and the effort of doing so nearly caused me to pass out. These boys were tough.

When we passed High Camp we could see the places on the bare ground where several tents had been erected overnight, and I was reminded that things could have been much worse. As we made our way toward the pass, crossing one false summit after another, we overtook some of the early risers who could have perhaps benefited from more sleep.

The earth around us was black and white in the absence of any living matter. At around 9:00, thinking that we were approaching another false summit, the earth sloped away in front of us and we realized that we had made it. I checked my watch and found that we were at nearly 18,000 feet. The clouds parted as they raced past the summits of the peaks surrounding the pass. An imposing summit stood to our left, while a massive red cliff jutted out to the right—once a part of the Tibetan Plateau, far below us. The clouds shifted and we could see down the valley to the dry desert ridges and rocks that made up the edge of the Tibetan Plateau, a place I never imagined I would see with my own eyes.

It was otherworldly; one of the most amazing places I had ever stood, not only because of what I could see, but also because of where I was, and what I had been through to get there. It was freezing, but my face felt hot.

We dropped our packs and walked weightlessly around the pass for fifteen minutes. Several other trekkers congregated there, ducking in and out of a rock hut for shelter from the wind. After the obligatory photographs, we again donned our packs and began the long slog down the other side.

The far side of the pass was another world altogether. Within a few hundred feet we had dropped below the snow line; we were now in the rainshadow of the Himalayas. The land ahead of us was parched and rocky all the way to Tibet, which spread out far below us. Nepal's northern border is defined by the edge of the Himalayan range, but we were now in the one small appendage of the country that lies beyond the Himalayas. Straight ahead was the former Kingdom of Lo, now a part of the restricted Mustang district, and beyond it the Chinese border.

We descended for hours, testing our knees as the trail wound down narrow ridges and through valleys in endless squiggles and switchbacks. By lunchtime we reached the first settlements and stopped at a yak corral for a bite to eat. We ate with Jake and Kendra, a guy named Stuss (who had by strange coincidence gone to school in my hometown and long ago worked with Kendra), and Lowell from California, who had made his own gaiters out of a grain sack and some string—a man who would have benefited our team about three days earlier back in Manang. We ate gluttonously, for we had earned it, and when we were done we donned our packs and strolled the final mile to Muktinath, the ancient Buddhist pilgrimage site. As we navigated through shrubs and boulders, our bellies full of Tibetan macaroni and cheese, I could hear Jake's voice.

"Yes, wild mushroom hunting can be a wet endeavor. I do very much enjoy it, but in the offseason it's easier to harvest my own by inoculating oak logs with fungal spores."

We stood on a rooftop on the edge of Muktinath and hung our laundry from the lines, glad to have put the grueling Thorong La behind us. A frosty wind cascaded down the canyon from the direction of the pass, stirred our hanging socks, and then swept into the canyon below. Behind us the Himalayas towered, miles high, and on the other side of the canyon in front of us was a different world altogether: the old Kingdom of Lo.

Crossing the pass had put us in Mustang, the isolated district of Nepal sandwiched between the imposing Himalayas to the south and a closed-off Tibet to the north. The people of Upper Mustang live a secluded life that has changed very little since the 15th century. Culturally, they are Tibetan, and the language, architecture, and customs are a reflection of this. Until 1992, the area was completely sealed to outside visitors. Upper Mustang was once an independent kingdom, the Kingdom of Lo, and was ruled by a monarch. This all came to an end in 2008 when Nepal became a republic, but access to Upper Mustang remained tightly controlled. The former King of Lo still lived out there, just twenty-five miles north of Muktinath, where life still went on just as it had for the last six hundred years, regardless of what was happening in world politics.

A rough jeep track weaved its way through the Himalayas to Upper Mustang, and I'd had my eye on it for months. It would have been the greatest driving triumph of our trip to drive this road, emerging five hundred years in the past on the Tibetan Plateau in a wild, shuttered Himalayan kingdom. But when the time came, we had been foiled by the cost of permits, which were $1,000, and would have only been good for ten days. Exploration of Tibet, like our desire to drive through China, was not to be. But by a stroke of luck the Nepalese government had very recently lifted restrictions on a small slice of Upper Mustang, and we were thus allowed to trek through it and witness what was considered by many to be the best-preserved example of traditional Tibetan life in the world on account of it being the only piece of Tibet not to have been adulterated by Chinese invaders in the 20th century.

When we left Muktinath, we didn't head east along the jeep road, as was the normal route. Instead we turned north, crossing several streams on log bridges, and within a half an hour we entered the formerly restricted portion of Upper Mustang.

As soon as we crossed the boundary, we were in a different world. Muktinath, having long been accessible to the outside world, was similar to many of the other villages we'd passed through on the trek. But the half-hour walk to Chhongkhar made it seem as though we had been transported to a far off land. Buildings were constructed in a completely different manner, tall and smoothed-over with plaster, flat-roofed, and painted with colorful vertical stripes. In places, people had formed balls of yak dung and thrown them at the walls to create a collage of manure discs, which when dried would be used as fuel. The people in Chhongkhar acted differently than other villagers we'd seen. They hadn't jumped on the entrepreneurial bandwagon yet, and simply went on with their lives while we walked through, gazing wide-eyed as if discovering Himalayan life for the first time.

We left Chhongkhar and soon arrived at the village of Jhong, which was dominated by an imposing but crumbling mud tower fort, built in the 14th century for the founding king of Lo. We climbed to the base of the tower and watched red-robed monks scurry about on the dirt paths below. Beyond the cracked and crumbling fortress, we descended through orchards where, not having found anything to eat in the villages, we scavenged a couple of famous Mustang apples from an overhanging branch, pairing them with a couple of packs of cranberry-flavored electrolyte chews for an impromptu picnic lunch.

As the hours passed, the weather soon began to turn, and by mid-afternoon a strong, freezing wind had set in. We topped a rise and were met by a shepherd with a herd of goats. The shepherd's face was withdrawn into the protection of his jacket hood, but he flashed a big smile at us as he passed. Before long, the wind brought pellets of cold rain. We donned our rain gear from head to toe and resumed a slow but determined march across the eerily damp and cold steppe, slowly descending into the bottom of a river valley, past clumps of dead grass and scattered pebbles and brown-sugar dirt.

At the bottom of the valley the rain let up just in time for us to down-climb through a chute carved in a dry mud cliff, but the wind continued to blow, whipping dust upward through the cleft in the rock. A half mile farther on we came to Kagbeni, the village marking our emergence from restricted Upper Mustang. We planted our weary selves at a guesthouse overlooking the river, where I sat in the sun-soaked dining room listening to the wind howl through the cracks in the walls. I gazed up the river, wondering what lay beyond the next bend where we were not allowed to go.

In the morning we proclaimed it a rest day. We had been on the trail for twelve days.

To the south the river valley snaked toward Jomsom under towering, white mountains, and beyond it, modern civilization. Behind us sat the secluded pocket of Upper Mustang, a region very unlike any other place on Earth; a place sandwiched between the world's most imposing natural barrier and one of the world's most politically guarded regions. It is one of the few places left where people still live as they have for centuries, cut off from the modern world. In a few years Upper Mustang will have changed forever; plans were already underway to run a highway right through Kagbeni and into the restricted area to provide another link between Kathmandu and China.

This weighed profoundly on my mind, and it was with heavy feet and heart that we departed to the south, promising ourselves to return in the not-too-distant future to explore the untainted Upper Mustang before it is too late.

Jomsom is situated eight kilometers downstream from Kagbeni, and is a popular termination point for less ambitious trekkers on the Annapurna circuit because of its accessibility by jeep, and the fact that it has a small airstrip. The stretch between Kagbeni and Jomsom was a pleasant jaunt along a wide and rocky riverbed, and as we approached the town, we could feel a marked difference between it and other villages as a result of its road access. There were buildings constructed of concrete, and the edge of town was demarcated by a thick line of parked jeeps in various states of disrepair. When we reached Jomsom it felt as though we'd been thrust back into civilization; mechanics rolled in the dust replacing wheel bearings and broken leaf springs, day-trippers and trekking tourists scurried between stores and restaurants. It was lunchtime, so we quickly grabbed a bite to eat and got out as fast as we could.

As we made our way down the dirt road out of town, we shielded our faces against dust kicked into the wind by jeeps and buses. We paused on occasion to watch the small prop planes jump shakily into the sky and perilously thread their way between snow-capped peaks, transporting trekkers back to Pokhara.

By late afternoon we had found our way off of the road and into the forest on a side trail. After leaving Kagbeni, the towns seemed more capitalist and commercial, and we already missed the wildness and desolation of Manang and Mustang.

For days on end we had been lugging around our camping gear, and every day Sheena reminded me, and everyone we met, just how big a moron I was for insisting we bring the tent along. Seeing the opportunity to escape the commercial towns and the road, and desperately wanting to prove myself not a moron, I seized the opportunity to swoop in and save the day. We sought out a clearing next to a small stream and happily built our own camp. After dinner we bundled up in our down sleeping bags as darkness and a stiff chill settled into the valley, and fell asleep to the sound of a light breeze rustling our tent.

After trading the jeep-riddled road for the alternate trail on the other side of the valley, we were very reluctant to trade sides again, a reluctance that saw us fluctuating wildly in elevation as we traversed the steep mountainside that hugged the edge of the river. After two days of climbing and descending pine mountainsides, we finally emerged at the busy hub of Tatopani.

Tatopani, as it turns out, is a popular jumping off point for myriad one-to-five day hikes, and as one can imagine, we found it full to the brim with people. We checked into a bustling guesthouse composed of a couple dozen shoddy bungalows and a busy restaurant.

In the evening I walked down to the river where I had heard about a hot spring, but was disappointed to find a concrete pool filled hip-to-hip with overweight Russian men. I stood there watching for a few minutes, angry for having allowed myself to get my hopes up. Some excitement trickled back as I noticed that the crowded pool was in fact not itself a hot spring, but that a hose lead down to a natural pool nearer the river from which the hot water was pumped. I carefully clambered down to the steaming pool amid the rocks and dipped my toe into it. To my surprise, the temperature of the pool had somehow been allowed to exceed the limits imposed upon liquid water by the laws of physics, and my toe very nearly caught on fire and burned off. I shrieked and limped over to the river to sit on a boulder and cry it out.

We awoke early for the final test of our trek, and headed for the hills. We began on the dirt road, but soon turned off to climb through a leafy forest toward Poonhill, whose summit, it was said, had the region's very best panoramic views of the Himalayan range. Since leaving Kagbeni on the northern fringe of the Himalayas, we had picked our way between peaks along valley floors toward the south. But to get back to Pokhara we would have to cross a high mountain ridge, regaining much of the elevation we'd lost since Thorong La, all in a single day.

The trail quickly assumed the form of a steep stone staircase, and for hours we climbed on. By midmorning we had caught up to two small Nepali girls dressed in school uniforms, so I rattled off some of the Nepali greetings I had been learning in order to impress Auntie Durga upon our return to Kathmandu.

"Kasto cha timilai?"

"Chikaicha. Kasto cha tapailai?"

"Ekdam ramro, dhanyabat."

Seeing that I was able to make and return a simple greeting, they assumed that I would be able to engage in a deeper conversation, but their squeaky banter—probably about string theory or molecular physics—went right over my head. I returned their attempt at conversation with a defensive statement I'd put in my lingual briefcase just for such situations, and which I had found myself using many times daily. As a result, I began to sound rather fluent as I rattled it off in Nepali.

"I'm learning Nepali, but so far my language skills are like those of a child."

This explanation of my handicap satisfied them, so they helped us out by switching to English.

"So where are you girls going?"

"We go to school," one of them squeaked. They strode with such energy, devouring the stairs like they were nothing.

"How far is school?"

"One hour."

"And you walk there every day?"

"Um, yis!"

The pair went on to tell us the Nepali names for everything they could think of: donkeys, bananas, rocks, trees, and various types of food. Suddenly one of them stopped, looked into the trees, and then raised both arms and started yelling and running towards the forest. A small family of monkeys saw her coming and scurried back into the undergrowth. She picked up a few rocks and threw them, although it must be noted that her aim was poor, clearly having to do with the fact that Nepal has no baseball culture. I decided to show her a little bit of American baseball prowess, so I picked up a rock, threw it, and very nearly fell flat on my ass and down the stairs on account of my two hundred pound backpack. The rock flew off in a direction approximately perpendicular to the direction of the monkeys, and the expression on the girls' face was one of utter pity.

We eventually made the call to complete the whole climb before lunch. We were back in the jungle, and it was no secret that jungle trekking did not rank high on the list of activities on which we liked to dawdle. Still, we later conceded that completing the whole climb before lunch may have been a mistake. At 1:00 we dragged our battered bodies into the ridge-top village of Ghorepani, having ascended 5,500 vertical feet of uneven stone stairs in a period of just six hours. We were the first trekkers of the day to reach the top, but we certainly didn't feel like we'd won anything. We settled into a guesthouse with a stunning view of 26,795-foot Dhaulagiri, the world's seventh tallest mountain. With a view like that, a soggy excuse for pizza never tasted so good.

The hike from Ghorepani to the Poonhill summit is an easy one-hour jaunt up a stone walkway, and there is something about it that brings out the inner Edmund Hillary in many a hiker. In a repeat of Thorong Phedi, dozens of our fellow trekking comrades awoke us at 3:00 the following morning by slamming their fists into the walls of the guesthouse hallway and yelling to nobody in particular about how psyched they were to bag this summit. I whimpered softly, mumbled a string of incoherent, half-asleep profanities into my pillow, and tried to reverse my unsolicited departure from the candy-cane-dreamland I'd just left behind. Two hours later we forcefully removed our zombie-like bodies from our beds and walked out into the darkness.

It was pitch black on the way to the summit, and we could trace the line of headlamps up the stone staircase before us all the way to the top. We emerged at the lookout a half an hour before sunrise and found a comfortable place to watch, taking note of those poor uncomfortable bastards who had so explosively departed at three in the morning, only to sit up there in the freezing cold darkness for two extra hours.

As people gathered around the summit, we reconnected with friends we'd made along the trek. There were the four Canadians we'd met shortly after Jomsom, and who had come to refer to as Team Canada. Then there was Lance, who had quit his job in California, and then built himself a house in Nebraska, only to realize that he'd just built himself a house in Nebraska, so he flew to Nepal to escape reality. There were Andriy and Olga, the charming Ukrainian photographers we'd met in Thorong Phedi while preparing for our shot at the pass. And finally, there were our ever-interesting, always-smiling, wild-mushroom-scavenging friends from Portland, Jake and Kendra.

On the day that we crossed the Mexican border at the very onset of our around the world drive, I noted a very memorable sunset. On that day, and perhaps it was made more beautiful by the fact that we were drunk with joy, the sky had exploded into flames like a cheap polyester suit. On this morning at Poonhill it happened again, only in the form of a sunrise. The sky slowly transformed from black to deep blue, the horizon began to glow, and then in slow motion Annapurna, Machhapuchhre, Dhaulagiri, and the rest of the Annapurna range was set alight by the crisp sphere of yellow rising from the eastern horizon.

It was a perfect end to the trek. We retreated to the guesthouse for breakfast, and then descended the untold millions of stone steps down the far side of the mile-high ridge. We grabbed a local bus back to Pokhara, arriving after dark, and then hailed a taxi for the final six miles back to our campground where Nacho awaited. It is needless to say that after 150 miles of high altitude trekking over the course of eighteen days, we slept like dead people.

When at long last we awoke, we found ourselves next to a clear pond in the middle of a golden field of rice.

41

Panchase Marga
at Pame Bazar

Sheena

A heavyset German man arrived at the campground in an antique Hannomark truck that he had driven all the way from Germany. He appeared to be in his late 30's and he had intense, crystal-blue eyes and a beehive of purple dreadlocks tied above his head into a crispy fountain of hair. We sat on a stacked rock that surrounded a small tree and inquired about his drive from Germany in the old truck.

"The trouble started when I got to Iran. The people of Iran I found quite agreeable, but someone stole my dog. You say, *kidnapped?* A man kidnapped my dog for the ransom of one bottle of liquor. I got the bottle and I traded it for my dog. But then I go to the police and I make a report. But then the police arrest me and throw me in prison for seven days! In the report I admitted to giving the man alcohol, but alcohol it is illegal in Iran."

I didn't see a dog anywhere, so I asked him where it was.

"Well, I don't have the dog any more. When I arrived in Nepal four weeks ago, I went searching for a place to host a yoga meditation retreat. It is hard to find the right place for this retreat, because the earth chakra must speak to my heart chakra. So I went through the hills with my dog to test the earth chakra of various places. One day, just over there in those hills, a tiger comes out of the trees and eats my dog. So now I travel alone." Later on he told us about his conspiracy theories, and we marked him as untrustworthy.

It was harvest season in the Pokhara Valley. While we were away, the rice fields surrounding our camp had changed from electric green to gold. Harvest season was the most time-critical period of the year, and everyone worked together to clear the rice paddies with their sickles,

245

beating the rice off the ends of their stalks by whipping them on the ground, and stacking the spent stalks in heaping mounds.

Past our campground through the paddies and over a suspension bridge lay the majority of the rice paddies, and once our legs had recovered from trekking, we began short explorations to the other side. Beyond the valley, steep hillsides covered in thick jungle rose up out of the rice. A few trails wove between the two contrasting terrains, put there by the coming and going of the villagers that worked the paddies.

Aside from it being harvest time, it was still the Nepali holiday season; *Dashain* had just ended, and *Tihar*, a five-day festival celebrating reverence for all things, was now at full tilt.

The giant bamboo swingsets that each village had erected for *Dashain* were still up, and the one for the village of Pame Bazar stood as a temporary landmark in a cleared field adjacent to our campground. The swing never stopped moving as children and adults continually came and went. Often they performed solo acrobatic tricks, while other times they doubled-up, two at a time on the little wooden plank at the end of the long hand-rolled grass ropes.

On the third day of *Tihar*, the people of the village garnished their cows with marigolds and fed them the best grass. In the morning, Brad left on a shopping run into the village, and when he returned he proudly showed me the mess of red powder and rice on his forehead. "I love this place," he said, smiling, "I was just walking back and I saw an old man applying *tikka* to his cow's forehead in a barn. He invited me inside to watch, and after he was done decorating his cow he did this and said a blessing for me."

On the evenings during the holiday the sleepy village of Pame Bazar awoke from its slumber and erupted into all-night dance parties. We listened from our campsite, and tried to imagine the modest, hard-working villagers cutting loose and dancing their hearts out. We had received an invitation to the big night, the final dance party blowout of *Tihar*, which would be in a couple of days. The invitation had been delivered to us by one of the village kids. She had approached us while we sat under Nacho's awning and handed me the little paper invitation, then smiled and quickly walked away.

One afternoon after the sun had passed its apex and began to slowly creep toward the western ridge of the valley, we walked beyond the rice fields and approached the place where the trail disappeared into the jungle. As we came around a bend in the trail where the foot of a mountain intersected the valley floor, we happened upon a group of villagers working the rice. A young boy approached us with a heaping bundle of stalks tied to his back, and when he reached us, he stopped in our way.

"Where you go?" he asked, timidly.

We didn't really know. "Just walking," I said, nodding my head toward the trees.

"No," he said. "Danger."

"What danger?"

He held his calloused hand up, clawed at the air, and attempted a shrill roar. "Today see," he said, pointing to his eyes, and then pointing to the trees.

Brad and I looked at each other. "You mean you saw a tiger?"

"Yes, big tiger."

Suddenly the purple-haired German conspiracy theorist's story didn't seem so unlikely.

Up ahead the villagers went on with business as usual, swinging their sickles and beating the grain from its husks. With all of the evidence falling into place to support the existence of a hungry tiger up ahead, we thought it prudent to take the warning seriously. We thanked the young boy and turned around, following the valley in the opposite direction, where the trail traced the line between the rice paddies and jungle. As we skirted along the valley wall, I kept an eye on the jungle's undergrowth, and soon I was overcome by paranoia. We were in the danger zone; vulnerable gophers defenselessly strolling in a garden, unknowingly in the crosshairs of a conniving feline.

"Listen," I said to Brad, "I watched a show once where a man in Florida was attacked by an alligator. He didn't have a chance to get away and he knew he'd die unless he was able to kill it with his bare hands. Just as the alligator jumped on him, he grabbed its throat and held onto it until it suffocated. I'm just letting you know that in case that tiger is watching us." I later learned that, in fact, panthers—not tigers—inhabit the forests of the Pokhara valley, and they kill several villagers each year.

On the way back to camp, Brad told me that he felt ready to go back to Kathmandu. And I suppose I did too.

We drove from Pokhara to Kathmandu on the fifth day of *Tihar*. That was the day on which sisters honored their brothers by placing multi-colored *tikka* marks on their foreheads, and strings of marigolds around their necks. It was the perfect day to be driving across the country. Every man, whether loitering by the roadside or zipping through

247

the canyon on his motorbike, added another splash of flowery orange to the scenery out the passenger window.

When we arrived at the Rai house, the windowsills and doors were decorated with marigold and chrysanthemum garlands, and in front of the door on the patio, Durga had created an artistic display of colored powder and flower petals arranged in a circular pattern. We drank tea and ate *selroti*, a special bread made of rice flour and sugar and is only eaten during *Tihar*, and we recounted our experiences from the Annapurna trek to the family. In the evening a group of kids sang *Tihar* songs on the street and fireworks exploded across the city.

42

Pasang Lhaamu "Highway"
to Syabrubesi

Brad

Pesal had spent a great deal of time teaching us about Nepal. To a certain extent I discussed the country's recent history with Bharat during our daily teatime conversations on the patio, but more often than not I ended up doing most of the talking, trying to come up with suitable answers for his difficult-to-answer questions. We well knew that the country had experienced a turbulent recent past, and that Nepal was still plagued by periodic Maoist assaults. It should have come as no surprise then, that as a function of Murphy's Law, no sooner had our friends Nathan and Claire booked their plane tickets to visit us in Nepal for a ten day vacation, the Maoist rebel leaders announced that the entire country would be completely shut down for a period of—get this—ten days, by force if necessary, coinciding perfectly with our friends' visit.

My eyes searched the ceiling for reasons as Pesal informed me of this impending calamity, and suddenly my mind became clear as an epiphany befell me explaining why so few people had gone out of their way to visit us during our circumnavigation of the globe. It was probably for fear of getting caught up in the unexpected and sometimes perilous, life threatening, or dim-witted situations in which we continually ended up.

"Don't you think you should at least tell them about this?" It was Sheena again, trying to override the cool and collected way in which I normally tried to conduct my business.

"Why? And risk them canceling their trip? I don't see any good that could come of it."

"You *do* understand that you're knowingly misleading our friends into going on vacation to a place that has been overtaken by violent rebels, right?"

She was always flipping things around and looking at them backwards. "Sheena, I'm not misleading anybody, I'm simply withholding information. There's a difference."

She showed me the whites of her eyes and the discussion was over, I clearly having emerged the victor. Somewhere deep down my conscience was trying to tell me something, but I was lost in the pleasure that comes with winning petty arguments, and I paid it no mind. It wasn't until a couple of weeks later, right around the time that Nathan and Claire's plane touched down in Kathmandu, that my conscience finally convinced me that I was a bad person. It was their smiles as they emerged from the airport that did it. I was leading these nice people to their deaths.

"Wow, that was a long flight. Do you realize we've been sitting in a metal tube for two days? They had free booze though, and I'd be lying if I told you that sitting in a metal tube drinking free booze was all that unbearable." Nathan's handlebar moustache conducted a symphony orchestra as he cheerfully rehashed his flight while I drove us back to our temporary hotel base in Bhaktapur.

"There's something I have to tell you—"

"Did you just say something? Wow, I'm so glad we're finally here. I haven't sat that long since—"

"I said there's something I have to tell you!" He stared at me, moustache frozen in suspended animation. "There's been a rebel uprising."

"Huh?"

"A rebel uprising. You won't look so nervous after I explain. You see, Nepal is coming up on elections and there's a somewhat nefarious group of unsavory hooligans, called Maoists, who won't rest until Nepal becomes a communist utopia." His moustache tips lightly quivered like divining rods honing in on water. He still looked just as nervous as before.

"The Maoists had several demands to be met before the elections, but you know, one thing led to another, and they weren't met. They were pretty pissed, naturally, and decided to prohibit the election from happening altogether by shutting down the whole country for ten days."

"What exactly does that mean?" He still hadn't moved his head or blinked, which was unnerving.

"It means that no businesses will be allowed to open, and nobody can drive anywhere. For ten days."

"When does it start?"

"In two days."

"And when are we supposed to start our drive?"

"Um. Also in two days."

"I see."

The following morning we convened in Nathan and Claire's room. Sheena's mother had sent a box of cookies in the shapes of letters, so we avoided our impending last stand against the rebels by spelling things with the cookies and taking corny pictures of ourselves. After the fun in that wore off, we ate most of the cookies and went out on the town.

Bhaktapur is a well-preserved medieval town of cobbled ways, carved-wooden windowsills, and tiered brick temples. I had parked Nacho in the small temple square at the center of the city, a stone's throw from or hotel, the night before. When we emerged in the morning we found the Communist Party preparing to stage a rally there, Nacho being the centerpiece by virtue of our parking place. Some men were trying to hide our van behind a communist banner, but couldn't find a place to hang it. Knowing that their little party would soon be the cause of much duress, we opted to leave Nacho there as the rally backdrop. I kept this small victory in my back pocket throughout the day, and every time I recalled it, I felt a little warmth in my heart.

Our doomsday came alas, and we had but one objective: to disobey rebel orders without being killed. We had to get from Bhaktapur to downtown Kathmandu to obtain trekking permits, and then drive several hours into the Himalayas where we would embark on the Langtang Valley trek. The rebel-imposed ban on driving had been in effect all of eight hours when we loaded our bags into Nacho.

A couple of police officers lingered nearby, so we approached them. While we had hoped that the Maoists would have simply changed their minds at the last minute, the officers shook their heads and verified that the *bandh*, as it was called, had indeed begun. No businesses would be open, nor would any cars be allowed on the roads anywhere in the country. The good news was that the business closures had been shortened to only one day, but the transport ban would remain unchanged.

"Well, do you think the rebels would mind if *we* drove today?"

The officers looked at each other, and then shrugged. "Maybe if they know that you are tourists they will let you pass."

"Do you really think so?"

"I don't know. What do they want from you? You are tourists."

My mind raced back to a period about ten years ago when the Maoists had blocked roads, pulled people from buses and cars, and set their vehicles on fire. Journalists had been kidnapped or killed. Tourists didn't factor much in the equation, because tourists weren't stupid enough to get in the middle of it.

We put our heads together and faster than you can say "Navy Seals" we had conceived and executed a plan to save our lives by scribbling in big, bold letters the word "TOURIST" on our windshield using a bar of soap. If our ugly van and white faces weren't enough to convince people that we were harmless, then surely this would. Barring a rainstorm or accidental activation of the windshield wipers, pretty much nothing could go wrong.

With that we set off and soon joined the Kathmandu Ring Road. On a street usually packed with hectic bumper-to-bumper traffic, it was absolutely dead empty. We traveled for miles as the only car on the road, and as we got closer to town, the highway became thick with scores of people walking. It was eerily silent and everyone stared at us as we passed. As we neared downtown, we passed a few Maoists standing on the backs of flatbed tricycles, waving their flags while yelling through megaphones. We passed by, avoiding eye contact, hoping that somehow they wouldn't notice us. Before long we arrived at the trekking permit office.

After buying our permits, it was game time. The plan was to drive six or seven hours into the mountains where we would leave Nacho at a small village while we went trekking. We snaked our way out of Kathmandu through streets without cars and finally climbed out of the valley and into the Himalayas.

The road skirted the valley wall, winding ever higher into the mountains, our progress periodically interrupted by ad-hoc military checkpoints. We made it through the first two checkpoints without incident, having only to stop and register our passage in handwritten ledgers. These ledgers, of course, would be used to report our last known whereabouts to international news outlets upon our inevitable disappearance.

The situation took a turn when we reached the third military checkpoint. We stopped and were surprised to see a small bus and a couple of work trucks there as well. I got out and registered our presence in the ledger, and then got back in the van, but nobody removed the barrier across the roadway. Soon an officer approached.

"*Namaste*. I have registered, may we go?"

"Maybe soon. One hour."

"What do you mean?" I asked, somewhat astonished. "We're just tourists. We've already passed two checkpoints, we'll be fine." He signaled for me to wait a minute, and then retired to his hut. A few minutes passed without word, so I got out and walked into the hut.

"Hi, we've already signed in, so can we go?" I spoke with conviction in the hope that they would simply wave us on. They indicated with hand gestures and rudimentary English that it wouldn't be long. One hour, they said. I moped back to the van feeling sorry for our guests and myself. We had hoped to arrive before nightfall, but by now the daylight was already waning.

As I walked back to the van I noticed that a group of men from the bus had congregated in the road, so I joined in. I introduced myself and tried to impress them with my Nepali language skills, by now about as advanced as those of a two year old. I very quickly exhausted my vocabulary and we settled on English, as always happens when people tire of my faltering infant blabbering.

"The officer has told me that we have to wait one hour. Any idea why?" They all nodded, clearly not upset in the slightest.

"The Maoists have blocked the road with trees. The military has gone in to open the road, and once they return, we will continue from here in a military convoy."

"Oh. Of course they did." My haste and self-pity evaporated in an instant and suddenly the time of our arrival was no longer of any consequence. I excused myself and went back to Nacho to explain to our guests that they were indeed in grave danger, but that everything was fine since we'd have a military convoy. Nathan's handlebar moustache quivered and his unblinking eyes stared straight through my face. We all came to a silent understanding that I was a bad person.

The group of men from the bus eventually came over and we spent the next hour chatting and laughing. Nepalis have such a positive air about them that even the gravest of rebel standoffs can be made to seem inconsequential.

253

Just as darkness fell, a military truck raced around a bend up the canyon and into the checkpoint. Suddenly the place was a whir with commotion as people loaded their vehicles and fired up the engines. Before we knew it we were racing in a snake of six or seven vehicles along a dark, winding mountain track. Military trucks carrying a half a dozen machine-gun-toting men in camouflage formed the head and tail of our road snake, and I pushed Nacho as fast as I dared around the winding corners so as not to create a gap in our convoy. We periodically crossed sections of road covered in twigs and leaves, very recently having been cleared of felled trees that the Maoists had used as roadblocks. I imagined the gun-slinging rebels watching us from the trees as we flashed past in the darkness.

Several times throughout the night, the convoy passed through tiny mountain villages, and each time we arrived at one we stopped, and the military men fanned out of their trucks. We presumed that they were gathering word about conditions on the road ahead, and without a moment's notice they would jump back into their trucks and we would race back onto the cliffhanging road.

After more than an hour we reached a village, and the soldiers walked more slowly from their trucks. The group of Nepali men from the bus emerged and came over to our van. It seemed we would have a longer rest there, so they invited us into a dimly lit concrete building for a cup of tea. They really did have a way of downplaying the seriousness of these things.

With half of our tea finished, we heard the call of the soldiers and everyone jumped up and made for the door. We ran out of the shack, jumped in Nacho, and sped out of town in between the machine gun trucks into the mountains.

As the night wore on, fatigue started to set in, and by eight o'clock I began to wonder where we would draw the line. Despite driving at speeds barely feasible for the tiny mountain roads, we weren't making good time on account of all of the stops. We were only halfway to our destination and we were getting tired. It was like a sign, and then, when the convoy suddenly stopped and the soldiers barked a few orders to the bus driver and a couple of other drivers who had made it that far. The bus started to turn around, so I got out and ran up to the soldier in charge.

"Excuse me, but what's happening?"

"You stay here. Follow the bus, he is going to hotel."

"Will the convoy go any farther?"

"No, after this it is too dangerous. You follow the bus and stay in the hotel."

"And what time does the convoy leave in the morning?"

"No more convoy. We go back to Kathmandu."

This sounded to me a lot like a death sentence, so I tried to come up with something more soothing to placate our visiting friends and maintain a façade of bravery and levelheadedness for Sheena.

"What's the word," Claire asked, looking sweet and innocent.

"Well, the soldiers think it's too dangerous beyond this point so they're going back to Kathmandu. We're following that bus to a hotel, and then we're on our own."

My soothing and euphemistic explanation had failed to placate the group. The hopeful mood in Nacho evaporated, and in its place grew a chilly desperation. Nathan and Claire were both engineers—very smart people—and upon hearing my explanation, it was clear that at that moment they considered me, also an engineer, not to be very smart at all. I had tricked them into flying across the globe, loaded them into my van, and used military force to get them a half-day's drive into the middle of a fiery poo storm. And now the troops were retreating, leaving us with no more than an ugly van with a message written in soap on the windshield.

The hotel was dank and our strangely shaped concrete room smelled like moist seat cushions. After unloading a few things I went out to lock up the van and noticed some commotion aboard the bus. Its sole passengers, a family of Ukrainians, were arguing with the driver, who tried in vain to get them off of the bus. I walked over to see what was going on.

"Hi," I said, poking my head into the open door, "is everything all right?" The driver, who didn't speak English, looked relieved and the angry Ukrainian matriarch explained the situation.

"We paid this man to take us to Syabrubesi so that we can go trekking, but he has stopped here tells us to stay at this hotel. Why should we stay here? It is probably his friend's hotel! We paid to go to Syabrubesi, and we won't get off of this bus until we arrive!"

I stared back at her, a little dumbfounded. It was as if we were speaking to each other from distant planets without a common basis for communication. The fact that we had ended up here was for me the culmination of two weeks of worry, education, and weighing odds. What was she talking about? We were going to have to start at the beginning.

"Well ... it's because of the *bandh*."

"The what?" She held onto her indignant tone, but for a moment it may have occurred to her that she had missed something.

"The *bandh*. It's like a strike." Blank stare. "Look, when you left Kathmandu, did you notice that there weren't any cars on the road?"

"No, I did not notice." Her crossed arms relaxed a little and her resentfulness started to give way to unease.

"Hmm, okay. Well, did you notice that for the last couple of hours we've been driving in a military convoy?" This news gave her a great shock, and the fact that she was shocked in turn gave me a great shock. How could an entire family have endured a whole day of this without even the slightest inkling that something were amiss? They had started the day as the only vehicle on the road in one of the world's most hectic driving cities, they had been stopped for over an hour at a military checkpoint while we waited for roadblocks to be cleared, and they would have seen armed soldiers running all around their parked bus every time we entered a village. I started at the beginning, briefly explaining Nepal's Maoist problems over the last ten years, and slowly worked up to the elections at hand and the situation in which we currently found ourselves.

When I finished, she was completely horrified. She turned to her family, who didn't understand English, and brought them up to speed while their faces transformed from angry to terrified. When she finished she looked at me again and complained, as though there were something that I could do about it, "I can't believe it! And here we have brought an eight-year-old girl into this!"

It was a welcome change not to feel like the most negligent person in the convoy, and I walked toward the hotel with my head held high. As I passed the bus driver he thanked me and looked relieved. I retired to my room, whereupon I informed Sheena that I was not as careless and harmful as previously thought, though my explanation did very little to change her mind.

In the morning we hoped that a new convoy would form, but one never did. We were truly on our own, so we loaded up and set out once more into the mountains. While we failed to see any Maoists at first, it quickly became evident that in fact the road itself might have posed more of a danger than the rebels. The paved switchbacks soon gave way to a crumbling dirt path that skirted several landslide paths as it threaded into the mountains, clinging perilously to an impossibly steep mountainside.

We slowly crept into the first slide path, kicking small pebbles off of the edge into a scary abyss and jolting violently as Nacho rolled over giant rocks. Claire, small and usually brave, was the first to lose her wits.

"Oh my god. Oh my god. Oh my god. We're going to die. Nacho can't handle this. Can Nacho handle this? This is too steep. We're all going to die! I need to get out!" Almost before I could come to a stop the sliding door was open and Claire was free of the death trap. "I'm running from here," she said, and then bounded off down the rocky path.

The three of us looked at each other and then started crawling over the rocks again, one wrong move away from tumbling to our deaths.

"I'm out too!" Sheena squealed. Her seatbelt clicked, the door slid open, and she was out. That left Nathan and me.

"You're not going to leave too, are you?" I asked.

"No way man, I used to be a Boy Scout. I'll keep an eye on this side and you do what you can to keep us from falling off the cliff." Sheena and Claire were perfect for each other. It was about time I had some quality bro time.

Nathan carefully instructed me where to put my right tire while I held my head out the window and watched pebbles fall off the edge on my side. At every opportunity to smash our oil pan with great force, we did so, and we frequently got out to inspect for damage. Before leaving Kathmandu I had designed an oil pan shield using a piece of sheet metal, and then gave my mocked-up design to a couple of pre-teen welding boys in an alley to build it out of solid iron. Now we smashed our way through the mountains, blow by crushing blow, and my hastily fabricated oil pan shield tirelessly performed its duty.

Suddenly the road pitched upward and curved to the right around a protruding wall of earth. To the left, beyond the road's jagged edge, there was nothing but atmosphere and blurry earth far below. The track was deep with dust and studded with embedded rocks. On our first attempt we spun our tires halfway up, and then Nacho's rear tires violently bounced and jumped toward the cliff's edge. I carefully slid back down the hill, weary of the exposure to my left. Nathan and I conferred, and decided that the best option moving forward was to gun it and do our best not to fall off the cliff. I backed up some more to get some momentum, breathed deeply, put it in gear and stepped on it. We slid and bounced up the hill, jumping from groove to groove, repeatedly smashing the oil pan as a waterfall of dust flowed off of the edge. We sailed around the off-camber corner in full Tokyo drift, and we came to a triumphant stop at the top of the incline, out of harm's way. Sheena had watched with clenched teeth from a couple of curves away, certain Nathan and I were about to meet our early demise.

At long last we reached the other side of the landslides where the crumbling pavement resumed, and a short while later we reached the next to last village of the drive. As we neared the village we were stopped repeatedly by one military checkpoint after another, only a few hundred meters apart. Within fifteen kilometers of our destination we reached the final military checkpoint. The officer approached my window and informed me that it was too dangerous to drive the final section alone, and we would have to wait for another vehicle to come along so we could drive together for safety. After ten minutes a beat up Land Cruiser arrived, and we set off together, Nacho out in front.

The road was in good condition, interspersed with short sections wiped out by landslides. Over the first five kilometers we put considerable distance between our safety buddy and us, so I pulled over to wait.

"At least he's in the back," I noted to the rest of the group, "so they'll be the sacrificial lambs in any kind of chase situation that should arise." A few minutes later, the Land Cruiser came up like a bat out of hell, flew by us, and then disappeared around a corner. I cursed myself for having waited and rumbled slowly back onto the road, now in sacrificial lamb position, verifying that no good deed goes unpunished.

Twenty minutes later, still alive and in one piece, we rolled into the small mountain village of Syabrubesi. As we arrived, disbelieving villagers and trekkers alike came out of their hovels to see us. A half dozen tour guides and stir-crazy trekkers stopped us on the road and asked a stream of questions in rapid-fire succession.

"How did you get here?!"

"Are there any others?"

"Are there any buses coming?"

"Can you take me back? I have a plane to catch!"

The shutdown had caused mountain villages to fill up with stranded trekkers, and there was no way for them to get back to Kathmandu. We made our way through the village, parked outside of an old hotel, and got ready to start our own trek into the Langtang valley, away from civilization.

We later heard that bricks thrown by angry Maoist rebels had showered other vehicles driving to Syabrubesi. Elsewhere in the country, buses and trucks that failed to observe the *bandh* had been attacked by Maoists who threw petrol bombs through their windshields, killing several people. Reports confirmed that no tourists had been targeted. In the end the elections went on as planned, and despite not having any motorized means of transport, a record-setting 78% of Nepal's eligible voters found their way to the polls to cast their vote.

While driving through the Andes Mountains of Argentina more than a year prior to our arrival in Nepal, we had passed through a small mountain town called Uspallata. This, as it turned out, had been the home base for the filming of the movie *Seven Years in Tibet*, and the surrounding Andes temporarily became the surrogate Himalayas. We had driven from Uspallata to the Chilean border, passing the imposing peaks of Aconcagua and others, and we had thought to ourselves, wow, these mountains are just like the Himalayas. Imagine that. Just like Tibet.

We were justifiably elated, then, to drop our packs outside of a rock hut in the Himalayas a year later, to eat lunch on our way back down from the Langtang Valley. Behind the hut stood a ridge, imposing and massive, and on the other side, only a couple of miles from where we sat, was Tibet. An excited Tibetan man—the same one that we had met on our way up into the valley—rushed to our sunny table, recognizing us at once.

"You remembered!"

How could we forget? Sheena had made this man a promise to return when we met him on the way up the valley, and had been guiltily stressing over her promise ever since.

"You guys, I promised him so we can't forget to stop for lunch. He would be so sad!" And then fifteen minutes later, "Do you guys remember that promise I made? We *can't* forget!"

"Sheena, that guy tricks everyone into promising to stop for lunch," I pleaded. Sometimes she could be too honest for her own good. Nevertheless, she had shaken his hand and promised to return for lunch and homemade yak yogurt, and she was sticking to it.

Yak yogurt, so rare and novel anywhere else, was as natural as anything in these parts. We spent our days on the trail passing yaks chewing their cuds and staring ahead blankly, dolt-like. Claire, while not so brave on Himalayan death roads, built her confidence and made it her mission to touch the shy yaks. She would walk close enough to remain unnoticed, and then inch her tiny frame closer and closer until the yak took notice and shook its gigantic ice-pick horns ominously in her direction. She would reach her little hand out and try to pet its head, but just before making contact she would lose her nerve and retreat.

We placed our order with the man to whom Sheena had made her lunch promise, and then we basked in the high-mountain sun.

"*Dai*, is there a toilet here?" I asked as the man passed us on the way to the garden to pick the ingredients for our lunch.

"Yes, in yak house," he said, pointing to the squat stone enclosure beyond the garden where his yaks presumably lived. I stood and followed him into the garden, and contorted my body into the yak house. Inside it was no taller than three feet and it was unclear how yaks could fit inside. Did they crawl? In any case, I would have had to crawl on my knees in the dark to relieve myself into the piles of yak dung. I opted against it and instead turned and walked back through the garden where the man was digging in the dirt with his hands.

"Digging to China?" It very quickly occurred to me that this piece of hyperbole wasn't so hyperbolic at our current location.

"No, digging for potatoes," he said, looking up at me as if I were perhaps a tinge stupid. We had asked for vegetable dumplings, and the first step in what would be an hour-and-a-half lunch (and well-worth the wait) was to dig up the ingredients. Fast food hadn't caught on with exiled Tibetans as well as crafty marketing techniques had.

The villages of the Langtang Valley don't sit on an ancient trade route, as do those of the Annapurna circuit. Rather, these villages grew when the Chinese invaded Tibet in the 1950's, ruthlessly slaughtering the locals in their thirst for conquest (a story rehashed in *Seven Years in Tibet*). Many who fled the torment ended up here, a couple of miles from the Chinese border, a stone's throw from their ancestral homeland. These villages became a place where Tibetans could continue to survive as herders and subsistence farmers—a land without a people for a people without a land. But in this case, it was actually true.

At some point, outdoor enthusiasts discovered the valley, and trekkers began ascending the valley, a few days' walk in each direction. The villagers soon recognized the opportunity to commercialize, and began offering room and board to weary trekkers.

The cost of living in the Langtang Valley, with its subsistence farming and herding, is almost immeasurably low. With an influx of comparatively rich trekkers looking for places to spend their money, the prospect of offering food and beds became irresistible to all but the staunchest holdouts, and as a result most structures in the Langtang Valley had been repurposed for trekking commerce. With so much supply and such limited demand, especially at that moment, given the near impossibility of trailhead access due to the Maoist uprising, enterprising villagers had devised inventive, persistent—if not somewhat annoying—strategies of rogue marketing.

Often, while ascending into the high glacial valley, we would spot Tibetan horsemen sauntering along the trail. We watched in awe as they approached, surreal beings snatched from the pages of the National Geographic. But the illusion would tarnish when the horseman reached into his tattered yak hide overcoat and produced a business card.

"My friend, pizza, lasagna, brownie, apple pie. Where you going? Stay my guesthouse."

Their tactics were copious and clever. Stopping somewhere for lunch or a night's sleep invariably ended in the proprietor seeing us off with strict instructions to stay or eat at a family member's place farther up the valley. Children would be sent by their parents down to lower villages to cling to groups of trekkers and lead them to the right place to sleep for the night. Failure meant a full day and a dozen miles of walking for nothing. If they did succeed, the guesthouse would usually provide a free room for the promise of eating breakfast and dinner there.

My favorite was when we passed through the village of Bamboo. We passed a family sitting in front of their guesthouse, when one of the young daughters ran up to me.

"Excuse me mister!"

"Why yes, my dear?"

"Can do big favor?"

"For you, my flower? Anything at all." At this she ran back to her mother and then returned to me carrying a small blue bag containing one apple. She handed me the apple and a small handwritten note with her aunt's name and the name of her guesthouse, which was several hours up the trail.

"Please deliver to my aunt. It very important." She stared into my eyes as she said it, gravely placed the apple in my hand, and curled my fingers around it with her dirty little hand. She was very deliberate in conveying a sense of deep importance, as though her aunt's very survival depended on it.

"I will deliver this apple to your aunt if it's the last thing I do."

"Promise?"

"I wouldn't lie about something like this," I said, and then turned and walked away, purposefully, for the benefit of my young damsel. I paused before turning the corner and looked back. The family was

261

watching me, their clothes rippling in the breeze, their eyes looking upon me with great hope. I nodded slowly, patted the apple in my pack, and walked on.

Of course the purpose of this charade was to trick us into going inside of her aunt's guesthouse. Once inside, we would be wooed by her aunt's home-cooking, and we would be offered a free room—an offer we would be unable to refuse—and we would make the whole family richer. I may be stupid, but I'm no dummy. I considered eating the apple, but thought better of it. Instead, we sought out the aunt's guesthouse later that evening and I approached the door with great purpose and knocked. A man answered the door.

"Good evening, good sir. I have come from the distant village of Bamboo bearing a great burden for your wife. Is she about?"

He stared at me. In a minute, his wife—the intended recipient of my apple—appeared and emerged from the hut.

"Hello ma'am. I have been sent by your loving sister, a resident of the far-away village of Bamboo, to see to it that you take receipt of this nutritious fruit." I produced the plastic bag containing the apple from my pack and handed it to her, along with the handwritten note.

"My duty is fulfilled," I said, and began to walk away.

"You want room?" she wailed in half confusion as I departed.

"No thank you, ma'am, but please enjoy the apple." We were bound for the next village anyway, but it was nonetheless fun to become a temporary thread in their marketing cloth.

On the third day, Claire was given the task of delivering not an apple, but a full-grown horse, to the uppermost village in the Langtang Valley: Kyanjin Gompa. To say that she was thrilled to be manipulated by a rogue marketeer would be an understatement. She was unable to wipe the maniacal smile from her face for the entire hour that she dragged that horse around by its rope.

"Come on Mr. Bo Jangles," she whispered, "You're a good pony."

Kyanjin Gompa consisted of little more than a smattering of huts that had been converted to guesthouses, and a few larger buildings that had been erected to hold larger groups of trekkers. Overwhelmed by the onslaught of villagers begging us to stay at their guesthouses, we hastily chose one of the larger guesthouses on account of it not having a hawker out front. It went against our general rule of not staying at a place with more than four rooms, and consequently we spent a freezing night in poorly constructed cardboard rooms smelling strongly of spilled kerosene.

Over a tasteless dinner, we made the acquaintance of two mountaineers who had just that day finished summiting a nearby peak, the first team to do so that year. The men, both glaciologists working a six-month stint in Nepal to study glaciers, had spent several days on the mountain eating meager rations, a condition illustrated by the number of tasteless entrees that they ordered, and by their orgasmic reactions to eating them. In between bites they conveyed cryptic advice to us for our upcoming exploration into the upper reaches of the valley the next day.

"I spent a lot of days in that valley," the older man said, stuffing a soggy pizza into his mouth, "and the Zen Garden is the bee's knees."

"Oh yes," the younger agreed, chow mein noodles dripping from his beard. "It is an oasis. There's a boulder with prayer flags, and below it is the Zen Garden." His blue eyes were like hypnotized discs, and the chow mein hung like worms in suspended animation from his wily beard.

The next morning we set off up the valley, leaving behind Kyanjin Gompa, the last civilization before the Chinese border and Tibet. The trail threaded along the edge of a deep groove set between endless ridges of peaks. Directly above our guesthouse stood Tsangbu Ri, whose 22,123-foot peak fell on the other side of the Chinese border—the only piece of China visible from the valley. As we trekked higher, Tsangbu Ri was hidden behind a succession of other peaks, and it was by the passage of peaks that we gauged our progress. The trail that we walked was not overly steep, but at around 14,000 feet we walked slowly and breathed heavily. The sun was intense at this elevation, and the sky a deep, crayon blue, but despite the look of summer, we wore down coats and wool hats to fend off the icy chill in the air.

In our search for the Zen Garden, we came across dozens of yaks, and each time Claire veered to intercept them. The yaks invariably shook their gargantuan, deadly horns and bolted. By lunchtime these unwanted advances had caused Claire to suffer the effects of glycogen depletion and she began showing signs of early onset hunger-anger, or *hanger*.

Just when we thought all hope was gone, we rounded a bend and saw, off in the distance, an enormous boulder perched on the side of the canyon wall, and from it a line of prayer flags. We hurried to its base, where we found a surreal garden-like area with pygmy trees, green grass, and a crystal-clear stream emerging from a spring beneath a boulder. We collapsed before the stream and stuffed our faces with the bread and cheese that we had procured from an artisan producer on the way up the valley, and afterward we all fell asleep in the grass. All except for Claire, who used her newfound energy to molest some nearby yaks. Our potato-digging lunch slinger would later tell us that a half dozen, overly touchy trekkers get violently gored each year by yaks along this trail.

As evening fell in Kyanjin Gompa I stood outside of our new guesthouse, having relocated from the large kerosene-scented one to a small four-room hut operated by a Tibetan husband and wife. I pulled my jacket tight against my neck to keep the blustery wind at bay. Suddenly, around a corner, a stampede of children emerged at full tilt, bucking and whinnying. They flew past me, two children with ropes in their mouths and jingle bells draped around their necks, pretending to be wild mustangs, and two more boys pretending to be the horsemen. The mustangs practically pulled their riders with their mouths, occasionally stopping to give a wild kick aimed at their tormentors. They disappeared behind a rock hut. A few minutes later they reappeared, circled, descended to a neighboring garden, and then returned to where I was standing. One of the young boys demonstrated for an older boy how to be a mustang: how to bite the bridle, rear his head back, and then kick the horseman. Once the older boy had the general idea, he placed the rope in his mouth and they all disappeared again, kicking and whinnying in a whirl of dust and snot.

That night Nathan, Claire, Sheena, and I gathered around the wood burning stove in the dining room, and were soon joined by the Tibetan woman who ran the guesthouse. She appeared to be in her late twenties or early thirties. Her English was rough, and she was almost completely unable to decipher my elementary Nepali.

"Sorry, my English not good," she said, "and Nepali worse."

We found this confusing, being that she had lived in Nepal her entire life.

"All villages Tibetan here," she said. "Nobody here speak Nepali. We speak only Tibetan, little bit English."

"And where did you learn English?"

"We learn English talking to trekkers. Not know much Nepali because not much Nepali trekkers."

I found this amazing. She had lived in Nepal her whole life but hadn't met enough Nepali people to be able to learn the language. Learning English through brief encounters with passing trekkers was no small feat either, having no access to computers or books.

"Do you live here in the village all year long, or do you go elsewhere during the snowy months?"

"Always live here, all life. Never leave. My husband find wood in summer so we can have fire in winter. My kids living in Kathmandu for school. Now hard for husband to find wood, because now mountains protected. He must walk very far. Can only bring one load of wood in one day, and carry ten miles." She was ruggedly beautiful, and had a tinge of a rasp in her voice and permanent rosy cheeks from a life spent above 13,000 feet in the cold, dry air. Her long black hair was contained within a woven shawl wrapped around her head. Her husband, whom we had met the previous day, was handsome and charismatic, and built like an athlete. To find these two living in the seclusion of the Himalayas was striking.

"I saw some children outside playing games this evening."

"Yes," she smiled, "two of them my children. They come home for *Tihar*, but cannot return Kathmandu because Maoist *bandh*. When *bandh* over they go back to school."

"And how do they get back to Kathmandu?" The hike from Kyanjin Gompa to the closest road in Syabrubesi had taken us three days.

"They walk on trail. Make it to Syabrubesi in one day, then take bus to Kathmandu. They very strong children. It take two days to get to school." Two days, including a day-long walk of nearly twenty miles, alone on a rough, high-elevation trail.

"And how often to you get to see them?"

The hint of a smile left her face and in its place came a look of sadness. "Only one time each year. They come home for *Tihar* holiday. School very important."

Talking to this woman, as talking with many Nepalis, made me realize that I had never really had to struggle for anything. I did well in high school and received a full college scholarship. I had attended university as if it were the natural progression for any person, and had easily found my way into the workforce after that. In talking to Nepalis about their struggle for education and their reasons for doing so made me feel self-conscious to admit my own breezy plight. Pesal's teenage cousin Barna, who lived down the street from Bharat and Durga's house, and who we had gotten to know pretty well, had recently said goodbye to her boyfriend; he had sent applications to universities all over the world, and was accepted by one in Ukraine. After learning of his acceptance, he

265

had six weeks to learn enough Ukrainian to start classes, and he went about it as if he'd won the lottery.

The wood burning stove kept the small dining room comfortable against the biting wind that pressed on the single-pane windows and seeped through the cracks in the rough-hewn hut. We relaxed around a wooden table next to the stove, on pillows on hard wood benches.

"So tell me about Tibet," I said to the woman, who had been staring softly at a pillow since speaking of her children.

"I never been to Tibet. If we go back, we in big trouble. We might be kill." She paused for a minute, and then her dimpled cheeks bulled back in a smile. "But we see our home in *Seven Years in Tibet*."

This was crushing. Not only would she be imprisoned or beaten by her Chinese tormentors should she decide to visit her homeland, literally a stone's throw beyond the ridge right outside of her window, but the image that she holds in her mind of her home is not actually her home at all. It is Uspallata, Argentina. I tried not to let my face show just how terribly sad I found all of this. I didn't dare tell her that the movie wasn't actually filmed in Tibet, and I hoped nobody ever would.

In the morning we packed our bags for the trek back down the valley. As we set our packs against the hut in the early morning sun, the woman's husband emerged from the kitchen and cheerily invited us for tea before our departure. We shuffled into the cramped kitchen and took our seats around the table, making small talk while his wife sat on a bench tending to the fire in their homemade clay stove.

The husband handed us tea and wished us luck on our trek. We asked a few questions about his plans for the day and then took some pictures of the family before he excused himself. She had turned her body back toward the stove and looked down at a stick in her hands.

"How do you say goodbye in Tibetan?" I asked

Maybe she was thinking about her children, and how long it would be until she would see them again. Or maybe about her husband, off to gather one solitary load of firewood from a faraway mountainside. Perhaps she thought of Tibet, one ridge away but forever unachievable. She turned to us, wiping her eyes with the back of her hand. Her face turned red and soon more tears streamed down her cheeks, and she spoke.

"Khalephe."

43

Jungle Track into Chitwan National Park

Sheena

We stood at the water's edge in our shorts and flip flops where six massive elephants rested on their sides in the cool water of the Rapti River. Each day the elephant riders, or *mahouts*, brought them out to the river for a bath, and we had been invited to help.

Claire stood before us, her eyes fixed on the elephants. "I'm going in." I followed.

The *mahout* we approached looked relieved to have help. The elephant's hide was thick and rough and covered in deep crevices that held in the dirt like a cracked heel. The *mahout* gave us a quick demonstration: lean into the beast and vigorously scrub its thick hide with a flat river rock. It wasn't a hard task, but it was a laborious one, with so many surfaces to clean. We found our own river rocks and began scrubbing. I did my best to scrape the dirt from the deep creases in its skin, but my efforts were futile and soon my focus shifted to creating a swirling, mud-streaked masterpiece on the elephant's back.

The *mahout* spoke to his elephant and it responded with a stretch of a leg or a full body rotation.

"Choop!"

This command told the elephant to blast me with a fire hose explosion of river water, which erupted from its trunk. The elephant looked indifferent to what he had just done. My mud art had washed away.

The *mahout* stood, proud and amused.

"You got me!" I shouted.

"Choop!" yelled the *mahout*.

Now it was Claire's turn to get soaked, I hoped. The elephant sucked in another five gallons of river water, but instead of aiming at Claire it again blasted me in the side.

"Choop!"

And then again.

"Choop!"

Finally Claire got her turn and she fell over in the water.

Farther down the river Brad and Nathan found an elephant to wash, and once they were done, we sloshed onto the clay riverbank.

"Hey, we didn't get sprayed," Brad pointed out, a little bit disappointed. "It must be because we're not ladies."

It was finally election day in Nepal and the locals seemed uncertain about how things would go down. This village, on the edge of Chitwan National Park, a wildlife refuge, was largely immune to the *bandh,* and so it had been more or less business as usual there. It was out of the way near the southern border with India, and not of much interest to the Maoists. Besides, nobody really drove there anyway, its people instead relying on bicycles or animals, and so the transport ban had little effect. On election day, all of the stores closed down at midday and the people went to the voting booths, a few hours later returning with black marker on their thumbnails to indicate that they had voted. Everything seemed to have gone smoothly, and it looked like the Maoists' efforts over the last couple of weeks had been fruitless.

As advised, we stayed clear of Kathmandu until after the elections. In the meantime we decided to head south to the hot, Serengeti-like lowlands, a region known as the Terai. Chitwan National Park. This park was the last natural habitat for one-horned Indian rhinoceroses, Royal Bengal tigers, and Indian elephants.

By now it was November, and descending from the ever-colder Himalayas into the low, flat Terai was heavenly; the weather was pure bliss and we were all ready to relax by the river in our lawn chairs. We also wanted to see the park; we just had to decide how we wanted to explore it: on the back of an elephant, by foot, or by jeep. It seemed that by elephant would be too slow, and by foot might be rather dangerous. Rhinos and tigers attacked people every year in the park, and that's not how we wanted Nathan and Claire's trip to end after what they had already endured. We also wanted to get farther away from the park's more highly frequented zone, so we settled on a full day jeep safari, which would allow us access to the more remote corners of the park.

On the morning of our safari we packed sack lunches of peanut butter and jelly sandwiches, fruit, and Oreo cookies as if we were headed off to primary school. Our guide met us at the hotel and walked us down the elephant-poop-splattered road to the river's edge. The river valley was enshrouded in a thick soup of fog, and there was a slight chill to the air. A narrow dugout canoe emerged from the soup of fog and we climbed in and sat down on wooden block stools. It was a surreal start to the day, and when we reached the other side, we had crossed into the park's boundaries where there were no active resorts or restaurants – just nature as it was intended to be.

Historically, however, it hadn't always been this way. Back in the 19th and early 20th centuries, the land had been used as a hunting reserve for rich aristocrats. In 1911, King George V and his son slaughtered thirty-nine tigers and eighteen rhinos in just one safari trip. But the greatest losses in wildlife populations came as a result of a diminishing habitat and illegal poaching during the Maoist insurgency. By the 1960s there were fewer than one hundred rhinos and twenty tigers remaining in the area.

Even up to a few years before we arrived, tourist resorts operated within the park boundaries. Then suddenly the government stepped in and mandated the shutdown of all such establishments.

We climbed out of the canoe, walked up the clay riverbank, and got into an old bare-metal jeep with our guide and a driver. We took off down a narrow dirt road, and already within a few miles we had spotted a number of the high profile animals: numerous deer with spotted backs and white, fluffy tails, a wild boar, a barking deer—short and compact with pencil-thin legs—and a plethora of birds. We visited a breeding ground for narrow-snouted crocodiles.

I silently held out hope of seeing a tiger. Our guide reported having seen one just a few days prior, crossing the road. We all stayed focused and hoped that we would be in the right place at the right time. We worked our way into the jungle, stopping here and there, and then came across a meandering stream with a small bridge across it. Another jeep was parked there with two people in the back; their guide had found tiger prints on the bridge and they were going to wait and see if it reappeared.

"Should we wait, too?" I asked our guide.

"No. What are the chances that the tiger will walk back the same way?" He shook his head. "It will not happen."

We pushed on, transitioning back and forth between jungles, thus providing us good visibility, and through open grassland thick with eight-foot-tall elephant grass. This grass can grow up to twenty-four feet high, and can conceal elephants and tigers. In just a few months the villagers would risk their lives to cut the grass to use it as material for home repairs and animal feed. Some villagers had already started cutting and I wished them safety from whatever lurked inside. The edge of the grass facing the road was dotted with thick cobwebs like shiny white freckles.

After twenty-five miles of dirt tracks we finally arrived at a wide riverbed and parked the jeep. We crossed the stream and set up our picnic lunch atop an overturned wooden rowboat in the shade of the trees, and our guide sat on a stuffed hemp bag at the water's edge.

"Pssst! Come quick!" our guide hissed. "Rhino!"

We dropped our sandwiches and ran to the river where I could hardly believe my eyes. A hundred meters down the shallow, pebble-bottomed river there stood a living, breathing rhinoceros. I had half expected it to look small and cute, but in reality it looked like a giant model of a prehistoric dinosaur placed out in the water. It was a predator for sure, bold and in charge and fearful of nothing. The massive beast slowly crossed the river to our side and then disappeared into the brush. The bushes moved in jerking waves as the rhino tramped through them, and we stared for a long time until the swaying stopped and the animal was gone, leaving me wanting more.

We finished our lunch and then crossed the river back to the jeep. Farther down the road we pulled over next to a narrow river smothered by the thick jungle, and we fought to make it to the water's edge. Our range of sight was rather limited and it seemed unlikely that we would spot much of anything. Now that I knew for sure that wild things prowled this jungle, I wanted desperately to see a tiger. I tried to will one to appear, focusing all of my energy until I wholeheartedly believed my wish would come true. My short attention span eventually got the best of me, and soon I was mindlessly staring out into the greenery.

Our guide, on the other hand, was honing in on something. We stood in silence panning our eyes between him and the jungle, wanting to be a part of the discovery. He shot a finger to the trees across the river, and from the greenery there appeared another rhino. This one was even more unbelievable than the last, and it was much closer than the other had been. I held my breath, afraid it would hear my heart beat. We stood dumbfounded and wanted a closer look. We crept along the bank until we were nearly across from the amazing creature.

Claire let out a sigh, and our guide shot her a look that said "Silence, foreigner! This rhino will kill you!" He had earlier explained that rhinos were incredibly dangerous, and you never wanted them to know of your presence. Not because they would run away, but because they were more likely to charge. I imagined myself trying to run away from the rhinoceros through the thick brush and the scenario did not end well.

As we bumped along the road toward the edge of the park, alternating between the tall grass and jungle, the sun cast its rays through the early evening dust, transforming our return trip into a sepia tone photograph. Had that really happened, I wondered? I looked around the jeep at the rest of the group, who were all lost in thought. They were probably wondering the same thing.

44

Kathmandu Ring Road

Brad

During a conversation I had with Bharat before we set off for Annapurna, we had discussed literature. He spent a good portion of each day reading, and the bookshelves in the living room were his window to the world. I had asked him what his favorite book was.

"The Fountainhead, by Ayn Rand," he had said, without hesitation. "It has become a manifesto for your Republican Party," he added.

While packing for our trek, I decided to bring it along. I had assumed that Bharat, a generation older and probably better read, must have found me a banal conversationalist, and I hoped that by reading his favorite book I could arm myself with something to contribute to a future conversation. Each night in the thin, freezing cold air of the high Himalayas I read the life story of an unpretentious genius-architect and his acceptance of being overlooked as a result of his refusal to exercise control over anyone else, and who made choices based on principles of simplicity, efficiency, and his own perception of beauty. It was a fulfilling read, although I spent many a daydream pondering how those principles had any practical connection to the Republican Party. It would be a good topic for my next conversation with Bharat when we got back to Dobighat.

Our return to Dobighat fell a few days before Thanksgiving, and during our treks we had talked about throwing a traditional American holiday feast for the family. However, soon after our return the hurdles began to mount.

"Pesal, is there a place in Kathmandu where we can buy a turkey?"

"What is a turkey?"

"It's like a very large chicken. Very large and bald."

272

"We have chickens in Kathmandu."

"Do you have turkeys here though?"

"We do not have turkeys in Nepal, I think so."

"Hmm. I guess a couple of chickens would do. What about ovens? Most Thanksgiving dishes are made in ovens."

"I do not think you will find an oven here."

"Isn't there a neighborhood *tandoor* or something where people can go to make naan?"

"We do not eat naan in Nepal. Actually, no bread at all. We do not have ovens in Nepal, I think so."

By Thanksgiving Day we hadn't managed to track down anything at all for an American-style feast, so we let it pass without mention and happily ate *dal bhat* with our hands. As usual, Pesal demonstrated that he was the fastest of the fast and excused himself by telling us that we could take our sweet time.

By the next day we felt ashamed of ourselves, and resolved to cook the next most American meal that we could think of: Mexican food. Pesal walked us to the various shops in Dobighat that sold chickens ("Can you please ask her to kill it for me?") and vegetables ("Brad, *dai*, in Nepal avocados are fruits!") Salsa and tortillas were no problem, as they were already staples of the Nepali diet, known as *achaar* and *chapati*, respectively.

In the late afternoon we pulled together a team of chefs in the kitchen; Sheena, Pesal, and Manika formed a *chapati* brigade, and Liza— Pesal's cousin from down the road—cut tomatoes for the *achaar* using a curved knife that she held in place with her foot, squatting on the floor. We threw together a bowl of guacamole, a recipe that we had used to win first prize in a guac-off way back in Costa Rica, and I prepared chicken and peppers to fry up for fajitas. Sheena cooked beans in the pressure cooker and mashed them up to approximate refried beans.

I tossed the chicken in a large frying pan with some oil and spices, and in a short while it was done.

"Pesal, go rally the family, the food is ready." He looked in the pan with some alarm, and told me that I didn't know how to cook chicken.

"Bharat and Durga will not like this chicken, I think so."

"Why do you say that?"

"Because it is not fully cooked. It should be cooked for a long time. This will make us sick."

In South Asia, meat is stewed for a long time until it nearly falls off of the bone, whereas in America we usually cook it just up to the point of it being done, and then we stop. Both ways work, but the American way requires more precise timing to ensure that it is cooked enough, but not so much as to become tough.

"Pesal, I assure you that this isn't going to make anyone sick." He reluctantly retrieved the family, and everyone sat around the table for our Mexican-Nepali Thanksgiving. The concept of fajitas, and of wrapping everything up in a tortilla together, was a foreign concept to our fellow diners, but they took to it like Japanese to hot dog eating contests.

"This *achaar* is so good with these beans!" I had never seen Uncle Laxman attack anything with such ferocity as he attacked his fajita burrito. I felt proud to have brought a little taste of the official food of the American southwest to our Nepali family.

As we all sat around afterwards massaging our bellies and softly burping, Pesal took inventory of the people at the table.

"Where is Barna? Oh dear, we have forgotten to invite Barna! Nobody must tell her!" But of course her little sister Liza, unable to resist, told her.

On the day before our final departure from Kathmandu, Bharat led me to the upstairs patio, as it was a particularly sunny day. Manika brought tea and we sipped it in silence—a comfortable silence, no longer awkward as it had been in the beginning. I looked out over the surrounding rooftops, all antennas and hanging laundry. There had been little planning in the construction of the buildings in the neighborhood, and as a result they all sat at odd angles to each other. A few prayer flags flittered in the breeze and I could hear the distant drone of traffic on the ring road. Kathmandu had the feeling of being an ancient outpost at the edge of the world. A pump was running at the house next door, bringing water up through a pipe where it splashed through a series of plastic buckets filled with sand—homemade filters—before falling into the large black plastic tank on the roof. Most of the families carried their water in large copper jugs from the neighborhood fountain. It reminded me that I wanted to talk about The Fountainhead by Ayn Rand. Bharat was ruminating something, staring off into space. When he finally spoke, he didn't ask a question.

"I read many books," he said. It seemed that he was trying to figure out where to start. "America is a great country, I think so. I read so many books about America." He was still concentrating very hard, still chewing over his thoughts.

"You people are very brave," he said. "You left your jobs to drive around the world." He sipped his tea. "You came here and you walked so many miles in the mountains. We Nepalis never go in the mountains unless we have to. I have never been to western side of Nepal. But you crossed Thorong La, so high and so dangerous. Why do you do this? You people have a different mind than the Nepali mind. You are not afraid to fail. There is so much risk, but you go anyway."

It was the first time that Bharat had led the conversation. Until then, he had presented only questions, and I had filled the void with words, but now, at the very end, I was hearing his side of the story.

"America is a great country, and I believe that there is something in the American mind that makes it this way. I read many books, to try to understand how it came to be this way.

"My son, Baroon, moved to America, and some years later he bought me an airplane ticket so that I could visit him for one month. It was my wish to sit down with Americans while I was there and hear them talk. I thought I could learn the American mind and then come back and teach it to my Nepali students. In this way Nepal could become great like America. Many Nepalis move to America, but they never move back, and the lessons are lost."

I had known that he had visited Baroon a few years before. In fact, it had been during the time when we all lived in Flagstaff. One evening, Sheena and I had gone out to the Himalayan Grill, which was owned by the uncles of Baroon's wife. We had seen Baroon at a different table with Bharat and Durga, but we hadn't known who they were at the time. How strange it would have been to have looked into the future and seen myself sitting on a Kathmandu rooftop with Bharat.

"When I got to America, I very much wanted to ask questions to American people, but it was impossible. People would come over and we would all sit together in the living room and have tea. Maybe we talked of small things, but then the people would get up and leave. I was there for one month, but when I returned to Nepal I had not talked in depth to any Americans. That is the way it goes when you are a visitor. It is hard to get to know people."

He leaned forward and placed his hand on my knee, as he had done on occasion. A few days before we had walked to a nearby shop to try buffalo meat dumplings, and he had held my arm while we walked, as we had seen Nepali friends doing.

"When Baroon told me that you people might stay at our home in Kathmandu, I felt very lucky. Now you have been here for two

275

months, and I have gotten my wish. Every day we sit here and I ask you anything I want. In these two months I have learned something about the American mind, I think so."

Bharat sat back in his chair and looked at me, smiling, and we sat there in silence. I was stunned. Since our first conversations I had taken his silence as a reflection of my banality as a conversationalist. I had assumed that he felt like he had to engage me in order to be a good host. I reflected back on all of our conversations and thought, if I had only known how much weight he placed on my responses, maybe I would have tried to think of something more profound to say. But maybe that was the point. He didn't want me to prepare any deep pontifications; he just wanted to peer into my brain, for better or worse. To see the foundation, how an American weighed risk and opportunity. He had asked me why America was the best country in the world (it isn't), why *we people* have so many guns (fear), and what we do with our old people (I didn't have a good answer). But he wasn't asking these things just to fill silence. He was solving a puzzle.

"What do you think about Nepal?" he asked after some time. Pesal had come upstairs with fresh tea and we had been staring out over the neighborhood rooftops.

"I love it here."

He was silent for a while, and again seemed to be contemplating something.

"I have a proposal for you, Mr. Brad. When you finish your world trip, move back to Nepal. We can start an English language institute. We can teach the American mind to Nepalis and the country can become great." I said that Nepal already was great.

On the morning of our departure the whole extended family was waiting for us downstairs. Liza and Barna, their sister Barsha, Laxman, Pesal, Manika, Bharat and Durga were all standing in the living room when we came down with our bags. The mood was solemn. We sat down on the couch. Pesal, and his father, Laxman, presented us with a Gorkha knife in a leather case, the typical knife used by the Nepali army.

"American life, Japanese wife, Gorkha knife," I said, and Pesal smiled.

"That is a good saying."

Liza presented us with a stamped-metal cutout of Nepal within a bamboo frame, and then Durga stood up and took the wooden clock from her wall and gave it to Sheena. Her command of English was still improving, and when she wanted to speak to us she seemed to rehearse it in her head before speaking. She moved her mouth as if practicing, and then she spoke.

"I hope you have so many babies, and you bring them to Nepal. We will take care of them, and you stay here!"

We stood and made our way out to the front patio, where Durga picked up two marigold garlands and placed them around our necks. Then she picked up a small tray of yellow and red powder and stood in front of us. She looked very sad, and I could feel a lump forming in my throat. Durga pressed her finger into the powder, and then made *tikkas* on our foreheads, a blessing for the road. When she finished she moved her mouth, silently practicing, and then spoke again.

"You are now my son," she said, placing her hands on my face, "and you are now my daughter." Sheena sniffled and let out a squeak, and then put her hands over her eyes.

We hugged Durga and then Bharat, and then each of the others in turn. Pesal, our trusted Nepali ambassador; Laxman, always so happy; Manika, who had finally warmed up to us and regularly gave me knuckle bumps; Barna, whose energy was contagious; and Liza, Sheena's Nepali sister. We walked somberly to Nacho and placed our bags inside, and then got in and turned over the engine. The family stood around the back alley behind the house and watched us back out, and then we slowly drove away as they waved to us. As soon as we were out of sight Sheena erupted into tears and I cleared my throat to make it seem as if I had a piece of food lodged there that was causing my eyes to water. It was as if the reason for us leaving home had been to find Nepal.

Our original intention had been to stay in Nepal for three months, and as we drove across the country to the west, we couldn't believe that we were prying ourselves away a full month early. We passed from one small region to the next, each completely different from the last, and we wished we could stop and discover what made each one tick. One could spend a lifetime in Nepal and never tire of it, despite its tiny size. For our third month we had intended to load the family into Nacho and drive over the mountains to their ancestral village in the east, where we would live in their old home and experience the village life. But we had received an invitation from their extended family in Delhi to attend an Indian wedding, and had decided to go for it. Either way we would be in for a profound experience, but we had to make a decision, so we chose the wedding.

That night we camped in a cool, foggy grove of gum trees near the Indian border, and enjoyed one last bout of solitude before returning to the human pinball machine that is India. In the morning we crossed the border over a narrow one-lane road on top of a small dam. Our progress was halted midway across the dam as a drunken Indian man sprawled out in the middle off the road and passed out. Several people pushed his body aside, but he repeatedly rolled back in front of our tires as hundreds of bodies poured around Nacho like flowing water. When finally we reached the other side, a corrupt official attempted to solicit a bribe from us for having been allowed to cross the border, and a dozen beggars approached us with their palms open to the sky.

45

Asian Highway 2
to New Delhi

Brad

It's four thirty in the morning and I am peeling my swollen eyelids open, stirred awake by heartburn and the jostling of a toothless old woman next to me. I am in the middle of the floor amid a sea of Indians. The air smells of stale oil and curry sweat. I fall back asleep. My finger is stabbing the strobe-lit air while I ricochet between jumping Punjabis. My eardrums hurt. I can't tell if I'm screaming or if I'm not making any sound at all. A man with a bejeweled crown arrives on a white horse amid the calamity of a marching band. A curled-up leper holds out her chalky, decaying arm stumps and moans through cracked lips. I lay down my cards and a man in a turban throws his head back and takes all of the money. I am wearing a dress. David Lynch couldn't write this dream. And anyway, it wasn't a dream.

We entered Delhi from the North and became part of the chaos of the ring road. The landscape surrounding the city was strangely reminiscent of South Phoenix, with its parched soil and dust-blown streets lined with shacks. Scraggly dry trees tangled with garbage stood in the rare places where ramshackle buildings did not, and the traffic lanes brimming with brightly-painted buses and yellow rickshaws and dilapidated cargo trucks whose sides had been decorated with blue Hindu goddesses. On the back of every truck and bus there was a message painted in block letters: "HORN PLEASE!" The horn is a do-all communication device in India: the driver honks to initiate a pass, to tell other drivers that he is behind them, or that he is beside them, or that he is completing a pass. Some honk for no reason, or because a moment may seem too peaceful, or because they remember that they have a horn and can't resist the temptation. Many trucks don't bother having side mirrors because driving is done by audible brail, not by sight. To drive in India is to be assaulted by noise, and the Delhi ring road became a giant loudspeaker enclosing the city.

People say that Delhi has the craziest drivers in the world. We heard this from Indians and foreigners alike, but we found it not to be true. Indians say this because they are from Delhi and perhaps they have never driven elsewhere in India, and the travelers who say it haven't been to the forlorn corners and in-betweens where the driving is truly life threatening. They take the train, or they fly, but nobody in their right mind drives across India. Delhi is a stinking, chaotic, betel-juice-stained, urine-reeking collection of cinderblocks and trash and people, but is one of the cleanest and most put-together cities in all of India.

When we arrived at Karan and Jyotsna's apartment, Jyotsna met us on the street. We parked between rickshaws under a pepper vine and the passersby stopped what they were doing to stare at us. At times we had feared for our safety in India—Sheena especially, as gang rape had become something of a national sport among India's urban youth—but vehicular security was not a concern. We were stared at because we were different, and nearly every interaction became a scam because we were perceived to be rich, and probably stupid. We were usually greeted not by wave of hand or bobble of head, but by upturned palms or by a gesture made with bunched, empty fingers placing imaginary food in the mouth with the repetitive rhythm of an oil derrick. But despite the scammers and beggars and gawkers, we couldn't imagine anyone breaking into our van. These were curious people, opportunistic askers, and crafty schemers, but most were not outwardly malicious aside from the rapists. We locked the doors and left Nacho on the street.

It was wonderful to see Karan and Jyotsna again. They greeted us with tea in the living room of their third floor apartment. The walls of their modest home were plain, and the place felt lived-in. A simple table, wooden chairs, a worn couch, a sofa chair, and a single bed in the living room. Karan's parents, grandmother, and sister lived there too, as is the custom. In India, the son traditionally lives with his parents forever, and brings his wife into his family home after marriage. Sisters remain at home until married, at which time they move in with their husband's family. Sons take care of their parents, and daughters take care of their husbands. We would see this transition with Karan's sister Suruchi, as it was for her wedding that we had driven to Delhi. We had been invited to have an experience that few foreigners get to have: to witness an Indian wedding from the inside. We would live with the bride and her family throughout the whole affair. We knew before it even began that it was a once in a lifetime opportunity, and for that we felt supremely lucky.

Seeing Karan and Jyotsna living in India was surreal. In America we had gone to restaurants, gone hiking and visited microbreweries. We don't often look at foreigners living in America, and consider how strange it must be for them to make the transition to our most unusual way of life. Maybe we don't even realize that we have a most unusual way of life. The person who takes your order at the Indian restaurant is a hero. He has made a series of bold decisions and somehow managed to get himself halfway around the world. He is making money beyond his wildest dreams, and his priorities and experiences—his entire paradigm for how the world works—are so vastly different from ours as to be unfathomable. The mindsets are incompatible. India and America are two opposite worlds somehow existing on the same planet. Hiking and microbreweries and big fluffy houses in the suburbs are just frivolous extravagances from American television.

Family from as far away as the Himalayas of northern India had already begun to descend upon the family's apartment for Suruchi's wedding. In this part of the world there are certain expectations of a host, one of which is the duty to house and feed all of the guests. I asked Karan's mother if anyone was staying at hotels and was nearly laughed out of the room. The foreigner asked if the family would stay in a hotel! This, I was told, would be profoundly unacceptable. Instead, Karan's father had temporarily rented the one-bedroom apartment below them on the ground floor. The family members, and we, would stay there.

"How many people will be staying in the one bedroom apartment?" I asked.

"I don't know, fifteen or twenty," Karan said nonchalantly, as if this weren't completely impossible.

At two o'clock in the morning my eyes felt like they were bleeding from fatigue. I squinted and bobbed my head, teetering on the edge of sleep as old Colonel Mohan, perched on a folding chair, recounted his glory days in the Indian Air Force.

"I tell you, Brad, those were the good old days. I flew just above the mountain tops, as free as a bird—"

"Is he telling you the surveying story?" It was the Colonel's wife. She had heard it a thousand times, and she rolled her eyes.

"—I have followed every state border in all of India, even Kashmir and Jammu. They are India, you know! I have seen India like

281

few others have seen India. I am like you, Brad, but in the sky like a bird!"

I wanted to collapse onto our thin mattress and recover from the long drive down from Nepal, but this was part of the experience.

"You don't say. Every border?" Sheena had passed out, and was splayed across our mattress as if she had fallen from the sky, her arms and legs in a lifeless tangle and her face straight down in the sheet. Earlier in the day a delivery of thin mattresses had arrived from a rental company, and we had lined every flat surface in the apartment with them, with the exception of the bathroom and kitchen. Another man had come by with a small boiler and spliced it into the water supply in the bathroom, providing hot water to the sink. The concrete floors were pitted and dirty, and the walls bore the collective stains of all of the previous inhabitants. The wallpaper was peeling in places and it smelled like mildew and dust. This apartment was the ugly duckling, left empty so as to be rented to visiting families during the wedding season. As such, it received no care, no maintenance, no cleaning. The drain in the kitchen sink was still clogged with green peas from a previous inhabitant.

All around our temporary apartment, family members happily bobbled their heads and smiled and chirped excitedly in Hindi. This was a happy time, not a time for sleeping. Every year Indian families look forward to the wedding season. It is as if they save up all of their energy throughout the year just for this. Astrologers choose the most auspicious date to be married, right down to the hour, and the country's one billion inhabitants listen. On the night of Suruchi's wedding, three days hence, there would be thirty thousand elaborate, over-the-top Indian weddings in the city of Delhi alone.

I didn't remember Colonel Mohan leaving. I only realized that I had fallen asleep when I heaved myself awake with curry-induced heartburn, helped along by the Hindi jabbering of several wrinkled Indian grandparents playing cards on an adjacent mattress. The lights were still on. It was four-thirty in the morning and we were the only ones who had fallen asleep. A smattering of Indians lounged about talking, playing cards, or in various states of repose. Karan's grandmother stared into my eyes as she slapped a card down on the mattress. Was she chewing gum? The expression on her face said, "You're a pussy!" And then I blacked out.

To describe an Indian wedding is to describe nighttime. Suruchi's wedding would be a three-day celebration, but a more appropriate description would be to call it a three-night occasion. The actual wedding ceremony was to occur in the wee hours of the morning of the fourth day, as dictated by the astrologers. Sheena and I awoke early, around nine-thirty, and took to the streets to experience the Indian morning: a food cart breakfast, a five-cent cup of pulled milk tea, and the smell of dust and ripe bananas and diesel fumes. We returned home as the sun climbed near its zenith in time to see zombie-like cousins, aunts, and uncles stumbling about clasping their heads with swollen eyelids. We all packed shoulder to shoulder into the upstairs apartment where Karan's mother served milk sweets and tea, followed by a spread of *chapatis* and rice and curry.

Until then we had become accustomed to being the sole guests in locals' households, and so those who knew the language carried out communication in English. But here we weren't the guests of honor. Rather, we were observers of an important family affair, and despite everyone knowing English, Hindi was almost exclusively spoken. We sat idly by, listening to a volley of Hindi, peppered with a few English words, unless directly spoken to. But this was good. These were Indians being Indians and we were flies on the wall.

Karan's grandmother was the one person who didn't know any English, and also the person who took the greatest interest in Sheena. She was short with glasses and long gray hair, and her chubby cheeks and protruding chin gave the illusion of an under bight. She adopted Sheena as her confidante and proceeded to tell her all of her best stories.

"Keyo batam kata la," she began, emphasizing her point by waving her hand. She maintained direct and deliberate eye contact with Sheena. "Hataijooba dza kando."

"I'm sorry," Sheena said, waving her hands and smiling, "I don't speak Hindi."

"She is telling you the story of Partition," Jyotsna interjected.

"Seekan jhai hudu bata…" the old woman began. Jyotsna pivoted to face Sheena, her young son in her lap, and translated.

"She says that in 1947 the British split India into two countries so that the Muslims could have their own territory. She lived in the partitioned territory, which was to become Pakistan, and was forced to abandon her home and relocate. Her grandfather had built their home, but she packed a suitcase and walked two hundred miles to India, leaving everything behind." The old woman paused often, her face calm. She chopped the air with her wrinkled hand at intervals to drive her point. "She started a new life here from nothing."

This old woman had every right to think I was a pussy.

On the first night of celebrations the bride's family would present expensive gifts of clothing and jewelry to all of the members of the groom's family in the banquet hall of a five star hotel. We piled into cars and made our way across the city, passing other wedding festivities for an hour until we arrived at the hotel.

"Why didn't you book a hotel nearer to your house?" I asked Karan as we approached the opposite end of the city. As the brother, he had been responsible for planning the entire wedding.

"Man, there are thirty-thousand weddings happening right now. Everything in Delhi is booked solid."

Karan and Jyotsna disappeared into the crowd when we reached the hotel, and Sheena and I gravitated to the fringe, the milk-faced wallflowers at the corner table. Colonel Mohan found us and joined us with his drink. He brought with him his nephew, Prateek ("Call me Patrick"), who had recently moved to Delhi from Brooklyn. Patrick was different from the others in that he had an American accent, and he dressed and carried himself like an American. He didn't look Indian to me, but perhaps Turkish or Italian.

Servers came around with plates of *tandoori* chicken, samosas, and chicken *tikka*. I gorged myself on the spicy Indian treats any time I they were offered, and washed them down with yogurt drinks. It was a gluttonous smorgasbord of Indian specialties. We talked America for a while, which bored Colonel Mohan, so he left us alone. The conversation turned to local issues and we asked Patrick why he had decided to move back to India.

"Wasn't my choice man," he said with New York exasperation. "I've lived in America since I was in high school. It's my home. I can't even remember living in India. I'm an American. Anyway, I went to university in New York and as my graduation date neared I started looking for work in the tech industry." He explained that, to remain valid, his visa required him to either be in school or have a full time job with work sponsorship. "I tried finding work everywhere, but nobody would hire me. At a certain point I realized that it wasn't going to happen. I thought about dropping off the grid and becoming an illegal immigrant, but I didn't want to have that hanging over my head." He decided instead to move back to India, a foreign place that he didn't know, to start over in a new life.

"I'm struggling here, to be honest. I don't understand Indian people. I don't understand interactions, and the women are a mystery to me. If I get a good job here I can probably expect to make a few hundred dollars per month. It's going to be a big change." He explained that he would probably get an arranged marriage, as he didn't feel that he stood a chance at wooing an Indian woman, given his lack of understanding of them. Suruchi's was an arranged marriage, as were most Indian marriages.

Over milk sweets and tea earlier in the day Karan had explained that his parents had found a husband for Suruchi through a community dating website that matched potential mates based on caste and income level, and that astrologers gave the final blessing. In India, inter-caste marriages are quite rare, as are marriages based on love. After her parents had consulted star charts and poured over the available grooms in the online catalog, Suruchi had been introduced to her prospective husband and was given one year to get to know him before the wedding. The couple could have chosen to call it off at any time if they couldn't get along. It all seemed very businesslike to me. Marriage based on measurable compatibility factors. But hey, coming from a country with a greater than 50% divorce rate, what did I know?

That night I was determined to show Karan's grandmother, and myself, that I was not a pussy. When Karan and his childhood friends headed up to the rooftop at three in the morning, I was right there behind them with a wad of Rupees in my pocket and a vague understanding of the rules of a strange Indian card game.

"Just follow along and we'll show you how to play," Karan said on the way up the stairs. It was a cold night. "You brought your money, right? But don't worry, it's a simple game, and we'll go easy."

Stupid, stupid, stupid.

We arranged ourselves in folding chairs around a plastic table: Karan; Puneet, the well-dressed proprietor of a chain of stores that very closely emulate the look, feel, and inventory of Office Depot; Gautam, who didn't say much, and looked almost exactly like Mr. Bean of British television fame; and Harjog, a dark-skinned Sikh man who wore a black jacket and a white turban on his head to contain his hair, which he was forbidden to cut on the basis of his religion ("I don't have to cut my hair, because it just falls out!")

I was dealt five cards, among which there was a two, a Jack, and a small flush of clubs. For this I was denied the pot, and asked to surrender several Rupees. Next my hand included two pairs and a lonesome face card, for which I was forced to ante up more cash than I wanted to, all of which I lost to Mr. Bean. I paused the game and demanded that the rules be explained again.

"Listen, Brad, if you get three of a kind you will win, got it?"

The next round was dealt and, what was this? Three Kings! I put on my best poker face and considered any possible way in which I might lose, but there was no possible way. I upped the ante twice until there was a great stack of Rupees in the middle of the table, and then I threw my cards down with a big shit-eating grin on my face. "Three Kings!" I said, triumphantly.

The man in the turban threw his head back and wailed into the night like a coyote, and then wrapped his arms around the stack of bills and pulled them in.

"Wait, but look, three Kings!" I said, "I win!"

Karan leaned over, shaking his head, and said, "No, you didn't win. See that? You also have a five and a seven. This hand is no match for Harjog's spades."

At five-thirty the sun began to rise, signaling the end of our game and time to go to sleep. We descended the stairs where I found Sheena sprawled out like a broken ski jumper on our mattress amid the sea of Indian bodies. She had spent much the night being regaled by Karan's grandmother with stories in Hindi. I wedged myself into the drawer of Indian spoons, wondering just how I would explain to Sheena in the morning how I had managed to lose such a great deal of our money while she slept.

The next day, like those before it, really began at dinnertime. The second day of celebration was to be held at a bar on the opposite end of Delhi, a dance party. It should be said that I do not dance. I think of dancing much too scientifically to be able to enjoy it. Music plays, sending sound waves into our ears, which the brain relays to the spleen, telling it to excrete some endorphins. Some of us don't understand how to deal with those endorphins, so we allow them to manifest themselves as flailing of our arms and legs. Show me a room full of dancers and I see a room full of people who have no idea how to simply enjoy the endorphins that Lady Gaga has given them.

Well in advance of the dance party, we loaded into Karan's sedan with a couple of his card-swindling friends, while some of the cousins loaded into another vehicle. We drove through Delhi to a nondescript strip mall of sorts, and we parked in a lot. There were various restaurants there, and the parking lot was full. We undid our seatbelts and made ourselves comfortable.

Karan addressed us over his shoulder from the driver's seat. "Do you two like whisky?"

286

The thought of drinking whisky after all of the milk sweets, tea, curry, and *chapati*, made my throat twitch. "I guess." We didn't want to be rude. Karan got out of the car and rooted around in the trunk, and then returned carrying a bottle of whisky.

He sat back down and began to educate us on the pastimes of India's modern adult middle class.

"Listen up guys, so you know how in America you have drive-thrus? Well, we don't have those in India. But lots of Indians have cars now, and eating in the car is considered high class." At this point, a dangerous-looking man interrupted him at his window. The man placed his hand atop Karan's car and looked into the window. Karan rattled off some Hindi and then turned to us.

"You like chicken *tikka*?"

"Of course."

More jabbering in Hindi.

"Do you eat lamb?"

"What idiot doesn't?"

More Hindi, this time with grandiose hand gestures. He pointed to us and to his friends and to his cousins in the other car. He pointed to his whisky and said more things in Hindi. People speaking Hindi always sound exasperated or angry, and sometimes both. The man turned and walked away.

"Right, so where was I? Oh yes, everyone wants to eat in the car, but there are no drive-thrus. Do you remember all of those people we saw on the side of the road near that samosa stand on the way here? They were all eating in their cars. They order their samosas and then someone delivers them to the car. Well, what we're doing here is similar, but better. You know that guy that just came over? He's sort of a waiter. We tell him what we want and he walks around and buys it all from the restaurants and delivers it to us so we can eat it here."

I had never been much of a fast food guy, but I could imagine that young Indians who were pulling in loads of cash as call-center workers and tech-savants would like to feel pampered.

"Also," he said, "the man will bring us supplies for our drinks. He can't get the alcohol, but he can get the cups and the ice. You should also know that drinking in the car is illegal. But in India, anything is possible. The police know this is happening—they're not as stupid as they seem—so the guy who delivers the food has to bribe the police. So people come here and eat and drink, and the police come by about once a day to collect their *baksheesh*, and everyone stays happy."

287

Soon the man returned with the ice and cups, and several tin containers of oily Indian food. Karan handed the man some Rupees and he left us alone, coming back on occasion to see if we needed anything else. We sat around drinking whisky and eating chicken and samosas until I felt as if I would hurl, and then we drove to the bar for the dance party, and I massaged my windpipe to suppress my now chronic heartburn.

Inside the bar the music was a meat cleaver to the skull, and this caused the Indians, decked out in their suits and their saris, to go hog-wild. The dance floor pulsated, the men stabbing the air with their fingers and women mouthing the lyrics to the eardrum-splitting Indian pop music.

Sensing my inability to dance, possibly tipped off by my abstinence from the dance floor and my dead-eyed stare (I was performing anthropology), Mr. Bean grabbed my arm and silently took me on as his protégé. He led me forcefully by the arm, and pulled me to the edge of the round swirling bowl of flailing Indians. Without speaking he demonstrated how to dance without actually dancing. It involved raising the eyebrows, hunching the back somewhat, and taking small steps forward while slicing the air in subtle motions with the hands as if cutting carrots. I thought it looked very funny, but I later realized that it is only funny if you are Mr. Bean; anyone else doing it just looks like a buffoon.

I repeatedly excused myself from the dance floor to nurse alcoholic beverages instead of dancing, only to repeatedly be dragged back in by a severely drunken man wearing a suit. I would display a few steps of Mr. Bean's dance, unambiguously marking myself as a buffoon, and then retire to nursing my alcohol. Before long my repeated nursing of alcohol caused my spleen to go out of control, squirting endorphins here and there like a garden hose, and I completely lost track of the anthropological study I had been conducting. The air was hot and I could feel myself bouncing off of bodies. Sounds had been replaced by ringing and the splitting of firewood on my eardrums. The strobe light froze my surroundings into static frames and the room was all at once a black and white slideshow. My hands in front of my face chopping carrots. Karan's cousin with her mouth open, probably screaming in fear. The severely drunken man's face directly in front of mine. My pistol fingers stabbing the air like a Punjabi dance master. Sheena suspended mid-air in the shape of a starfish. Blurry. Loud. Dizzy. Heartburn.

I sat up clasping my bloated head amid a dispersion of sleeping Indians. I batted at the sunlight from the curtainless windows with club hands to blot out the sun, but it was futile. I stumbled to my feet and tripped over mattresses to the bathroom. I placed my hands on the sink and wailed like a yeti. Stop ringing that bell!

The big day had arrived, and with consecutive four-hour nights of sleep under our belts, everyone wore on their faces a look of boxing match defeat. Kirtan hunkered down in the corner wearing sunglasses over his swollen eyes. Pradip's hair poked out in all directions, and despite being rail thin, exhibited a double chin. Colonel Mohan's shirt was partially untucked and he walked with a slight limp. We drank tea and ate milk sweets in silence, except for Karan's grandmother, as fresh as can be, entertaining Sheena with an unintelligible anecdote in Hindi. By now they had developed their own system of communication through sign language and sounds, and Sheena made whale calls at the old woman while lightly waving one hand and wiggling her fingers. Her eyes appeared to be swollen shut.

"All right, Sheenaji, are you ready? Come up to the rooftop!" Jyotsna splayed her fingers so as not to smudge the freshly applied henna on her hands. Delicate lines swirled across her palms and fingers, and curled in intricate patterns up her forearms. Sheena stumbled out into the sunlight and made her way to the rooftop overlooking the surrounding chaos that makes up a typical Indian morning.

By midday Sheena's hands had been covered in paisley, and Karan's aunt had squeezed her into a traditional Indian sari ("This is the most uncomfortable thing I've ever worn—I'm going to pass out!") Karan set me up with a traditional man-dress—literally, a dress—with long black tights to go underneath and a frilly feather boa to make my neck look fabulous.

"I'm telling you, man, this is what Indian men wear to weddings."

"I believe you, but I'm a *farang*. Are you sure people won't think this is weird?"

He thought about it for a second and without answering sent me downstairs to have my dress ironed.

"But how do I—" before I knew it he was gone on another errand. I walked downstairs cradling my dress, assuming that something would present itself, perhaps an ironing board or a sign. When I reached the parking lot I cornered a young girl and, trying to communicate my needs, pretended to be ironing something and then shrugged my shoulders and looked around. Her face was confusion mixed with fear as I swirled my fist in the air over an imaginary surface. Sensing her confusion I motioned as if I were touching an invisible iron, which was very hot, so I shook my finger and put it in my mouth and then continued ironing. Next I held up my dress and regarded its crispness, and then held it in front of my body and ran my hands down the front of it, displaying how flat it had become. She stared at me, her mouth agape, and then held her limp finger out in the direction of a dark alley.

I brought my dress into the alley, the feather boa around my neck for safe keeping, and was surprised to find a skinny Indian man next to a large flat stone with an iron, which must have been a hundred years old, filled with red hot coals. Odd, but we had come to expect this sort of thing in India. I handed him my dress and at once he began splashing water on it from a bowl and deftly sliding the hot iron over it. In a moment he handed it back to me and returned to his state of repose. I offered him a couple of Rupees and slowly retreated, bobbling my head in thanks in the way that Indians do.

At night the banquets halls along the ring road emitted pink and yellow halos of light as we passed. Marching bands and throngs of people surrounded men on white horses adorned with jewels and streamers, and the sounds of horns and drums shook the windows of Karan's car. I had questioned the claim that so many weddings were happening on a single night in the same city, but the proof was in the traffic. Suruchi's wedding venue was five miles away, but after an hour and a half we were still driving. Or more appropriately, not driving.

As time went on, the number of wedding-goers on the road increased exponentially, and Karan became restless. He revved the engine, and then all at once pulled into the oncoming lane. Drivers swerved and honked as we sped off in the wrong direction down the busy divided street. His face was that of a possessed man. He turned to me, taking his eyes off of the impending head-on collisions and said, nearly yelling, "Welcome to Delhi! Craziest drivers in the world!"

Stepping into the wedding venue was like entering a fantasy world; the chaos outside the high walls ceased to exist and we were enveloped in a scene as atmospheric and luxurious as any I have ever witnessed. The courtyard seemed like that of a Raj's palace, and was designed in such a way as to block all evidence of the outside world. The vast court where the wedding would take place had a perfectly maintained lawn with paved walkways, open to the night sky. At its center there had been erected a giant four-post canopy draped in fabric, which could shelter a hundred people. Against one wall a stage boasted a two-person throne. Various sofas, chairs, tables, and verandas dotted the grounds, while an enormous outdoor kitchen lined the western wall. A thick vaporous haze had settled into the courtyard, and the subdued lighting ignited every airborne molecule in a soft pink glow.

We arrived at ten o'clock at night and already the temperature had dipped to jacket weather, at least according to Sheena and me, having spent the previous two years in a state of near-perpetual summer. Sheena tucked her bare arms into the polyester folds of her sari and I rubbed my exposed thighs through the waist-high slits in the side of my man-dress, and tightly constricted my feather boa around my neck. We regarded the setting with amazement, and pondered the extremes to which the Indian culture has gone with its weddings.

The origin of dowry – a price paid by the bride's parents to the groom's in exchange for their son's hand in marriage – is hard to trace in India. By many accounts, the practice only began in the 20th century, and was rather insignificant at first. This contrasts with the practice in modern India, as evidenced by the endless expenditures we witnessed. I had asked Karan about the monetary aspects of Indian weddings, and he informed me that the day a daughter is born in India, the parents begin saving for her wedding, and even then they will take on a great deal of debt for the occasion. That is because it is the responsibility of the bride's family to pay for the wedding and to present new outfits and gifts of gold to all of the extended members of the groom's family (this had taken place on the first night at the hotel). To show restraint would be shameful, and so the practice is carried out behind the façade of a smile, like it is nothing. The display of material wealth at wedding time, regardless of whether the family actually possesses such wealth, is of paramount importance. Karan told us that a bride's family is expected to spend on the wedding the same amount that the groom's family had spent in raising him up to that point in his life.

We made ourselves comfortable under the giant canopy, and I quickly filled up on food brought around by the well-dressed wait staff. Not yet fully appreciating the extent to which Suruchi's parents had gone to impress their guests, I failed to realize that these were just the appetizers. A vast assortment of main courses awaited us at a buffet inside of a giant food hall, but by the time I realized this, it was too late. In short order I had eaten myself into a food coma, and my Indian food heartburn had flared up and was clawing at my esophageal sphincter. I alternated between massaging my windpipe and squeezing shut the side slits of my dress to shield my upper thighs from the creeping cold.

From the corner of my eye I spied Mr. Bean arguing with his wife, and it occurred to me that he was in fact a real person, one whom could speak, and not just a figment of comic relief.

Notably absent from the congregation had been Saurabh, the groom. From a distance we heard the shrill wail of horns and the deep thud of a bass drum. We joined a stampede of people and emerged from the courtyard to a side road where we were met by a most unusual scene. A decorated marching band of mustachioed, dark-skinned men slowly approached, their big raccoon eyes reflecting the strings of overhead lights strung between poles and carried above the procession. Mixed in with the band was the groom's entire extended family, led by his father. Bringing up the rear, Saurabh rode atop a white carriage led by a white horse decorated with jewels and frilly harnesses. Saurabh wore a gold crown and his face was concealed behind strings of dangling crystals. Every so often his father would throw a handful of money into the air and the music would momentarily stop as the marching band dove to the ground to pick it up. The family danced and swirled and the father threw money and the band intermittently delivered its thudding, shrieking tune in a minor key as if leading a gladiator to the ring.

Meanwhile the bride's extended family created a human barricade to the courtyard so as to prohibit the groom from gaining entrance. The groom's father approached the barricade and began the traditional negotiation with the bride's female cousins and sisters-in-law to allow the groom into the wedding.

Until an Indian woman gets married, she will have spent every day of her life living with her family. On her wedding night she goes home with the groom, never to return to her old way of life; her future will be spent caring for her husband and her husband's parents. Thus, the negotiation that we witnessed was for a monetary payment to the bride's family to let the groom come inside and take her away for good. Tonight, Suruchi would assume a new life.

The negotiation was hot and Jyotsna led the shouting match in trying to secure the best price for Suruchi. She and the rest of the ladies displayed a supernatural sassiness in their haggling, something truly Indian, and were able to take eight hundred dollars in cash off of the old man to share between them.

At around three o'clock in the morning, Saurabh and Suruchi finally tied the knot. They sat on pillows under a veranda while my knees shook with fatigue. They pressed *tikka* dots onto each other's foreheads. Sheena fought to keep her eyes open while being regaled by Karan's grandmother with stories of the old country. Hindu priests said blessings and threw flower petals into a candle. I whimpered. The couple encircled a fiery shrine seven times, very slowly. Karan's grandmother stared at me and silently mouthed the words "You're a pussy!"

And then it was done.

In the morning Sheena and I slept in. After three solid days of sensory abuse and sleep deprivation, our brains finally ceased to function and we lay there, euphorically tangled in the sheets like John and Yoko on a flimsy rental mattress in the middle of the dirty floor. A column of sun slanted through one window and for a moment, as I began to regain consciousness, I imagined I was camping on a deserted beach. But when I opened my eyes there were different people milling about than the ones that had been there when we went to sleep. They stepped over us and clanged pots and pans in the kitchen. I jerked my pale, bare torso into an upright position and looked around in fear. A big-eyed Indian girl stared at me, adjusting her sari.

"Psst! Sheena, wake up! What is going on?!"

Sheena blinked a few times and then flinched and recoiled. The same stains adorned the walls and floor, but the mattresses had all been stacked against one wall and Karan's family had evacuated. In the meantime, while we slept, a different family had taken over the apartment and decided to leave us there in the middle of the floor. We quickly gathered our things and made the walk of shame upstairs, hair poking wildly in all directions, to Karan's apartment.

"You're just in time," Karan said when he met us at the door. "Saurabh's family will be here any minute."

It is customary on the day following a wedding that the bride and groom, along with the groom's parents, return to the bride's family home for a private lunch. We insisted to Karan and his parents that this was a family affair, and no place for a couple of milky-faced intruders. We would make it awkward. But they wouldn't have it, and insisted that we stay. Sheena and I sat down on the bed in the living room and began nervously wringing our hands while Karan's mother neatly laid out lunch on the table.

A knock sounded on the door and Karan's father stood up, paused and took a deep breath, and then opened the door. Suruchi and her new family entered and Karan's mom pointed them to the living room. They situated themselves around the coffee table, taking their places on the couch and chairs. Very little was said. Karan's father stood and retrieved gift boxes filled with sweets, which he handed to Saurabh's parents. They accepted them without speaking, and set them on the floor. Everyone looked at one another in the festering silence—these two families now joined, but still with sweaty palms.

Karan's father rendered some confidence and bravely spoke a short sentence to Saurabh's father.

"Keenan jabu hannan tikka."

Saurabh's father shrugged. "Jamlu tikka."

The silence simmered, and my insides reduced to an uncomfortable paste that seeped through my pores and coalesced on the surface of my skin like dank sweat. I scratched my stomach through my shirt and reached for a milk sweet on the coffee table.

"Seema boota epdoo?" Karan's mother asked. The question was acknowledged but nobody responded. Sheena shifted her weight on the bed and I scratched my stomach again. My mouth was dry. I needed some water, but I didn't want to say anything. I wanted to be invisible.

"Ekdam baji emroo foreigners?" Saurabh's father asked, pointing with his chin in our direction.

"Ekdam," Karan's father responded, shrugging his shoulders. I cleared my throat and Sheena's breathing became labored. I hoped she would pass out so I would have an excuse to scoop her up and say that we were going to the doctor. She remained upright. My belly was becoming raw, but still I nervously scratched at it. This went on for an hour and a half, during which time no English was spoken, nor was much said at all and then the family left.

That evening Jyotsna stayed home to take care of her son while Karan, Sheena and I headed into Delhi. Karan wanted us to have the temple experience, and we were happy for the change of pace. We drove to a nearby train station and left the car there.

When the train arrived, it was filled to the gills and we squeezed aboard.

"Sheena," Karan said, looking a little uneasy, "maybe you should ride in the women's car."

Looking around we realized that this train was completely filled with men, most of who were staring at us, which we had become accustomed to.

"I'm fine, that's all right," she said. But Karan insisted that maybe she should, so she asked why.

"Because these men might rape you."

"Right here? But I'm with you guys."

"Yes," Karan said, "but there are more of them than there are of us." It was the sad state of affairs in India, unfortunately. In the years leading up to our arrival, the headlines had been littered with stories of gang rape on public transit and elsewhere. In India, a rape occurred every thirty minutes. Even foreign tourists—and not just women traveling alone—had fallen victim. One brave husband was no match for five or ten out-of-control Indians, and potentially helpful bystanders had been notoriously passive. Months later we would read a news story about the Indian Prime Minister using his biggest speech of the year to encourage his countrymen to "reset their moral compass" and stop raping people.

When we arrived in the center of Delhi it was dark, and we wound through crowded streets lined with food hawkers and beggars. The gutters were filled with the usual garbage and the noise of honking cars, and rickshaws stabbed at us from all directions. We weaved our way through crowds of people toward a Hindu temple. At the base of each of the plaster columns leading to the temple's entrance there sat slouching lepers with chalky, decaying arm and leg stumps. They had gauze over their eyes and their lips receded from their bloody gums. Their limbs were literally falling off and they heaved their hideous, chapped stumps at us as we passed, their mouths agape in agony.

We stepped into the dark temple and were at once whisked into a torrent of sweating, pulsating bodies. The crumbling moldy walls had been painted in layer upon layer of blue paint, scenes depicting elephant-headed, multi-armed gods and goddesses perched cross-legged or floating midair. At the back of the maze of corridors we came to an opening where, in the middle of the concrete room, sat a statue of a monkey god. This being the temple of the monkey god, and it being Tuesday—the day on which Hindus were meant to give offerings to the monkey god—this was the prime destination for Indians from all walks of life. People pushed and shoved their way to the monkey statue, where they smeared their foreheads with pigment and said a quick prayer. They lit incense or touched the statue, and then they pushed and shoved their way to the door. It was a hectic, violent place.

We left the temple and walked past the lepers and beggars, and past pushy rickshaw drivers and people with their palms up. We crossed the street, past honking buses, fuming trucks, and sputtering rickshaws to a side street where there stood an imposing white building with domed roofs: the Sikh temple.

We entered the temple gates and were met with a scene of serenity: a placid pond, and pensive men and women pacing the grounds.

Few people spoke, and those who did were calm. Nobody pushed and there were no beggars. We removed our shoes and walked through a stream of water to clean our feet before approaching the entrance. At the top of a flight of stairs we took scarves from a basket and used them to cover our heads.

Inside the temple, couples or individuals sat on a carpeted floor facing the central pillars. Some bowed their heads in thought, while others watched and listened to a man speaking. We sat for a while, and it reminded me how hard it is to find refuge from chaos in India. At last we stood and walked outside to stand by the pond.

"Did you notice that the people at the Hindu temple were all in a hurry?" Karan asked. "Many of them treat their religion like a business. They feel obligated to go through the motions, so on Tuesday they come to the monkey temple and give an offering to forgive their misdeeds for the week. Then they go off and do whatever they want. It's like a free pass." He said he came to the Sikh temple often.

"I'm sure you've noticed the beggars everywhere." That was an understatement. "People give a couple of Rupees because they're supposed to, but for the most part people feel that it isn't their problem. The government banned the caste system, but it's still alive and well. Here in India it's every man for himself. But you'll never see a homeless Sikh, or a begging Sikh. The Sikhs take care of each other because they're taught that it's the right thing to do."

Sikh temples serve free meals every day, and anyone without a place to stay is given a bed. Karan had once taken a bed at a Sikh temple while traveling. At the top of the hour we queued up and, when it was our turn, a man dipped his hand into a giant bowl and scooped out a ball of oily paste, transferring it into each of our hands in turn. We found a quiet spot and I made myself place the oily peanut goo into my mouth, certain that I would finally fall ill with food poisoning, although that never did come to pass.

As outsiders just passing through, it was easy for us to assign labels and point to the aspects of Indian life that seemed flippant, idiotic, or frustrating. Mixed in with it all there were also hidden gems that made us smile, but really the emotions we felt toward India were just data points with non-interchangeable units plotted on an unlabeled scale. India had evolved from a different primordial soup, one brewed up by blue-skinned gods with elephant heads, and loin-cloth-wearing wise men. Our mindsets are incompatible. India and America are two opposite worlds somehow existing on the same planet.

46

Westbound Highways
to Rajasthan

Brad

After the chaos of Delhi, we embarked in search of calmer pastures. We wanted more than anything to return to Nepal, but our Indian visa wouldn't allow us to leave the country again unless we didn't plan to return. The Himalayas extend into the disputed territory of Kashmir and Jammu in northwestern India, but it was by now December, and the mountain passes had been closed down due to deep snow. If it was possible to find warmth and solitude in India, the deserts of Rajasthan seemed like our best bet.

We went out of our way to make a pit stop at the Taj Mahal near the city of Agra, a building said to be the most impressive ever built. I will not contest the fact that it was an impressive building, but to say it is the most impressive building ever built is laughable hyperbole. Still, once we got past the relentless touts and camel drivers that surround the complex, the Taj Mahal was a worthy stop. Perhaps equally interesting was the Red Fort, only a few kilometers away amid the putrid squalor of Agra.

When we finally arrived in Rajasthan in the far west, we found something that we had long ago given up on in India: solitude. We skipped from one desert fort to another until we arrived at Jaisalmer, a far-flung fairytale outpost when viewed from afar, near the Pakistani border. It seemed like a giant sandcastle as we approached, and within its walls we found the most visually pleasing facades and cobbled streets, filled with the most annoying touts selling camel safaris.

Each night in Rajasthan we drove off on some dirt track and slept in the desert. It had become a real novelty to camp in the wild, but in India wilderness was still relative. Each night we were found by shepherds tending their sheep, or by men in turbans riding rickety motorbikes through the desert. All were curious but pleasant, though none left without putting a palm up for a handout. Feeling particularly nice, perhaps on account of our relative solitude and the relaxation that it brought, we obliged each visitor's begging with copious amounts of Indian milk sweets that we had brought down from the wedding.

When it finally came time to leave Rajasthan, I was stricken with a great idea: rather than take the highway south to Gujarat, we should have an adventure. Maps of the region showed a salt flat called The Little Rann of Kutch spanning a large area just to the south of us. It began just thirty or forty miles away, and we could get quite close to it by taking rural dirt tracks toward the Pakistani border. Based on the maps, it appeared that there would be a 150-mile stretch of salt flats without any roads, and if it was anything like the salt flats of South America, then we could simply drive to the Pakistani border and then follow the border southward across the crispy ground using our GPS as a guide. Eventually we should end up in Gujarat, where we could find our way back to a road. What could go wrong?

We purchased a week's food provisions in Jaisalmer, and then set off to the south, toward the Pakistani border on a small paved road. When the GPS showed the end of the road, we stopped at a ramshackle village to fill up our water tanks. Nacho became quite heavy when fully loaded with water, so we had waited as long as possible to fill up. We had also forgotten to buy eggs, so I parked, and while Sheena set off on foot to find someone with eggs to sell, I inquired about filling up our water tanks.

I asked several people, and each one pointed back toward the edge of town and indicated that I should ask for a man named Rajesh. When Sheena returned with the eggs, we headed back in the direction from which we came, and repeatedly asked villagers where we could find Rajesh. They stared at us confusedly at first, and hesitantly pointed to the last house.

Scraps of garbage and pieces of rusted metal surrounded Rajesh's house. I parked Nacho next to a concrete platform in front of the house and got out. A man wearing a stained tank top—Rajesh, I presumed—approached me holding a tiny plastic cup full of tea, which he tipped into his mouth then threw on the ground.

"Juju gablib nadar?" he asked.

"*Pani?*" I asked, using the Hindi word for water and tipping my thumb into my mouth. I walked to the side of the van and unscrewed the

298

cap on one of our water tanks and pointed inside. He nodded and pantomimed that I would need a bucket, so I went to the rear bumper and retrieved our blue jerry cans, which we used for filling our water. He led me over to the concrete platform and lifted a rusty lid, which lay on top of it. There was water inside, but it was covered in a layer of green scum and bits of flotsam.

"No, no," I said, waving my hands, "For drinking." I indicated again with my thumb. He nodded vigorously and made a demonstration. He put one hand into the tank and pushed the scum out of the way, and then took some of the water in his hand and put it in his mouth. He smiled and nodded profusely, and put his hand out to take my jerry cans. Not seeing any other options, I handed one to him.

Rajesh set the jerry can on the surface of the water, and then pushed it under to submerge it. When the fill nozzle broke the surface of the water, all at once the layer of green scum dove into the can, and when it was good and full he lugged it over to me and took the other one to fill. I decided just to go with it. We had been in India and Nepal for nearly five months, and hadn't gotten sick, so why not? I poured six jerry cans full of scummy water into our drinking water tanks and handed Rajesh a few Rupees for his trouble. He poured me a tiny plastic cup of tea, and I tipped it into my mouth, severely burning my tongue, but I played it cool and handed the cup back. He flipped it to the ground, and then we said our goodbyes and set off.

While the GPS didn't show any more roads, a small dirt track continued for a while past a set of sand dunes. Just before we reached the Pakistani border, we came to a tiny crossroads of two dirt tracks bordered by a couple of stick huts. We stopped there to review the GPS before setting off into the desert. Within seconds a dozen villagers surrounded us, pressing up against our windshield and windows. They stared at us as if they had never seen foreigners before—which they probably hadn't—and we stared back. By now we were well used to the dead-eyed stares, but this was different. The men wore brightly colored turbans around their heads, and large, golden hoop earrings. The women had pierced noses, with metal chains connecting their nose and their ear piercings, and they wore vibrant saris with shawls over their heads. They stared at the strange foreigners, and we stared back at the pages of the National Geographic.

We asked if it was possible to drive to Gujarat from there, and hearing the name of the adjacent state, they all enthusiastically shook their heads no, pointing back in the direction we'd come. We thanked them and drove on, turning left just before crossing the border.

At first we followed a dirt track that seemed at one time to have been a road project, but it quickly petered out and we followed tire tracks in the dirt. We passed a shepherd who was wearing a dirty white *lungi* and leading a flock of sheep. As we passed, he smacked his stick into the ground to clear his sheep from the track. As we passed him, his face was pure confusion. A hundred meters later we passed two men dressed in Lawrence of Arabia costumes leading a herd of camels into the desert.

Soon we reached what was supposed to have been the salt flat, but were surprised to discover that it was in fact an expansive dry tidal marsh. To drive across it was to drive across Velcro, and our tires sank two inches into the semi-dry muck while we drove, sapping our power. Occasionally we came to spots where the underlying mud was still wet, and we sank deeper. We had the feeling that we were driving on ice, the wheels sliding and squirming as we drove. As evening fell on the first day we pointed toward an island in the tidal marsh and set up camp on its edge. At highest tide it would have been a beach to a very shallow ocean inlet, but for now the ocean was fifty miles away to the southwest. We were surprised that we hadn't gotten stuck, having driven a two-wheel-drive overloaded van into a hundred-mile-wide tidal marsh.

First thing in the morning, after coffee and breakfast, we got stuck.

It happened not in the mud, but in sand. We had driven out of the marsh to cross a small, dry island, when we reached several stretches of deep sand. Feeling cocky, I flew at top speed into a long stretch of sand, and midway through came to a stop. Sheena cursed me, but I had learned my lesson about getting stuck in the sand back in Argentina when I had attempted to camp in the bottom of a sandy wash. I dug the sand away from the engine, deflated the rear tires, placed our sand ladders in front of the tread, and easily drove out of it.

It was at this point that the poo really hit the fan.

The GPS showed several little rivers that we were to crossover the width of the tidal marsh, and each had turned out to be dry. But when we came to the very last one—the only thing standing between off-roading conquest, and us—things took a turn for the worst. We saw it from far off, and as we approached it our hearts sank. This tidal inlet was still full of water, and there was no telling how far we would have to drive to get around it. We were smack in the middle of nowhere, right on the Pakistani border, and we didn't have enough gas to go back. We would have to cross it. I doffed my shoes and waded in, noting that the bottom was deep, sticky clay. This was bad news. I walked upstream and downstream, and as I did, the first people we'd seen in two days—a couple of dark-skinned men—came up behind us on a motorbike. They stopped and took off their shoes, and then walked the bike across, pushing and lurching it through the clay. They stood on the other side and offered encouragement.

"You can do it!" they chanted, bringing to mind images of gymnastics coach Bela Karoyli. What came next fell far short of Kerri Strug gloriously flipping through the air. I got in, told Sheena that I knew what I was doing, and then very slowly and deliberately drove right into the clay river, where we would remain for the rest of the day. I spent a great amount of time digging in the clay and strategizing, but in the end Nacho just wasn't the 4x4-at-heart that I had imagined.

After an hour a jeep arrived, adding another dozen people to our audience; one is never alone in India. I asked the driver if he would be so kind as to pull me out, but he solemnly shook his head no. The clay was too deep, and we were far too stuck. Instead, he produced a bucket of peanuts from his jeep and we all sat around looking at Nacho and eating peanuts in the sun in the middle of the endless, flat desert. At long last, as evening approached, a man arrived on an antique tractor. The man with the jeep had called him, and it had taken him an eternity to reach us. I hooked our short tow rope to Nacho's front bumper and looped the other end on the tractor, and we very nearly destroyed both Nacho and the tractor in trying to pull us out. But at the end of the day we drove away and eventually found a road. We had made it to Gujarat after all.

Two days later we reached the Gujarati coast, and crossed the bridge to the island of Diu, an old Portuguese outpost, where we would spend Christmas. We drove the perimeter of the island and miraculously found our very first secluded Indian coastal camp atop a cliff overlooking the Arabian Sea. It was marvelous, something we hadn't experienced in more than a half of a year. We rolled out the awning and set up our chairs, and listened to the waves crash against the cliff below.

In the morning Sheena and I took a drive and parked at one of the island's popular beaches. As we strolled along the main section of beach, out of the corner of our eyes, we noticed a man walking toward us. Middle aged, respectable. We walked on, chatting about all manner of joyous Christmassy things, when all of a sudden the man cut us off, and, literally fifteen feet in front of us, dropped his pants. We froze. He folded his body in half and plopped an enormous shit right on the beach in front of us. We stared, dumbfounded, before wincing and reeling back, and then hurried off in the opposite direction. It was only then that we began noticing that, every fifty feet or so, other people had left their own little prizes all over the otherwise pristine beach. We needed to get out of India.

Our original intention had been to spend six months driving through the Middle East to get to Europe. In fact, it had been one of the regions I had most looked forward to on the trip. As soon as we began planning our escape from the rat race I started devouring books about Pakistan and Iran, and about the old Soviet republics of Kyrgyzstan, Tajikistan, Uzbekistan, Turkmenistan, and Azerbaijan. Our wish was to pass through northeastern Pakistan into China, and then to enter Kyrgyzstan and follow the Silk Road through the old Soviet republics, cross the Caspian Sea on a ferry, and then make our way down to Turkey. Our fallback plan, having equal potential to be fascinating, was to cross Pakistan and Iran to get to Turkey.

While we were in Delhi, we had tried to plan the Middle Eastern portion of our route. Our first choice proved impossible, not only on account of China wanting a king's ransom for permission to drive through, but because Pakistan had very recently seen a rise in al-Qaeda activity aimed at foreigners, and had temporarily stopped issuing tourist visas to Americans. I spent considerable time on the phone with the Pakistani Embassy, but they would not budge.

Unfortunately, Pakistan's refusal to grant us visas also killed our backup plan. Not that it really mattered anyway, because Iran also refused to issue us a visa on account of us being American and wanting to drive our own vehicle there. And so it was that we found ourselves in the same situation as in Southeast Asia: cut-off from the rest of the world by political borders. Our only choice was to place Nacho in a shipping container—again—and ship from India to Turkey. And since we were on India's west coast, that meant shipping from Mumbai.

We followed the coast down from Diu, and lo and behold, as soon as we entered the city we were pulled over by a cop. Indian cops are nothing more than common criminals, and this one fit the stereotype perfectly. After pulling us over in the a thickly-trafficked Mumbai street, he got off of his motorcycle and waddled over to my window, his moustache like a smudge of barbecue sauce on his bulbous face. He quickly got to the point by informing me that we had committed a heinous crime.

302

"You have committed a heinous crime."

"And what crime would that be?"

"Your windows are tinted."

"Ha!" For a moment I thought that perhaps it was a bad idea to laugh in his face, but then I remembered that I wanted to strangle him to death, and laughing was a much better release of energy.

"That's really funny," I said, making sure he knew that I could not take him seriously.

"What is the solution?"

"Excuse me?"

"I said, what is the solution?"

"The solution to what? To me having tinted windows?" It should be noted that our front windows are not tinted. As I argued with him several vehicles drove by with full blackout tint, but when I pointed them out to the fat cop, one after another, he made excuses. It didn't matter, because he hadn't pulled me over for my windows, he had pulled me over because he thought I was stupid.

"I guess you'll have to write me a ticket."

He looked confused, and tried again. "What is the solution?" He repeated. I slowly mouthed the words to him as if speaking to a deaf person.

"I – guess – you – should – write – me – a – ticket."

The conversation went around and around and I practically begged him to give me a ticket. I knew that he wouldn't; it would be too much paperwork, and all of the money would go over his head. He wanted a bribe, and even went so far as to tell me that I could just give him a monetary "gift" to make it all go away. The he showed me a laminated page stating why tinted windows are illegal: to keep people from concealing criminals in their cars. I handed the page back to him.

"This says that tinted windows are illegal because they can be used to conceal criminals. I promise I'm not a criminal – I'm just a tourist. But if you think I'm a criminal, please just write me a ticket so I can stop wasting your valuable time."

At this, he once again asked me what the solution was, and then put his face close to mine and stared in my eyes. Classic. I stared intensely back at his eyes, studying myself in the reflection of his aviator sunglasses. After thirty seconds it started to get ridiculous, two men silently staring at each other in the middle of Mumbai traffic, waiting to see who would crack. I focused on not blinking, just as I did when having staring contests with my kid niece. Finally, he cracked. He

303

mumbled a few more words and folded some papers to save face, and then he left. I watched with great delight as he waddled back to his motorcycle, his pride shattered, and situated his grotesque paunch on his gas tank. I stared at him with laser beam eyes, like a disgruntled gang member trying to instill fear in his rival, and then I pulled away.

The next couple of weeks in Mumbai passed in a continuous parade of days in which we dealt with shipping logistics, punctuated by small endeavors of tourism. Over one weekend we had nothing to do, so we headed for the hills. I had done some internet research and found that there was a campground nearby—the only campground we had heard of in India—and set out to see what it was all about. At first we were unable to find it, and we passed through several small villages where the people stared at us as if their eyelids were glued open. We eventually found our way into a nice forest on a mountainside, where we drove through a dry riverbed for a while, and then found a secluded camp spot in the trees.

In the morning, several men surrounding Nacho awakened us. They rudely demanded that we leave, and stood next to our door until we had packed everything up. The leader of the pack, some kind of officer, was the most assertive and rude, barking orders at us nonstop. He took copies of all of our vital papers and called them in to his main office, then came back several times asking for more papers. Birth certificate, marriage license, auto title. His demands were ludicrous, and exemplified India's infamous crippling bureaucracy. The man ended a phone call with his office and barked that he had to photograph us and all of our things, so he lined us up like criminals and took several photos. In the end, just before we pulled away, he blew my mind in a way that only Indian authority figures can.

"Excuse me, one more picture."

"Why? You already have pictures of everything."

"No, picture of you for my Facebook."

"Hey Sheena, this guy says he wants to take his picture with us to put on Facebook," I yelled.

"You can tell him to go to hell!" she screamed.

"My wife says she's not interested," I said, and then pulled away into the riverbed, furious and flabbergasted.

Back in Mumbai, we stumbled headlong into the shipping process and quickly entangled ourselves in a dehumanizing web of inane Indian bureaucracy. Amid all of the inefficiency, scamming, quarantines, and rickshaw riding, we received an invitation to join some friends in

Goa for a few days of sun and sand before waving goodbye to India for good. Goa is a small state about 350 miles south of Mumbai, consisting of miles and miles of idyllic beaches. Our friends would be staying just north of the last coastal town we had driven to several months earlier before having cut inland to Hampi, where the worst drive of our lives had begun. We had managed to make a near-complete circle of India over the course of our three months in the country, and by reaching Goa we would close the circle. What the hell, we figured, why not give India its full pound of flesh?

With Nacho safely sealed inside of a shipping container, we found our way to the train station, bought our tickets from a man with a giant old-fashioned ledger, and settled in for the fourteen hour ride south.

Mumbai had been the most normal and modern city that we had visited in India. It had its beggars and scammers, its touts and sidewalk sleepers and slums, but for the first time we could almost blend in with our surroundings. For two weeks we had strolled the city, sat along the sea wall, and eaten popcorn while watching movies at the cinema. It is foreigners and its proximity to Mumbai that make Goa such a strange place.

Goa is located within India, but it really isn't Indian at all. It is India's resort destination, a place where Mumbai's elite escape the city for a weekend of disco and flesh-watching, and where foreigners flock by the thousands to eat cheap Indian food on idyllic coconut-palm-fringed, white sandy beaches. The influx of money from vacationing middle-class call center workers and foreign tourists created an incentive for Goa's beach towns to pick up their garbage and put the kibosh on the touts and beggars. We saw that as bittersweet for the region's cultural depth: bitter because there were hardly any Indians in Goa, yet sweet because it was actually a place that people might actually want to go.

After hailing a cab from the railway station—which seemed to have been partially reclaimed by jungle—we arrived late in the evening at the house of our vacationing friends Jeff and Sharo. The house was a short walk into the palms from Palolem Beach in a small community of rentals filled mostly with long-term foreign visitors. Jeff was an American who worked for Amazon, and had relocated his family to Singapore for work, which was where we had met him several months before.

Our forays to the beach were at once wonderful, for the idyllic location and relative peace and quiet, yet disappointing, due to the lack of cultural sensitivity demonstrated by the visiting foreigners. Yoga tourists strolled around town, ate at restaurants, and zipped around on motorbikes in skimpy bikinis, baring their breasts and bottoms to a backdrop of ultra-conservative villagers. That was Goa: located *in* India, but nothing *like* India, and therefore a very strange and confusing place indeed.

We only stayed for two days; long enough to stretch our legs, sleep in, laugh, and smell the ocean breeze before it was time to return. It had been a last hurrah, our swan song, a fling.

Our sleeper car for the return trip consisted of several tightly packed shelves of thin cots inside of a repurposed wooden cattle car. It was a haunted library whose dark shelves held not books, but rather prostrated bodies and bags stuffed into every crevasse. The air inside of the sleeper car was a thick vapor of body odor and damp wood, and you could smell the galvanized steel where a thousand dirty hands had rubbed the bed rails smooth. Sheena climbed to the top cot and I took the second one down; they were stacked three high. I pushed my overstuffed backpack onto the tiny mattress and it took up nearly half of the bed. I wedged myself on top of it, put in my earphones, and fell into a fitful sleep.

The sleeper car didn't have any windows, but in the morning I could see the overspray of reflected sunlight speckling the floor at the end of our haunted library. I clawed my way out of the overstuffed row, which had by then become filled with extra parcels of belongings secured with twine, and emerged into the covered breezeway at the end of the car.

I leaned against the doorway and gazed upon the world that night had birthed. Our train slowly drew a line up the coast, through an endless thicket of coconut palms. We passed tilled fields and rice paddies. A skinny, shirtless boy whipped a water buffalo with a handful of weeds and stopped to watch us as we passed. Stick huts demarcated the edge of each field that the coconut palms encroached upon. The morning smelled of dry clay and hot grass and coconut husks. A breeze wafted into my covered viewing gallery, causing my hair to twitch against my forehead. I was watching India go by, person-by-person, hut-by-hut. A pig pushed its nose into a garbage pile at the edge of the tracks, but we were gone before I knew what it was after. A boy tilling a field waved at the train. The breezeway on the overnight to Mumbai was the place to be.

I lowered myself into the doorway and let my legs dangle out the side of the train, and the warm air brushed my skin. The train slowly rocked and swayed, and I anonymously, hypnotically, watched the world go by.

My coconut-palm-hypnosis was interrupted when a couple of Indians approached and I could feel them behind me. They stood there for a minute, and then one of them touched my shoulder.

"Excuse me," he said. I acknowledged him with a nod. They were passengers.

"You should be moving your legs."

I craned my neck to see them. "Excuse me?"

"You should be moving your legs inside the train."

I said okay, and lifted my legs into the train and stood up. Just then, without any warning, the concrete platform of a rural train station whooshed by, just inches from the edge of the train where my legs had just been. I watched, dumbfounded, as the platform flashed by and the space in front of the door became once again a breezy void. *That would have ripped my legs off*, I thought to myself. I turned around, but the men were gone.

Brad is the most interesting man in the world, as evidenced by the throngs of Indian men that surround him as he performs basic auto maintenance.

Even Chennai's street-dwelling children see our subjects as extraterrestrials, and attempt to establish a means of communication.

While walking from her guesthouse in Chennai to the beach, Sheena is handed a bare-bottomed baby and proclaimed an honorary member of the clan.

Santhanam (right) and Gopal Krishna (middle) see Nacho and crew off as they depart their campsite in front of the temple at Mahabalipuram.

Only 2,200 kilometers of this bomb-crater road stand between Hampi, India, and the Nepali border. India's National Highway 7 can go fork itself!

Indian highways are a model of safety, efficiency, horn-blowing, and inventive overloading configurations.

An entrepreneurial shakedown artist on a motorcycle leads us on a very long alternate route around a giant swimming-pool full of mud, which has somehow ended up right in the middle of India's National Highway 7.

Men stand on the *ghats* and bathe in the Ganges, Hinduism's most sacred (and perhaps its most polluted) river, in Varanasi, India.

311

Human bodies are burned all day, every day, on the *ghats* in Varanasi, India. The ashes are swept into the Ganges, but the fire is never extinguished.

Brad experiences the happiest moment of his life when, emerging from the dust and chaos, Nacho reaches the Nepali border at the end of India's National Highway 7.

Nepal proves to be a kingdom of rainbows, unicorns, and little old men hanging around wearing matching hats and vests. This isn't a Krispy Kreme employee picnic, it's heaven.

(Left to right) Pesal, Durga, Manika, Barna, and Bharat—a subset of the Rai family—in front of their home in the Kathmandu suburb of Dobighat.

Sheena begins the ascent of 18,000-foot Thorong La Pass on Nepal's 150-mile-long Annapurna Circuit trek through the Himalayas.

On the morning of the *bandh*, Sheena, Brad, and visiting Nathan and Claire convene in Bhaktapur's central square and decide if they should ignore the orders that have come down from the Maoist rebels prohibiting all driving.

Someone has a great idea involving a bar of soap that will surely keep the angry Maoist rebels from throwing petrol bombs through Nacho's windshield. Those rebels can read English, right?

After being abandoned by the military convoy, Nacho takes to the cliff-hanging Himalayan mountain roads like Batman to rogue justice.

You want an X-box? You want a radio-controlled car? Here's a dirty rope and some jingle bells, now get the hell out of here and use your imagination.

Our Tibetan hosts in the remote village of Kyanjin Gompa, nestled against the Chinese border deep in the Himalayas. They live only a mile from Tibet, but have never been there, and perhaps never will because of political issues involving the Chinese.

Rajasthan is the closest to wilderness that can be found in India, but even in the emptiest deserts, wandering shepherds are never far away. Here, two shepherds engage in a wordless visit that inevitably ends in them departing with pockets full of milk sweets.

Each night of camping in Rajasthan came with its own shepherd visit. Brad became well-practiced at standing around in silence with them.

Brad and Sheena pass a herd of camels on their way to the Little Rann of Kutch, a 150-mile stretch of desert tidal marsh without any roads, a place where nothing could possibly go wrong.

Two days into their road-less crossing of the tidal marsh known as The Little Rann of Kutch, something finally goes wrong.

In between bouts of sensory overload, heartburn, and sleep deprivation, Brad and Sheena tag along as Suruchi and Saurabh's wedding unfolds all over Delhi.

Karan's Punjabi grandmother kisses Sheena's henna-tattooed hand as they walk together across the grass of the wedding venue in the early hours of the December morning.

Part 3

Middle East to
the Dark Star

47

Atgecmez Sokak 10, Istanbul

Sheena

After getting used to seeing landscapes and people change slowly over distances, airplane trips made transitions abrupt. On the night before we left Mumbai we took a rickshaw ride down a chaotic street in the warm, sticky evening air to a hole-in-the-wall restaurant where flies swirled around our table and the Indian waiters bobbled their heads. As evening fell, we had gazed out over the rooftops from our hotel and watched as hundreds of kites filled the sky like delicate bean sprouts, and the sky lit up in brilliant orange and pink before darkness fell. In the early morning we were on a flight, and by lunchtime we were having tea with an orthodox Jew named Ishmael at the airport in Amman, Jordan, staring out the window at an endless sea of sand. In the evening we emerged from the airport in Istanbul, Turkey, to the biting chill of winter on the dividing line between Europe and the Middle East.

Setting foot in Istanbul was the start of a love affair. With Nacho still on a ship, and desperately needing to take a few breaths after five months on the subcontinent, we had rented an apartment sight unseen. When we hailed a cab near the city center and told the driver to take us to Balat, the neighborhood where our apartment was located, he looked at us a little strangely. He then set off to the west along the Golden Horn—a finger of water that juts off of the Bosporus, pointing toward Europe. After a while, he cut left away from the water, and when his little taxi struggled up the steep cobbled alleys until he could go no more, he let us out.

"You walk from here," he said in his strongly accented English, pointing up the hill.

From that day on, whenever we told someone where our apartment was located, we got the same response.

"Why do you take apartment in Balat?!" They pronounced *Balat* with a heavy B and a subdued second A, the way a Russian person might pronounce "bullet."

We had unknowingly stationed ourselves for the next month in *Little Tehran,* as it was called, Istanbul's most traditional and conservative Muslim neighborhood. But it didn't take long to begin loving our neighborhood; it was quite literally like no other place in the city. Our apartment was on Balat's fringe. One block downhill put us in a scene of old-world Istanbul, while one block uphill was a scene plucked right out of the Middle East. Women strode down the cobblestone streets in shapeless black burkas, their eyes and noses peeking out of small triangular openings in the fabric, while their fathers, brothers and husbands sported thick beards and were dressed in long, gray trench coats and finely-embroidered flat-top hats.

Altug drove a four-wheel-drive Volkswagen van that had once been used as an ambulance in Austria. He had gotten in touch with us as we neared Turkey, and offered to show us around when we got to the city. On the day that he came to our apartment to meet us, he echoed the confusion of so many others in our home base choice.

"Why?" he asked, dumbfounded. "Why *Balat?*" His bearded-face was a picture of pure bewilderment. "You have chosen the most conservative Muslim neighborhood in all of Istanbul. You should have asked me first!" And then he added, "Besides, it is very poor and dangerous here."

I looked out the window at the wall of decrepit buildings and it made sense that one would think that, yet I had observed life on our street every day and it just didn't feel the least bit dangerous. There were the neighborhood kids who played soccer well past midnight every night; a colony of happy street cats; and a slew of charming families who spent countless hours breaking apart old bed frames, fruit bins, shipping crates, and furniture to use as firewood in their homes. I hadn't realized why they broke furniture apart all day, but came to understand that they did it out of necessity. Altug said that hardly any of these old stone homes had been built with a means to heat them, and given that many of the people in Balat lacked the financial resources to buy wood to burn, they had to look for it instead.

Much of the charm and personality of the neighborhood came from the mobile businesses that made their way down our street every day. Each vendor had his own call, and since we didn't speak Turkish, it took a while for us to distinguish who was passing by without first peeking out the window. There was the old man who sold the ever-popular *simit,* a sesame covered bagel; another man who sold potatoes and onions; and someone else who just pushed around a flatbed cart with old electronics on top, each day an assortment of new things. I reported the daily inventory to Brad as the cart passed by.

"It's the junk man! Today he has an old computer screen."

The next day: "It's the junk man! He has wires today, and an old rotary telephone."

Altug said that he was a recycler. He picked up old electronic junk from people, fixed it up, and then sold it for profit.

The recycler was interesting, but my favorite vendor came every Saturday around four-thirty. He had a big farm truck and sold all of the typical in-season Mediterranean fruits and vegetables with a selection that changed a little bit every week. He was my only consistent weekly appointment and I was always ready when he appeared.

Brad and I went for a run each morning dressed in sweatshirts, winter hats, and gloves to fend off the cold. We would begin by threading through the alleyways and staircases that led from our street down the hill to the waterfront, and then we turned left and ran along the boardwalk of the Golden Horn for a few miles. We ran past the small dinghies and fishing boats that lined the boardwalk with names like *Asmay* and *Balıkçi Amka.* We passed the old city wall, the funicular, and the graveyard before turning around at a small island inhabited by ducks. It was during one of those runs, just after leaving our apartment but before descending the hill, that we had walked right through a film crew shooting a scene in which two young boys played soccer on the cobblestone street. We told this to Altug.

"Yes, this area is pretty famous," he replied. "My friend who works in the movie industry knew this exact street when I told him where you lived. He said he's filmed in this neighborhood many times." Balat was considered the last remaining neighborhood in Istanbul that retained the charm of the old city, and whenever a commercial or television show was supposed to feel like "the real Istanbul," it would be set there. It felt like we lived in a movie set, and we both quite enjoyed it.

Aside from the ultra-conservative Muslim attire, the bookshops selling Qurans, and the ladies' black garment boutiques, our neighborhood contained all of the institutions of secular Turkey. There were the butcher shops, bakeries loaded with warm bread and honey-soaked baklava, tea shops, kebab shops, and natural beauty shops selling chunky blocks of handmade olive oil soap.

The two shops I frequented most were the pastry shop and Kharem's grocery store, which were conveniently only separated by an old brick wall. The pastry shop had the best chocolate-covered-pistachio-speckled meringues on Earth, which I bought and ate daily, while the grocery store was filled with all sorts of gastronomic delights, and was operated by the loveliest man in all of Balat. Kharem had wooden barrels of aged olives, sausages, braided stringy white cheese, crumbled goat cheese made in his home village in Kurdistan, baskets of brown eggs, fresh grape leaves for making *dolmas*, logs of thick-rolled clotted cream (to be eaten slathered with honey), bulk bins of fig and strawberry jam, chocolate-hazelnut and plain hazelnut spread (both chunky and smooth varieties), and honey—available in either pre-filled jars or expertly ladled by Kharem himself into a container from a massive tub beneath a slab of honeycomb. I nearly passed out every time I walked into Kharem's grocery.

At checkout, Kharem gave me instructions on the proper handling of my triple-plastic-wrapped container of honey.

"Now *do not* put this in the refrigerator. Yes you understand? No refrigerator." He also gave advice on the cream we purchased.

"You have two days. Two days and then goes bad. Yes, you understand?" He treated the food that he sold with the same reverence as if he were letting us care for his beloved cat.

Besides grocery shopping at Kharem's and people-watching from our apartment window, we spent considerable time exploring the city. A thirty minute walk down the Golden Horn in the opposite direction of our morning runs led us past the clusters of private boats that sat in the jellyfish-infested waters, and past old men who casually watched their fishing lines as they drank cup after cup of black tea. Every so often they would rise from folding chairs and pluck a sardine-sized fish from their line and deposit it into their repurposed five-gallon yogurt buckets. In Turkey, yogurt was such a staple that they actually procured it by the five-gallon bucket. Just a bit farther down the Golden Horn there sat bigger passenger boats at anchor serving *balik ekmek*: fish sandwiches.

We made the obligatory stops to the city's most famed destinations: the mosaic-filled, domed church from the sixth-century known as Hagia Sophia, as well as the Blue Mosque and the Grand Bazaar, which is the world's largest bazaar with over 4,000 shops and several miles of lanes. The nearby spice bazaar contained a plethora of spices, nuts, honeycombs, figs, dates, and Turkish delight, which are sweets made from rolled dried fruit and honey. We also passed through the Basilica Cistern built in 532 AD, an underground water storage place that was forgotten for nearly a millennium, only to be rediscovered by a scholar in 1532 through a trapdoor in a neighboring house.

On the same day that Altug came to see our neighborhood, we went to go see his. Like ours, it was devoid of foreign tourists. It was bustling with locals whiling away the afternoon in cozy cafes and on the benches that lined the waterfront. The walkway leading out to the water was lined with vendors selling stuffed-potatoes, so we each ordered one and chose from an array of odd toppings like pickled vegetables and couscous. Aboard and empty banquet boat, and with potatoes in hand, we found shelter from the wind and ominous clouds. The boat departed shortly thereafter, taking us on a cruise up the Bosphorus. From the boat we watched the sun set over the European side of the city—the Bosphorus strait splits the city between Europe and Asia—while Altug shared his local insight on everything from the historic buildings we passed to Turkey's troubled past and recent political unrest. At the time that we had arrived, Turks in Istanbul—Altug included—had just taken part in protests to maintain the country's longstanding separation of church and state. The protesters had taken to the streets after the current administration had overturned numerous laws ensuring secular government, and it seemed that the country was slipping into a pre-Ataturk state of non-secularism. He and his wife had long been trying to get pregnant, and one night, a short while before our arrival, they had gone to a protest and had been caught up in a violent interaction with police. They had been pepper sprayed and had to run away in a fit of coughing and gagging. When they got home, just before bed, his wife found out she was pregnant. It was a joyous time amid uncertainty and chaos in the country.

Before we departed ways for the evening, Altug stopped at a shop whose inventory spilled out into the street. He rummaged through a few bins, found what he was looking for, and held up two blue glass beads, each embedded with a black dot surrounded by a white ring.

"Which do you prefer?" he asked. "Round or square?" He asked if we had ever seen these before. We hadn't. He explained that they were ubiquitous in Turkey, and were used to reflect other people's envy by hanging them on one's most treasured things. They were placed in homes, in new cars, and especially on newborn children. "This one is for you," he said. "Hang it in Nacho."

A few days later we took the ferry to the Asian side of the city and met up with Eileen, Brad's childhood friend, who happened to be living in Istanbul. She had been there for nearly a year, and had long established her favorite eating haunts. For lunch we ate *lahmacun,* a typical Turkish flatbread covered in minced meat and vegetables, rolled and filled with mixed greens, parsley and cheese. Afterwards, to my utter joy, I discovered that Eileen was on a year-long search for the best baklava in Istanbul. We tagged along, sampling the flaky desserts while we explored her neighborhood's outdoor market, which was brimming with cheese and sausages, paper thin sheets of filo dough, severed goat heads, fresh fish, dried eggplants, and peppers.

By the time Nacho arrived at the port in Istanbul, it had been three weeks and we were itching to hit the road and explore Turkey's backroads. Brad spent nearly a week zipping around to the port and various shipping offices to try to set Nacho free. He rode around town for two days with a couple of Turkish port workers who didn't speak English, filling out paperwork and doling out money to various agencies. Meanwhile, I tried my best to fit in with the burka-clad ladies around the neighborhood, while frequently popping in to grab a few meringues from the pastry shop or a refill on hazelnut spread from Kharem's grocery. Finally, after a week of headaches and tea drinking in various port offices, Brad emerged from the port driving Nacho. With mud still clinging to its sides from being stuck in the tidal marsh on the Pakistani border, and dust from our backwoods explorations around Mumbai, Nacho wasn't garnering much envy from the well-dressed Turks on the trans-Bosphorus ferry, over from the Asian side. Nevertheless, when Brad pulled up in front of our apartment I hung Altug's envy bead from the rearview mirror, just to be safe.

When Altug learned that we were leaving Istanbul to drive toward the stone gardens of Cappadocia, he put his hand out and placed it on the table between Brad and me.

"My good friend Eren lives near Ankara – he will be happy to host you. He drives the same car as you!"

As it turned out, we had actually spoken to Eren a year and a half earlier while still driving through South America. He had emailed Brad with a question about a computer-aided design file. After Brad helped him out, Eren had invited us to look him up if we were ever in Turkey, but we had completely forgotten about it. It was only by luck and coincidence, then, that just a few hours after leaving Istanbul, we passed by Ankara and followed our map down a long and winding dirt road to Eren's childhood home. We passed through a gate and drove into a tunnel of fruit and nut trees to what would be our first campsite in Turkey: Eren's driveway. We parked and walked to the front door, where Eren and his fiancée Rabia greeted us with warm and welcoming smiles. It was a serendipitous moment that left us thinking about the influence that seemingly inconsequential encounters can have.

Eren asked if we had gotten a message that he had sent, but we hadn't. "Rabia is cooking tonight," he said. "She has been preparing all day."

When we walked inside, the air in the house was heavy with mouthwatering aromas, and while Rabia finished cooking, we warmed up next to the wood burning stove in the corner of the living room. A nutcracker and a basket of shelled nuts from the yard sat on the floor near the stove—signs of a cozy, good life.

Tea came quickly, as we had expected. Altug had told us that on camping trips, Eren's van was the place to go for tea. A good friend to have around, and as he had put it, "His kettle is always on the burner." Çay (chai) is Turkey's hot drink of choice, served in small tulip glasses with a cube or two of sugar, but never with milk.

I asked Eren how many cups of tea the average Turkish man drinks per day and he said that he himself consumes about twenty cups. This comforted me, because Brad had gotten into the habit of constantly harassing me for my habit of having two-to-three cups of coffee each day. Now I would have a piece of humbling data to throw in his face at the first sign of harassment the next time I felt the caffeine itch.

Brad and Eren became fast friends. They were both mechanical engineers, and so the two of them spoke the same language. They had a small engineering project to work on as well: to build an adapter for our propane tank. We had run out of propane while camping near Mumbai, and in Turkey we had been unable to find a propane station with a nozzle to refill our American tank. Altug had given us a metal contraption that would adapt a European thread to an LPG filling station nozzle, but it needed to be adapted to fit to our tank. Eren thought he could figure it out in his machine shop at work, so he put it with his things to bring to work the following day.

Rabia and I literally didn't speak the same language, but it didn't matter. We talked in charades and laughter, and when things got really tough, like when she tried to relay the cryptic quote on the inside of her mastic bubble gum wrapper, we tried to use her smart phone to translate but it only produced garbled gibberish.

Before bed, Eren and Brad strung an extension cord across the yard and plugged in an electric heater to keep us warm through the frigid night. It was silent in our orchard camp under clear, starry skies, and we couldn't have been happier to be back in a sparsely populated countryside.

An exuberant rooster awakened us the next morning, and through our rooftop tent window, we could see the orchard bathed in the day's first light. The heater had kept us warm throughout the night, but it made me wonder what it would be like once we left Eren's house. We were supposed to have been crossing the Middle East, but instead we had been deposited in Europe in the wintertime.

It was a weekday, so Eren left for work with Altug's propane adaptor in hand, and we remained at the house with Rabia. She was an actress, and her most recent theater production had just ended, leaving her with a few weeks of recovery time. She spent much of the morning going all-out on a traditional Turkish country breakfast: an omelet made of freshly-gathered eggs from her chicken coop, whipped and poured over a healthy dose of thickly-sliced local sausage, and garnished with dill. The omelet puffed up like a giant marshmallow, the result of the flour she had mixed in with the eggs. Genius! She served the omelets with freshly baked bread, a variety of white cheeses, homemade cherry jam made fresh from their cherry tree, hazelnut spread, and coffee.

In the afternoon we lounged around the living room watching a television series in which Rabia starred as a nurse. In one scene she began to cry during a tense surgery, and the surgeon slapped her. "Wait, watch!" she said. "Now he slap me! Ha!" After the dramatic slap she laughed herself tired and then put on a movie in which she played a prisoner's wife. "This funny! Oh, not so funny. My husband in jail. But that man very funny in life!"

We practiced cracking walnut shells(a therapeutic activity, I discovered), and we roamed the orchard and played charades to uncover what fruit or nut tree we were standing under. I tasted almonds and new fruits like the Asian olive, a small berry indigenous to Turkey. Most of the trees were without leaves—as expected for the time of the year—but like many places in the world, that year the winter had been unseasonably warm, causing the ground to be bone dry instead of having its usual layer of snow. Eren had said that he had never seen anything like it; winter had never arrived in Turkey. We retired indoors and ate canned peaches from Eren's mother, topped with *kaymak*, Turkey's delightful clotted cream.

We toiled away in the kitchen for the rest of the afternoon making a classic family recipe. We roasted an eggplant over the stovetop flame, and then mixed its insides with a concoction of butter, flour, and milk, turning the mixture into a decadent eggplant puree. We then placed a large dollop of this puree on each plate, and to that we added a healthy scoop of beef and vegetables, serving it with a simple shredded carrot salad with lemon and oil. Turks really seemed to love their salads, and their homemade seed-covered bread. For good measure we added a box of *helva* to the table, a dessert made of semolina flour and nuts, topped with more clotted cream.

We all woke up early the following morning and ate breakfast with Eren before he departed for work. Rabia served *menemen*, a traditional Turkish breakfast of eggs cooked in a sauce of tomato, onion, and green pepper, accompanied by fresh bread, black olives, white cheese, and slices of cucumber. Our visit with Rabia and Eren was too short—only two days—but Nacho's import permit for Turkey would expire in less than three weeks, and we had a long way to go.

A few hours after Eren left, we followed the curving driveway past the fruit and nut trees, and through the gate. Rabia saw us off with a freshly baked cake in hand, creatively decorated with a big blob of cocoa powder in the center, a stamp of love that she had made using a heart-shaped cookie cutter stencil. A few miles down the road we stopped at a gas station to test out our new propane adaptor, and breathed a sigh of relief when Nacho's stove successfully produced a glowing orange flame. My kitchen was back in business and we were off to Cappadocia.

48

The D300 to Cappadocia

Brad

Sleet had been falling on and off all morning. In the village the men huddled around a tea shop next to a barren mountain in the gray, bleak Turkish countryside. Inside—that is, inside of the mountain—I was precariously wedged midway up a thirty-foot vertical shaft that connected two levels of a vast, hidden underground city. I paused in the darkness and looked down into the abyss, a lone useless rope dangling between my legs and disappearing into the black emptiness below. A flashlight held by a mustachioed man in a leather jacket, a Turkish Burt Reynolds, illuminated the space above me. The chute was no more than twenty-four inches square, with little pockets dug into its walls to serve as toe and finger holds, carved into the solid rock by villagers seeking protection from invading Hittite tribes some 3,600 years ago. I tried to imagine how I might utilize the rope should I lose my grip on the walls, seeing as how both hands and feet were busy keeping me wedged in the shaft, but every mental scenario ended with me lying in a crumpled heap, the dangling rope faintly tickling my lifeless body.

Being the only visitors to the underground city at Mazi that day, and finding a complete lack of security, we had simply walked into a cave at the base of the mountain and found ourselves in the midst of the underground system. We quickly decided that a guide might help to keep us from getting lost in the extensive underground city spanning multiple levels separated by chutes and tunnels, so we had solicited one of the men from the tea shop to accompany us. After crawling through a kilometer of tunnels, moving from room to room, we had ended up at the vertical shaft, where I clung on to dear life by my fingernails. As I hung there in the darkness, suspended over the abyss, it occurred to me that this would never fly back home in litigious America, and that these

332

were the types of things that made the rest of the world so much fun to explore.

Cappadocia lies amid the barren grassy hills and canyons of Central Turkey. The drive from Eren's house had brought us past a giant salt lake and over hours of rolling, windy hills under the constant threat of rain, although the precipitation hadn't materialized. As we had approached our destination, the landscape had become crisscrossed with canyons and pillars shaped by millennia of erosion, giving it the feel of Cedar Breaks National Monument in Utah, only this one extended for miles in every direction. To the west a sentinel volcano stood watch over the valley, imposing and snow-covered. We had arrived in the evening and had set off into the hills on a dirt road to find a place to camp.

For the first two days we drove from site to site in this once thriving civilization, from the hand-carved rock cities in the Ihlara Valley to the underground city at Mazi, each night pulling off onto a dirt road to find a secluded camp site. It was the first time since leaving South America, more than a year prior, that we had been able to find truly isolated and wild camp sites away from people. It was, in a word, glorious.

All of the fresh air and peace and quiet seemed to be messing with Sheena's mind. One evening while camped above a deserted collection of cliff-dwellings, she sat on the couch and I on the captain's chair in my matching down shorts and down jacket.

"You look like that long gray guy. What's his name?"

"Gray guy? I have no idea what you're talking about."

"Dumbo!"

"The elephant? I thought he was pink. Then again I'm color blind, so you're the expert."

"No, not Dumbo. You know, from the TV. Is he green? He's stretchy and has long arms and legs."

"You mean Gumby?"

"Yeah, him! I used to watch that when I was little. You look just like Gumbo!" She stared blankly ahead, having deeply confused herself, until she spoke again, almost in a yell. "Who the hell is Gumbo?!" I sipped my beer, amused by this little woman.

After three days Sheena identified a valley on the map where she wanted to go hiking, so we decided to find a place to camp somewhere along the way. Our GPS showed two roads leading to the valley, and between them a vast expanse of canyon wilderness. We set off on one of the roads and kept our eyes out for a way to drive into the boondocks. A small dirt track on the left hand side of the road led into a dry riverbed, and then up and around a small hill, so we took it. After a short jog through an orchard, the road wound up the side of the hill to a cave home carved into the side of the hill. Outside, its inhabitants had just killed a sheep, and as we came to a stop, the last signs of life twitched from its body, blood pooling in the dirt under its neck. A man walked up to my window, bloody knife in hand, and through charades he motioned that there was no way to get through to the valley without taking the paved roads. He smiled and waved us off and then walked back to his dead sheep.

A short time later we found a muddy 4x4 track leading off through a farmer's field, so we turned onto it. After a sloppy jaunt through the field, the track curved around a hill and began a long, bumpy descent along the edge of a small canyon. We slowly crawled over rocks and straddled gaps in the track until finally coming to an area littered with large cone-shaped stone spires. There seemed to be a flat spot between two of the spires on a nearby hillside, so we aimed Nacho toward it.

After setting up camp in the waning light, I took a quick saunter around the stone spires, and to my surprise, found that many of them were hollowed out. Most of them had no clear entry point except for holes high up on their sides, and a few dozen meters in front of our camp there appeared to be an old church carved into the hill.

In the morning we set off with flashlights to see what we'd stumbled upon, and were amazed to find an entire community of cave dwellings. The hill next to our camp had been partially hollowed out to form a church, complete with domed roof and columns, but the main dome had recently collapsed. Along the walls and ceiling, ancient Christian frescoes depicted saints and angels.

I remembered from an art history class I'd taken in college that at a certain point in history artists had figured out how to draw in perspective to give depth to their paintings. Before that point, it hadn't occurred to them that shapes could be drawn obliquely to show depth, and so landscapes and buildings appeared oddly two dimensional and disproportional. The turning point when perspective was generally adopted was in the 13th century, and could be easily observed by looking at halos over the heads of saints in old Christian paintings; pre-perspective paintings depict the halo as a perfect circle behind the saint's head, while post-perspective artists drew a more realistic oval. The frescoes on the church we'd found depicted saints with circular halos, so it seemed that they must have been more than seven-hundred years old.

We moved on to the hollowed-out spires that jutted up around the hillside, and found our way into a few of them. They were mostly basic habitations with a couple of rooms and windows, though a few of the more elaborate ones had multiple rooms and kitchens with underground cooking vessels that looked just like Indian tandoor ovens. We came across one spire with a high door accessible by climbing part way up the side and shimmying along a ledge. Inside it was the most elaborate dwelling of the whole complex, with multiple rooms, various shelves carved into the walls, and a series of divots in the floor where giant clay jars would have stood to hold wine, oil, and dry goods.

On the way back to Nacho I noticed a small hole at the base of one of the hills near the church, partially closed up by dirt but still big enough to squeeze through in a crawl. Sheena wailed a fear wail and refused to enter, so I turned on my flashlight and squeezed inside, finding not a room but a tunnel. I crawled along on my knees as the tunnel sloped steeply downward, and before long I arrived in a room underneath the hill. An enormous rolling stone door protected the entrance to the room. It must have been a shelter for villagers during raids, and once closed from inside, it would be impossible for the rock to be moved from the outside. Another small tunnel took off from the back corner of the room, but very quickly ended in a collapse. We later found that the other end of that tunnel emerged in the back corner of the collapsed church.

Our time in Cappadocia passed as a parade of mostly sunny days spent exploring, punctuated by cool nights camping in the countryside. We hiked canyons, hills and orchards, all the while discovering little bits of the old civilization: aqueduct tunnels cut through cliff walls, shepherd shelters carved into rock spires, and whole communities carved in rock. We visited a couple of the better-known tourist sites in Cappadocia—the open air museum and the Rose Valley—but found them to be overbuilt and over commercialized. Their frescoes had been restored, making them look too fresh.

After a week of exploring dirt tracks and backroads, we finally stumbled upon the jackpot. It came about as Sheena sat in the passenger seat softly moaning about the dinner time hunger welling up in her belly.

"We need to find a camp," she whimpered. I knew that this would be my only warning, and that she would quickly slide into a state of intense hunger-induced unrest and aggravation. We sailed around the bends in the road and then, on our left, a dirt track took off down a hillside. I passed it, on account of Nacho's high speed and poor braking combination, and then flipped back around and took it. The road wound its way around a few hills before stopping at a turnaround spot, a perfect place to camp. Off in the canyon to our right there sat a multistory ancient stone village carved directly into the canyon wall. Small window holes pocked the face of the cliff, and a stone arch extended over the creek below. A section of the cliff had sheared off, exposing the once-hidden rooms within.

Throughout the evening we peered across the canyon, imagining the adventure to be had exploring the rooms within the canyon walls. We drifted off to sleep in a silence accented by the faint sound of trickling water from the creek below.

In the morning we took to the canyon, summoning our inner Indiana Joneses. Crossing the creek posed the first challenge, and I daydreamed of Indiana Jones fearlessly whipping a snake and then swinging across the creek on a vine, probably holding a helpless damsel under one arm. I looked at Sheena and thought better of trying to hold her under my arm, and anyway I couldn't find any vines. I suppressed my fear and then made a valiant leap across the water and onto a big sandstone boulder. My style was good, but that was all that could be said. Failing to move my center of gravity over my feet, my body teetered and then I instinctively pushed off with my legs, sending myself, airborne, into the middle of the creek. I sighed and walked through the water to the other side while Sheena made clucking sounds with her tongue and shook her head.

We found our way into the cliff dwellings through a squat tunnel, flashlights illuminating the way, and climbed through a complex of small rooms and makeshift stairways carved into the soft rock. It was amazing to think that once a civilization had thrived there. We found kitchens and storage rooms and habitations, all bare but clearly well-used. It was like finding an enormous ruined Native American habitation back home, except that this had been completely untouched by modern managerial infrastructure, and was much better preserved on account of being carved in stone. We were free to explore as if discovering it for the first time.

We hiked around the cliffs and down the creek, and eventually came across a church carved high into the canyon wall. Its interior was still adorned with frescoes depicting ancient Christian scenes, but they were covered in the scratchings of visitors who had wanted to leave their marks. On one hand it was a shame that the frescoes had been defaced, but on the other hand the graffiti served as a fascinating chronology of the visitors who had passed through the cave. There were Greek letters, Arabic scroll, and Roman characters, and dates spanning the centuries. In 1732, forty four years before America's declaration of independence from Britain, a little Greek punk stood in that very place and scratched a message into the cave wall. In a way the graffiti was just as interesting as the fresco that carried it.

On the way back we discovered a new entrance to the cliff, only accessible by approaching it from a different ridge. We lit our flashlights, put on our Indiana Jones fedoras, and entered. Before long we located a vertical shaft leading up into the darkness, just like the one from the underground city we'd visited with the mustachioed Turk. We had thus far been unable to find access to the upper stories of the cliff dwelling, and this looked promising.

Sheena, sensing danger and possible bodily harm, encouraged me to go for it. I pulled myself into the ceiling with Jean Claude Van Damme swiftness and style, and wedged myself in place. From there I nervously and clumsily inched upward, the shallow toe and finger holds and my Van Damme musculature the only things keeping me from becoming a crumpled corpse on the floor below. I inched upward, and finally emerged thirty feet higher in a bright room overlooking the creek from high up on the cliff face.

It became immediately evident why a piece of the cliff had fallen off adjacent to this room: a two-inch-wide crack ran across the floor from one corner of the room to the other, and continued up both walls and across the ceiling. It seemed that any weight placed in the outer half of the room could cause the whole chunk to shear off. I nervously, stupidly, sphincter-puckeringly, and with feline-like agility tiptoed across the crack to have a look out the window, then quickly retreated, jumping back to safety like Indiana Jones, or Jean Claude Van Damme.

We spent two days at our canyon campsite, and in those two days the only other visitors to the canyon were one car load of local boys. They had come to sit around on rocks and drink soda from a two liter bottle. A few minutes later they loaded up and left. No tour buses, no visitors, no fences, no signs. It was just us and our little roving home, left alone to admire an ancient scene, like Indiana Jones and that little Asian kid, or Gumbo and his trusty clay horse.

49

Backroads to Gökçeovacık Köyü

Brad

As the months passed and we continued to wake up each morning in a van, our sense of adventure rose and fell like phases of the moon. One day we would wake up in a Colombian junkyard and it could only get better from there. Then, over morning coffee we would regard with amazement the way that the jagged tip of Tierra del Fuego sliced into the sea right before our eyes, the very end of the Americas, the end of the road. But for every momentous morning coffee view there was a nondescript parking lot or a filthy Indian petrol station. Still, no matter where we woke up, or how our desire to carry on was tested, I always came back with the same suggestion to my sweet and forgiving wife.

"Just hear me out, Sheena," I said time after time. "You know how we're sitting in our van right now? And how there are thirty creepy Indian men staring at us through our windshield? And how your hair is matted and the air in here is fetid and stagnant?" She nodded. "Well just think how much better it'd be if we had a sailboat. The open water, the great unknown, the deep sea fishing, the silky, sun-streaked hair. We could sail around the world!"

And to this she always had the same response:

"Bradley, if you want to sail around the world, you're going to have to find a new wife."

"But think about the adventure! The fresh seafood! And anyway, I would never trade you in for a new wife. That is, unless Shakira wanted to marry me."

"Do you see this matted hair? This is your fault. Do you know why? Because you made me move into a van! And Shakira? Do you really think that Shakira wants to live on a tiny boat?!"

338

And so I saw it as both a minor victory and a chance to sell Sheena on the idea of a "next adventure" when our new Turkish friend Engin invited us to go sailing around some Turkish Mediterranean islands on his sailboat.

"There's no pressure, Sheena," I said. "But while we're out there just remember this: there are no Indian highways out at sea, and no public defecation. Every day is paradise!" To this she shot me a look that said *you'll be living in this van long after I divorce you!*

Eren had put us in touch with Engin, his friend on the south coast, assuming that we would be fast friends on account the fact that we all drove the same car. And of course he was right; we had found that overt kindness and generosity were prerequisites to VW van ownership. Engin had been anticipating our arrival, and when we arrived at his mountainside home he put us up in his guesthouse overlooking a sweeping canyon that led to the Mediterranean below.

It was the very end of the winter offseason and so the sail on Engin's sailboat had been removed, leaving a naked mast and no choice but to motor sail. But no big deal, he had told us, we would simply motor-sail to a different island where another boat was parked, this one having a sail, and we would simply swap boats for a couple of days. We loaded two days rations into the boat, and precariously crossed the narrow wooden gangplank from the dock to the boat with armloads of supplies. Before long we set off under ominous skies, the bow slicing through the calm waters around the harbor at Göcek.

While Sheena and I had once been aboard a sailboat, it should be noted that it never left the dock. This time would mark the first time in our lives that either of us had ever been on a *moving* sailboat. I would have to gather my sea legs, or else do a knockout job of faking it, to convince Sheena that I would make a capable captain of an around-the-world seafaring vessel. I scrolled through my memory for an example of seafaring triumph that I could emulate, and came up with several recollections of the film *Titanic*. Not a sailboat, but close enough. I got up and walked to the front of the bow, stood in the very front so as to give myself the feeling of being a low-flying coastal bird, and tried my best to look like Leonardo DiCaprio. I stopped short of holding my arms out to the side, as that maneuver is decidedly only cool when you are simultaneously spooning Kate Winslet. After displaying to the crew (Sheena and Engin) that I was seaworthy, I took my seat in the back where Engin, clearly surprised by my seaworthiness, gave me the steering stick and told me to drive.

Some time later we rounded a bend and entered a hidden channel leading to a calm bay in the middle of an island. The island's hills surrounding the bay were covered in old knotted olive trees, flowers, and the ruins of a very small and old island community consisting of a farmhouse, a few outbuildings, and the remains of a church. It was disgustingly cute and quaint. We docked the boat in the tiny harbor and quickly discovered that the boat we had intended to commandeer had also been stripped of its sail. Seeing no other elegant solutions we sat back and had a picnic onboard, drank a beer, and then Sheena and I set off on foot to explore the island while Engin took a nap.

The island, as it turned out, was still inhabited by a Turkish family who had taken to living in the old farmhouse, and whose goats and cows wandered around the stables behind the ruins. We made our way through the stables and past the church, the crystal clear bay to our left, and the low, rocky, olive-covered hills to our right. Over a small rise we came to an outward-facing cove and sat down to soak in the isolation of this too-good-to-be-true, quintessentially Mediterranean island. We sat. Time passed. Waves lapped. Breeze flipped hair. Storm moved in.

The weather had been touchy since we had arrived in Engin's village near Fethiye on Turkey's south coast three days earlier. Nacho had braved deep mud to get to his house high up on the side of the mountain and the sky had threatened rain each day. We had kept the heater in our bedroom cranked to fend off the chill in the air. By day we had worked on Nacho projects: we redesigned the broken rear bumper mounts, which had fallen victim to India's National Highway 7, we reduced the size of the box on our bumper that held our extra water and gas cans to save weight, we beefed up our shoddy awning mounts, and we re-welded a broken exhaust mount. Those projects had been carried out in between spats of cold rain and occasional gusts of chilly wind, and each night we gathered around Engin's wood burning stove to enjoy dinner, a beer, and each other's company.

To add variety to our days filled with van repair projects, we would all load up in Engin's Land Rover and explore the dirt roads crisscrossing the mountains between his home and the sea. On Turkey's southwest coast there exists a combination of mountains and sea that we never knew existed; rugged snowy peaks cascade down from the sky in pine-covered ridges and rock faces where they prematurely meet the sea. This meant that one could drive forest roads that looked like those found in the high pine forests of the American West, but the roads would abruptly end at the sea and the pine trees fanned out onto the beach. Our arrival in late spring, with the accompanying rain and overcast skies, made us feel as though we were in some Mediterranean version of Oregon. With so much uncertainty in the shifting springtime weather patterns, it should have come as no surprise that we ended up in a minor island emergency weather situation.

At first sign of the impending storm we stood up and headed back over the rise toward the secluded bay, but our attention quickly shifted from safety-seeking to exploring the olive grove on the hillside. We turned left and walked up the hill, and before long the wind picked up and the rain started. We sought refuge under an old olive tree, and reminded ourselves that, storm or no storm, being stuck on a deserted Turkish island with a sailboat full of food and drink was far better than most days one might experience in life. When a lull in the rain came, we fled from the shelter of the olive grove and made way for the boat. When we reached the boat we found Engin seeking refuge in the belowdecks.

Just then the rain began to fall biblically in sheets, and we had to make some decisions.

"I spoke to the people at the marina before we left," Engin said, "and they reported that if the storm did arrive today, it would probably last for three days." He looked stoic, like many Turks do, and we couldn't quite read between the lines. Was this a bad idea? I thought back to *Titanic* but didn't remember any scenes involving storms.

"We can stay the night if you want. But if the storm does come, we might be stuck here for a few days. And we really only have enough food left for one more meal." This kind of thing clearly didn't bother Turks, who, admittedly, are far tougher and more resilient than we Americans are. I had apparently grossly exaggerated the amount of food on hand. Engin's warning of meager times ahead weighed heavily on our minds, and after some contemplation and indecisiveness we all agreed that it would be best to head back to the mainland where food and shelter abounded.

This time Sheena was enlisted to steer the boat with the steering stick, which left me ample time to walk back and forth along the sides of the sailboat holding onto rigging to keep my balance just like the experienced sailors do in the movies. I nearly lost my balance as Sheena attempted a minor correction with the rudder, jerking the boat at a tight right angle, and putting us on course to Greece. She corrected her course in a series of sloppy zigzags while Engin massaged his temples and lightly shook his head. I stood in front of the boat like Leonardo DiCaprio again and imagined that I lived on a boat, and that this was just another

341

day in a carefree sailing life. I imagined the tasty seafood frolicking below me as the bow of the boat sliced through the deep blue waves that steadfastly marched across the surface of the sea. I imagined Sheena and myself sitting on our boat couch, which would be modern in style and probably white, positioned in the tidy living room of our fancy catamaran. We would be sipping wine, laughing about a joke that we'd heard in port, and I would go out for a moment to check the line to see if any mahi mahi were waiting to be made into fish tacos.

I turned and looked at Sheena, who was nervously steering the boat, and then made my way over to her by deftly clinging to the rigging.

I spoke with the idealism and toothy grin of a boy scout. "Hey Sheena, can't you just imagine how great it would be to sail around the world? Can you *imagine*?" It didn't need any more explanation. She would be feeling the same sense of freedom, the wind in her hair, almost able to taste the mahi mahi tacos.

"Listen...to...me," she said in an uncharacteristically assertive voice, staring directly into my eyes with all of the wild intensity of a spouse who really needs to convey an important message. "WE–ARE–NOT–GETTING–A –SAILBOAT!"

I slunk down onto the wooden seat and I watched the waves march by, the rain trickle down, and my dream of sailing the high seas wash overboard and sink into the deep blue water of Fethiye Bay.

50

Transcontinental Marathon to Morocco

Brad

Turkey's spring days were surprisingly chilly and the nights cold. Beyond Anatolia we knew it would only get worse; we had been to Europe in the springtime and knew that the experience would be, to our Arizona-bred bodies, the equivalent of living in a van in the Arctic Circle. It was with this thought in mind that we decided to drive as quickly as possible from Turkey to Morocco in northern Africa, where we could wile away the spring in the warm Sahara Desert until better weather transpired in the north. But we faced a more immediate challenge: we had only three days left to legally exit Turkey, and we were a full three day drive from the border.

Before departing from Engin's house, we had made the passing comment that whenever we waited until the last minute to do something—as in leaving only barely enough time to exit Turkey within the bounds of the law—if something could go wrong, it most certainly would. This of course is the universal principle that governs our lives known as Murphy's Law. That Murphy must have been a real bastard.

Day one started off innocuously enough, but soon the clouds overhead thickened into a whirling soup and threatened rain. It began as a soft drizzle but very quickly escalated to a deluge. Within minutes Nacho's defrost fan blower cut out and the windshield started fogging up, so I resorted to desperately toweling the windshield off to retain visibility. Minutes later on a curvy mountainous highway, the windshield wipers also cut out and we were suddenly passengers aboard a flying danger Twinkie, barreling through the rain completely blind. We had no choice but to stop and wait for the rain to subside lest we blindly plunge to our deaths.

343

Day two also started off fine, with us having spent a cold and windy night camped at the end of a finger of land jutting out into the stormy bay of Bodrum, where violent waves erupted into upward-flowing waterfalls right outside of our windows. We set our sights on the ancient Roman ruins of Ephesus and started driving, and before long there came a violent knocking sound coming from somewhere in Nacho's frontal suspension area. I opted not to mention it to Sheena, who was again busy reading her coming of age princess novella in the passenger seat. It seemed to me that the very mention of trouble would make it real, and hence give rise to the need to deal with it. The sound got progressively worse until we reached Ephesus, where I finally felt the need to get out and see what was the matter.

I stopped the van. A torrential rain began to pour. I got out and performed a maneuver I like to call the "wet-jack-it," which consisted of me jacking up Nacho in the pouring rain. The "wet-jack-it" is described in a clause in Murphy's Law. You can look it up.

I noticed that the driver's front wheel seemed a little wonky, so I disassembled the hub and found the outer wheel bearing to have what seemed to be more play than usual. I swapped out the bearing and we pulled away, but within seconds the knocking resumed, naturally. It was raining too hard to explore Ephesus, so instead we flipped a u-turn and parked on the roadside, where I proceeded to perform a wet-jack-it on the passenger side of the van. It was only then that I realized that the upper ball joint was completely destroyed. India's highways had not only killed our morale, but apparently our upper ball joint as well. I consulted our trusty GPS (who, it bears mentioning, we had named "Ruth," and when on rare occasion we drove without it, it could be said that we were "driving Ruthlessly") which told us that there was a parts store in Izmir, about eighty kilometers to the north. By then it was evening time, so we drove a few kilometers to the beach to camp.

We arrived safely at the parts store the following morning where we found the right part. I bought two of them just in case, as well as more wheel bearings and a spare tie-rod-end on a whim. It began to rain as soon as I got to work replacing the ball joint, but this time I was working on the passenger side, so I extended the awning to reduce the amount of wet-jack-iting to be done. Under the supervision of the parts store manager and a wily old Turk with a gray moustache, I swapped out the ball joint, and then turned down an invitation to go to the manager's house for dinner—we were working toward a deadline, after all—and instead settled for tea in the store. We then carried on northward.

By nightfall we were back on the coast and we consulted Ruth for a suggestion of a place to sleep. The screen indicated a wayward dirt road along the beach so we headed in its direction. When we arrived it was dark, and after winding through a steep grove of trees, we were suddenly driving downhill on a very muddy, rutted clay track through an open field of dead weeds. The outlook was not good.

"Damn you, Murphy!" I yelled as we came to a stop in the mud. Sheena was looking nervous.

"What do we do now?!" she wailed. She was right to wail rather than talk in a regular voice, as we were obliged by law to remove Nacho from the country by the following day. Yet now we were stuck in the mud on a steep abandoned road, miles from civilization and many hours from the border.

"Damn! Murphy! Blah!" was what came out of my mouth next.

I will try not to brag, but what followed could only be described as pure driving genius on my part. Against all odds—nay, against the laws of the universe, among them Hooke's Law, Kirchoff's Law, the Second Law of Thermodynamics, and even Murphy's Law itself—I managed to squirm Nacho's slick tires sideways to a patch of weeds, expertly manipulate the clutch, rev the engine like a race car driver, and set Nacho into a mud-slinging, wild-bronco-like, bucking, swirling rampage—in reverse—which culminated in us becoming free of the quagmire! Sheena squealed with joy, her teary eyes staring admiringly at me as I slapped my chest and whooped like Howard Dean at a pep rally. Our hearts thumped like the legs of a thousand itchy rabbits as we came to rest at a more sensible camping spot along the bay, where we calmed our nerves with a modest intake of hard alcohol, and retired to bed.

In the morning we set off to the north, a day's drive from the border, with a marathon of *This American Life* episodes on the stereo to keep our minds occupied as we sailed along through the rolling Turkish countryside. By evening we reached the border, just in time.

It was an easy procedure to be stamped out of Turkey, and it would have been easy to get into Greece, but suddenly, for some inexplicable reason, I decided to ask the customs officer where we could buy Greek car insurance.

"You no have Greek insurance?" he asked, surprised. I knew immediately I had made a grave mistake.

"Actually yes, we do. Never mind!" I said, backpedaling, and quickly rummaged through our papers and handed him the fake car insurance papers I had made in Photoshop for just such situations.

"This no worky," he said, and handed it back. "Only green card worky. You come tomorrow and buy green card from man." And with that our operation was shut down. We had already stamped out of Turkey, and didn't have a re-entry visa to get back in. Having been denied entry to Greece, we had no choice but to set up camp in "No Man's Land"—the short stretch of road that sits in between each country's border control posts. It is lawless land, the gaps in between international borders, and for one night we were countryless drifters.

In the morning I found the customs man who was responsible for selling car insurance, and it turned out he was one mean sonofabitch. It had been a long time since we had come across a border guard with a chip on his shoulder, but this guy had it. He yelled at me a couple of times and then disappeared in a flurry to make some personal phone calls, and then began passively filing away papers instead of selling me insurance. After a half an hour we became tired of his game, and decided to dart across the border without insurance and just hope that no official types would notice that we had not been stamped into Greece. But just as we got into the van to leave, the customs man emerged and yelled at me to come into his office, where he proceeded to sell me one month's insurance for $250, a full three or four times more than we had ever paid for insurance at any border. We reluctantly paid, and then drove into Greece.

Arriving in Europe was both a triumph and a shock to the system. For the past two years we had explored the Earth's faraway wild places with wonder and amazement. Every time we moved we were moving into the unknown, and with it came a sense of adventure and uncertainty. To enter Europe was to emerge from the unknown into a world that we knew. Yet, while arriving in Europe was intended to provide relief after the assault of a very long trip, what we experienced instead was something unexpected.

Given that our goal had been to drive to Morocco quickly so as to escape the winter chill, we consciously but begrudgingly sped through Greece. Over the course of two days we drove from the Turkish border to the mountains of Meteora, where monasteries topped rocky spires like stone hairdos surrounded by impossibly sheer cliffs on all sides. After a night camped among the stone monasteries, we continued our westward trajectory with the intention of crossing Albania and driving the Dalmatian Coast to Italy.

346

A few miles before the turn to Albania, Sheena noticed that our overpriced car insurance policy was invalid in four key countries: Albania, Montenegro, Macedonia, and Serbia— some combination of which must be crossed in order to reach the Dalmatian Coast at all. Quick research on Sheena's part revealed that individual insurance could be had at the Albanian border for an extortionate price, and we decide that for the short duration of our mad dash, extortion was unjustifiable. We reluctantly drove to Igoumenitsa on Greece's west coast to catch the ferry to Italy.

We set up an impromptu camp on the ferry for the overnight trip, and arrived late the following afternoon in the eastern Italian town of Ancona. Camping in Italy, we quickly realized, was a much less private affair than it had been in Turkey and Greece. We spent the night in a parking lot between the ocean and a busy road while being periodically awoken by the screech of train wheels right outside our window. In the morning we set off through picturesque towns and small mountain villages of peeling paint and rustic villas into Tuscany, where we spent our second Italian night in a parking spot behind a gas station next to a big fuel storage tank. La dolce vita!

One might beg the question why—given that we were already in Italy, and that we were only following a self-imposed requirement of reaching Africa as soon as possible—we didn't just slow down. Perhaps bum around under the springtime Tuscan sun for a while, just for kicks. The answer lies in the Schengen agreement.

It is because of the Schengen agreement that goods and people may pass unrestricted between most countries in Europe without customs and passport control. Upon our arrival into the Schengen Zone—that is, the grouping of countries that allow free passage between each other—we received a Schengen visa good for all of Europe. The trouble with the visa, though, is that it was only good for three months, and it could not be extended. In order to receive a new visa, we would have had to leave Europe for at least three months within a six-month period before returning. Therefore, the longer our drive to Morocco took, the less time we would have been able to spend in Europe upon our return from Africa when the weather warmed up. Thus, our story continues where we left off, wherein we were crossing Italy in just two-and-a-half days.

We stopped in Lucca, a typical, picturesque city in Tuscany, and walked through its historic center. We regarded the pastel walls and narrow cobbled alleys, and the smell of fresh bread and sausage wafted to us from open doors, but that sense of adventure that we had felt before was missing. We sat down and enjoyed two small coffees on a terrace, and then received a bill for $12.50. Twelve dollars for coffee?! The chicly-dressed barista shrugged her shoulders at my look of confusion and waited for me to hand her what, since arriving in Asia, had constituted two full days' food budget.

Hanging out in familiar places and paying premium prices for things like coffee suddenly felt strangely unadventurous. We started to feel, for the first time, not like brave adventurers but like homeless people.

We cut to the coast and drove to what we had always considered one of Italy's best gems: Le Cinque Terre, a series of five small villages perched on the rocky cliffs overlooking the Mediterranean. We drove the winding cliff-side road from village to village, stopping in Riomaggiore and then in Vernazza for the sunset.

We parked Nacho and made our way out to the waterfront where we stepped out onto a rocky outcropping that extended into a small bay surrounded by crystal clear water. The Mediterranean unfolded before us, and the pastel Italian fishing village climbed the canyon wall behind us, but we felt a great deal of nothing with a hint of boredom. We noticed an American girl in her twenties perched on a rock, glowing as if entranced by her surroundings and the view. It only made us feel as though we didn't belong there. Like maybe we weren't quite ready to appreciate the western world, and that perhaps bee-lining it to Morocco might actually be just what the doctor ordered.

In the morning we pointed Nacho's big blunt nose toward the French border. As we approached Genoa on the Italian Riviera, we hopped on the motorway to speed things up through the foothills of the Alps and into France. But after two hours on the motorway we were completely exasperated by what felt, literally, like highway robbery; in only two hours we had racked up eighty-seven dollars in road tolls. This, combined with gasoline costing nine dollars per gallon, meant that our drive was costing one dollar and fifteen cents per mile, and we had over a thousand miles to go before leaving Europe. We exited the motorway, agitated and stressed, and returned to the slow, but toll-free, surface roads.

By evening we had made it to Provence, and we trundled off on a dirt track into a vineyard to sleep for the night. France was surprisingly beautiful and tranquil, and we began to feel much more relaxed. Italy, despite always having been my favorite European country, had left us feeling a little overwhelmed, and perhaps in a minor state of reverse culture shock.

In the morning we took to the road, where we happily bounced along southern France's backroads past farm stands selling fresh asparagus and strawberries, and past vineyards and quaint villages. We had become emotionally fickle, like a couple of fourteen-year-old girls.

"My soul feels hollow! I can't afford to drink coffee! Ooh, is that asparagus? Do you think the French would approve of this cute pants-hat combo?"

By late morning we crossed the border into Spain and felt something of a homecoming. We had marked the beginning of our new life nearly three dozen months before by crossing the border into Spanish-speaking Mexico, and over the first year of driving came to feel at home in Spanish-speaking lands. In Spain, we felt it again. For the rest of the day we plodded along Spain's backroads and highways through dry hills, and then skirting the Mediterranean coast before cutting inland and finally stopping for the night at the base of the Sierra Nevada mountains.

We awoke to crisp air under blue skies, and Sheena headed off into a juniper forest for her morning run. The ability to exercise comfortably in Europe had left Sheena elated; she had missed her morning runs for a long time. She had developed a consistent regimen back in Argentina where it was easy to get into nature and away from people. But as soon as we got to Asia, it had all come to a halt. It was either too hot or too congested to run, and when we got to India it became impossible for her to go out alone for fear of being assaulted by creepy men. In many places where people struggled to survive each day, it seemed a mockery to be seen running for sport, and so she had refrained. Now she was in her element and she was a happy copilot. She returned an hour and a half later with her pockets full of wild thyme that she had picked in the forest. Then she fired up Nacho's onboard hot shower and washed away the dust and pollen, emerging clean and ready for the day.

We packed our things and hit the road under sunny Spanish skies, traversing the edge of the Sierra Nevada, and then snaking along the edge of the Mediterranean until we arrived, at long last, at the port of Algeciras. We stopped at the grocery store to stock up on cold beer, Spanish sausages, and other Iberian specialties before heading out to the port. In the distance the shores of Morocco stood watch over the Strait of Gibraltar, and as the ferry disembarked, we looked south toward a new journey: the Dark Continent, a dose of chaos, and a new-found

349

sense of adventure. There would be a time to appreciate Europe for what we intended it to be: our last hurrah. But first, one final blast of dirty street carts, mud hut villages, and the unadulterated unknown.

51

Moroccan Highways
and Backroads

Sheena

It only takes forty-five minutes to get from Europe to Africa. Just a quick jaunt across the Strait of Gibraltar, and we were almost in Morocco. Almost in Morocco because the arrival port on the African side is Ceuta, a Spanish city. This made our arrival to the fifth continent of our road trip somewhat anticlimactic at first because it still felt like Spain, but as evening turned to night, we crossed the border into Morocco and were met by another world altogether.

I was more than a little bit excited to be in Africa, even if only for a few weeks. The reason for my excitement had something to do with exploration and new faces and the unknown, but more than anything it had to do with the culture of food. It was five years earlier on a trip to Spain that we had tasted Moroccan food for the first time: a life changing meal served in a *tagine*, a shallow clay pot with a cone-shaped lid. Inside the *tagine* there was a chicken thigh covered in a thick, honey-sweet broth topped with sticky, dried apricots and whole almonds. As soon as we got home we purchased our own *tagine,* and Moroccan dishes became our go-to comfort food.

With few expectations beyond good food and desert camping, we headed southward in the general direction of the Sahara Desert, driving alongside the Atlantic coastline where men rode horses down the beach. We passed through patches of forest where women wore funny hats with equidistantly-spaced pom-poms hanging from the brims, and past agricultural fields where donkeys were busy pulling big-wheeled buggies loaded with grain or passengers. In the town centers, *tagines* made their appearance, supervised by a cook and attended by young boys who added water to the stew as needed. Whole goats and cow legs hung from

351

hooks outside of ramshackle butcher shops, and groups of men congregated on the patios of tea shops. The ever-present *jellabas*, loose-fitting ankle-length robes with pointed hoods worn by both men and women, added to the country's visual aesthetic. The men's were mostly made of natural-colored wool in solid or vertical-striped print, and the women's were made of shinier synthetic fabrics, sometimes in bold patterns like cheetah or floral print.

Night after night along the Atlantic coast our camps overlooked remote beaches, and our drives were kept interesting by frequent encounters with exotically-dressed locals performing their daily chores in the fields and villages. We passed Chefchaouen, Casa Blanca, and Marrakesh, then climbed up and up into the High Atlas Mountains. The drive into the dry, rocky, and treeless mountains brought on a change in both village construction and dress, as the construction materials and fibers available to the mountain people were different from those available on the coast. We summited the mountain range and dropped down the other side to the edge of the vast Sahara desert.

On our first night of desert camping, we situated ourselves on the side of a rocky red cliff dotted with dry scrub, and where shattered, red boulders were strewn about. Across the valley from our camp we watched the sun set over a hillside just above a mud brick village that blended in perfectly with its surroundings. It was a typical village for the area, created from mud quarried on location and left natural in its color with only the perimeters of some windows painted peach or white. The result was a village that became almost completely invisible in the absence of shadows, disappearing into the hillside each night with the setting sun.

Being that our camp was visible to the entire mud-brick village, in the morning two young men came up to visit. One of them lived in a red mud home in the village across the way, and to our surprise and delight, he invited us to his home for tea. Our new friend, named Brion, hopped in the passenger seat of Nacho and led us down the hill, across a dry wash, and into the village on a dirt track that squeezed through a narrow passage between huts that led us to his home. His mother greeted us at the door, and then made us a pot of wild thyme and rosemary tea. After a while we emerged from the house, and Brion walked with us to the edge of the village where a small grove of date palms and almond trees grew. Next to them sat the "old village" consisting of a gigantic mud tower dotted with random peep holes and tiny triangular windows. Most of the rooms in the old village had fallen into decay but what still existed was used as a manger for livestock.

Back on the road we soon came to Ouarzazate, an isolated city known for its 1,000-year old *Kasbah,* or walled citadel, which once served as a Hollywood backdrop for *Star Wars.* Within a few minutes we wandered into a shop filled with beautiful old pieces of antique furniture and textiles, embroidered bamboo mats, and fancy painted pots—some for sale and some just for rent to the movie industry to be used in sets. I scoured the stacks of embroidered rugs and pillowcases made by the Berber people, while Brad searched for a wool striped *jellaba.* At the top of the four-story shop there sat a balcony with a commanding view of the *Kasbah.* It was there on the balcony that the shopkeeper, Mustafa, served us tea. We watched the neighborhood storks, and admired the antique clay jugs that filled most of the balcony in toppling stacks. Before we left, Mustafa invited us to return in the evening for a *tagine.*

When we returned, Mustafa had converted the balcony into a cozy hangout with blankets and cushions. To provide some background music for our evening together, he went through great pains to plug in an old metal radio, stringing an extension cord down all four flights of stairs to the only electrical source in the building on the ground floor. We drank tea, and Mustafa began dinner preparations by first filling the *tagine* with water and then setting it aside to soak. In the meantime, he peeled and chopped vegetables, and then set them aside.

"Come," he said. "We need bread."

We stood and followed him downstairs and onto the street, where we ducked into a back alley and found our way into a small neighborhood. He led the way, ducking into a low door into a dirt-floored, one-room mud hut where three women sat around an earthen oven making giant discs of flatbread. One woman flattened the dough into a circle, placed it on a metal sheet, and then set it on the ground. The second woman grabbed a handful of pebbles from a bucket and scattered them on top of the flatbread, and then the third woman placed the dough in the oven.

Mustafa handed the women the equivalent of ten cents, and they handed him a large round of bread, still warm and still covered with rocks—which served to keep the bread from rising while baking—and we left the hut. On the way back to Mustafa's place we picked the rocks from the bread and threw them on the ground.

When we returned, Mustafa emptied the water from the *tagine* and placed a chicken thigh in the bottom and then layered the chopped vegetables on top of it, piling them up until they created a large mound that nearly filled the cone-shaped lid. He sprinkled the vegetables with herbs, added a little oil and water, and then set the dish precariously atop a tiny burner screwed on to a propane tank. It was simple and delicious—nothing like the big complicated endeavor I once thought it would be. The evening turned to night, and night into the wee hours of the morning while we lounged around under the stars. The desert breeze filled the terrace with cool, dry air while Mustafa regaled us with stories of life at the edge of the Sahara.

In the morning we drove east through "the valley of a thousand *Kasbahs*," and then turned into the Dadès Gorge, a canyon oasis lined on both sides by almond and fig trees, leading north into the Atlas Mountains. Toward the top of the gorge we came to a set of winding hairpin switchbacks that brought us out of the bottom of the gorge and onto a plateau below the canyon rim. We stopped at the top and were immediately invited to have peanuts and tea with a man who owned a café. We sat down, and no sooner had Brad given the man a casual compliment on his blue turban, than the man zipped into action. He grabbed another identical blue turban—seemingly out of thin air—and began to wrap Brad's head in it. It all happened so fast that Brad didn't even have a chance to react, and he soon found himself dressed like a Moroccan camel rustler.

After tea, Brad unwound his fancy headgear and we continued up the valley, turning onto a rough, steep side trail for a lunch break. We found a relatively flat place to stop. Brad set the parking brake, and then took off to explore the road ahead on foot. I slid Nacho's side door open and got to work making tuna salads. Before long an old, ragged-looking man carrying a small wooden box approached the door. He perched himself right outside of the sliding door, squatted down, and watched me make lunch. There we were, miles from civilization, and this man sat at arm's length from me, silently watching my every move, and it dawned on me that I didn't mind. In fact, it didn't seem strange or uncomfortable to me at all. Those months in India during which our every move had been scrutinized by the staring masses in close proximity had changed me.

After a while Brad came back and saw the man staring at me, and approached him. Brad spoke to him in French.

"Good afternoon, what do you have in the box?"

"They are fossils from the mountains." Brad bent down and began to sift through the man's box, which contained a fairly substantial collection of fossilized shells and trilobites.

"Are they for sale?"

"Yes, you can pick the ones that you like." The man's face was worn and leathery; he had clearly led a hard life.

"How much are they?"

"You can pay whatever you like," the man said.

Brad picked up each shell in turn, keeping the ones he liked. "Do you live around here?" he asked.

"No, I live over the mountains," the old man said, pointing westward. "Every day I walk the mountains looking for fossils to sell so that I can feed my family." He smiled and said, "I have ten children."

"Are there a lot of fossils out here?" Brad asked.

"Not so many, but I can find them. I walk ten or twenty kilometers per day and I find a few."

His feet were calloused and hard, straining the cracked straps of his plastic sandals as he sat hunched over on the rocks. We chose several fossils and paid the man more than they were worth, and then handed him some food while we ate our salads in silence. When we finished, we cleaned our plates and closed up the van.

"Can we take you anywhere?" Brad asked him.

"Maybe just up to the next ridge," the man said, and he got into the passenger seat.

Morocco is forty-five minutes from Europe, but the two are entirely different worlds. This occurred to me when I had watched Brad tossing back peanuts and tea with a toothless African man in a turban, when I had watched the women covering flatbread with rocks and baking it in their dung-fired oven, and again while we drove through the Atlas Mountains with the ragged fossil collector. Those forty five minutes are a small barrier, but one that has succeeded in helping Morocco to sustain its cultural identity so close to Europe.

We stopped on the roadside to prepare lunch. To our right the Sahara Desert unfolded before us, while to our left the foothills of the Atlas Mountains rose steadily in boulder steps. Off in the distance, just a few hundred feet from Nacho, two camels wandered through pebble-strewn desert between shrubs. They appeared wild and uninterested in developing a friendship with Brad, despite his desperate attempts to hand-feed them a branch he had picked from a low shrub. He soon enough realized that the camels were best viewed from afar, and gave up his pursuit. We set up our chairs to point in their direction and had lunch, fully recognizing our good fortune.

"What do you think the chances are that we'll have a view like this again in our lives?" I asked Brad.

"Dunno. Probably never." He smiled. "Unless we keep going and drive to South Africa." He was trying to trick me into doing something crazy, I could tell.

After lunch we continued driving while mirages danced ahead of us across the desert. It was a glorious day and I couldn't stop smiling, an emotion fueled by knowing how far removed we were from the modern world, witnessing the most stereotypical of desert images: camels and mirages.

Our general destination for the day was the Todra Gorge, which runs parallel to the Dadès Gorge directly into the High Atlas, famous for its natural features formed by a massive fault line that runs beneath it. There is one spot in particular that everyone comes to see, where the road threads through a slot canyon next to a stream. But for us, the entire gorge was quite something to see. Berber mud-brick villages stood back to back with ribbons of palm groves, young children ran down the streets wearing headscarves, and women went about their daily activities dressed in strange attire, which appeared to be bed sheets wrapped over their regular clothes.

We had passed the last of the mud-brick villages when all at once the canyon walls rose up a thousand feet; we were driving through the famed narrow slot canyon where sunshine only reached the bottom for only a few minutes each day. Tourist buses parked at the mouth of the canyon, and tourists emptied out and walked through the slot canyon to take a few pictures and buy carpets from a selection of dozens of vendors.

We continued on in search of something less populated, and just five minutes up the road the gorge was all ours again. Nomadic shepherds called the Todra home for the season and we spotted some of their encampments high up on the canyon walls and out in the open flats. We eventually climbed out of the gorge and drove off into the desert at top of the mountains on a faint jeep track leading into the wilderness, then set up our own camp near a walled-in stone corral left unused for the night by the shepherds. Brad was excited to find the remains of a half-buried clay pot near Nacho's front bumper, and spent much of the remaining daylight hours trying to piece it back together.

After breakfast we backtracked out of the gorge and continued east into the Sahara where every so often a green island would come into view on the horizon, and eventually we would arrive at a small date-palm oasis in the desert. Amid the oases men sat along the road and sold succulent dates that hung from their branches like grapes on a vine. In one village we bought a five-pound box—the smallest size—for four dollars, then went on our way. We popped the dates into our mouths like candy, smiling like Prozac children.

Our resting point for the night came thirty miles from the Algerian border at Erg Chebbi, one of the places I had been most excited to visit in Morocco. We left the tarmac and headed down a badly-rutted, sandy road, which soon turned into faint tracks and then disappeared altogether. Camels lazed around in the distance, and only a few hundred feet away the surreal landscape went from pancake-flat blackish sand to a four-hundred-foot wall of golden sand dunes. We were at the base of one of Morocco's two Saharan *ergs*, or massive sand dunes, created by windblown sand. The dunes at Erg Chebbi were fifteen kilometers long by fifty kilometers wide. We drove Nacho as close as we dared and then set up camp for the night. Luxurious resort camps dotted the edge of the dunes off in the distance, and tourists took off on camels to explore the dunes at sunset. We watched from our camp as the towering sandbox lit up in unreal hues of fiery orange and red.

"What do you think the chances are that we'll have a view like this again in our lives?" I asked Brad.

"Dunno. Probably never." He smiled. "Unless we keep going and drive to South Africa." A dirty trick!

We awoke to a crisp blue sky and a chilly wind, and walked into the dunes to explore what we had always held in our minds as the stereotypical Sahara. We spent much of the morning happily running across the ridges of the dunes with bare feet, setting off sand avalanches along the way.

At last we said goodbye to the Sahara and set off to the north. We drove away, passing through the last swaths of desert oasis and sand castle villages where burka-clad women ambled along the roads on foot and men zipped around on donkeys and bicycles. The dunes at last gave way to rocky foothills, and then we climbed back over the High Atlas Mountains, transitioning out of the desert and back into Morocco's rolling agricultural fields. Desert castles and camels disappeared, replaced by dark clouds and sheets of rain. Between the sudden bursts of precipitation, we explored Volubilis, an old Roman city decorated in tile mosaics—a place where Roman columns had been overtaken by storks that used them to support their massive nests.

Toward the end of our quick three-week tour of Morocco, we reached Fes, a 1,200-year-old masterpiece of a city with a central *medina*—a walled, maze of streets containing market stalls and residences—that is said to be the largest living Islamic medieval city in the world. It is also happens to be the largest car-free urban environment on the planet. We drove inside the walls of the medina and paid a parking attendant to allow us to set up camp under a row of ancient trees for a few days.

The medina comprised a mesmerizing spider web of tight cobblestone streets full of markets and tiny open squares, food stalls, and tiny ramshackle homes. The markets held my attention for hours at a time, and I periodically lost my bearings, thus needing a local's assistance to point me back in the right direction. I went grocery shopping in the produce market, which had the most incredible selection of goods, especially its varieties of figs and dates and buckets of chickpeas and hand-rolled couscous. I bought ground, spiced beef for making shish kebabs, and then paused in front of the display of camel steaks, but decided against the idea. In the spice market I loaded up on *hanout*, a forty-spice mix used for flavoring vegetables and meat, and then passed through the pottery market where one could buy painted bowls and plates and clay *tagines*. I returned a number of times to the bronze and copper pot district to watch old men and their apprentices pound out copper pots over charcoal fires.

The most unique aspect of the medina was the tannery—the world's oldest—where leather had been tanned by hand for the last millennium. We viewed the operation from the commanding view of the balcony of a leather shop, taking in the sight as the smells of raw skin and sulfur wafted into the air. The shopkeeper gave us sprigs of mint to place under our noses so as not to become nauseated by the odor. The tannery was organized by task: the back corner contained wash basins and a giant roller for rinsing, while the adjacent white-stained basins were filled with a concoction of pigeon guano and cow urine used to soften the leather. The other basins were used for coloring, each filled with natural dyes for staining the leather: blue from indigo and red from saffron. Yellow, made from poppies, was the most expensive and labor intensive, and men on rooftops applied the yellow dye to the leather by hand.

In a world where most things are machine-made and rarely touched by the human hand, Morocco was like a glimpse into a simpler time. After I got my fill of medina life, we completed the last leg of our trip back to our starting point in the far north end of the country. As darkness descended on our last day, we stopped at one of the many roadside pottery factories and bought a set of individual *tagines*. With our purchases safely stored next to our everyday pots and pans, we loaded Nacho back onto the ferry and made the forty-five minute trip back across the Strait of Gibraltar, finally committed and ready to descend on Europe.

Brad frees Nacho from Istanbul's Hydarpasa Port with a little help from his Turkish sidekicks and esteemed tea-drinking buddies and their bolt cutters.

While Brad and Sheena are labeled as fools by their Turkish friends for having rented an apartment in Istanbul's most conservative Muslim neighborhood ("Little Tehran"), they enjoy their time there immensely, and embrace their status as infidels.

An old Turk eyes a display of fresh fish at Istanbul's spice bazaar, determined not to botch the task bestowed upon him by his wife to "buy some fish" without "screwing everything up." Brad can sympathize with this old Turk.

Sheena prepares for her all-out, week-long, Indiana-Jones-esque exploration of the far-off corners of Cappadocia, whose stone "chimneys" once housed an entire civilization of Hittite-fearing country folk.

Sheena stands inside of a church building that a past civilization has carved into solid rock in Cappadocia, Turkey.

After following a dirt track through a farmer's field, then descending a rough track, Nacho and crew stumble across an off-the-grid cave community. One of these holes leads to an underground series of chambers.

By crawling into a random hole at the base of a giant rock hill, Brad discovers an underground system including a "safe room" with a rolling stone door. He is unable to roll the door shut on his own, and is invaded by a marauding Sheena.

Sheena and Engin relax near Engin's home on the south Turkish coast; behind them, a sprinkling of uninhabited islands dot the Mediterranean Sea.

Brad wanders to the front of Engin's sailboat to do his best Leonardo DiCaprio impression as the boat leaves the hidden bay of a Mediterranean island.

Having wandered from a hidden bay to an outward-facing beach on an island off of the Turkish coast, Sheena considers how to break the news to Brad that she will never permit him to buy a sailboat.

"...Because you'll be living in a VAN, down by the (Mediterranean Sea)!" Motivational speaker Matt Foley would be proud (at Bodrum, Turkey).

Sheena considers her major folly at not having brought a skateboard on which to descend the switchbacks in Morocco's Dadès Gorge in the Atlas Mountains.

After being complimented on his stylish turban, a Moroccan man correctly guesses that Brad would like nothing more than to have a stylish turban of his own.

Brad and Sheena take a lunch break in the high Atlas Mountains of Morocco, where they are later found by a roving fossil hunter.

Brad goes into full *tranquilo* mode on the rooftop terrace of Mohammed's antique bazaar, while a late-night tagine dinner balances precariously atop a propane cylinder.

Camels crossing the Sahara Desert in Africa? So cliché.

Part 4

Europe, Alas

52

Camino del Sacromonte, Granada

Brad

The grass along the banks of the Rio Darro hung tall and still under the roasting midday sun. Below the dipping reeds the water flowed crystal clear without hint of turbulence, like air with the viscosity of motor oil. A group of orange and white cats passively surveyed the river from under the drooping stalks along the bank. They lived as if in a vacuum, free of responsibility, no place to be, nobody to please. The laziness that underscored their daily affairs was a natural defense against Granada's heat. The locals knew this as well as the cats, and they responded to the searing heat with a daily *siesta* within their whitewashed homes or in the shade of the jacarandas that grow along the river.

Above the grassy riverbank a pair of ancient stone retaining walls jutted upwards, enveloping the river in a slot between the old town center and the Alhambra palace—the Moorish stone masterpiece adorned with arched windows and curly Arabic inscriptions, whose walls seemed to grow out of the earth creating a vertical extension of the finger of land extending down from the snow-capped Sierra Nevada. On the wall above the river in the shadow of an imposing alder, I sprawled my body out in a state of lethargic repose, my legs dangling lifelessly from the wall while my body absorbed the coolness of the rocks. Sheena leaned against a stone pillar at the end of the wall near my feet. I watched the cats, who in turn watched the clear water as it passed under an arched stone bridge.

Standing opposite to the towering Alhambra to the South, the ancient whitewashed neighborhood called Albaicín extended up the hillside to the north in a web of tight cobbled lanes and winding stairways. A few feet away from us in the plaza at the base of the

371

Albaicín a man played *tremolos* and *rasgueados* on his flamenco guitar, the nylon strings reverberating through planed spruce to fill the air with the sound that defines the spirit and history of Andalucía. Men and women wearing light pants and skirts and sunglasses—the attire of a hot climate—relaxed in chairs under vine-covered trellises in the plaza, sipping wine and casually eating olives, manchego, and slices of cured chorizo.

We left the plaza walking along the river, and then turned up a street toward the Alhambra. We passed shops selling postcards and decorative tiles, and several workshops where flamenco guitars had been manufactured continuously for centuries. Inside, the men hunched over their workbenches, tapping into place the frets that would one day be deftly manipulated by the city's flamenco performers to produce the region's haunting music. The music would, in turn, be danced to in caves and bars, making Andalucia characteristically Andalucian. The calloused hands of the guitar makers shaped the character of the city.

We circled back around to the bottom of the hill, stopping in a bar of varnished wood for a drink to temper the afternoon heat, and sat amongst old men who watched soccer on television. We wandered out of the bar and up the hill on a small cobbled lane into the Moroccan district on the edge of the Albaicín. Men and women of a mocha complexion ducked in and out of shops selling saffron and leather, while the smell of tea and flavored tobacco floated from within the ubiquitous tea houses and hookah bars. A Moroccan man sat on a stool beside a board displaying various decorative paper sheets and a cup containing quill pens. We handed him one Euro and, in exchange, he wrote "Nacho" in Arabic calligraphy using a hawk feather—our little way of supporting a micro-entrepreneur. We left the Albaicín through the old city walls, wandering into the gypsy quarter known as Sacromonte, where migrant *Gitanos* had dug cave homes into the hillside hundreds of years ago.

In Sacromonte there is a bar inside of a cave on the north side of the road opposite the alders and willows lining the Rio Darro. Outside of the bar under cover of an overhanging tarpaulin we took our seats at a table next to a man and his young daughter, who was perhaps eight years old. She had long, dark hair, and in between sips of her juice, which she clung to with both hands, told her *papá* about all sorts of things in the squirrel voice that little Spanish girls have. Her name was Nina.

The bar man walked outside to take our order.

"Dos cañas, porfa," I said. He nodded and addressed the girl and her *papá*.

"Hola guapa," he said to the girl, "algo mas para vos?" The girl shook her head and the bar man smiled and went back into the cave to retrieve our beer. While we waited, an older woman approached from down the canyon and smiled at Nina.

"Hola guapa!" she said. Nina smiled as she sipped her juice through her straw, causing her dimples to deepen and her eyes to squint. The bar man emerged with our beer and *tapas*—a plate of cold meats with cheese, olives and bread. In Spain, a bar is the place to go for a light lunch. The cost of a draught beer is around two Euros, and a free plate of tapas worth more than two Euros always accompanies it. How Spanish bars manage to make any money is a mystery, but it is the way it has always been and hopefully the way it always will be.

Why a culture of tapas emerged in Spain and not elsewhere is a mystery. Long ago in Spanish bars, the barkeep would serve beer with a small plate situated atop the glass to keep the flies out. At some point someone thought to place a small snack on the plate before serving the beer, not only keeping the flies at bay but providing something to snack on as well. "Tapa" literally means "cover," and is so called simply because they were originally used solely as a cover for the beer. Tapas are no longer served on top of the beer, but they are proudly delivered with every round; cold cuts, paella, *bocadillos*, chorizo sausage, fish, or any number of other dishes may be delivered with your drinks, *gratis*.

Eventually we finished our beer and tapas and stood to leave. Just as we did so, an old man approached Nina and bent over to address her. "Hola guapa," he said, smiling. Everyone in Sacromonte knew Nina.

In the late afternoon we walked out past the caves of Sacromonte along the river away from Granada. The sides of the narrow road were lined with sprawling agave plants, prickly pear, flowers and grass, and we caught periodic shade from the occasional overhanging tree branch. We had parked Nacho in a pullout carved into an embankment below a strand of agave, and when we arrived there, I set up the shower. It was my thirty-first birthday and we had reservations at a flamenco show in Sacromonte. We took turns taking hot showers as the cool evening air settled in, and then put on our best clothes, which after more than two years on the road were nearly indistinguishable from the clothes worn by Granada's street gypsies.

As evening settled in we strolled along the road through Sacromonte in the direction of the Albaicín. As we did, the slanting rays of sun gave one last pass through the atmosphere, and then dipped below the horizon, causing cool air to wash into the valley like water from the canyons that descended from the snow-capped Sierra Nevada. By the time we reached *Venta El Gallo*, a gypsy-cave-turned-flamenco-bar carved into the hillside, the air outside was cool enough to allow the wearing of long sleeves.

Inside the small cave we found our seats near the wall among several rows of simple chairs. It was cool and dark inside, and a wooden stage had been constructed at the base of a wall decorated with hanging antique ladles and copper cups. An old street lamp illuminated the stage from within an arched recess in the wall. The roof of the cave traced a low arch all the way to the floor like a half-tube, its rough earthen bulges having been whitewashed. The room filled quickly while a woman walked around filling glasses with sangria for everyone in attendance. Our heads soon became light from the wine while the air became increasingly heavy and warm from the collective exhalations of the waiting audience. The artists took their places at the front of the cave, and at once smooth, rhythmic plucks of the flamenco guitar filled the air.

The first among the group of three dancers—a young woman wearing a traditional black dress and polka dot blouse—took her place at the front, staring intensely straight ahead. Her dark eye shadow and red lipstick portrayed a sultry intensity. At once her body snapped into motion, her arms writhing and twisting in the air as her feet stomped the wooden floor in time to the guitar and the chants of the two singers behind her. Her hips twisted to the music and her face strained with the effort to sustain the sewing-machine-tapping of her feet on the floor. She seemed to float in place as her feet moved faster and faster, her arms uncontrollably grasping at her dress until her face could no longer mask her intense concentration; her eyebrows flattened and her shiny lips became thin. The veins in her neck hardened, and she struggled to keep her eyes open. The sound of her feet tapping the floor became a steady vibration and then her hands splayed open, leaving her dress wrinkled where she had held it in her small fist. She began slapping her thighs and chest with her open hands, wincing at her own self-flagellation. At just about the time that it seemed she would explode into flames, she jerked her head back, stomped her feet one last time, and threw her arms into the air, her chest heaving, sweat dripping from her face, and her long black hair hanging in loose strands. She collapsed into her chair and the next dancer stood up.

As we walked back home in the dark, the breeze carried a hint of agave and dry soil, made into perfume and whisked through the canyon by the currents of cool, moist air rising from the banks of the Rio Darro.

53

Carretera Nacional 135 to Burguete

Brad

With limited time to spend in Europe I would need to think of something sneaky and clever to get Sheena to let me have my way. While she wanted to walk around fancy European trinket markets looking at shiny objects and sampling candied fruits and nuts, I had it in mind that we should be spending our time fishing instead. And when it came down to a choice between fish wrangling and lady time, lady time always won. Fortunately I had classic literature on my side, and everyone knows how much ladies like classic literature.

"Oh Sheena, my sweet," I said encouragingly as the dry Spanish countryside marched past our windows, "do I have a treat for you!"

"Oh?" she said.

"Yes, actually. You see, I've been planning a special fishing tri–"

"What? Does it look like I want to go fishing right now? Is that what this looks like?" She bobbled her head like a sassy hip-hop singer while wildly pointing to various parts of her head and abdomen with her whipping index fingers.

"But my pea, hear me out. We'll be following the path of Ernest Hemingway from *The Sun Also Rises*, in which Jake and Bill escape the hustle and bustle of Paris and steal away to the relaxing trout streams of the Pyrenees. It's really more of a reenactment of a very important story from classic American literature."

"Ernest Heming-who? And *where* was his fishing trip?"

"Well I'm not exactly sure, but I think we can piece together the clues and retrace his steps. But in the end they catch twelve fish. Can you imagine? Think of all the fish tacos we could make!"

There is no other explanation except that she must have found me too charming to resist, as she reluctantly agreed to my shoddy plan of following clues from a ninety-year-old fictional novel. The fishing trip in the book was based on an actual trip that Hemingway had taken to Spain, so I figured it was worth a shot.

"There's Roncevaux," I said.

"Where?"

"Way off there where the mountain starts."

"It's cold up here," Bill said.

"It's high," I said. "It must be twelve hundred metres."

"It's awful cold," Bill said.

The bus levelled down onto the straight line of road that ran to Burguete. We passed a crossroads and crossed a bridge over a stream. The houses of Burguete were along both sides of the road. There were no side-streets. We passed the church and the schoolyard, and the bus stopped. We got down and the driver handed down our bags and the rod-case.

The pages were littered with clues, and in no time I had pinpointed our starting point destination: the small Basque mountain village of Burguete. A quick search of the maps revealed our destination as a mere asterisk amid the giant Pyrenees range.

We passed Pamplona on its eastern outskirts and ducked off onto a winding one-lane road snaking upward into the mountains, bisecting fields of yellow gorse as it went along. We of course knew the yellow flowers were gorse because of my gumshoe sleuthing skills.

Ahead the road came out of the forest and went along the shoulder of the ridge of hills. The hills ahead were not wooded, and there were great fields of yellow gorse.

We climbed out of the valley into the cool forest pocked with farmhouses, and drove up a winding road into the forest to camp for the night. While our trip across Spain had been generally warm and sunny, the Pyrenees were overcast and it rained on and off, making everything seem clean.

In the morning we drove into Hemingway's Burguete. The road into town was indeed straight. We passed a crossroads, just as described, and found very old homes lining both sides of the street. We passed the church, near where Jake and Bill disembarked from the bus, and found a parking place.

It was time to prepare Sheena for our adventure. She had never read *The Sun Also Rises*, so I opened it and flipped to the part about the fishing trip. If we were to be successful sleuths, she would need to be brought up to speed with all of the clues at our disposal. I sat in the driver's seat and she in the passenger's seat, and like a couple of book dorks, I read aloud to her.

"This is stupid and embarrassing," she pleaded.

"It's only embarrassing if someone sees us," I reassured her.

First, I read to her about the hotel in Burguete. If we were to capture the spirit of Hemingway and leverage it to catch a bunch of fish, we would need to see where he stayed.

> We went up the street, past the whitewashed stone houses, families sitting in their doorways watching us, to the inn.
>
> ... We washed, put on sweaters, and came down-stairs into the dining-room. It had a stone floor, low ceiling, and was oakpanelled. The shutters were all up and it was so cold you could see your breath.
>
> "My God!" said Bill. "It can't be this cold tomorrow. I'm not going to wade a stream in this weather."
>
> There was an upright piano in the far corner of the room beyond the wooden tables and Bill went over and started to play.

By this point I was getting pretty excited. I was like one of those dorky twelve-year-olds who reads Harry Potter aloud to his parents as if they were actually interested in hearing about hobgoblins and haunted broomsticks. Sheena rolled her eyes and I continued bringing her up to speed with all of the clues that Hemingway left behind.

We locked up the car and wandered around Burguete, Sheena taking photos of old doors and windows while I wandered from building to building trying to find the inn. At last, a few hundred meters up the road from the church we wandered into a hotel. On the wall of the low-ceilinged, stone-floored, oak-paneled dining room hung a painting of none other than Ernest Hemingway himself. I whooped with joy at having found the inn while Sheena rolled her eyes and slowly shook her head.

In *The Sun Also Rises*, Jake and Bill set off early from the inn to walk over the ridge on foot to the Irati River where they would spend the day fishing. Jake rose early to dig worms behind the inn and then they set off.

> We packed the lunch and two bottles of wine in the rucksack, and Bill put it on. I carried the rod-case and the landing-nets slung over my back. We started up the road and then went across a meadow and found a path that crossed the fields and went toward the woods on the slope of the first hill...

Given our history of getting lost and causing international missing persons incidents, we opted not walk blindly into the woods, but rather to include Nacho in the adventure by driving. We left town and skirted the ridge, descending after a few kilometers into the canyon through which the Irati River carved its path. During the descent I spied a small dam on the river far below, and imagined that it must have been the fishing spot where the story took place. The subjects found their way over the ridge and down to the river, stopping at a dam. Jake opted to fish from the dam using worms, while Bill wandered downstream to try his luck flyfishing.

> *There was a field of buckwheat on the hill. We saw a white house under some trees on the hillside. It was very hot and we stopped under some trees beside a dam that crossed the river.*

> *Bill put the pack against one of the trees and we jointed up the rods, put on the reels, tied on leaders, and got ready to fish.*

> *"You're sure this thing has trout in it?" Bill asked.*

> *"It's full of them."*

> *"I'm going to fish a fly. You got any McGintys?"*

> *"There's some in there."*

> *"You going to fish bait?"*

> *"Yeah. I'm going to fish the dam here."*

At the base of the canyon we found the small village of Aribe, where we parked Nacho to investigate our options. We wandered around and found a small but promising dirt road taking off along the opposite bank behind a small stone bridge. Near the church we found a placard with some information about Hemingway. Our detective work was spot on—a fact that I reiterated to Sheena with enthusiasm, and I sensed a small hint of admiration in the eyeball-roll that followed.

I asked someone how to get to los Baños, and was pointed down the riverbank toward the dam I'd seen. We got back in Nacho and turned onto the dirt road, which wound its way along the bank and then climbed above the river valley through the thick beech forest. At about the point where I had remembered the dam being, we parked. The locals had reported that Hemingway used to bring with him a basket of beers, so I hastily grabbed the basket we'd bought on the roadside in Thailand for carrying sticky rice, and put a couple of beers in it. I was willing to go to great lengths to make this trip as historically accurate as possible.

In the book, Jake and Bill each bagged six rainbow trout in a relatively short period of time on the afternoon that they spent at the dam. In short, we were more or less guaranteed to be eating fish tacos by nightfall.

> *I did not feel the first trout strike. When I started to pull up I felt that I had one and brought him, fighting and bending the rod almost double, out of the boiling water at the foot of the falls, and swung him up and onto the dam. He was a good trout, and I banged his head against the timber so that he quivered out straight, and then slipped him into my bag.*
>
> *While I had him on, several trout had jumped at the falls. As soon as I baited up and dropped in again I hooked another and brought him in the same way. In a little while I had six.*

When we arrived at the dam I set down the basket of beers and began to assemble my fly rod. Below the dam on the eastern side of the river there was a still pool, while the western side of the river fanned out over some submerged rock ridges before ducking below some overhanging willow trees. I fished both sides of the river, flicking my fly out into the current or into the still pool. After a while, not having any luck, I switched flies. I didn't have any McGinty's.

Sheena put down her coming of age princess novella and broke the silence.

"Any luck?" she asked.

"Nope, not yet."

"What are you using?" she asked. I was pleased that she was finally showing a real interest in our literary detective mission.

"I've tried a couple of different flies," I said. She stared at me for a minute, as if to say, *Are you stupid or something?* At last she spoke.

"Seriously? A fly? I thought Ned Hemington used worms!"

"Ned Hemington? Are you kidding me, woman? Are we talking about a literary legend or a Simpson's character?!"

"I just think that if he used worms then maybe you should use worms too."

"Some things are better left to the experts, understand?"

The afternoon passed without a single bite. We leaned against a tree in the shade, keeping to strict historical accuracy, and drank our beer.

In the morning the rain had moved in, but we weren't to be discouraged. We left Nacho parked by the riverside in Aribe, opting this time to walk the riverbank out to los Baños, fishing the bank along the way. The river's edge was pretty well socked in by groves of low hanging willows, making it difficult to fly-fish without waders, but I tried nonetheless, knowing that this river was brimming with the grandtrout and great grandtrout of those caught by Hemingway all those years ago.

While I fished, Sheena distracted herself from the mission by taking photos of grass, flowers, trees, water, and slugs, among many other things. When finally we reached los Baños, a place designated by a couple of old abandoned buildings on the water's edge just a few meters upstream from the dam, I resumed fishing. I tried several flies, alternating between the bank, a sandbar, and the retaining wall in front of the old building, but after a few hours came up completely empty handed.

Having photographed everything within a three hundred meter radius of los Baños, Sheena finally meandered back to the waterfront where I noticed her standing there with her hands on her hips.

"Where are my fish, boy?!"

"I think they're all asleep today," I said.

"Do you want to know what I think?" she wailed in disbelief. "I think that Ned Hemington is full of crap!"

54

Rue Michelet, Paris

Brad

When we left the United States, we began to witness the world changing around us, a world hardly recognizable from the one we left behind at the Mexican border. At first the changes came hard and fast, but after a while we started to forget how things were back home. By the time we arrived in Europe we had managed to forget many of our old Western habits, and had not only become accustomed to seeing things done differently, but came to see many of the alternative ways as superior. In Europe, at long last, some of those old nonsensical Western memories came flooding back. One deeply disturbing difference between the West and the rest of the world reemerged like a lurking character in a nightmare.

The stroller.

The moment we left US soil, strollers became almost nonexistent. With the exception of a few sinister nonconformists here and there, parents around the world carried their children on their backs in a sheet, which was secured by a knot in the middle of the parents' chests. The babies would spend each day pressed up against their parents while they sold goods at the market, walked around, ate, harvested rice, or zipped through traffic on their motor scooters.

But in Europe, we were suddenly confronted by hordes of parents pushing around those gigantic monstrosities of mechanical engineering: road-worthy and crash-tested behemoths with locking wheels, bump-neutralizing four-wheel independent suspension, retractable awnings, cup holders, toy storage bins, and cushioned hand grips.

Inside of these ridiculous rigs, the babies writhed in their padded seats crying, trying to escape, wondering where on earth their parents had gone and why in the hell they'd been strapped into overbuilt plastic capsules with five-point safety harnesses. Meanwhile the rest of the world's babies went about their business comfortably conforming to their parents' curves inside of their cocoon-like sheets, never crying, and silently chuckling at their silly Western baby counterparts. I just assumed that everyone who had seen *the other way* would share my distaste for strollers, and this included our Parisian friends Benoit and Aude, whom we had first met, along with their four children, on the misty mountaintop in Laos.

That evening back in Laos, as the light dwindled and we prepared to settle down for dinner, their daughter Jeanne had bopped around the parking lot pushing a little luggage rack that resembled a stroller. It was probably the only stroller-type apparatus in Laos.

If I had remembered that incident, then I might have opted not to go into my anti-stroller rant over dinner at Benoit and Aude's house in a suburb of Paris a full year after our first meeting. Perhaps it was the wine, but in any case I launched into my rant, frequently seeking reassurance from our hosts that we agreed about the frivolity of strollers, to which they nodded and shook their heads at those poor pitiful people with their silly over-engineered baby cars.

"In France we call them *pushchairs*," Benoit said, sipping his wine and lightly shaking his head in disgust.

Benoit and Aude lived in Asnieres, a neighborhood in the northwest quarter of Paris, along with their children Alexandre, Emma, Blanche, and Jeanne (self-proclaimed "*Jeanne la Plus Forte*"). We had grown quite fond of them during the week that we spent together in Laos. Back in Asia they had invited us to stay with them when we got to France, and so we set aside a week to reacquaint ourselves with Paris and spend time with our friends. Alexandre, the oldest, led us up the stairs to his room, which he had graciously donated to us for the duration of our stay—a true gentleman, I must say—and he temporarily adopted the attic as his living quarters. He was the kind of chivalrous young man whose good character could only be the result of a childhood not tainted by time spent in solitary confinement, strapped to a prison cell on wheels.

In the mornings, Emma and Alexandre would walk or bike to school, Aude would zip off to work in the car, and Benoit would load Blanche and Jeanne onto the back panniers of his bicycle, disappearing down the street in a flurry of backpacks, swinging legs, and pigtails in the slipstream of Benoit's business-casual attire. On those days during the week, Sheena and I were on our own to explore.

We walked the backstreets and avenues of Asnieres, and we acquainted ourselves with the Metro. In Montmartre we climbed the hill to the *Sacre Coeur* past peaceful parks filled with people lounging in the grass, and rested on the steps under the cathedral while we watched a performer hang from a street lamp and juggle a soccer ball with his feet. The street corners in the iconic neighborhood were dotted with pubs and chic restaurants, while nearby shops sold quirky trinkets. In the shade of a giant tree, a group of Spanish men played their guitars and sang traditional songs.

In between home-prepared meals of *foie gras*, cheese plates, and Benoit's throwback preparation of Thai curry, which he had perfected while traversing Thailand in the RV, we found time to dine at the *Côté Bac*. It was a new, chic neighborhood restaurant owned by a friend, on its second day of operation. Over the course of one amazing meal, I made four observations about France.

After studying the small selection of available dinner options for the night, which would change based on seasonal availability of meats and vegetables, three of us ordered the lamb, while Aude ordered a tomato salad. We sat back and talked, and quickly noticed that everyone in the packed restaurant knew everyone else. Each time a new couple came in the door, they cheerfully said hello to everyone, walked to our table, gave Aude and Benoit a *bise* on the cheek, chatted for a moment, and then sat down.

The first observation: France is like that bar in the 1980's television show *Cheers*, except the French are better dressed and don't have the ugly hair. It must be nice, I thought, to live in a place where everyone knows your name.

When our dinner arrived I noticed that Aude's plate didn't seem to have much food on it. Poor Aude, I thought. As we dug in, a man walked in the door and let out a boisterous yell in the direction of the owner, clearly his friend. My first thought was, *I feel right at home! This is the way Americans are! We're not so different after all!* All of the diners stopped eating and looked at the man. He walked through the restaurant, continuing to speak at an elevated pitch, and gave the owner a hug before sitting down. The chatter resumed.

"This is a kind of joke," Benoit said, chuckling. "This man is the neighborhood butcher, and every time the restaurant owner comes into the butcher shop he disrupts his business by yelling. It is very funny. Now that the butcher has come to the restaurant, he is doing the same thing to disrupt his friend's business by yelling."

The second observation: We Americans really are loud, and the French are probably annoyed by the fact that we're not joking.

The arrival of the butcher shifted our conversation toward butchers and butchery in general.

"This man," Benoit said, pointing his chin at the butcher, "he is something of a world famous butcher." He pronounced *butcher* as *boo-chair*. "He is known all over France, and people come from abroad to apprentice with him. A few months ago, he did an exchange with a popular boo-chair in New York City. The New York boo-chairs would come to Asnieres to see how we do it, and then the Asnieres boo-chairs would go to New York." He thought for a minute and chuckled. "When my friend went to New York, he said that the boo-chairs would throw the pieces of cow on the table, and then quickly cut them with an electric saw. An electric saw! The French boo-chairs showed them how to boo-chair a cow with only a very sharp knife—you know, here our boo-chairs cut around each muscle very carefully—it's like an art."

The third observation: While we Americans may make fun of the French for being soft-handed and fashion-aware, they really are much cooler than we are.

As the meal wound down and evening turned to night, we sipped wine and talked. It was after ten o'clock, and the place was still packed with diners. Seeing that we were nearly ready to leave, the owner came back to the table to see how everything was. Being that the restaurant had just opened, and that they were all friends, he was looking for honest feedback.

"We really liked the menus. The weight of the paper was perfect, and your font is very attractive." The owner thanked them and waited for more. Benoit continued. "One critique that we can make is regarding the portion sizes." Aude knowingly nodded her head, and I looked on, proud that I had made the same observation. Poor Aude with her little tomatoes. "The dish that Aude ordered, the tomato dish, was perfect, but the lamb portions were too big. You should reduce the amount of meat, it was just too much."

The fourth observation: Heavy butcher paper makes a fantastic backing for a menu. Now if we could just figure out how these French people stay so svelte and healthy.

The weekend rolled in under blue skies and we packed a picnic lunch to accompany us on our "Rediscovering Paris Walking Tour," which would involve all eight of us navigating the Metro to the river Seine, and then meandering around the streets of central Paris. I was upstairs getting ready while Sheena helped with lunch preparations downstairs with Benoit and Aude.

"Shall we bring the pushchair for Jeanne?" Aude asked Benoit.

"Shhh! No way! You saw how much Brad hates pushchairs!" Benoit said in a hushed voice, recalling my earlier tirade, in which I may at some point have referred to strollers as "a catalyst to the imminent downfall of Western civilization." Aude sighed and placed an apple in the picnic bag.

The ride on the Metro went off without a hitch, despite our group's size and the fact that it contained an energetic four-year-old not constrained by leash or harness. The feeling of emerging from the underground into a sunny Parisian morning along the river Seine can be described as nothing less than heavenly. We meandered from street to street, past the Notre Dame, peering into ancient courtyards and stopping to rest at tastefully artistic fountains and parks. Sheena and I observed Aude and Benoit's parenting style, and the maturity and independence of their children, with a great sense of admiration, much as we had all week.

From time to time we would see a parent with a stroller, and we would all pretend to ignore it. When we reached a park with very few strollers, Benoit would regard, "There are not so many pushchairs here, no?"

As we walked, Benoit and Aude acted as our tour guides, while Alexandre pointed out things of interest and Emma roamed around taking pictures with our camera. Jeanne, meanwhile, zipped between streets and alleys and into any and all shops containing shiny things or pretty dresses. At one point she stopped to watch a street sweeper, following him down the length of an entire block, entranced by the translation of debris along the gutter. Whenever she strayed more than a block or two from us, nine-year-old Blanche, in her ballerina tutu, would corral her through the crowded streets, back to the group before the cycle repeated itself. Benoit and Aude showed no concern of child abduction or disappearance of little Jeanne, a fact that only strengthened my distaste for strollers and the wussification of children who are forced to sit in them.

A bonus observation: Hanging out with French parents and children is dangerous for non-French parents-in-training because they make you forget just how monstrous and difficult some non-French children can be.

We sat down and leaned against a rock wall next to a walking path along the Seine and spread out our picnic lunch. Across the way the drooping boughs of old trees and several ornate domes and towers decorated the skyline. Boats floated by and we were warm and comfortable in the sun. Emma, Blanche, and Jeanne danced together and played games while the rest of us gazed across the river at the Notre Dame cathedral.

After lunch Jeanne whizzed through the crowded sidewalks for another few minutes before finally running out of steam, and fell asleep atop Benoit's head for the remainder of the day.

When we arrived home in the evening, I went upstairs to drop my things in Alexandre's room, and Sheena listened in on Benoit and Aude chatting in the kitchen.

"That was fun, wasn't it? The kids did very well for such a long day," Benoit said.

"Yes, it went quite well," she said.

"So, what did you think about not taking the pushchair?" Benoit said hopefully, having somewhat bought into my point of view regarding these asinine eyesores.

Aude looked deep into Benoit's eyes and uttered two words: "No comment."

55

Benelux Backroads

Brad

With the foam mattress cover folded back out of the way, I laid the last of our contraband out on our bed. I leaned back, wiped the sweat from my forehead, and inspected my work. I carefully rolled the mattress cover out over the bed, concealing the bounty in a foam sandwich. Would a border guard think to look there? I hoped not. I spread a yak hair blanket over the whole mess, smoothed it out, and then climbed down into Nacho's living quarters where Sheena had just finished stuffing the rest of our illegal contraband under the couch. Using a power drill I ran two screws through the bottom of the seat and tested it to be sure it couldn't be opened. I got out, picked up the ugly chicken wire cage that I had built on the bank of the canal, and slid it into place behind the front seats. I hoped it would deter the workers in the shipyard and the customs agents from going into our living quarters while Nacho was in the port.

"Let's just hope they don't find any of this," I said. Sheena nodded, nervously wringing her hands. A rower sliced through the dark water of the canal, barely taking notice of us inspecting our work. Scraps of chicken wire and wood littered the ground around the van. This was the result of an ill-conceived plan long in the making, one that we set into motion as soon as we left France in the north.

Belgium—flat, muddy, cold, and windy—is a Petri dish of hardened souls from which a smorgasbord of culinary decadences were spawned, among them the world's finest chocolate and beer. Since the ninth century, Trappist monasteries have been brewing beer as a way to support their abbeys. The monastic order fell apart during the French Revolution, and only seven monasteries had survived in Benelux: six in Belgium, and one in the Netherlands. My goal upon arriving in Belgium was to visit them all, but most importantly to get my hands on the uncontested holy grail of beer from Abbaye Saint Sixtus in the tiny village of Westvleteren.

Westvleteren 12 had long been considered the best beer in the world, but it had never been distributed outside of the region, and its sale was tightly restricted to a few dozen cases per week. In order to get it, one had to make a reservation a week in advance, and then pick it up in person from the monks somewhere out in the windy cattle pastures of western Belgium.

By the hundredth time I tapped out the ten-digit number on the keypad, my fingers acted without instruction. I squatted on my heels in the center of the tourist information office in the village of Rochefort, and had been doing so since the phone line had opened. After thirty minutes, the old woman behind the counter whose phone I was using shook her head and muttered in French "That's enough," but I pretended not to understand and continued tapping. A good thing, because five minutes later someone picked up on the other end of the line.

"Hello, this is Saint Sixtus. Can you be here next Monday at 2:30?"

"Oh god, I almost hung up! Yes, I'll be there."

"What is your license plate number?"

"It's AHK 2531."

"Okay, I will see you on Monday." *Click.*

I let out a restrained whoop, gave the finger pistols to the old lady behind the counter, and then walked outside into the cool, overcast Belgian morning, flaunting my social retardation in its most unbridled form.

We should have been ecstatic to be in Belgium, but since we had arrived it felt bittersweet. Three years earlier when we had scratched out our rough plan for worldly discovery, it all culminated here. Leave home. Machu Picchu. Catch fish. Himalayas. Drink beer in Belgium.

This was a big one, but it was also the last thing on the list. In a little more than a week we were to load Nacho onto the fifth and final ship in Antwerp, whereupon he would brave the high seas one last time en route to North America. After having put down tracks in thirty-one countries throughout five continents over the course of two and a half years, this was it.

On the first day of our self-driving tour of all of the Trappist beer-brewing monasteries, I bought a special Orval beer goblet. Later on when we set up camp in the mosquito-infested woods, I walked into a stinging nettle, and then Sheena broke my special Orval beer goblet by carelessly knocking it into the sink with her elbow.

"Damn it, woman!" I said. "You just broke my special beer goblet!" On her face there was a frozen look of terror, all clenched teeth and raised eyebrows.

Our long path to that point had taken numerous twists and turns, and the stinging nettle and broken glass happened when and where it did as a result of everything that had come before. There were certain points that changed our trajectory entirely, like when Nacho's transmission failed and purged its life-blood all over the road while climbing through a very remote part of the Colombian Andes. A couple of hours later a passing truck had towed us to the decrepit lair of a malicious mechanic who touched Nacho inappropriately and did unspeakable things. Under cover of darkness a farmer had helped me to steal Nacho away to the safety of his farm, where we would remain stranded for nearly two months.

Over those two months we would get to know the little old lady who navigated the trail each day behind the farm near the rock that had been painted for the Battle of Boyacá, the pig farmer who lived up the hill, the boy who filled our pitcher each morning with fresh milk straight from the cow's udder, and the coca farmer who stopped to say hello each time he passed Sheena in his truck during her morning runs above Chicamocha canyon. But above all, we got to know Hernando and Cos, the lovely couple who ran the farm where we stayed, and whose kindness made it very hard to leave Colombia, even when we were mechanically able.

It was to our great surprise and delight, then, that we received a message from Cos while we were in Rochefort stating that Hernando would soon be in Köln, Germany to visit his daughter for a few days. We updated the route on our GPS, adding a lightning bolt trip to Germany after our upcoming stop at Westvleteren.

To get to Westvleteren, where the world's best beer awaited, we set off across Belgium toward the western coast. Along the way we stopped at Chimay, the best known of the Trappists, and spent a day milling around the idyllic town of Brugge, hitting a couple of small farmhouse breweries along the way. After leaving the premises of a steam brewing operation whose labels featured illustrated pigs in seductive poses, we stopped by the Dubuisson brewery in Pipiax, where Bush beer was brewed. Inside we chatted with one of the workers.

"What brings you to Belgium?"

"Just driving around, mostly."

"Very good. Where are you from?"

"The United States."

"Oh! We hate George Bush around here!"

"Yeah, most people in the world do."

"Yes, yes, but we hate him for a different reason. After he was elected he sued us for having the same name. Can you believe it? We have been brewing since 1769! And do you know what? With all of his high-powered lawyers, he beat us! We had to change the name on our labels for American distribution. It was a very expensive time."

"That guy must be some kind of bastard, brother. Some kind of bastard."

When Monday finally rolled around we awoke with a sense of haste and purpose. Well one of us did, anyway. Sheena didn't seem to care that the day had arrived to pick up our two cases of Westvleteren 12, the Holy Grail in my beer crusade. She slouched in the passenger seat reading her coming of age princess novella while I closely followed the turn-by-turn instructions on our GPS through farm pastures until we finally reached the monastery. I pulled into the driveway, and there before us sat a giant stack of wooden crates full of the coveted beer. Next to the crates there sat a monk in a small office, and as we drove up he checked our license plate against his paper and then instructed us to grab two crates.

"You can grab two crates," he said.

"I love you," I said, realizing too late that I was speaking my thoughts aloud. But there was no time to explain; we had to get to Germany.

When we first met Hernando in Columbia, we were at a low point. During our first week on his farm, having just experienced a long stretch of mechanical failures, we had considered ditching the whole plan and flying home. But after weighing the options, we had reluctantly persisted, a decision that certainly transformed our lives for the better in the years that would follow.

I thought back on the trove of experiences that we'd gained since deciding not to quit. I knew what it felt like to cross the Andes in the back of a rattletrap chicken truck. I knew how the heat felt rising off of the Atacama Desert. I could still taste the Patagonian rainbow trout cooked over a campfire, and I could recall how I felt when my eyes first saw the tip of Tierra del Fuego disappearing into the icy waters of the Beagle Channel. I knew the fragrant heat of the Malaysian jungle, the

Muslim call to prayer, and the sizzle of Thai street food and the spices stinging my lungs. The salty air rising from the sea on the Cambodian coast, filling the inside of our home, and the Tibetan Plateau stretching out before us from a Himalayan pass. The way my fingers turned yellow from turmeric while eating lamb *biryani* out of a crumpled Indian newspaper under the stifling Tamil Nadu sun. The sight of Turkish pines fanning out onto the beach, and the feeling of being swallowed by a bustling North African souk. The uneasy feeling of setting off, having chosen the tougher option, from the Colombian farm as Cos and Hernando waved goodbye, turning right when we could have just as easily turned left.

Hernando and his daughter Tatiana met us on the sidewalk as we approached her apartment. Tatiana's picture had hung in the room where we stayed in Cos and Hernando's city house in Bogotá, and we had thought she looked very pretty then. In real life she was even more beautiful, and her face reminded us of her mother, Cos, back home in Colombia.

"Hernando! Que tal?!"

"Todo bien. Ustedes llegaron a pesar de Nacho!" You arrived in spite of Nacho. Touché.

We opened Nacho's door to let the two of them peer inside, Tatiana for the first time, and Hernando for old time's sake.

"It looks just the same," he said. "It's like no time has passed at all. Is this Westvleteren beer? I've heard about this beer!" I shot an "I told you so" glance at Sheena, for she hadn't believed me when I told her that this beer was a big deal.

Over the next day and night we caught up with Hernando and got to know Tatiana. He told us that the same young couple still worked on the farm, milking the cow each morning at six-thirty. The only difference now was that there weren't any stranded gringos waiting bleary-eyed with their pitcher in hand for their morning milk. Our quaint little cabin still stood in the grassy meadow, at the base of the hill where the trail climbs past the rock that was painted for the Battle of Boyacá. And Cos still zipped around the village and occasionally back to Bogotá in the same car that Hernando and I used to steal Nacho away from the molesting hands of the deranged mechanic.

Our time was running out on account of a shipping deadline, and in a whirl we were back on the road, driving toward the Dutch border. While the next stop was the Trappist monastery at Achel, where I would be sure to buy a special Achel beer goblet, the real destination was the town of Eindhoven, where there awaited another blast from the past.

We had run across Jan several times since splitting up in Kuala Lumpur; we had run into him at the beach barbecue in Terengganu, at the sidewalk restaurant in the Cameron Highlands, and finally at the night market in Krabi, Thailand, after we had watched the transvestite fashion show. He had ridden his motorcycle throughout Southeast Asia for another six months before a string of mechanical issues signaled the natural end to his trip, and he had flown home to resume his life as a tax lawyer.

A full year after our last encounter in Thailand, we brought Nacho to a stop in front of Jan's home on a quiet street in Eindhoven. When he answered his door, we hardly recognized him without his white wifebeater shirt.

"Is that Westvleteren beer?" Jan asked, peering into Nacho. "That beer is very good, you know. We can drink some tonight, along with the rest of the beer that I want you to try."

As evening rolled around, we proceeded to be driven into the ground by our Dutch friend. By the end of the first or second beer, Sheena and I were three sheets to the wind. By the fifth or sixth we were swimming in a pool of jell-o with magical narwhals and mermaids, all wookie-eyed and red-nosed. We each finished off the evening with a Westvleteren 12, but my state of mind prohibited me from remembering anything about the beer. What I did recall was that my feet looked like dueling submarines, Sheena reminded me of a cartoon, and my head felt very heavy.

Jan prepared breakfast and chatted with Sheena while I set the table on the back patio. He hadn't used his patio set since summer had arrived, and so I spent a few minutes cleaning it up for the new season. I wiped the accumulated dust from the tabletop, and walked to the garage to look for the chair pads. When I opened the man door on the side of the garage, a wave of warm air smelling of fertilizer and old motor oil hit my face. When my eyes adjusted to the light, I saw, in the corner of the garage, Jan's motorcycle covered in dust. The sight of it made my heart sink. How could someone go back to a normal life after such an experience? Was it possible to go home, unpack, and eat a sandwich?

The ordinariness of American life did seem appealing at times, and perhaps there is a point in every open-ended adventure at which the desire for the ordinary begins to overpower the desire to keep going, and maybe that is the turning point where you know it's time to go home.

Since leaving Asia, the stimulation of the road had slowly been declining, but perhaps it was because we were slowly and unwittingly returning to a sense of ordinariness by virtue of rejoining the Western World. Jan had adapted very well to his new life at home, and perhaps that was because he had reached the tipping point on his trip, and he had acted upon it. What was unclear to us was whether we had hit the tipping point, or if the real solution would be to turn around and go back into the unknown. It was too late to change our minds now, though. Our ship was waiting in the port.

On the final night at our canal-side campground, just over the Dutch border in Belgium, we finished packing for Nacho's final trip across the Atlantic. We were allowed to pack up to two bottles of alcohol, and that was going to be a problem, seeing as how we had just taken ownership of forty-eight bottles of Westvleteren, not to mention Sheena's wine collection that she had accumulated while traversing Europe. We lined the mattress with contraband bottles and Sheena placed the rest under the couch, and then I locked the couch down with screws so that it couldn't be opened. Since we were shipping Roll-On-Roll-Off for the first time, a process in which someone else would drive Nacho onto the ship without us being present, I placed the wood and chicken wire barricade I had built behind the front seats to separate the cab from the living quarters. The whole operation was something of a desperate Hail Mary.

Once everything was secure, we fired up the engine and pointed toward the port at Antwerp.

56

European Route 20 to Shmirgin

Brad

We had gotten to know Sven through email correspondence over the course of a couple of years. Like so many others we had met in our travels, our connection had transpired on account of us driving the same car, and shortly after our first conversation he invited us to stay at his house when we got to Sweden. Great, we thought. This would be the perfect opportunity to execute a pilgrimage twenty years in the making.

I had always wanted to go to Shmirgin, which of course rose to fame following the release of *Wayne's World 2*. While it had been an eternity since I'd seen the film, one scene had always stuck with me. In the scene, Wayne flirts with a buxom Swedish secretary named Bjergen Kjergen, who hails from the Shmirgin fjords. I immediately took a liking to the place, and when I was in high school I even chose Shmirgin as my Yahoo Chat screen name, which I used to converse over the newly popular interwebs with Sheebee223, whom I would eventually trick into marrying me.

It therefore broke our hearts to tell Sven that we wouldn't make it to Sweden, even though we were already in northern Europe.

"Dearest Sven," we had written, "it breaks our hearts to inform you that we won't be able to come to Sweden." We went on to explain that the trip from Belgium to Stockholm would add three thousand kilometers to our trip, while the impending expiration of our European visa would mean that we would have to turn back shortly after arriving.

"Hey cool dudes, why don't you just fly here? The airplanes work too, and are much faster than Nacho. Besides, what else are you gonna do, sit around and twiddle your fingers?"

Honestly the thought had never occurred to us, given our obvious inclination to drive everywhere. When we told Sven that we would take his advice, he seemed pretty happy.

"I'm happy to be your guide, host, chef, or anything else except pole dancer actually...I can't wait to have you here! I feel like Hammy in Over the Hedge."

We purchased our tickets to Stockholm, where we would stay with Sven and his family for two weeks before flying onward to meet Nacho at the port in Halifax, Nova Scotia. I informed Sven of our itinerary, and reiterated how excited I was to finally eat Swedish Fish in their country of origin.

"Swedish Fish is an American candy invention, but when you get here I will feed you real Swedish fish."

When our plane touched down, we collected our backpacks and emerged from the arrivals gate into the chilly Scandinavian night.

"Hiya cool dudes! See how the airplanes work?" After loading our bags into the back of his wife's Prius, Sven looked at me from the driver's seat with shifty eyes and told me to open the glove box. As I did so, two large, white, unmarked bags fell into my hands and we sped off.

"One for you, one for Sheena," he said, weaving between cars as we sped toward the city center. "This is real Swedish candy—you will find no American candy fish in there!" Sven lived twenty kilometers outside of Stockholm on an island, as do many Swedes, given the fact that their country literally has over 200,000 islands—30,000 in the Stockholm archipelago alone. We left the airport and drove through Stockholm, and when Sven stopped the car on the side of a large thoroughfare overlooking the city, we got out.

"This is my city," he said, staring out at the string of colored lights reflecting off of the bay in between moored sailboats. "It really is a beautiful city. I'm not just saying that because I live here." We looked out in admiration at the scene before us for another minute, and then Sven broke the silence. "We should get the heck out of here before some cop decides to give me a super-big ticket for parking in the middle of the street."

In the mornings, Sven would head off to work and his wife, Annmarie, would load their two sons, Wilmer and Walter, into a bike trailer and pedal the twenty kilometers to work, dropping the boys off at daycare along the way. Sheena and I were on our own, and were given two bikes to use. We ate breakfast with the family and then pedaled out across the bridge and onto the bike path, which stretched all the way to downtown. You could get anywhere on the bike path. As it neared the city, the path became even more impressive, having its own curving flyovers to cross major thoroughfares, and frequently cutting through

396

parks and along the shoreline. On a couple of evenings we loaded up the paddleboards in Sven's VW van and brought them to the edge of the island to explore his corner of the archipelago. Given our latitude, which was approximately as far north as Anchorage, Alaska, the evening sun sliced nearly parallel to the horizon, causing the sunset to last a great long time. We paddled across the calm saltwater as the nighttime sun projected a kaleidoscope of color across the sky. Sweden was all right.

"You think *I'm* crazy?" Sven asked as he paddled between us. "You should see those crazy bastards who speed skate from here all the way to Stockholm to go to the work when the ocean freezes!"

One evening over a dinner of barbecued Swedish fish on the patio, Sven and Annmarie regaled us with horrendous stories of their life under their "oppressive socialist regime," as we in America like to call it. The 480 days of paid parental leave for each child. The free daycare, the free healthcare, the free university education, the forty-one days of annual paid vacation for every worker. It was every terrible thing that our political pundits back home had warned us about. That day Annmarie had come home with a new carbon fiber pump for her bicycle. When asked where she got it, she said that they were being handed out to everyone who was riding on the bike path during rush hour to thank them for not driving. The heavy-handedness! The human rights abuses!

It occurred to me that all of those times back in India when kids would come up to us and say, "America number one!" the appropriate response would have been, "No, you must mean Sweden."

"So Sven, have you ever heard of a town called Shmirgin?" He paused mid-chew, Swedish fish hanging from his fork, and his eyes became slits. He took another chew, thinking hard.

"Your pronunciation of our Swedish towns is terrible, man. Do you mean Smögen?" The pronunciation was similar, although my source was Wayne Campbell, so it was no wonder that I'd botched it. The Ö was pronounced in the way that a British person might say the middle of the word "work," a sound that doesn't really exist in American English.

"Yes! That's it! It is the birthplace of Bjergen Kjergen! Is it far?"

"Hmm. Yes, it is somewhat far. But listen up dudes, you know next week I have to go to France to go windsurfing, right?"

"Right. Because of the forty-one days of vacation for every worker."

"That's right cool guy, it ain't easy being Swedish. Anyway, why don't you take my Vanagon and do a Swedish tour for the week. It will be like a Smögen quest." I envisioned buxom Bjergen Kjergen sitting at her secretarial desk.

"Yes, a Shmirgin quest!"

Sheena and I drove west from Stockholm under blue skies streaked with wispy smears of cloud. The road slowly snaked through a wide swath cut through the forest, gently rising and falling over hills scraped smooth by glaciers. As the hours ticked by, little changed in the landscape. The road continued its trajectory through dense forest, a landscape that the last ice age ensured would offer no mountain vistas. By dinnertime the sky was no darker than at midday, but we stopped at a serene roadside lake anyway and fired up the camp stove to make some pasta with sparkling bottled water.

Normally, had we been driving Nacho, we would have filled our water tanks before hitting the road. But with Sven's tankless van, and given that we couldn't seem to find a large water container to fill up, we found ourselves at the mercy of using bottled water for the week. Apparently bottled water isn't a thing in Sweden, and the only bottled water we would find for the duration of our Smögen quest would be sparkling water. And unfortunately for us, despite Sweden's oppressive socialist regime, the country's economy was far healthier than America's, causing our dollar to be virtually worthless in the land of Abba. The cost of the water used to boil our pasta had been approximately equal to an entire day's food budget in Asia.

At eleven o'clock we called it a night. We brushed our teeth and washed our faces with designer sparkling water, pulled the couch into a bed, rolled out our sleeping bags, and lay down. After thirty minutes of tossing and turning, Sheena bellowed crankily from within her sleeping bag.

"It's too goddamn bright! Glarb!"

Without any curtains, and given the nearly twenty-four hours of sunlight, we were essentially sleeping right out in the open with light streaming in from 360 degrees. I got up and propped various objects near the windows, hanging towels from fishing poles and leaning pieces of foam against the windows, but it was all for naught. At just after midnight it became dark enough to fall asleep.

At three o'clock in the morning the sun blasted through the van windows, bludgeoning us into consciousness against our will. We sat up, bags under our red eyes, which were swollen with fatigue. I took an expensive swig of sparkling water and blinked hard a few times to stop the vertigo. I wailed like a yeti as I clawed my way out of my sleeping bag, slid the door open, and stumbled out into the bright sunshine in my wrinkly underwear.

As we emerged from the forest at Sweden's west coast, the landscape abruptly changed from dense trees to windswept, low rolling rocks and bare hills. Giant, low, smooth boulders dotted the coast like sleeping turtles, their surfaces covered by deep scrapes inflicted by the slow-motion passage of glaciers. We arrived first in Gothenburg, where we stopped at the market to restock on a new case of sparkling water and some food, but just enough to keep us alive and scurvy-free, so high was the cost of everything.

"Bradley, these little cucumbers are four dollar each!"

"Sweet Jesus! What else can we eat?"

"How about these ten dollar crackers?"

Between the eight-dollar-per-gallon fuel, the small fortune required to buy food, and our reliance on designer sparkling water, our Shmirgin quest had turned into a battle of simple economic survival. Our first warning should have come when we had gone to lunch with Sven's boss, and the bill for our modest lunch of reindeer and herring at a simple café had come to $150. Passing a pub in Stockholm, I had noticed Westvleteren beer on the menu—of which forty-eight bottles were tucked into our bed inside of Nacho—for $100 per bottle.

"Keep in mind, dearest Sheena," I said as we waited in the checkout line in Gothenburg. "This is our Shmirgin quest, and I've been waiting my whole life for this. We will make it at any cost." The checkout lady placed our salad greens in a bag, slid our designer water to the side, and requested in return the GDP of a small island nation, which we begrudgingly handed over.

The Swedish coast was something from a fairy tale. Stereotypical, weathered wood-shingle homes painted in primary colors or whitewash dotted the shoreline. Fishing boats bobbed in the bays while small sailboats tacked in and out of coves. Fishermen sorted their nets on the docks set against windswept, smooth-boulder backdrops. On our first night on the coast we slept in front of a beach overlooking a cove, where I passed the evening fishing from a dock into the crystal clear water before retiring to the van for the world's most expensive salad. At around midnight we washed our faces with sparkling water under the twilight pastel-streaked sky, and then crawled into our sleeping bags where we tossed and turned until one in the morning, our movements illuminated by the twilight.

At three o'clock in the morning the bright sun awoke us through the windows, and again I wailed like a yeti, signaling the premature start to a new day. After a breakfast of crackers and pickled herring we were on our way northward, our swollen eyes regarding the windswept landscape as it passed our windows. We were finally Shmirgin-bound.

"Oh my god I'm so tired, Sheena," I said, bobbing my head from side to side.

"Oh me too, what are we going to do?" she said as she rolled over in the passenger seat and went to sleep. I stared ahead, blinked my eyes several times and tried not to fall asleep at the wheel. I cursed our latitude and the omnipresent sun. When at long last we pulled into Shmirgin, or rather, Smögen, there was a jubilant and victorious air about the van. We rounded a bend, crossed a bridge, and then came upon a wonderful coastal village set among the smooth boulders. Simple white and red homes clung to the rocks; they had shingled or plank siding, peaked windows and weathervanes, the kind of homes one would imagine to exist in a quaint Swedish fishing village. Bjergen Kjergen was one lucky lady to have been born here. We parked the van along the waterfront and I could almost hear Wayne Campbell's voice saying "Excellent!" We flung the doors open on our Mirth Mobile and tiredly faltered about, all in a whirl of high fives and whoops.

"Party on, Sheena!"

"Party on, Brad!"

Several days later, after having decided on a whim to drive to Norway, we finally arrived back at Sven's house. It had been a magical week of near-sleepless camping in forests, along coastlines, and on lakeshores. We had seen a bit of Scandinavia, and in doing so had made a pilgrimage to an important place from my childhood. We had made it to Sheena's ancestral Norwegian homeland, but that came in a distant second to the Shmirgin quest.

"Sheena, I'm so sleepy I could hurl," I said, tilting my head to the side and flashing a big toothy grin.

"Brad, you need to stop pretending to be Wayne Campbell."

We pulled the curtains in our bedroom and fell into a deep, comatose sleep. When we finally awoke, and were reunited with the internet for the first time in a week, I decided to re-watch the clip from Wayne's World in which Wayne flirts with Bjergen Kjergen of the Shmirgin fjords. I loaded the clip and we huddled around the screen in anticipation. Wayne opened the door and walked toward the buxom secretary, played by Drew Barrymore...

"Hi, um, we're here to see Handsome Dan. My name is Wayne Campbell."

"Ja, I know, ve've been expecting you, Vayne Campbell. I am Bjergen Kjergen."

"Wow, I love your accent, where are you from?"

"I am from Sveden."

"Oh really, whereabouts in Sweden?"

"Knjergen, near the Bjergen fjords."

"Wow, nice to meet you Bjergen Kjergen from Knjergen near the Bjergen fjords. Hmm...Knjergen, that's in the Klargen province, near the Bebjergen river?"

"Ja!"

All at once my heart sank and I could feel Sheena staring at the side of my head. My stomach felt weak and I thought I might hurl. This couldn't be.

"Um, Brad, did she just say she was from Knjergen? That sure doesn't sound anything like 'Shmirgin.'"

I sat there silently as it dawned on me that my whole life, or at least the last twenty years of it, was built on a lie. I searched for the words, but none came. We sat stunned, watching the rest of the clip. Wayne listed off the annual rainfall and chief exports of the Klargen province for Bjergen Kjergen.

"...And your chief export is modular furniture. I did a project on Sweden in the eighth grade."

"Vell, I am impressed by your quest for knowledge. Educated men are rare."

"It was really hard, I stayed up all night workin' on it. And then the next day in gym class I was on the mini-tramp, and I got diarrhea ... I really wish I hadn't told you that."

"Vell, I am sorry to hear of your illness, but since you have sacrificed your health for knowledge of my home country I find you very attractive, and I hope to make love to you in the near future."

The camera cut wide and a smile grew on Wayne's face. He began to walk away, and as he did he spread his arms wide and did a pelvic thrust as he said the word:

"Shmirgin!"

Sheena turned back to face me, a look of disbelief on her face.

"Do you mean to tell me that Shmirgin isn't even a real place? That we drove all the way across Sweden because of a pelvic thrust?"

I supposed that is just how things happen. All of us were borne, just as our arbitrary pilgrimage, of seemingly insignificant pelvic thrusts.

"I guess so," I said. "But what else were we going to do, sit around and twiddle our fingers?"

Sheena glared at me and shook her head. "It's true, you know," she said. "Educated men are rare."

A Spanish flamenco dancer performs in a cave in Granada's Sacromonte neighborhood.

A flock of Spanish sheep keeps an eye on Nacho, as Nacho's inhabitants in turn keep an eye on the lake somewhere in Andalucia.

Having followed clues in Ernest Hemingway's 90-year-old classic *The Sun Also Rises*, Brad fishes from the same bridge where Jake and Bill fished in the book. Brad, it turns out, is not the trout slayer that Jake and Bill are.

Nacho lugs his 6,000-pound heft into the clouds enshrouding the Pyrenees on the Spain-France border.

"Nacho is reaching into his briefcase of courage and coming down this finishing straight like a Grand Prix motorcar!" Brad narrates Nacho's time trial up the famous Alpe d'Huez (in the French Alps) in his best Phil Liggett voice.

Repacking or replacing Nacho's wheel bearings every couple thousand miles might have been the bane of Brad's existence were he not such an understanding guy. Here, he hones his art in Annecy, France.

Nacho momentarily interrupts French traffic for a beauty shot next to the Eiffel Tower.

The Lassarra family, who Brad and Sheena first ran into on a Laotian mountaintop, make great Parisian tour guides. Here they enjoy sandwiches on the bank of the Seine behind the Notre Dame. Notably absent is a stroller for *Jeanne la Plus Forte.*

Brad makes the somewhat irresponsible, yet irresistible decision to buy two cases of Westvleteren 12 beer from the monks who brewed it, somewhere in the Belgian countryside.

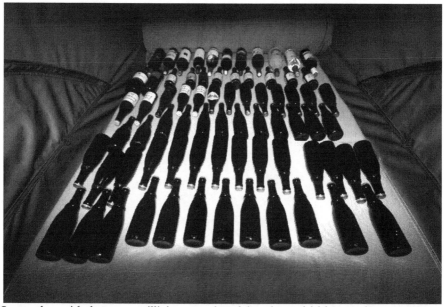

It can be said that more illicit contraband has been hidden under mattresses. Where else would one hide 73 bottles of beer and wine in a humble hippie van?

The man, the myth, the legend: Swedish Sven gives Brad and Sheena a late night paddling tour around the Stockholm archipelago before they set off for the mystical land of Shmirgin.

Shmirgin: the actual hometown of lusty office lady Bjergen Kjergen; or is it?

Part 5

The Long Way Round

57

Atlantic Compass
Container Vessel to Halifax

Brad

On a snowy day nearly three years ago I shat my last shit in my own house. Soon thereafter we crossed the border into Mexico and I saw a cinderblock shanty on the side of an embankment. It had a broken down truck next to it and there were various rusty signs in Spanish around it littering the roadside. I thought to myself, I have shat my last shit in my own house, and I've stepped out of my comfort zone for the next three years, and there will be nothing I can do about that. Our driftwood raft had lost sight of land, and one day, *inshallah*, we would find land again.

It was skydiving. A first kiss. The last click of the climbing roller coaster car before gravity takes over, and then the acceleration. It was that feeling of pure unbridled ecstasy, and we went to sleep with it. And then we woke up with it. We surfed with it, ate tacos with it, and brushed our teeth with it. We shat behind cactus in the desert with it. And behind palm trees, and on volcanoes and beside rivers with it. We were walking into the unknown with a thousand days ahead of us, and nowhere to be except farther. So we drove farther and farther and farther, and wherever we went, it was always farther. But Galileo was right, and when we arrived in Nova Scotia after driving almost all the way around the world we were no longer driving farther, but each day drawing nearer. The chute had been pulled. The rollercoaster was decelerating. There was no more farther, only nearer.

When we landed in Halifax, David was there to meet us at the airport. It was one of the unforeseen joys of long-term travel in the information age: we had developed a global family. We drove an hour out of town to where he and his fiancée lived, and promptly fell asleep on their couch.

Sherry prepared breakfast in the morning. She set the plates out on the table, shuffled around the kitchen, and then sat down nervously.

"I have to tell you guys," she said, "when David told me that he was bringing over some people who live in their van, I was pretty nervous. What if you guys were murderers or something?" I stared into Sherry's eyes, letting an awkward amount of time pass before speaking.

"You were right to be nervous," I said. I forked some egg into my mouth and continued to stare at her with my beady eyes, wondering if she would catch on that I was joking, or if she would call in the Mounties.

"Oh my. Do you want a coffee? I have some K-cups."

K-cups were just one of many things that had risen to common household status while we were away, and which made our arrival back in North America feel much like the emergence from a mother's womb to gaze cluelessly at an unfamiliar world of new and strange things.

There was Instagram, for example, to further complicate one's digital life, and TaskRabbit to manage to one's already overcomplicated physical life. The resurgence of foods once enjoyed by devolved humanoids during the Paleolithic era, like squab quiche and walnut coconut tofu shakes and lobster eggs Benedict. Kale. Leggings as pants. E-cigarettes. Phones with no buttons.

David and Sherry introduced us to the Canadian side of North America, which, despite having spent nearly ten thousand days living within two days drive of it, we had never experienced before. Maple syrup. Funny accents. Tim Horton's. Fish 'n' chips. Ellen Page. Being nice. Maple syrup. And as the days passed we came to regard Halifax, despite its reputation as the wild and lawless eastern outpost of the Dangerous North, as the coolest city in North America east of the Rockies. Sorry Cleveland.

When the slow boat arrived from Belgium, we collected Nacho at the port and carried on down the coast. In Lunenburg we were invited for more Canadian hospitality, and our new hosts Dave, Paula, and Paula's daughter Claire, treated us like family. With each passing day we hiked through coastal forests, went cliff diving from waterfalls, and cooked up freshly caught lobster and scallops with Paula's parents. Meanwhile Claire, an up-and-coming singer-songwriter, took time between local performances to drive up and down the coast with Sheena.

Dave, a television stuntman, tried throughout our stay to convince me to run over him with Nacho.

"But Dave, Nacho doesn't have a hood, so you wouldn't be able to buckle and roll."

"Yeah, but maybe I could jump right before you hit me and I would fly over the van."

"But what if you smash our solar panel?"

He later suggested that I wear a special stunt hat that would allow him to break a broomstick over my head, which I was keen to try. But in the end we settled for a real life stunt, in which the two of us attempted to install new rear suspension springs on Nacho, after having driven all the way from Bangkok with nearly bottomed-out rear suspension stuffed with tennis balls. In this stunt, Dave lay on his back and forced one spring into place with his feet, after my usual improvisational and highly dangerous ratchet-strap-spring-compressor failed to work. I foolishly put my hands in the way, and ended up smashing my fingertip when the spring released its energy and snapped into place. When we moved around to do the other spring, our factory VW jack buckled, causing Nacho to fall down onto the sidewall of the tire, which I'd pushed under the brake drum just moments before.

Canada was indeed a dangerous place.

At last, after a few more days of exploring Nova Scotia on our own, we found ourselves in the parking lot of a grocery store with a bag full of maple syrup and tea towels featuring pictures of hockey players and lumberjacks. There was nothing left to do, nowhere left to go, except America. Sheena mustered some courage and then spoke.

"Bradley, it's time," she said, scratching at the ground with the toe of her Mary Jane shoes.

"Time for what, my sweet?"

She mumbled something under her breath.

"Excuse me?"

"I said I'm ready to drive."

Up to that point I had driven every hard-earned mile since leaving home 45,000 miles earlier. From time to time I had encouraged Sheena to try, but she always declined.

"I hate driving this thing, it's too quirky!" or "I never learned to drive a manual!" A lie!

She had recognized that we were in the final throes of our trip, and she would need to put down some miles lest I hold it over her head for the rest of her life. We situated a sleeping bag behind her back, the

413

cable on the seat adjuster having broken long ago, and she familiarized herself with the controls.

"So I press on that and that at the same time, then push that stick and release that?"

"More or less. Just like riding a bike," I said.

She turned the key and Nacho lurched forward and stalled. I reminded her that the clutch must always be pushed in when stationary, and then she successfully started the engine. We were parked on a hill, so she coasted backwards, then put it in first, and lurched forward.

"I'm driving!" she wailed, and as she made a hard right turn, her door flung open. Being that she hadn't fastened her seat belt either, she very nearly fell out the open door of our moving vehicle while driving in the parking lot.

"Whoa! I almost fell out the door! Did you see that? Jeez! Now how do I get out of here?" I instructed her to do a two-point turn and exit the parking lot, but instead she crept forward and dropped off of the pavement at the back of the lot in between two orange cones, heading for the back of the store through mud and grass.

"What are you doing?!"

"I can't stop! I need to keep it going or I'll never get started again!"

We bounced along behind the store as I shook my head disapprovingly, and then we emerged on the other side and headed toward the street.

"Make sure there's nobody coming. I can't stop!"

Before I knew it we were careening onto the highway to New Brunswick, and beyond it the US/Canadian border. It had been two-and-a-half years since Nacho had slipped through the giant border fence protecting America from the treacherous outside world. And while we were gone, so much had changed.

We had certainly changed. Our worldview, our approach to problem solving, our patience. We had discovered that most of our homeland's fear and negative misconceptions about the rest of the world were home-brewed, bubbling and stewing inside of that big protective fence. And of course we were concerned about the rules. Usually when we crossed a new border it involved some degree of ignorance of the rules on our part. The difference was that America took its rules pretty seriously, and this naturally had us a little worried, given the cargo hidden in Nacho's mattress. We reached the border and stopped.

Three cars in front of us.

Two.

One.

"Good morning," I said as I came to a stop in front of the border guard.

"Passport," the uniformed guard said. He grabbed our passports with a scowl on his face, trying to seem as intimidating as possible.

"Which places have you visited while outside of the United States?"

"Umm. Canada," I said. The whole story was a bag of worms, and I didn't want to unnecessarily rouse suspicion. He began flipping through the pages of my passport and his eyebrows lifted in a Homeland Security kind of way. I interjected an explanation.

"Well, before that we drove through Europe." Eyebrows still raised, still flipping pages. "And before that we were in India. And Nepal. And also Southeast Asia. And South America. And Central America. And Mexico. It was a very long trip, as you can imagine."

"All in this thing?" he asked, nodding his head toward Nacho. He panned the van with his eyes, noting the Indian, Iranian, and Turkish beads hanging from our rearview mirror, the broken side mirror from the overzealous bus in Kathmandu, the dented cargo box from the road marker in Cambodia, the Malaysian front license plate, and the big scrape from when I sideswiped that bus in Varanasi. This prompted a full explanation, which took a couple of minutes, during which time the border guard ran us through his mental screen to determine how likely it was that we were terrorists.

"Do you have any alcohol or tobacco?"

"What, us? Inside of here? Why, just two bottles of beer in the fridge, you know, for drinking in times of non-driving."

"Can I search the van?"

Not seeing an elegant way to decline, we obliged.

"Where do you sleep?" he asked, peering inside the sliding door.

Oh boy. I started to point at the couch, intending to tell him that we slept there, until I imagined him requesting that we demonstrate how the couch pulls into a bed, which would be impossible since I used power tools to ensure that the cushions would be unmovable. I shifted my finger upward.

"We sleep up there. The roof lifts up." Sheena shot me a panicked glance, not remembering that I was the Garry Kasparov of border tacticians, and was thus already anticipating four moves ahead.

"Hmm. That's crazy," he said, and looked at the upper mattress for a minute. "You can close this thing up and go inside to stamp your Carnet."

And with that we entered Maine, back in America after all of that. But it wasn't long before the initial elation of reaching the final country of our drive wore off. As we drove in a straight line on the well-groomed highway, unengaged and bored by the perfectly smooth surface and wide shoulders and tidy signage, I was overcome by a kind of sad realization.

I had shat my last shit in the wild.

I would no longer shit behind cactus and palm trees, on volcanoes and by rivers. The rollercoaster car had arrived at the unloading platform; the parachute had gone slack. Our raft had, after more than nine hundred days at sea, bumped into land, but we had found comfort adrift. Soon, I would begin a routine of shitting in my own climate-controlled house, each time staring at the same beige heater vent on the wall. This was my old comfort zone, but now I recognized that I had mistaken comfort for complacence. What I really wanted was a cinderblock shanty, a broken down truck and some rusty signs, and nowhere to go but farther.

58

A Place With No Roads

Brad

On the day that I quit my job, my company's CEO invited me to lunch, and then proceeded to do his best to convince me not to leave. He even suggested I see a shrink. He also invited along the company's former CEO to join us, as it was he who had hired me, and he thought he could help to convince me not to quit my perfectly good job and move into my van. But something funny had happened.

Throughout our meal at the Himalayan Grill, the new CEO, Scott, was unable to wrap his head around my logic. He would clasp his head in his hands, be silent for a few moments, and then repeat the same exasperated questions.

"You're moving into your *van*? You're quitting your job to *move into your van*?" Throughout the conversation, he had several other win-win ideas that seemed more logical.

"Here's what you should do," he said at last, as if he had finally solved the problem. "You want to drive your van around the world, right? And it's a hunk of garbage on wheels, right? Right. So look, just go home. When you get there, completely disassemble your van—what do you call it? Nacho? Disassemble Nacho down to the last nut and bolt and spread it out on the floor of your garage, right? Then reassemble it all. That should be very frustrating, and it will take care of your dreams of mechanical conquest. Next, take three months off, buy a bunch of plane tickets, and fly to every place in the world that you ever wanted to visit. Then come back and get back to work. Right? Can you do that instead?"

As Scott went through his suggestions, interspersed with clasping his head in his hands and laughing hysterically, I could see Dixon, the former CEO, sitting back and not saying much, with a hint of a smile on his face. Something was going on in there. Finally, right after he

417

suggested that I see a shrink, Scott sat back in his chair, threw his hands up, and said, "What do you think, Dixon? You've been awful quiet!"

At this, Dixon leaned forward, his gray moustache curved into a comforting smile. He looked at Scott, and then he looked at me.

"I get it," he said. "I think he should go." He leaned back, smiling, and then continued. "When I was about your age I wanted to travel, too. Of course we didn't have the money, so I got together with some friends and we wrote a proposal to Volkswagen. We told them that we wanted to drive a VW bus down to Central America and back, and we wanted to film our trip for a VW commercial." Scott squinted disbelievingly at Dixon, his mouth slightly agape. "Volkswagen liked the idea, so they gave us a VW bus and a video camera and some money. For six months we drove around having the time of our lives, and when we got back we sent our film to Volkswagen, and they turned it into a commercial. So I get it. Life is short. When you get back you'll have no trouble picking up right where you left off. Go out there and have the experience of a lifetime while you're still able."

When faced with tough decisions, I often ask myself which path will least likely result in me looking like a dumbass, me getting arrested, or my early death. After passing that initial screen, I get to the second level of decision-making, which involves me imagining what other people with more sense, and who have achieved a higher level of success, would do in my situation. Sometimes I think about my friend Jay, and sometimes I think about Dixon.

"What would Dixon do?" Usually this gets me on the right track. He had risen through the ranks to become CEO of a division of Ford Motor Company, and of Scott Paper Company, among others, and he was the one who hired me to do the job that I would quit in order to embark on our circumnavigation. And that's exactly what Dixon would have done.

The speed limit was twenty-five miles per hour, but we sailed through the rain at double that, hugging the shore of Maine's Damariscotta Lake on a winding road through the forest. We were late, owing to Sheena having been unable to pry herself away from a roadside antique shop that sold all manner of shiny frippery, and books whose smells could only be described as historical. We rounded a bend and skittered onto a dirt road leading to the water's edge, which we could hardly make out in the downpour. Two figures approached us wearing heavy-duty fisherman's rain suits. One approached my window and looked out from under his hood, and I could see that gray moustache.

"Dixon! It's been a long time!"

"It sure has! So this is Nacho, huh? Park this thing and follow me to the boat. Meet my son, Alec." We followed the two of them out of the trees to where a small motorboat waited. Once we were aboard, Alec fired up the engine and we set off into the driving rain and waves toward Dixon's island.

I had long known that Dixon owned an island, but never knew much beyond that. People at work would mention it from time to time, and it gave him an air of James Bondian enigma. He worked hard and traveled often, always smiling and beaming confidence and positivity, meeting with investors and business partners and trying to crack new markets for our company. And then, when the Energizers finally needed a recharge, he would disappear for a few days to his island, reemerging later at full tilt, all smiles and forward momentum.

Our first two nights in America had been spent in Walmart parking lots, which had only compounded our reverse culture shock, causing us to question how advanced our home country really was, and to ask why, exactly, we had voluntarily returned. We soon learned our lesson about campsite choices and their impact on our reintegration, and began wandering off down logging roads to camp in the woods. Our plan had been to drop by Dixon's place for dinner, and then be on our way. The rain began to let up and Alec swung the boat around in a well-practiced arc as we reached the dock.

The island was roughly four acres, flat, and a near perfect circle. From any point on the island one could see the end of the trees and the water emanating outward. A campfire ring and some walking trails provided the only evidence of man's existence on the island, with the notable exception of two cozy wooden cabins at its center.

"That one on the right is our place, and you two get to stay in the Ritz. That's what we call the guest cabin. Stay as long as you want, but in a couple of months you won't want to be anywhere near Maine!"

The Ritz was comfortable and tastefully decorated inside, with views of the lake from the three windowed sides of the cabin. A pillow with our initials embroidered on it had been placed at the head of the bed. A nice touch, we thought. We had only planned to stay for dinner, but how could we pass up an offer to stay in our own cabin on a private island? One with our very own monogrammed pillows? I considered what Jay would do, and then I considered what Dixon would do. It was unanimous. Just one night would be okay.

That night after dinner we crawled between clean sheets into the comfortable bed, a fresh breeze flowing through an open window, and fell asleep to the sound of singing frogs and lightly lapping waves. One night turned into two and then three, and each day we felt less urgency to move on. Alec and I would take the boat out to go fishing, and then the five of us—Dixon, his wife Gail, Alec, Sheena and I—made trips back to the shore to explore the quaint village of Damariscotta, or to visit the summer camp where Dixon had gone as a kid. We took ourselves on a margarita cruise, prepared paella over the campfire, and drank sangria. We contemplated Dixon's half-joking offer to stay until the lake froze over, and walk back to Nacho.

On the morning of our third day I decided to dust off a kayak that was kept under the Ritz and go out for my own fishing excursion. I grabbed a fishing pole and dragged the boat to the water's edge, and then pushed off. Once clear of the land, I made a short cast, and then continued out across the lake, trolling a lure behind me, en route to a hidden cove. Just as I reached the middle of the channel between the island and the hidden cove, I was surprised to see a Game and Fish warden, way out there in the middle of nowhere, pull up beside me in his motorboat.

"Good morning, sir. Please hold onto the side of my watercraft."

"Oh, hello, and good morning to you!"

Perhaps I had grown naïve with so much time away from American soil, but it didn't occur to me that anything was amiss. I just figured the guy was bored and needed someone to talk to. I gripped the side of his boat and smiled up at him.

"Where have you come from today, sir?" he asked. I pointed to the island a few hundred yards away.

"From that island," I said.

"And to whom is this watercraft registered?"

"I don't know, probably the guy who lives on the island." I thought back to all of the homemade floating crafts I'd seen while driving around the world, and it seemed a bit absurd to require the registration of a simple kayak.

"Is that right? And do you know the individual that lives on that island?"

"Um. Yes."

"Do you have a fishing pole on board with you, sir?" I looked down at the fishing pole sitting right next to me in plain sight.

"Yes, I do."

"I know. I saw you cast back there. So you're fishing and you have a pole on board, we've established that, because I just saw you cast and you just admitted to having a pole on board this watercraft." At this point it occurred to me that some people have a rather socially retarded way of communicating with other people.

"Yes, it has been admitted and witnessed that there is indeed a fishing pole in use aboard this watercraft, sir," I said.

"And do you have a fishing license in the state of Maine, sir?"

I finally saw where he was going with this. My mind jumped into action. What would Jay do?! No response. What would Dixon do?! Again, no response. I imagined that neither Jay nor Dixon would have gotten themselves into this mess to begin with.

"No, I don't. It just hadn't occurred to me that I needed one I suppose."

"Where are you from?"

"I'm from Arizona."

"And in Arizona, are you required to have a fishing license to operate a fishing pole?" I scoured my memory, and then settled on an answer.

"Yes, I believe so."

"Then why didn't it occur to you that you should have a fishing license in the state of Maine?"

"Because I haven't been to Arizona in a long time. I've been living mostly in South America and Asia. I just forgot."

"Well do they require fishing licenses in South America and Asia?" he said, sarcastically.

"Not in most places. People there fish to survive, and charging someone to fish for survival would be unthinkable."

"That's very interesting. Well here in the state of Maine we mostly fish for sport, and for that we require a fishing license. I'm going to have to write you up for that. Now tell me, do you have a life jacket aboard this watercraft?" I wished he would just call it a kayak. I looked around and didn't see anything I could convincingly call a life jacket.

"No, there doesn't appear to be a life jacket aboard my watercraft."

"Well sir, it is required by law in the state of Maine that all watercraft have a certified life jacket on board. What do you think would happen if this watercraft were to capsize?"

"I think I would just swim back to shore. Or maybe I would try to roll the kayak back over and get back on it. I guess I'd have to see how it all played out and make a decision when the time came."

"So you're a pretty strong swimmer, eh? You think you could survive a rollover in this watercraft?"

"I guess so. I mean, I surf without a life jacket, and that usually involves me getting repeatedly pummeled by giant ocean waves. I guess if I can survive that, I could probably survive a rollover in this watercraft."

He stared at me for a minute, not speaking. I imagined that he must have been admiring me for what I had certainly described as superhuman water survival skills.

"Look, I'm going to write you up for the fishing infraction, but I'm just going to give you a warning for the life jacket infraction. The fishing penalty will be one hundred and forty dollars. Now, do you need a ride back to that island?"

"No, I think I'll manage."

"All right, well I'm going to wait here and watch you until you've reached the island just in case your watercraft capsizes."

He wrote me the ticket, which I put in my pocket. I thanked him for correcting my bad behavior, and then began paddling back to shore.

"Sir!" he shouted after me, "Please reel in your line!" he slowly shook his head, mimicking the reeling in of my line. As I paddled myself back to the island under the supervision of the fish warden, it occurred to me that I'd forgotten just how rule-driven life in America was. Not that there is anything wrong with a strict adherence to law and order, we just hadn't been exposed to it for a while.

That evening we all sat around in the living room of the main cabin talking, Sheena and I having finally decided to leave in the morning. Alec swiped through photos on his tablet that he'd taken at a recent horse race. After a while the conversation turned to Nacho. "Doesn't Uncle Sam have a van like Nacho?" Alec asked, referring to Dixon's brother. Dixon thought so, and so Alec pulled up his uncle's Facebook page and verified that, in fact, Sam did have a Vanagon.

"You should ask him if he's ever heard of us," I said. The Volkswagen community is pretty tight-knit, and most people with the patience to keep these old vans on the road were in some way involved in the community. He sent Sam a text, which Sam quickly returned.

Of course I know those guys. I've been following their progress for years!

At this, Dixon's eyes lit up. "Give me your phone, Alec!" he said, and quickly dialed Sam's number.

"Brother Sam, you'll never guess who's sitting right across from me out here on the island. It's Brad and Sheena. Yes, I'm serious. No, why would I make this up?" He held the phone out to me.

"Brad, Sam wants to talk to you."

"Hi, this is Brad."

"Yeah right! How can you prove to me that you're really Brad? Tell me something that only you would know." I thought about it for a minute, as nobody had ever asked me to prove that I was me.

"Um, our transmission failed in Colombia."

"Oh come on, everyone knows that! You could have gotten that from the internet!"

"I don't know. I promise it's me. Can you hear Sheena squealing here in the background?" Sheena squealed a hello. After a while he was adequately convinced that we were who we said we were, and I promised to stop by for a visit when we rolled through the Seattle area. I handed the phone back to Dixon.

"You guys just scored me some major cool points with my brother! He said he couldn't believe that I know real people!"

In the morning we loaded our things on the boat and crossed Damariscotta Lake to the dirt pullout where Nacho was parked. We said our goodbyes, and snapped a photo to send to Brother Sam. As we drove off, I looked back and saw Dixon waving, his gray moustache curved up in a comforting smile.

423

59

Interstate 83 to Baltimore

Brad

Telecommunication was not our strong suit. We'd owned Blackberries in our past lives. Mine was set up to vibrate whenever I got an email, and I could surf the web on it. Pretty basic, but it slowly siphoned my attention until it became something of a needy child. I would feel the vibration on my leg and I couldn't resist looking at it. For the first couple of months after we had crossed the border into Mexico, after we had ritualistically thrown our Blackberries in the garbage, I would get phantom vibrations on my leg and instinctively grasp at my pocket, but there was nothing there. But after a while they went away. If someone wanted to hear our voices, they would have to come and find us. It was glorious.

In a moment of idealistic weakness, I convinced Sheena that it would also be a great idea to drive around the world without any maps. We would simply ask people for directions wherever we went; it would be great! It would get us in touch with the locals; we would get our finger on the pulse of *la raza*. In the end this turned out to be a terrible idea, and many gallons of fuel were wasted in driving off in the wrong direction for hours on end. As it turned out, *la raza* didn't own cars, and thus usually had no idea how to get from Point A to Point B, except for the part about how to find the bus that went there. But still, the people of Latin America were too proud to admit that they didn't know the way, so invariably they made something up and delivered it with conviction. We drove all the way to Panama without a map, and then finally cried uncle and bought a GPS at a mall in Panama City.

When we reached Colombia we thought it prudent to be able to contact each other in case we became separated, so we bought two cheap phones in Bogotá. That necessitated that we buy new SIM cards in every country, and we ultimately found that we never used the phones, making the purchase of said cards an exercise in futility. After a few countries we retired the phones, virtually unused. We revived them briefly in Nepal when we discovered that calls to America were only a penny a minute, and we occasionally called our families. After that we retired them again for good. Getting used to life without a phone had been like getting back in touch with real life. We relearned the art of striking up a conversation, and it was deeply satisfying. But once we returned to America, we suddenly had to coordinate with people. We made it to Boston, and then Sheena put her foot down.

"I don't care about your ideals anymore, we're getting a damn phone!"

I had become a little shocked at the degree to which people had become disconnected from one another, and strongly resisted our inevitable reintegration. Everywhere we looked, people had their faces buried in their smartphones, and they didn't notice each other. I felt like Brooks upon his release from the Shawshank Prison; I didn't want the burden of a phone, the hassle of health insurance and bills and rent, or to have all the answers at my fingertips. I was standing on a chair with a pocketknife, carving "Brooks was here" into a rafter, wishing for the way it was. I reluctantly agreed to get a phone, but I was determined not to let sneaky marketing tactics sway me into buying a smartphone. We found a RadioShack in Harvard Square, and approached the front desk. I wore no emotion on my face and brandished my conviction like a switchblade.

"Good morning," I said, "We would like to buy a phone—but something ghetto. I want the shittiest phone you have."

The young sales clerk, clearly a smartphone user, looked surprised. She paused for a moment, probably trying to think up a sly sales tactic, and then pointed to her display case.

"Well, uh, we have that one," she said, pointing to a gray rectangle with rubber keys.

"Nice try, but I want something even worse. Do you have one of those old brick-looking ones?" I wanted to be ashamed of my phone. That would keep me from wanting to ever use it outside of a sheer emergency. I didn't trust myself not to waste my time. She shifted a little and tugged at the collar of her polo shirt.

"Well, we do have...*this* one," she said. She slowly reached under the counter and pulled out a dusty box and placed it on the glass countertop.

"How much is it?"

"It's twenty-five dollars."

"Does it have the internets?"

"No."

"Good. I just want an apparatus that will allow me to place telephone calls. Nothing fancy. Does it have a touch screen?"

"No, it's a really bad phone."

"It's perfect, we'll take it."

And with that we were birthed into the 19th century. We promptly called our friend Sunday, in Rhode Island.

"Hello?"

"Sunday! It's Brad. Sheena and I got a phone."

"You didn't already have one?"

"No. You're the first person we've called in over a year."

"Did you get an iPhone?"

"No, it's one of those with the plastic buttons."

"They still sell those?"

"Yes. At the RadioShack. But anyway, we're on our way to see you. I wanted to ring you up on my handset to communicate that."

"Your what?"

"Handset. It's an archaic term for a telephone."

We had known Sunday since our university days. He had been a roommate with Mike, whose death in an avalanche had awakened us to the idea of changing our lives, and that ultimately led to us quitting our jobs to drive around the world. Sunday had made the trip to northern Mexico to see us off, and had hoped to visit us in Panama or Peru, but neither trip had come to pass. When we reached his house in Narragansett, we parked in the shade of an overhanging tree in the driveway. He wasn't home, so Sheena took a nap on Nacho's couch while I walked across the street to practice my conversation-striking skills with an elderly couple sitting in Adirondack chairs in their front yard.

At last Sunday arrived and he showed us inside.

"Where's your American flag?" I asked. He said that he didn't have one. "But every house here has an American flag. Are you some kind of America-hater?" He said he hadn't noticed. Was I sure? "Yes, look around, everyone has one."

"Damn it," he said, looking out his window. "You're right. Now it's going to drive me crazy. I haven't noticed that in all the years I've lived here, and now all I'm going to see are American flags."

I hadn't spent a great deal of time on the East Coast before and didn't really know what it was all about, but I had immediately noticed the flags, and it seemed rather strange. Every country has a flag, but I hadn't recalled seeing a single one flown over a private residence anywhere. I imagined each homeowner ritualistically rolling down their flag each night and folding it in sharp motions into a triangle, and placing it in a wooden box for safe keeping. America was a strange place indeed.

When Sunday's roommate got home, he stormed through the front door with a big smile on his face, and threw his keys and sunglasses on the counter. He drove a shiny black car, had good posture and white teeth, and was chipper like a personal banker. He was into motivational self-improvement audio discs, and he listened to them in the car on the way to and from work. Sunday introduced us, and then his roommate got to work making himself a shake in his new Vitamix blender.

"I've been experimenting with different ingredients for my green smoothie recipe, and I've almost perfected it. I use coconut milk and some berries, a bunch of kale, and some agave. But the secret ingredient is cocoa powder. Just a pinch to take the edge off." He was an energetic fellow.

"Remember when I made us those smoothies the other day?" Sunday asked.

"Don't remind me. That was the most disgusting thing I've ever tasted." He paused and shook his head to rid himself of the thought, and then poured his whipped kale into a glass. Sunday shrugged his shoulders.

"I don't know, I thought it was kind of good. I've been doing some experimentation of my own. I used peanut butter and some sesame seeds and milk for the base. But you know how sometimes you hear about really good recipes having unexpected things in them? I decided to add some mustard and a little bit of curry powder. And I really like Mexican food, so I finished it off with a few jalapeño peppers." His roommate shuddered and then took a sip of his green shake.

"Sunday told me about your big trip. Very interesting," he said. He took a big gulp of kale and wiped his mouth with the back of his hand. He was silent for a minute, and then he looked up and said, "So, what is the pulse of the world?"

It was perhaps the most succinct, all-encompassing question anyone had asked us about our experience. But it seemed impossible to answer, as it would require the distillation of volumes of observations and realizations into one easily deliverable oratory nugget.

"I don't know," I said.

"So many American flags," Sunday said, shaking his head as he looked out the window. "Damn it."

427

After a few days in Narragansett and Newport, and a weekend trip out to Cape Cod, we pulled ourselves away from our good friend and continued down the heavily trafficked eastern seaboard. The route was a repeating set of cities bordered by buffer zones of strip malls and modern glass office buildings, and separated by stretches of thick deciduous trees. Our primary goal was to get to Baltimore in time for Barna's day off. The fact that she had moved to Baltimore was a pretty big deal. When we got to the city, we passed around most of it on the ring road—just as we had done to get to her house in Kathmandu—then exited on the west end into a suburb.

The first door we tried was the wrong door, and a Pakistani woman wearing a bright green sari answered. She didn't speak English, but invited us in for tea so that we could wait for her husband to come home, as he would certainly be able to help us. This was the kind of hospitality that we came to know in South Asia, and being in Baltimore made it stand out even more. In America we are skeptical of door-knockers, a natural reflex that is a result of generations of door-knocking Jehovah's Witnesses with pamphlets, Mormons with nametags, Girl Scouts with cookies, and Avon ladies with catalogues.

While I attempted to deduce the location of our Nepali friend's apartment by making robotic motions with my hands and speaking universally-recognizable grunting sounds, Sheena spied Sunil around a corner, who was smiling and waving. We thanked the woman in the green sari and excused ourselves. Sunil enthusiastically shook our hands and led us toward an open door where Barna and Kalpana waited, smiling. In Nepal, the line between family and neighbor isn't always strictly defined. While walking through Dobighat, Pesal used to chat with everyone we passed by. When we asked who they were, he would always say, "That is my cousin." Soon we realized that everyone in Dobighat was Pesal's cousin—not by blood, but because they all hailed from the same village in southeastern Nepal and had all migrated to the same place. They love and respect each other like family, and every door is an open door. We had come to see our Nepali friends as family much in the same way. Barna is our Nepali sister, or *bahini*.

Barna had lived in the house just down the street from Bharat and Durga's house, and was Pesal's cousin by blood. She had spent all eighteen years of her life in Nepal, but had the best grasp of English of anyone we had met in the country. Not only was she fluent in the language, she was also well versed in American pop-culture, and could

428

easily transition between her Nepali accent and her California valley girl impersonation. She had been especially excited those days, because she had just won the lottery.

Every year America holds a lottery for a small number of Diversity Visas, which provide an instant green card and permanent residency for those drawn. Barna had miraculously won the first year that she applied, meaning that she would get to live out her wildest dreams of moving to America. This fact had made her valley girl accent sound especially bubbly when we discussed it back in Nepal.

The last time we had seen her, along with the rest of her family, was in the alley behind the house in Dobighat as we departed for India. In the time that it took us to drive Nacho from Nepal to America, Barna had said goodbye to Kathmandu and had flown halfway around the earth to take up residency in a Baltimore suburb. We found her living there with her cousin Sunil and their friend Kalpana, in the building adjacent to that of the Pakistani woman in the green sari, who probably had her own inspiring immigration story.

We had promised Barna that we would take her out for Mexican dinner when we arrived. This held a particular significance, on account of the fact that we had forgotten to tell her that our Mexican food Thanksgiving dinner had been served, causing her to miss out on what would have been her first American holiday celebration. Shortly after our arrival at their Baltimore apartment, Barna and Kalpana sneakily usurped our plan by preparing a traditional dinner of *dal bhat*. She wasn't going to let our Mexican dinner plans get in the way of her being a good hostess.

In between chatting with us and helping in the kitchen, Sunil sat on the couch typing a journal entry on his tablet. He told us of his work as a delivery truck driver, and Barna excitedly told us about her new job at the 7/11 convenience store. She had just received her first paycheck, which amounted to about half the annual income of an average Nepali person. Life was good.

We had been curious to hear Barna's first impressions on life in America, so as she worked in the kitchen, Sheena inquired. I think we were both expecting some profound insight about struggle and opportunity, or that perhaps the move from the Himalayas to Baltimore had caused her to feel a nostalgic homesickness for the simple life.

"Oh my god, I *love* it here!" she said, excitedly waving a wooden spoon.

"What do you love about it?" Sheena asked.

Barna put her hand on her hip and wagged the spoon as she spoke. Her answer came without hesitation. "Well for one thing, we have electricity twenty-four hours a day. I can just switch on the light any time and it always works." She flipped the light switch on and off and shrugged her shoulders. It was true. In Kathmandu there hadn't been enough electricity generation to meet demand, and so for eight hours every day there wasn't any electricity. She put the spoon down and opened the dishwasher where she sifted through a stack of pots and pans.

"Do you store things in your dishwasher?" Sheena asked.

"Yeah, we don't understand this thing. It's easy enough to wash the dishes by hand, so we use it for storage. I don't even know how it works, actually." I considered showing her how to operate it, but there was something wholesome about not succumbing to the allure of unnecessary gadgets. It was interesting to gain a perspective on America from a new immigrant for whom coming here was a lifelong dream.

When next the opportunity arose, we let there be no mistake that we were taking Barna out for Mexican night. That evening she dressed up in her cutest of outfits and we hit the road. As we drove, she told us that despite having been in America for three months, she had yet to go out to a restaurant. Eating out is a luxury, after all, and she was still trying to get on her feet. As it turned out, we had chosen a restaurant in a fancy neighborhood where her boss lived, which made it all the more exclusive.

We were seated under a faux thatched cabaña near the mariachi band, and soon our waiter arrived to take our drink orders. He was a typical American waiter, in that he seemed overly chipper and introduced himself, saying that he would be "taking care of us" for the evening. Barna jokingly ordered a beer, to which the waiter teased her for looking fifteen years old. She made a sassy comeback, and Sheena and I looked on like proud parents as our brand new Nepali transplant verbally sparred with the waiter. He lightheartedly accused her of being an illegal immigrant, which she took in stride, and without skipping a beat, accused him of being Canadian.

When it came time to place our order, and Barna being unable to decipher the Spanish names of the meat options—*pollo, carne asada, carnitas,* and the like—she asked if they had any *buff.* This, of course, is what Nepalis call water buffalo meat, and after I explained this to the waiter, he let out a belly laugh. Barna was clearly having a great time.

After dinner we strolled down the main street in the dark, passing by the bars and restaurants. We prodded her for more first impressions of America, and she told us how the women were all so beautiful, and that Americans apologize too much. Just then a girl walking in the other direction brushed Barna's arm, and then spun around and loudly apologized. This caused us all to erupt in laughter. A minute later a group of college-aged couples approached, and as they neared us one of the girls in the front caught Barna's eye and said, "Oh my god! Your skirt is so *cute!*" You could nearly see the happiness exuding from her every pore. Our Barna *bahini* was going to do just fine here. As we headed back toward Nacho, Barna turned to Sheena and said, "This has been the best night of my life."

When we had first arrived at the apartment, Sunil had been writing in his journal while the girls made *dal bhat* in the kitchen. After dinner, I asked him what he had been writing about, and he offered to read it to us. We gathered around the table and he read aloud in Nepali, pausing at intervals so that Barna could translate.

> *I still remember the day when my brother, Dr. Baroon Rai, mentioned his friends Brad and Sheena, who were getting ready to drive around the world. They all lived in Arizona then, and my brother was on his way to achieving his second master's degree. I love the idea of traveling, so this was not merely a piece of information, it meant a lot more and was very exciting for a person like me. The fact that they are not just traveling to a place, but the entire world, I had thousands of questions welling up inside me. Will I ever travel the world someday? No answer, but the excitement ran down my spine. I had done my research over the internet and had gained a thorough knowledge about travel, like the story of walking to the North Pole, and the motorbike world tour of Ewan McGregor and Charlie Boorman.*

> *Brad and Sheena named their journey Drive Nacho Drive, as they called their beloved white Volkswagen van "Nacho," and started posting updates to the web. I liked their Facebook page and started observing them. After completing their journey to Argentina, they shipped their Nacho to Malaysia. I could not take my eyes off after viewing the photos they had posted from Latin America of the mountains, hills, rivers, streams, roads and the local people around. They were very beautiful indeed.*

> *They reached Nepal after resuming their journey from Malaysia. After their arrival in Nepal, they were meant to stay at my brother Dr. Baroon's house. During their stay, they visited my home too, which was a few blocks away. They were introduced to my family members and especially the kids; they loved them and are more familiar. While they were in Nepal, I believe they had a wonderful journey. I still have their pictures of Thorong La captured within me.*

431

After two months of stay, they headed for India. Once again through internet, we started receiving beautiful pictures and writings from their journey. With every passing day, they completed more miles of the world in their van, our very own Nacho, with joy and gusto, while I silently studied them. When I traveled back to Nepal, Brad and Sheena would be remembered and talked about all day by the children, and especially Liza (my brother's daughter) would retell all her experience about Sheena.

Today, two and a half years later, the Nacho traveling the world is parked in front of my house here in Baltimore, USA. Brad and Sheena are sitting right beside me at our dining table having coffee with me. As I look at them, or to be more precise stare at them, I feel they are different from anyone I come across walking in the streets. Still I cannot get enough of them. They are chit chatting about their experience from when they were at my house in Nepal, and I keep imagining myself in their shoes. I am trying to think about all the possible things one might know about after traveling the whole world, but it's easier said than done, as I cannot even come up with an idea of what might have happened. My niece, Barna, who met Brad and Sheena in Nepal, welcomed them in the US and is cooking Nepali dishes for them. Sheena says that they still have three thousand miles to go before they reach their home in Arizona.

To be honest, for me they are not just my brother's friends staying at my house, but are an ordinary couple that dared to become extraordinary travelers. In Nepali, there is a famous saying, "We should treat our guests as God," and today, I am actually realizing Brad and Sheena to be God in the form of our guest. Watching them constantly, I feel like I have traveled the world myself. Dreaming of traveling the world—billions of people do that every second, but actually doing it, very few can achieve that. From the bottom of my heart, I salute Brad and Sheena for their valiant and audacious determination.

-Sunil

We hadn't known that Sunil had been following our progress at all, let alone from the beginning. As he spoke and our Nepali sister translated, it reaffirmed our love for this family and their country. One year after leaving Nepal, we were reunited with a piece of the family, but this time the hectic sounds of Kathmandu had been replaced by the silence of an American suburb after dark, interrupted only by the occasional passing car. Sunil had said that he couldn't begin to imagine what we must know after a trip like this. But he came from the place that taught us more about the purpose of living than any other place had.

Sunil, Kalpana, and Barna were living examples of untainted positivity, kindness, and determination. I considered my conversations with Bharat, and I wondered if perhaps we ought to be studying the Nepali mind to improve ourselves, instead of the other way around.

60

Interstate 10 to the
End of the Road

Brad

The farther west we drive, the straighter the roads become, their curves dying out as the mountains sink into the ground, and by Louisiana both the roads and the mountains have flat-lined. I have been rattled awake from my daydream of road-line-laser-beams by a flat tire, whose exact moment of eruption has been a result of accumulated abuse over the potholed roads of India's National Highway 7, the rocky mountain tracks of the Himalayas, and many others. As I fix our flat tire, the stagnant swamp air rises from the tarmac like liquid heat. Cars fly by at warp speed, dusting my legs with bits of dirt and wafts of hot air. The breeze through my open window has whipped the tips of my hair into a wild jerry curl. Sheena naps in the shade of the passenger seat. We pull back onto the road and the side mirror begins to rock loosely on its mount, a result of the overzealous Kathmandu bus driver. Our Turkish envy bead swings from our rearview mirror next to Santhanam's prayer necklace.

At the edge of the marsh, we come to a few forlorn buildings and I pull off the highway to have our extra spare tire mounted on a rim at a dirty shop cluttered with greasy tools by a man wearing overalls, and who speaks as though he has no jaw muscles and a ball of wax in his mouth. We head onto the main drag and stop at a southern diner for a lunch of assorted deep-fried nuggets on a thick white platter with a side of gravy. Four enormous women banter boisterously from the next booth. The food is bad, bland, unidentifiable. There is a small plastic trough of saltine crackers at the center of the table. We stop at an antique shop on the other side of the highway. Baseball pennants, wooden roosters, tin signs, a jukebox. And then we are back on the road, headed out west.

We pull into a truck stop on the Texas-Louisiana state line for the night, and I go for a late-night walk along a gravel road next to a hayfield. Sheena stays behind and goes to sleep. I wonder if walking alone at night along a gravel road leading away from a Louisiana truck stop is considered wise in these parts. I wonder if there are alligators in the bar ditch, because I clearly know nothing about alligators. After a while mosquitoes discover me, and I systematically rub my hands all over my body as a natural defense against them as I speed-walk back toward the truck stop. It is midnight, and I find a light on in one of the buildings. A sign on the door declares it a *Tourist Centre*. Inside there are toilets and a vending machine selling Pop Tarts and Gatorade, and a magazine rack with real estate pamphlets and brochures welcoming visitors to Texas and Louisiana. I sit in a chair and flip through a real estate pamphlet. All of the realtor headshots look the same. They are all women with puffy blonde hair and too much makeup and bleached-white teeth. They are selling mostly banal tract homes painted pastel seafoam green and turquoise. On the way back to Nacho, the sole of my shoe comes unglued and begins to slap against my foot. These were my "fancy shoes," to be reserved for special occasions. The tread is completely gone and they look like hobo shoes. I only realize this now that I am back in a place where the roads are perfectly straight, every surface is cleanly swept, and everything old has been destroyed. I throw my shoes in a dumpster and go to sleep.

We stop in Fredericksburg, Texas, where I lived for one year when I was in third grade. Sheena finds the town quaint and kind of nice. She can't blame my mom for having relocated us there on a whim, although she had soon found it too conservative for we wild Arizonans and we had fled. We walk into some shops selling trinkets and doo-dads and candles. There is a popcorn store and several restaurants in the style typical of the Texas hill country; everything is hewn of large logs and there are horns mounted on things. Budweiser and Coors are available.

We drive by my old elementary school, and I remember sitting next to a concrete wall with Christopher Dooley, finalizing our plans to construct a gigantic paper airplane, which, when finished, would carry us from the top of the school to some faraway place. I had returned my overdue library books on the last day of school, and the old hag of a librarian had scowled at me, and then barked, "I hope you're *happy*!"

We drive up and down the Llano Highway until we find our old house. Its front yard is full of weeds and it looks despondent, empty. I hadn't realized at the time that we only had one neighbor, and then

435

nothing. Just hayfields and oak trees. In our family photo in front of the house I am wearing psychedelic shorts that go all the way to my shins, and my little brother and I are holding baseball bats. My mom has one leg bent and both hands in the air as if to say, "Ta-da!"

We buy a peach-pecan pie to bring home for the family. Won't that be something? A peach-pecan pie from Fredericksburg.

For the evening we drive out to Enchanted Rock—possibly the tallest mountain in Texas, but it is just a great big granite rock. We reach the parking lot and it is twenty-five dollars to park there for the night. It is a parking lot seventeen miles outside of town next to a great big rock. Sheena and I talk it over and I decide to ask a park ranger if we can avoid the fee by staying in our van and leaving first thing in the morning. I flag down a passing ranger, and he informs me that we will have to pay or leave, so we leave. We drive five more miles and then find a dirt road that seems to go into the middle of nowhere. We pull off into the dead grass next to a wall of juniper trees and go to sleep.

The flashing lights of a police car awake us in the early hours of the morning. I slide the door open as Sheena tries to make herself presentable. I feign a smile through my delirium, but I can't see anything for the blinding flashlight shining in my eyes. He makes us get out of the van in our pajamas and tells us that he received a call about some suspicious people. He takes our papers and license and goes back to his patrol car. He returns having studied the law, and—fortunately for us—our camp is deemed to be within the eight-foot easement extending off of either side of the road. Imagine our luck! More than twenty miles from town on a dirt road and we have parked with the eight-foot legal zone. We are non-prosecutable.

In the morning I walk farther than eight feet from the road and then I come back. I am a Texas outlaw.

We set off early for the mind-numbing drive across West Texas, and arrive at El Paso by early evening. The tail end of the drive is made interesting by punishing rains that give us the impression of driving in a river. El Paso presses up against the Mexican border, creating a segmented city whose counterpart is Ciudad Juarez on the other side of the Rio Grande.

Since leaving Canada we have been planning for El Paso. We secretly hoped that when we arrived we would be unable to resist the southerly pull, a chance to touch home, turn left, and keep on going. We manage to talk ourselves out of it. We have a peach-pecan pie to deliver, after all. We stop at a Mexican dive restaurant and enjoy a taste of heaven. Mexican polka drifts out from the kitchen, old men hunch on stools, and a little girl drinks horchata at the next table.

We drive into the city center, which sits right along the border fence—the enormous behemoth of a protective barrier erected eighteen feet high to keep the outsiders from taking what we have fought so hard to build for ourselves, this wonderful life in the Great White North. But El Paso is dead. We roll into the center as evening falls; the lights are all on, streetlights go through the motions: green, yellow, red. Neon signs identify businesses and restaurants, but there are no people. The sidewalks are empty, save for a few lone stragglers. We pass a bus stop where three people wait. A homeless man is crumpled up next to an overturned shopping cart. We look at each other, confused. What happened here? The people seem to have shuttered themselves away, or else abandoned the place altogether.

As we reach the border, where a great sky bridge climbs over the protective steel-grated wall and crosses the Rio Grande to Mexico, we catch our first glimpse across the river. The opposite riverbank is lined with cantinas and taco shacks, and we can hear vibrant music: accordions and mariachis hooting and tweeting. Groups of friends and families walk on the dilapidated sidewalks while a couple of jalopy cars vroom past carrying smiling passengers. We turn and drive along the imposing border fence, and through the woven steel cables we see houses, brightly painted and small with peeling paint, and with their doors wide open. People stand in front of the homes and talk. A boy bounces along a dirt road carrying a box, an old man leans on a wall, and a group of teens kicks a soccer ball in a dusty lot.

Someone had warned us that to look across the border fence to Juarez was to look into a rat's nest of filth and chaos. A slum. But to us that is not the case at all. When I look across I see friendships waiting to unfold, open doors, a collection of hands that know hard work and families that stick together. Conversations about nothing that might lead to something. Beyond the wall there aren't any slack-jawed cannibals clicking their tongues. I have met them, and they are familiar. Their kindness and sincerity is humbling, and the more we have gotten to know them, the more we have seen ourselves changing to reflect their impact on us. Beyond the wall there is a world filled with amazing people living fulfilling lives. They kick soccer balls around dusty lots. They congregate at pad Thai restaurants and drink orange juice. They converse on patios overlooking the Kathmandu Valley. They fly kites from Indian rooftops. They drink beer together on pine-covered hilltops above the

437

Mediterranean Sea, and they listen to music in the dry air under the Saharan moonlight. They could make their bread alone, but instead one makes it flat, one places the pebbles on top, and one slides it into the oven. A machine could process the rice, but instead one woman chops it down, one man beats it on the ground, and a boy carries it away, warning the wary foreigners of tigers in the jungle. They do not work in high-rise buildings, and they are not models of efficiency. They eat what they grow, and they are happy to share it. They have time. They have each other. They are rich.

And that is the pulse of the world.

After 927 days, 45,822 miles, thirty-four countries, and five continents, we have arrived right back where we started.

Made in the USA
San Bernardino, CA
08 May 2015